A John Hope Franklin Center book

A book in the series
Latin America Otherwise: Languages, Empires, Nations
Series editors: Walter D. Mignolo, Duke University
Irene Silverblatt, Duke University
Sonia Saldívar-Hull, University of California
at Los Angeles

MODERN INQUISITIONS

Peru and the Colonial Origins of the Civilized World

Irene Silverblatt

DUKE UNIVERSITY PRESS   Durham and London 2004

Printed in the United States of America on acid-free paper ∞
Typeset in Carter and Cone Galliard by Tseng Information Systems, Inc.
Library of Congress Cataloging-in-Publication Data appear
on the last printed page of this book.
Duke University Press gratefully acknowledges the support
of the Program for Cultural Cooperation between Spain's Ministry of
Culture and United States Universities, which provided funds toward
the production of this book.

In the spirit of Guido Delran
and for Nan Woodruff, George Vickers,
and Aaron, Elan, and Sarah Silverblatt-Buser

CONTENTS

ABOUT THE SERIES

Latin America Otherwise: Languages, Empires, Nations is a critical series. It aims to explore the emergence and consequences of concepts used to define "Latin America" while at the same time exploring the broad interplay of political, economic, and cultural practices that have shaped Latin American worlds. Latin America, at the crossroads of competing imperial designs and local responses, has been construed as a geocultural and geopolitical entity since the nineteenth century. This series provides a starting point to redefine Latin America as a configuration of political, linguistic, cultural, and economic intersections that demands a continuous reappraisal of the role of the Americas in history, and of the ongoing process of globalization and the relocation of people and cultures that have characterized Latin America's experience. *Latin America Otherwise: Languages, Empires, Nations* is a forum that confronts established geocultural constructions, that rethinks area studies and disciplinary boundaries, that assesses convictions of the academy and of public policy, and that, correspondingly, demands that the practices through which we produce knowledge and understanding about and from Latin America be subject to rigorous and critical scrutiny.

In this pathbreaking study, Irene Silverblatt makes a number of interrelated arguments. She takes Hannah Arendt's insights into the origins of a modernity that allowed "civilized" peoples to embrace fascism and applies them to the sixteenth and seventeenth centuries, when Spanish colonialism dominated the globe. Professor Silverblatt joins Latin American scholars like sociologist Anibal Quijano and philosopher Enrique Dussel in arguing that "modernity" originated with the Spanish/Christian victory over the Moors, the expulsion of the Jews from the Iberian peninsula, and, simultaneously, the colonization of "Indians" and the slave trade. This confluence of events set the stage for the development of a capitalism that used race thinking to justify the exploitation of labor (through serf-dom and slavery), linking ideas about race and Christianity to bureaucratic control of colonized populations.

Describing how the early modern state was formed in conjunction with colonialism, Silverblatt argues that the barbaric underside of the modern world was born in the subsequent mix of bureaucratic rule, race thinking, and the capacity to rationalize violence. She uses records from the Spanish Inquisition in Peru to illuminate these modern processes: Inquisition trials show the modern side of an institution we customarily brand as pre-modern and provide material to understand the civilizing/modernizing processes from the perspective of the colonies. Chronicling the interplay of bureaucracy and race, colonialism and statecraft, *Modern Inquisitions* confronts our assumptions about civilization, its origins, and our role in its creation.

ACKNOWLEDGMENTS

The written word always belies the many hands that have gone into its making. This project has been a long time coming, and many people over the years have been midwives to its extended birth. I hope I remember to acknowledge you all.

Without the generosity of several funding sources, I would never have been able to fully research this book—track down the Peruvian Inquisition records, find early-print books, and uncover other relevant documents and records. A Rockefeller Foundation fellowship at the University of Maryland's Latin American Studies Center, whose director is Saul Sosnowski, gave me support and encouragement when the project was in its earliest stages. A Guggenheim Foundation fellowship, coming just when I needed it, let me finish all basic research and delve into the analytical process. Finally, with a fellowship from the Radcliffe Institute for Advanced Study at Harvard University—and benefiting from the great encouragement of and conversations with Drew Gilpin Faust, the founding Dean of the Institute, Judy Wishniak, Director of the Fellowship Program, and all my pals—I managed to finish a first draft.

Several conferences and edited volumes provided the deadlines needed to jolt me into writing. The McNeil Center for Early American Studies and the Omohundro Institute of Early American History and Culture co-sponsored a conference exploring comparative colonial histories that resulted in *Possible Pasts: Becoming Colonial in Early America*, edited by Robert Blair St. George. "The Inca's Witches: Gender and the Cultural Work of Colonization in Seventeenth-Century Peru," much improved by Robert's help, forced me to confront the witchcraft trials. Wonderful discussions at the Johns Hopkins Women's Studies Seminar contributed much to the revised version published here, and I owe a special thank-you to Jonathan Goldberg and Michael Moon for their insights and generosity.

The present book's chapter "New Christians and New World Fears" benefited from several hearings: It was first presented, in very rough form, at
the 1995 meetings of the Institute of Early American History and Culture at the University of Michigan; followed by a presentation at the
John Carter Brown Library's 1997 conference "Jews and the Expansion
of Europe: 1450–1800," ably organized by Norman Fiering; and then by
a lecture at the University of Illinois for the Sheldon and Anita Drob-
ney Program for the Study of Jewish Culture and Society, where I was
afforded the insights of Helaine Silverman, Fred Jaher, Michael Shapiro,
Nils Jacobsen, and Cynthia Radding. This paper was revised again for the
Historical Anthropology Seminar at Emory University's Anthropology
Department, headed by Don Donham, and it appeared in the ensuing collection *From the Margins: Historical Anthropology and Its Futures*, edited
thoughtfully by Brian Keith Axel. "Becoming Indian" began as a paper
presented in Trujillo, Spain ("El surgimiento de la indianidad en los andes
del Perú central: El nativismo del siglo XVII y los muchos significados de
'indio'"), and published in *De palabra y obra en el Nuevo Mundo*, vol. 3, *La
formación del otro*, edited by four towering scholars, Gary Gossen, Jorge
Klor de Alva, Manolo Gutiérrez Estévez and Miguel León-Portilla. The
Shelby Collum Davis Center seminar at Princeton University, organized
then by Natalie Zemon Davis, was an extraordinary place to refine this
paper—as was the ensuing volume *Imperial Aftermaths and Postcolonial
Displacements*, edited so well by Gyan Prakash. Ideas about American tri-
umphalism were first tried out in Bogotá at the Pontificia Universidad
Javeriana, and then published in *Reestructuración de las ciencias sociales en
los países andinos*, thoughtfully and incisively edited by Santiago Castro-
Gomez. In Bogotá, I met some of Latin America's pioneering philosophers and social scientists, from whom I had much to learn, and I deeply
appreciate their abundant intellectual generosity.

Several other symposia have enriched my thinking, and I want to
thank participants for comments that helped me enormously: Mary Kay
Vaughan, Barbara Weinstein, and other fellow seminarians at the Univer-
sity of Maryland's Center for Historical Studies symposium "The Body
and Latin American History" who read my chapter "States and Stains";
Meg Greer, Maureen Quilligan, Walter Mignolo, and participants in Duke
University's "Rereading the Black Legend" conference who heard me out
as I tried to pull together Peru's conspiracy theories; as well as Susan
Rogers, who organized the Holy Cross College conference "Practicing
Catholic: Ritual, Performance and Contestation in Catholic Faith." A
Dumbarton Oaks conference—leading to the publication of a volume of
essays coedited by Elizabeth Hill Boone and Tom Cummins, *Native Tradi-*

tions in the Postconquest World—started me thinking about the interaction of racial and sexual politics. And again, my hat goes off to the fellows of the Radcliffe Institute for Advanced Study at Harvard University for the ongoing seminar series.

It is a true pleasure to work with a publisher like Duke University Press, committed to the highest standards of scholarly publishing. I owe much to its editors. A special thank-you to Valerie Millholland, my editor, who kept me going with patient understanding, great advice, and valued friendship. Luckily for me, Charles Purrenhage, who copyedited my first book, agreed to work on this one as well. Charles is the best, and I know his fine eye and facility with language have saved me from embarrassment—and made this a better book. Mary Mendell has added beauty to it with a superb design. Mark Mastromarino has patiently shepherded the manuscript through the production process. And Duke's editor-in-chief, Ken Wissoker, who has led the way in building an important press, stayed in my corner, in spite of my "glacial" pace. Duke University Press also engaged two of the finest reviewers in the field—Kathryn Burns and Barbara Weinstein—to critique the manuscript; their considered criticisms and wise advise changed the shape of this book. My appreciation for their time and effort is boundless.

The staff at the Archivo Arzobispal of Lima, at the Archivo Histórico de la Nación, in Spain, at the Biblioteca Nacional of Peru, and at the Archivo Arzobispal of Cuzco were always helpful (even in difficult times), as were the librarians at the John Carter Brown Center, the Luis Alberto Sánchez collection at Pennsylvania State University, and Duke University's special collections. Obviously this book could never have been written without their insight, doggedness, and assistance.

I am one of the fortunate few who works in a department—Cultural Anthropology—where faculty members actually like one another. I relish our many serendipitous conversations, the hallway and office give-and-take, that make intellectual life a pleasure, and I want to thank our department chair, Anne Allison, for setting the tone. Thanks also to Holly Frances and Pat Bodager, who keep us in line. I have benefited enormously from my colleagues in other departments: History, Latin American and Caribbean Studies, Women's Studies, Romance Studies, and Literature. We also have wonderful interdisciplinary seminars at Duke, seminars I wish I attended more of, but that have been inspiring nonetheless: Marxism and Society, Imperial Reason, and Transnational Feminism, to name a few.

Wonderful friends and colleagues have bravely read different sections of the manuscript, patiently listened to my ideas, and then gave me new ones:

Ann Wightman, Lisa Henderson, Paul Harvey, Daniel Beaver, Guido Ruggiero, KumKum Chatterjee, Michael Moon, Jonathan Goldberg, Peg Spears, Alan Derickson, Bill Pencak, Isabel Knight, Bill Blair, Lori Ginzberg, Gary Gallagher, Richard Burger, Lucy Salazar, Enrique Mayer, Jing Wang, Sue Larsen, Danny James, Lynn Dipietro, Jeff Quilter, and Kay Warren. At Duke, special thanks go to Laurie Shannon, Jan Radway, Thavolia Glymph, Margaret Greer, Wahneema Lubbiano, Jan French, Kathy Rudy, Bill Reddy, and all of my colleagues in Cultural Anthropology. Claudia Koonz has read portions of the manuscript and provided, as always, rich and fruitful commentary. Barbara Weinstein, in addition to being a reader for the Press, has gone over ideas with me at great and wonderful length over coffees and dinners. Orin Starn, an extraordinary colleague, has generously read the entire manuscript and provided the kind of detailed, engaged criticism that is any academic's dream. In Peru, Henrique Urbano was the first to strongly encourage me to pursue this project, and he generously gave me books and microfilm to get me started; Eli Selem's political engagement and sharp intelligence have lit my way for years; Mari Solari, a wonderful friend, has always given me a second home in Lima; and Teodoro Hampe Martinez, one of Peru's premier historians of the Inquisition, has graciously invited me to be part of his intellectual circle. Several years ago I co-taught a course and seminar with Walter Mignolo, and the impact of his creative thinking and that of our students can be scanned in these pages. I was fortunate to be co-teaching a graduate seminar with Deb Thomas. She along with our students were shamelessly forced to read the manuscript, and their insights and sturdy criticism have given me a new lens through which to understand what I wrote. A truly exceptional group of upper-level and graduate students in my seminar on ethnohistorical methods annotated and analyzed the Francisco de Avila sermons, published by the Carolina and Duke Consortium in Latin American Studies as Working Paper no. 29. My advisees at Duke have helped me more than they probably realize: Gonzalo Lamana and Tracy Brown (with much-appreciated grant assistance from the Duke Arts and Sciences Research Council) contributed in significant ways by researching some of the correspondence between the Lima office and Spain and by challenging me with their ideas; and Leigh Campoamor went over the manuscript with a fine-tooth comb, offered insightful suggestions, and compiled the index. Many thanks are due. I count my blessings to have such wonderful friends and colleagues—and I hope I can learn from their example.

Miski Silverblatt, along with other members of my immediate family— Hilda Silverblatt, Helene Silverblatt, Bob Buser and my late father, Salvin Silverblatt—have made me laugh, cry, enjoy, and think. Their wise counsel and warmth have illuminated my life. Two people, in particular, accompanied me on this journey, and without their wisdom, love, and abiding sense of humor I could never have finished. I dedicate this book to them: to Nan Woodruff, my dear *compañera*, whose friendship, ever-ready ear, and engaged scholarship have kept me on track, and to my husband, George Vickers (he actually read the entire manuscript!), whose gifts of intellectual clarity, healthy skepticism, plain talk, unflinching commitment to social justice, and good loving mean more than I could ever put into words. *Modern Inquisitions* is also dedicated to Guido Delran, whose spirit infuses this book, and to my nephews and niece—Aaron Silverblatt-Buser, Elan Silverblatt-Buser, and Sarah Silverblatt-Buser—in the hope that they can help carry this world forward in peace and justice and create a space, for all of us, where a modern inquisition can never exist.

Modern Inquisitions

Good Government: The Inquisitor.
From Felipe Guaman Poma de Ayala,
El primer nueva corónica y buen gobierno (1613?).

PROLOGUE

We can no longer afford to take that which was good in the past and simply call it our heritage, to discard the bad and simply think of it as a dead load which by itself time will bury in oblivion. The subterranean stream of Western history has finally come to the surface. — HANNAH ARENDT, *The Origins of Totalitarianism*[1]

PUZZLING OVER THE RISE OF FASCISM, Hannah Arendt searched for a precedent in Western history — a form of government supporting worldwide dominance by a would-be master race — that might have eased the way for civilized peoples to embrace barbarity. She found it in the global imperialism of the nineteenth century, when northern European nations like England were putting the machinery in place to rule their colonies around the globe. That machinery included an organization for absolute political control and an ideology of social superiority. Imperial powers governed their colonies as despotic bureaucrats, argued Arendt, and racial ideologies turned mere bureaucrats into members of a superior caste. Her fear was this: intertwined, "race thinking" and bureaucratic rule could unleash "extraordinary power and destruction," a destruction all the more terrible since it was bathed in an aura of rationality and civilization.

Colonialism's governing principles, however, were not launched by nineteenth-century imperialism. That honor goes to Europe's first wave of colonial expansion, spearheaded not by northern Europe but by Portugal and Spain. From the sixteenth century through the mid-seventeenth, Spain was in the vanguard of the modern world, installing cutting-edge bureaucracies along with templates for race thinking in its colonies dotting the globe. This book is rooted in Arendt's insights but applies them to the Spanish empire and its workings in the Viceroyalty of Peru. If we take the first wave of empire as the origin of the "subterranean stream of

Western history," we have a better grasp, I think, of its complexity and depth: the dance of bureaucracy and race, born in colonialism, was party to the creation of the modern world.

We trace our modern beginnings to the efforts of European monarchs to extend their power and consolidate their victories—the initial moments of state-making. What we often forget is that history wedded these domestic efforts to incursions abroad. Spain is a prototype of this double-edged politics. Castilian monarchs were vying to increase their authority over the Peninsula when they triumphed in the Americas, struggling to control Iberian principalities when they worked out details of colonial government, battling the English when they established Indian courts, and skirmishing with the Dutch when they defended colonial borders. The Spanish experience—fashioned out of colonial efforts and European conflicts—colored all the West's state-building projects. European state-making, then, was bound in various ways to imperial expansion; this link is hidden if we date colonialism to the nineteenth century and not to the sixteenth.[2]

To make a Spanish colony out of what had been the Inca empire was an extended process. Although begun in the 1530s when Spanish conquistadors, led by Francisco Pizarro, overwhelmed Cuzco's native forces, it wasn't until the century's end that royal authorities—having confronted civil wars, rebellions, and settlers' raw ambition—could successfully root the institutions of government.[3] The Crown quickly learned that successful colony-building pivoted on control over immigrant colonists in equal measure to control over native peoples, and it instituted bureaucracies to curb and administer both. Learning from pitfalls on the Peninsula, the Crown consolidated colonial state power in ways that would have been unthinkable in Europe. The Crown gave royal officials (as opposed to Spanish settlers) jurisdiction over Indian commoners and had royal officials broker relations between Peru's colonizers and colonized natives. The Crown appointed magistrates to supervise Spanish–Indian relations, designated local headmen to represent native communities before the royal authorities, and established courts, armies, and district governors to oversee the rest. It fell to the Crown's ally, the Church, however, to instruct Indians, as well as colonials, in the ways and necessities of civilization.

Like all bureaucracies, that of colonial Peru functioned through a cultural matrix, and race thinking was its scaffold. Royal authorities, grounded in the experiences of a developing absolutist state, imposed broad, racialized classifications on their imperial subjects. They created two unequal "republics" as the foundation for colonial rule. Native Americans and their descendants—regardless of origin or ethnicity—were classed as Indians; Iberians and their descendants—regardless of origin or ethnicity—were privileged Spanish colonists. With the exception of the native nobility, all Indians owned tribute and labor to the Crown; Spaniards in the colonies, unlike lower-class Spaniards in Europe, had no such obligations. When Indian populations, decimated by disease and upheaval, could no longer meet labor demands, the Crown turned to slavery, spurring the creation of a third abstract category, *negro*, which included all Africans brought to Peru and their descendants—regardless of origin, ethnicity, or social rank. Ancestry determined the official categories of colonial government. But, as authorities were soon to realize, colonial realities could not be contained within colonial categories, and "hybrid" racial classes (like *mestizo, mulato,* and *sambo*) entered the Spanish political ken. This was Spanish legal theory's flat presentation of colonial order—a caste trio of *español, indio,* and negro along with mixtures.[4] Like most categorical descriptions, this one too concealed the historical processes—and the contradictions—at its heart.

For something akin to a cultural revolution was taking place: a revolution of social selves, social relations, and social understandings, a revolution mapped by the great transformations in political order and economic power during the sixteenth and seventeenth centuries. The new human beings of the modern world—español, indio, negro, mestizo, mulato, sambo—were born out of the same upheaval that made "nations," "bureaucrats," "slavers," "global merchants," and "colonies."[5] It was the modern world's signature to etch economic dominance and political supremacy into a radical cultural design. It was also its signature to hide the social relations that were brewing supremacy and conflict behind a semblance of "race things."

The Modern Inquisition

Most anglophones regard the Spanish Inquisition as an implacable, premodern institution, manned by greedy fanatics who gleefully and brutally defended Spain's religious purity. This stereotype, with origins going back to Queen Elizabeth's propaganda wars against King Felipe II, has blinded us to the fact that the Inquisition was one of the most modern bureaucracies of its time. It has also blinded us to the fact that the tribunal's function as defender of the faith and nation was inseparable from its bureaucratic structure.[6]

The Spanish Inquisition was established at the end of the fifteenth century to meet a perceived threat to national security: namely, the undermining of the Spanish state; first by Judaizers, and then by all manner of heretics. In spite of its religious demeanor, the Inquisition was an institution of state, under the jurisdiction of the Crown (not the pope), and like other organizations it was subject to the bureaucratic and judicial norms increasingly shaping the governmental institutions of the modern world. Like any bureaucracy, the Inquisition was run according to procedures and rules, and its workings were overseen by bureaucrats, i.e., credentialed *letrados* (learned men, university graduates). Although not a court of law, the Inquisition was guided by the legal practices of contemporary judicial systems: it was subject to regulations regarding evidence and the use of torture, and its procedures were weighted in favor of the prosecution, in spite of some legal protections for the defense.[7]

But the Inquisition was startlingly different, too. It was, perhaps, the most modern of Spain's bureaucracies. Not only absorbed by rules and regulations, not only structured by offices in a clear hierarchy of command, the Inquisition's mandate extended to all members of society (except Indians; see below), regardless of social standing, wealth, or power. Nobleman or slave, governor or laborer, Spaniard or black could be brought before its bench and strapped to its racks. In this sense, the Inquisition was the empire's fairest court.[8] It was certainly the empire's most extensive court, for it was the only Spanish institution with dominion throughout the empire, headquartered in Madrid and with branches across the globe.

Spain brought this renowned institution to the Americas, establishing branch offices in Lima (1569–71), Mexico (1569–71), and Cartagena (1610).[9] The Lima Inquisition was launched during the tenure of Viceroy Francisco de Toledo, a prepotent administrator often credited with solidifying Spain's presence in the viceroyalty. His attitude toward the tribunal, like that of many royal authorities who followed, was one of studied ambivalence. On the one hand, Toledo never doubted the colony's serious religious needs and took great delight in the tribunal's arrival; on the other, he was wary of the tribunal's incursions into the domain of secular power—that is, into his domain. Toledo wrote to the Council of the Indies that the Inquisition "would be a factor of great importance in the preservation of these kingdoms" and that the inquisitor Servando de Cerezuela, "occupies the most important and needed office in this land";[10] however, Toledo also warned of the difficulties faced by the viceregal government "because [the inquisitors] were extending their jurisdiction much more than they should."[11]

In Spain, where the Inquisition believed its mandate was as pivotal to the empire's survival as that of any other imperial bureaucracy (and with officeholders just as arrogant), the jostlings between royal authority and Inquisition were legion. Drives, ambitions, and egos of individual protagonists could inflame, or mollify, discord; nonetheless, the conflicts between tribunal and viceregal government were, first and foremost, institutional battles over the character of the emerging state. And, like the rest of European state-making, the balance ultimately tipped in favor of secular power.

Nonetheless, because of its authority over pivotal aspects of religious life—in a country where Catholicism was akin to a nationalist ideology—the Spanish Inquisition and its episcopal counterpart, the "extirpation of idolatry campaigns," were commanding figures in colonial life. As the state structure responsible for cultural security, moreover, the Inquisition was a significant arbiter in race thinking designs.

The Inquisition was one structure of many that were involved in the colony's moral regulation, but it was nevertheless responsible for the empire's rawest displays of cultural force. In the great theater of power, the *auto-da-fé*—and, in smaller, daily theaters of reputation and fear—the Inquisition clarified cultural blame by presenting who, among the colony's non-Indian populace,[12] held beliefs or engaged in life practices that were considered threats to the colony's moral and civic well-being. These threats included a range of heretical crimes—from blasphemy, sexual misconduct (including the solicitation of sexual favors by priests), and witchcraft to the capital offense of worshiping within non-Catholic religions, whether Islam, Protestantism, or Judaism.

Most of us presume that the inquisitors always got their man or woman, that the verdict was fixed, that the tribunals were, if anything, mere show trials. We commonly expect that a combined weight of prejudice, greed, and fanaticism determined trials from the start. This is a plausible reading, but a simplistic one.

The accused were severely handicapped, it is true. Presumptions of guilt, the character of testimony, the nature of evidence—all worked to the prisoner's disadvantage. Disadvantaged, however, is not the same as predetermined. Inquisitors did not act as a concerted group, executing the will of their superiors; verdicts did not catapult themselves forward. Lima inquisitors, who were midlevel bureaucrats, were a quarrelsome bunch: they quarreled among themselves and they quarreled with their superiors. Magistrates, albeit rarely, had to publicly admit to errors of judgment; they had to publicly concede mistaken arrests. Men and women accused of heresy and imprisoned—sometimes for years—while waiting for their case to run its course, might find that their case had been "suspended"[13] or, in the end, that they had been exonerated. These exceptions help us see the obvious: the Inquisition, like all state institutions, was not a monolithic, coherent body; the Inquisition, like all state institutions, was structured by bureaucratic exigencies; the Inquisition, like all state institutions, was only, or all too, human.[14]

After the Inquisition ran roughshod over native Mexicans in the early years of colonization, the Crown prohibited the tribunal from sitting in judgment over Indians. Nevertheless, indigenous beliefs and practices did not go unmonitored. Church mandates put Indians under the direct surveillance of local bishops and, sporadically throughout the seventeenth century—at different times and in different places—those bishops sponsored missions to investigate whether heresies still poisoned the souls of their native congregation. In Peru, the most vigorous crusades were waged in the Archbishopric of Lima; at least that is where we find the most abundant records.[15] The trial transcripts, housed in the Archbishop's Archive, paint the idolatry campaigns as smaller, restricted versions of the Inquisition itself. First, "inspectors" were sent out into the countryside, where they read an "edict of faith," posted it on the church door, and warned the by now baptized flock about their religious obligations. Natives were encouraged to confess idolatries and to name sinners: as with the Inquisition, personal testimony and denunciations were the principal sources of evidence. As with the Inquisition, too, judicial policies encouraged further confessions and further denunciations (and further false testimony?). As with the Inquisition, family and friends often ended up being pitted against one another. And, as with the Inquisition, colonial subjects were participating in a bureaucratic institution whose rules and procedures, internal conflicts, and political allegiances were enmeshed in the possibilities of a particular time and a particular place.[16]

Bureaucracy and Modern Life

"Bureaucracy" holds special sway over the West's social theorists, who have considered it crucial for shaping modern lifeways and sensibilities: bureaucracy stands for modernity. This argument's most famous proponent, Max Weber, believed Western bureaucracy to be the most fully rationalized organizational type—and therefore the most modern—in the contemporary world.[17] Weber, like others before and many since, divided history into two periods, characterized either by "modern" forms of social organization or by "traditional" ones. Traditional bureaucracies were everything modern ones were not; traditional officeholders, mired in patronage and chosen without regard to merit, were corruptible, biased, partisan. On the other hand, modern bureaucracies, in Weber's vision, were professional, rationally organized, impartial, and impersonal. Bureaucracy, then, became a line in the social sand, dividing societies into the modern and the not modern, the progressive and the backward. Weber didn't write about the Spanish Inquisition, but I bet he would have put it in the "not" category.

Two contemporary theorists of power and culture, Michel Foucault and Pierre Bourdieu, had a somewhat different take on Western bureaucracies. Like Weber, they connected bureaucracies to modern ways; but their interest was the advent of the modern state and, for them, bureaucracies were significant because they helped fashion the state as an autonomous entity—with a rationale apart from the sovereignty of kings. Unlike Weber, Foucault and Bourdieu were drawn to the sixteenth and seventeenth centuries by their concern with the erosion of dynastic power. Yet, like Weber, neither one talks about Spain's contributions to state-making.

Foucault, exploring the evolution of what he called the "arts of government," believed the seventeenth century marked a watershed in European state formation and in the history of the West. The seventeenth century not only witnessed the birth of large-scale administrative units that would come to challenge the sovereignty of kings, it also witnessed radical transformations in political vision.

In the seventeenth century, for the first time, the "state" was something to talk about.[18] It was a meaningful concept, understood as an independent entity, born out of dynastic rule but significantly different from it. Seventeenth-century philosophers and political thinkers wrote about the state, describing what a good state should do and be, the obligations subjects owed the state, the obligations the state owed its subjects, the essentials of proper state comportment. This new thing, with its own logic, its own way of being, its own conceptual expression, was "governed according to . . . principles . . . intrinsic to it," according to "its own form of rationality." State rationality, Foucault pointed out, was practiced and structured through administrative bureaucracies: namely, the bureaucracies of the absolutist state. Schools, "manufactories," armies—these were the institutional forms, the techniques of government that, for Foucault, constituted the seventeenth century's emerging "society of regulation and discipline."[19]

Like Foucault, Bourdieu focused on the processes making the state an autonomous entity, emphasizing its structures of existence, rationale of being, and patterns of classifying the world—its imposing epistemology. Bourdieu untangled the dialectic between bureaucracy and state, arguing that while the state constructed bureaucracies to administer populations, bureaucracies constructed the state by ordaining its format, its categories of order. Bourdieu's concerns were at once cognitive and structural: his intention was to chart the dynamic making these two facets of social experience inseparable, to focus on the emerging ideologies and institutions which, jointly, opened the political space known as the "state." Bureaucracies were central to Bourdieu's scheme, given their capacity to frame institutions while at the same time monopolizing information, knowledge and, indeed, moral sensibilities.

Bourdieu called bureaucrats a "state nobility," the state-era equivalent of an aristocracy. They formed a charmed circle, he argued, for they enjoyed a monopoly over productive means—now knowledge, rather than land. They even acquired a cloak of divine mystery, having the power to bestow identity cards (credentials) and to control admission into their elite ranks.

Bureaucratic claims jostled with dynastic privilege during state-making's early stages, and Bourdieu suggested that this conflict accounted for ideological changes both accompanying and spurring the autonomy of state institutions. The state nobility, working against the hegemony of dynastic power, developed a special vocabulary to frame its version of political morality and political imagination. The emerging idiom was that of universalism and rationality—a new theory representing special interests in the language of "the public." Public good, public will, and public order were, in Bourdieu's words, "working to autonomize reason of state from dynastic reason."[20]

Bourdieu understood the growing legitimacy of state institutions to be part of an emerging "habitus," implicit knowledge framing a societal common sense. And, as the reach of bureaucracies grew, a growing number of human beings would share a new sensibility vis-à-vis the world, a sensibility defined by categories both produced by and producing state bureaucracies.

So Weber placed the birth of modern bureaucracies in the nineteenth century, and Foucault and Bourdieu placed that birth two centuries before. What are we to make, then, of the Spanish Inquisition's rules and regulations, its appeals to public welfare and to an ethos of public service, its letters to headquarters and displays of deference, its clashes with secular authorities over jurisdiction, its glorious pageants and spats over ritual place, its clever evasions, its backstabbing, its detailed records of torture practices, its jousts over the right to sword and dagger, its appeals to national security? No surprise here. I'm with Foucault and Bourdieu— but I would add the Spanish Inquisition to any list of modern bureaucracies. As an institution it was developing a structure and logic apart from dynastic boundaries; it was formally organized according to principles of rationality; it was imagined as being greater than the sum of its individual officeholders; and it was careful to legitimate its practices through an appeal to public welfare. In sum, the Inquisition was a bureaucracy that typified the evolving institutions of the emerging modern world: it was a state structure in the making. Later, we will take a closer look.

Foucault and Bourdieu provide a handle on the enormous changes—the truly great transformations in power relations—producing contemporary life. They give us the big picture, and their work is insightful and pioneering. Like many big pictures, however, theirs can be painfully abstract, a bit pretentious, and, in the end, a bit lifeless. There are few human beings in their story, in the main, just institutions: bureaucracies make the state, bureaucracies make categories, the state makes bureaucracies. And the state, in these imaginings, is like a juggernaut, rolling over any body or object in its way.

Now, to be fair, Bourdieu and Foucault are theorists working on a level of abstraction that precludes historical detail, and since their subject matter, the modern state, is more than its constituent individuals, it is hard to find linguistic terms other than abstractions to express the state's persistence and broad reach. But there are theorists who talk about the "state," recognizing its structured persistence, who do make the "state" come alive: that is because human beings, living in social relationships, acting in history, are central to their grasp of what a state is all about.

The "State," Illusion, and History

Philip Abrams tackled this very problem, the abstraction of the state, by arguing that an abstraction was all the "state" was—an illusion, an ideology, a portrayal, but not a concrete entity. Not to say that the "idea of the state" wasn't real, for Abrams would be the first to underscore its profound political effects; but the concept itself was not a tangible being. The idea of the state was, rather, a misrepresentation of what states are: "politically organized subjection," a complex of institutions governing economic and political dominion. The "state," Abrams argued, presented these institutions as if they were a coherent and unified entity, as if they acted in the common interest, as if they were morally legitimate, as if the violence committed for reasons of state were inherently justified.

Abrams turned to history to get the state and state systems right. The only way "not to take the state for granted" was to "understand its historical construction"—to understand the development of a particular "state" portrait in relation to the power systems it legitimated.[21] Since relations of political dominion in absolutist states were more transparent than in bourgeois-liberal variations (additionally padded, as they are, by ideologies of political equality), Abrams pointed to the seventeenth century for clearer-cut examples of how the "state-idea" emerged as part of the reorganization of European power relations. Abrams, like Foucault and Bourdieu, also focused on the state as it came into being; but, as a more articulate dialectician, Abrams insisted on process, on the dynamic between state illusion and political practice: "State . . . starts as an implicit construct [within political relations], then is reified—as the *res publica*—and acquires overt symbolic identity progressively divorced from practice as an illusory account of practice."[22] The records of the Spanish Inquisition in Peru are both witness to and part of the process making the "res publica" we have come to take for granted. They unveil what Abrams called the real state secret: "the secret of the non-existence of the state."[23]

Philip Corrigan and Derek Sayer added historical fiber to Abrams's analysis with their momentous book *The Great Arch*, a study of the lengthy and complicated cultural upheavals (over nine centuries) transforming feudal England into a modern nation. Corrigan and Sayer want British state-making to be understood, in their words, as a "cultural revolution": as an enormous transformation of social identities, dispositions, and meanings produced by the "forms, routines, and rituals" of state-making. We are speaking here not only of the institutional changes we commonly associate with the state (constructing parliaments, defining voting rights, imposing standardized legal systems, raising armies, raising taxes), but also of the more mundane activities of life (filling out tax forms, getting a license to drive or to teach, marching in parades, celebrating national holidays). This entire range of activities, they argue, is a means to regulate behavior—a means to define what is acceptable and what is not, what is encouraged and what is not—within a broader context of the organization of power. State routines and rituals punish, but they also serve as moral signposts, creating the vision, sentiment, and disposition for acting correctly in a hierarchical world.[24]

Standing on Foucault's and Bourdieu's shoulders, Corrigan and Sayer underscore that the processes of moral regulation are "projects of normalizing"—taking for granted and internalizing the social categories that organize power by making them appear to be intrinsic to life. Thus, structures of inequality—of race, gender, religion, class—articulated through state systems, can become as natural and as invisible as the air we breath. Abrams's "idea of the state," Corrigan and Sayer warn, is found inside of us.

Just how the mix of routines and morality, of forms and legitimacy occasioned state-making in England is their book's scope, and the pleasure is in the details. Corrigan and Sayer understand state-making to be a centuries-long endeavor, and they go back to medieval, premodern England to find the cultural grounding of emerging "modern" institutions. In the arena of recordkeeping, for example, they find that the development of Church institutions stimulated an increase in written records, which in turn spurred a need for literacy among administrators, which in turn intensified the dominion of the written word—now archived and retrievable, defining "facts" and reality—a condition, in turn, buttressed by a formal authority (clerisy) instituting its own "routines and rituals" of legitimation. In another realm, that of Church and punishment, we find the beginnings, at the same time (ca. 1400), of a Western tradition damning heretics to the stake.[25]

The Great Arch goes from the medieval cultural matrix to the Tudor period—an interval of extraordinary transformation rivaling the changes in cultural politics experienced in Spain. The English trajectory, however, tracked a different path. Here, the Crown broke from Catholicism (and its entrenched political hierarchy) to found its own church (the Church of England), thus converting Protestantism into a banner of nationalism, and the English into a self-consciously "elect" people. This spirit of "national sovereignty," once unleashed, fostered the extension of governmental reach and the strengthening of state institutions. Treason's compass was expanded in the 1530s to include "treason by word" (i.e., the refusal to take the Oath of Supremacy to the king and to the Church of England) and again, fifty years later, to include religious treachery (i.e., ordination into the Roman Catholic priesthood). Meanwhile, the Crown set up a secret service to track down and monitor Catholic clergy and their disciples (as Corrigan and Sayer point out, the use of paid agents for information gathering marked a "new development in policing methods").[26] Government censorship grew with the suppression and monitoring of publications, and from 1538 through most of the seventeenth century domestic and imported books were under the Crown's surveillance. As the number of criminal offenses grew, one "serious addition," to quote Corrigan and Sayer, was the crime of witchcraft. With the expansion of courts, torture was on the rise as an instrument of "information gathering." Also on the rise were other phenomena: onslaughts against Gypsies, the embodiment of immorality; anti-Catholic sentiments to strengthen Protestant nationalism; and appeals to national security and "reasons of state."[27] Corrigan and Sayer characterized the first part of the seventeenth century as a period when "the density of government" increased: the nation's reach extended, definitions of "Englishness" sharpened, and the state's institutional presence—the means (often violent) through which the nation was organized—thickened.[28]

English and Spanish state-making thus followed different courses, but both entailed political realignments that were cultural at heart. The state, along with its "reason," became a rhetoric of the times; religion and nationalism were wedded as ideology; boundaries defining membership in the national community were solidifying, as were exclusions; government institutions—organizing power and displaying nationhood—were expanded and consolidated; the very sense of what power looked like, felt like—as well as what it should look like and feel like—was transformed; political legitimacy took on new meaning, as did political possibility; and, not least, bureaucrats—and their human subjects—were social beings in the making.

Violence and Civilization

The "state-idea"—riding on the "forms, routines, and rituals" of state systems—masks a reality of political subjection. Or we could say, bringing Hannah Arendt into the dialogue, that it camouflages the West's "terrible underside." Arendt does not flinch: violence is as much a part of our Western legacy as the most uplifting of civilization's values, and we forget that at our peril.[29] Violence and civilization: they are inseparable. They need each other, they feed on each other—a realization that can stop your heart.

Michael Taussig also refused to ignore that terrible fact and, at his best, presented the West's hidden violence with a frightening sense of immediacy. He traveled to the Amazon basin to reveal the horrors carried out in the name of civilization during the early twentieth-century rubber boom, when the British savagely tortured (dismembered, hung, burned) Indian laborers in the Putumayo.[30] Taussig argued that the brutality was so severe, so profound, that the standard rationale given for such behavior—labor control, profits—was trifling. Torture might have been triggered by a concern for control (or information), but that alone could not explain the gratuitous cruelty shown by British managers to Indian laborers. That kind of savagery, Taussig believed, had a cultural logic rooted in the "epistemic murk" at the marrow of Western being—not a logic of ideas, but one of feelings, fantasies, and hidden terrors. I can't do justice to his argument or style but, for Taussig, that dark, infernal core, capable of unleashing such enormous cruelty, was the violence begotten by power, by the ability of some Western men to command the very being of others.[31] This is Arendt's fascist precedent.

Taussig, like Arendt, understood that Western rationality could perfume violence in the colonies and violence at home. He is at pains to make us see the discomforting union of violence and reason, along with the contortions we go through to deny their collusion: all those "legal niceties" that are part of the "necessary attempts to rationalize violence."[32] For it is terrifying for those of us who rest our superiority as a nation on its founding as a "rational legal state" to recognize how we "imbue violence with the greatest legitimating force there could be."[33]

The state, the "legitimating force" for all kinds of obscene acts, became, in Taussig's rendition, the modern equivalent of Emile Durkheim's "society"—that entity drenched in awe, devotion, and fear which is the object of traditional peoples' religious devotion. As did Durkheim in his rendition of society, Taussig stressed the constraining force imposed by the state: no matter how unbodied or conceptual, the "state" exerts force just as coercively as any material being. Taussig, in other words, saw the state as a modern fetish, and with that he surpassed Abram's metaphor of state as mask. Although the state's fetishized power might be illusory, it is, Taussig discerned, preeminently real: it is no less than the means through which we apprehend, grasp, and make sense of our political world. "Mask" does not do the state's wizardry justice.

We hold that modern states are rational institutions, bearing little resemblance to the traditional states of the past. Ancient states, unlike our own, were shrouded in religious speculation, ruled by mortals become gods, and governed through patronage. But our belief in the essential rationality of the modern state is, Taussig underscores, part of Western creed: the modern version of the "sacred quality of violence/reason [that] we will impute to the ancient states."[34] This belief stops us from seeing the sectarian interests behind official deference to the public good.[35] The belief in "reasons of state," in a "rational legal state," is our faith, and it is a faith we won't admit.

But reality is a worse nightmare. Inquisitors, though stewards of Catholicism and Christ, did not necessarily appeal to a divine image to justify their acts of state terror. They appealed to reason and to the public good, to the necessities of national security, to the mysteries of the State. The Inquisition was not on the traditional side of the modern divide. It was at the cusp.

We would probably consider Spain to be the most fantastical, the most awe-driven, the most phantasmagoric of European absolutism, and we would probably consider the Inquisition—one of the epochal strands in our social imagination of evil—to be its star icon.[36] The divide partitioning the ancients from the moderns, separating our "rational legal state" from early modern history, declares (to our comfort) just how long a way we have come.

State fetishism—transforming the "state" into an entity with a life and power of its own—casts a wide net: it obscures the subjection of people, and it also obscures the subjection of nations. It creates the remarkable historical illusion that European nations developed autonomously, with pasts independent of the larger world community. It encourages the fiction that European countries (make that northern Europeans) were self-made and that successes enjoyed since the time of conquest were rooted in their preferred position on civilization's highway—apart from any integral relationship with peoples outside their borders. Put another way, this version of state fetishism denies any intrinsic, relational hierarchy between nations (or peoples); it denies that states and colonies were party to each other's creation, including the re-creation of structured inequities; it denies that Western state-making, along with its basic mechanics of rule, was honed in the colonizing process. State fetishism denies history.

Fernando Coronil brilliantly described this Western mythology as "occidentalism"—the conditions underlying those Western portrayals of selfhood that made "orientalism" (our often violent, uninformed, partisan, and distorted representations of "others") possible. The way we express cultural differences or "otherness," Coronil argued, must be understood historically; that is, in relation to the political and economic disparities kindled by Western dominance. The "hierarchization of cultural difference"—the fantasy making the West both superior to and isolated from the rest—is embedded in global geopolitics.[37]

State fetishism, in its occidentalized format, wrested Western nation-building from its roots in global politics—a fictional divorce just as characteristic of seventeenth-century fetishism as it was of the more commonly discussed nineteenth-century version. The modern world, from its inception, was transnational in scope and hierarchical in structure. And perhaps nowhere are these characteristics more evident than in the categories ordering the newly globalized humanity: the categories of race thinking.

Race thinking, Bureaucracy, and Nationalist Spirit

Tracing the modern world back to the sixteenth century, when Iberia was simultaneously building a state and an empire, lets us get a better grasp on another of the modern world's deceits. State fetishism—veiling our origins in a globalizing, hierarchical world—has also veiled our origins in race thinking; it has made us lose sight of our colonial foundations and of the antagonistic social relationships at its core. Yes, race thinking, nationalist sentiments, bureaucratic rule, colonialism—and the nascent capitalist economic order girding them—had different roots and different pasts; but history joined them five hundred years ago, and history accordingly paved the way for an onslaught of often deadly confusions.

Hannah Arendt, choosing her words carefully, didn't so much talk about "racism" as about "race thinking." "Race thinking" cuts a wider swath than "race" because it moves us behind and beyond racism's narrow, nineteenth-century connotations. It takes social processes that we have categorically divided and places them within the same frame: instead of studying ethnicity and race, or caste and race, or nationalism and race as autonomous social forms, we can, under the rubric of "race thinking," better grasp how they have interpenetrated and shaped one another over time.

According to almost every major historical text, Latin America was a society of castes. Spain divided conquered peoples into corporate groups —Spanish, Indian, black—each with associated rights, privileges, and obligations. Ideally, castes were endogamous and, since caste-mates were to marry one another, membership was, in principle, determined by descent. The caste system was patently a device of political order; and even though descent played a part, even though color ("negro") was singled out as one constituent, caste is understood to be a legal or social (as opposed to biological) construct at heart.

If we follow the traditional/modern divide, caste would be the old way of marking inequalities; race would be the new. Unlike caste, race is understood to be principally a question of ancestry and phenotype, a biological phenomenon (or so goes the ideology), and, consequently, to be independent of social or political regimes. Race emerged as the root cause of social differentiation in the West's "modern," liberal age, and the nineteenth-century revolutions in the natural and human sciences provided its explanatory frame. Race was inherited, and since human capabilities were linked to race, human capabilities, according to racist doctrine, were also inherited. Race was apparent (or at least it was supposed to be) because race was color-coded. It seems that nineteenth-century race ideologies forgot the "preliberal" origins of "negro" when they devised the "modern" color trio of white, brown (or red), and black.

Race thinking does not negate the colonial caste system, nor does it deny that caste and race systems represent two different modes of organizing and explaining inequality. Race thinking, however, does help us see what the race vs. caste division hides: that race and caste were not separate systems, but interpenetrating. Race thinking helps us understand how race and caste might, chameleonlike, slip in and out of each other,[38] how a relatively innocent category (like color) could become virulent, how politically defined differences (like nationality) could so easily become inheritable traits.

"Race thinking," then, broadly refers to any mode of construing and engaging social hierarchies through the lens of descent. It represents a potential way of sensing, understanding, and being in the world, a cultural possibility that can become part of social identities and social practices. Its most significant property, though, is its most difficult lesson: race thinking is invariably tied to other expressions of power, other forms of social antagonism, and is best interpreted in dialectic with those relations.[39]

Arendt was especially concerned with how race thinking could become embedded in the bureaucracies of state and colonial governments. Like her, I center on this dynamic, recognizing that I have done so at the expense of others. This book, then, is by no means meant to be a comprehensive study of race thinking in the Viceroyalty of Peru: it is a look into race thinking and its consequences within the frame of a nascent, colonial state embarking on bureaucratic rule.

Bureaucrats control knowledge, and, as social analysts have pointed out, therein lies a source of their power.[40] But inquisitors dominated a special kind of knowledge, for they could determine the most profound of societal truths—membership in a human community. Inquisitors were charged with certifying Spanish "purity of blood" (i.e. the absence of Jewish or Moorish ancestry); and they oversaw religious orthodoxy—a determination often attached to purity of blood—that, in its modern form, was linked to a budding spirit of Spanish nationalism. Inquisitors, principal arbiters of imperial culture, buttressed the race thinking on which it rested.

Peru's inquisitors (as little gods) were producing the "state" at the same time that they were inscribing race thinking into institutional practice. And the processes were remarkably similar. Just as the inquisitors (among others) were conjuring diverse government institutions into an abstract state, diverse social relationships were being conjured into abstract race categories. By the seventeenth century, magistrates and other functionaries were officially dividing people into Spanish–Indian–black boxes as a matter of course; and "Indian," "black," and "Spaniard" were taking on the appearance of a thing—of a self-evident quality of human being. For, like the "state," "race" was a phantasm. Part of the mystique of race thinking and its categorical practices was to present indio or negro or español as if it were either a category or an individual, and not a social relation produced in the political and economic turmoil of colonialism.

Marx taught that a concept like "individual," and the social practices giving it life, could have come into being only in dialectic with the "state,"[41] and I believe we can say similar things about "race." Slaves and citizens, Marx argued, were not as they appeared (i.e. individuals with inherent personal qualities); rather, they were individuals living in and constituted by a set of defined societal relations. So too were indio, español, and negro—individuals living in and constituted by a set of defined societal relations.

Racial categories not only come into being with "state" and "individual," they embody an analogous dialectic. Colonial race thinking was at once a "universal" designation, marking out a formal slice of global humanity, and an "individuating" one—one that bureaucrats got to by stripping away social bonds in search of a personal, inherent truth. All were fetishes: perceived as material things, avenues through which reality was understood, yet fictions of the social relations spawning them.

Seventeenth-century inquisitors (like other colonial bureaucrats) inherited a world whose humanity was increasingly understood in racialized terms, and magistrates played a significant (if unwitting) role in deepening and consolidating race thinking as a way of life. Through their practices, inquisitors were delineating the very terms of social experience: the terms by which the world was to be judged, the terms framing any individual's social truth. But even though tribunal magistrates were some of the most powerful players in the processes defining colonial life, neither they nor any other official had the only word; neither they nor any other official could impose their own terms, cookie-cutter style, on the hearts and minds of their subjects. So, even as we focus on how tribunal practices inscribed race thinking and how magistrates helped build the scaffolding of a modern, colonial cultural order, we must never forget to keep an eye on how their subjects, within these bounds, embroidered race thinking into the fabric of living.

Spain, Spaniard, Spanishness

Nationalism and race thinking, in concert, propelled the modern world's most destructive beliefs; yet we have trouble visualizing the depth of that connection because our historical sensibilities rarely put colonialism at the core of modern life. Spain, Spaniard, and Spanishness suggest we do otherwise, for their dialectic was at the center of debates about what, at the biological and spiritual core, a Spaniard and the incipient Spanish nation were to be.

There was no Spain (as government and nation) in the seventeenth century. What we now call Spain was composed of regional principalities, including the New World colonies, under the dominion of the Hapsburg dynasty of Castile. Still, by the first century of modern state-making, when the concept of "state" was coming into being, the Peninsula's philosophers and policy advisors were nonetheless writing about a Spanish character and a Spanish people. What our theorists of the state—Foucault and Bourdieu—do not put into the picture is that Spain's philosophers and policy advisors were doing so as Castile was conquering and colonizing around the globe. Investigations into "Spanishness," then, were taking place at the same time that colonizers were calling themselves "Spanish" in order to distinguish their ancestry from the lower orders of Indians and blacks. Something of the nation must have been made with every use of the term "español" in the colonies; and, reciprocally, Madrid's discussions of the Spanish character must have drawn on a vision of the colonial Spaniard. For not only was "Spanish"—as a colonial category—racialized, so was its hidden partner, the potential Spanish nation.

Hannah Arendt's history of English colonialism points a finger at the tensions within a category like "race." Colonialism required a superior caste of bureaucratic rulers who could find a peer wherever the Union Jack flew. "English," she argued, had to be a global phenomenon. Yet "Englishmen" were not all equal; they did not share the same possibilities in life. Race thinking had to obscure these internal divisions; at the same time, though, it had to leave them in place.

"Spaniard" played a similar role: it defined a unifying experience for all colonizers (españoles did not owe tribute or labor service), gave that experience substance as an "unmixed race," and portrayed the kingdom and people as God's chosen over all others. But, as Lima's authorities —who, like their English counterparts, harbored elite expectations and pretensions—were to discover, the notion of "unmixed race" stretched precariously over the internal hierarchies it was supposed to mute. Peruvian Spaniards, as viceroys and inquisitors bemoaned, had forgotten their place. Tensions between Spaniards—between metropolitan and creole, between noble and commoner, between aristocrat and merchant—were unbearable for many metropolitans at work civilizing Peruvians, and some of the Inquisition's most grievous tragedies were the result.[42]

The Setting

"In Lima and throughout Peru," wrote one observer of Peruvian life, "there live people from the best places in Spain, and there are Portuguese people, there are Galicians, Asturians, Vizcayans, . . . Valencians, Murcians, and French, Italians, Germans and Flemish, Greeks, people from Ragusa, Corsicans, Genovese, Majorquens, . . . English, Moriscos (Christians of Moorish ancestry), [and] people from India and China and many other combinations and mixtures."[43] Peru, then, was a cosmopolitan place, and Lima a cosmopolitan city, a potpourri of nations and "races," of wealth and poverty, and alive with the energy of newness. Lima was a modern city where, in the words of the seventeenth-century Jesuit priest Bernabé Cobo, "the ocean was like a road."[44] It was a modern place where King Commerce anointed aristocrats, Indians owned slaves, all Spaniards (not just the nobility) could have servants, and women both sued for divorce and "wanted to be equal" (or so it was said).[45] Lima's ebullience was noted by travelers: it was a city bustling with goods from China to Cuzco and dotted with *pulperías* offering Indians, blacks, Spaniards, and "mixtures" a good time in exchange for money; a city where churches were grander than Europe's, public celebrations more distinguished, and the population more sophisticated;[46] a city where, contrary to how it was supposed to be, pure castes mixed—and mixed with "mixtures"—in pubs, markets, church events, and "witchcraft" sessions. Lima was also a well-ordered and rational city, with streets in a grid plan and inhabitants counted in government censuses.[47] It was also a city where a few were very privileged, many were disadvantaged, and most were increasingly dependent on market goods for sustenance. It was a city where the homeless wandered its elegant plazas.[48] It was a city that bore the scars of early capitalism.

Peru was a land of hope and promise, and as our chronicler pointed out, all sorts of migrants were drawn to its major cities. These migrants were joined by migrants of another sort: men and women who had no choice but to work, as slaves or drafted labor, in cities like Lima or Cuzco or in the mining centers of Potosí and Huancavelica. According to a 1614 census, slaves dominated Lima's population: blacks constituted nearly half of her roughly 23,000 inhabitants (10,386); Spaniards were the second-largest group (9,616), followed by Indians, now living in a quarter reserved for native Andeans (1,978); and mestizos and mulatos made up the smallest group (936).[49] Twenty-six years later, a creole priest estimated that Lima had nearly doubled in size to 40,000;[50] and, while we can't offer numbers, its "mixtures" grew concomitantly. But with all of Lima's pretense, Potosí was perhaps the viceroyalty's most remarkable urban center. Seated on top of the silver mines that produced much of Spain's wealth, Potosí boasted 120,000 inhabitants in 1572 and 160,000 by 1610—making it one of the world's largest and richest cities.[51] Inquisition documents suggest that it was also a center for heresies.

Religion absorbed the lives of men and women living in the viceroyalty. Much more than a set of beliefs, religion was a worldview, a model for living in the world—reinforced in daily practice—that both specified the boundaries of community and one's place within it. But the viceroyalty was a world in the making, with equivocal boundaries and puzzling definitions of place. No wonder, then, that Catholicism could become a battleground of debates around personhood and sanctity.

The viceroyalty, while not uniquely so, was at the center of several religious storms over the shape of colonial Catholicism. Saints emerged, and sanctuaries bloomed. But which were true, and which were frauds? Lima and the highlands produced several potential (but equivocal) saints along with potential (but equivocal) sinners; along with them came potential (but equivocal) holy shrines and potential (but equivocal) carved images. Andean Christianity, exuberant and creative, produced its share of holy apparitions and postulants to sainthood. The Church gave its blessing to some, and the most famous of these were anchored in colonial life: if God smiled on all his people, he could certainly allow a Peruvian, the Spanish creole Rosa of Lima, to become a saint, or, in recognition of indigenous Catholicism, allow a virgin carved by a native, the Virgin of Copacabana, to make miracles.[52]

Colonial religious life glittered in spectacular devotions. But saintly standing was not a certain path in the colonies; someone's saints could be someone else's devils. The Inquisition, as supreme judge over heretical matters, found itself in the middle of bitter disputes over the sanctity—or perfidy—of colonial subjects.[53] And its ecclesiastic counterparts found themselves facing similar disputes over the nature of native beliefs and customs. The starkly contradictory status of religious sentiments—and the starkly contradictory passions they stirred—reflect the Church's growing pains, symptomatic of a restless, modernizing world.[54]

Coming to Terms

Hannah Arendt spoke about the terrors born in the union of race thinking and bureaucratic rule—a union intrinsic to the West's development and the source of its "subterranean stream." The principal concern of *Modern Inquisitions* is to come to terms with the historical depth of this terrible union, to come to terms with the colonial origins of the modern world. The coming chapters examine different aspects of the seventeenth-century dance of bureaucracy and race, but we will look at these broad processes through a specific lens. We will focus our attention on women and men living in the Viceroyalty of Peru, caught up in the Spanish Inquisition or in analogous campaigns to expunge native heresies; on women and men becoming Portuguese, Spanish, Indian, black, or a "mixture" while learning both the ways of state and their place in the globe.

Modern Inquisitions draws on a range of sources: sermons, catechisms, diaries, official correspondence, and (most consequential) on Church records from Peru's Inquisition and from the corresponding extirpation of idolatry campaigns. The trials of three persons brought before the tribunal—Doña Mencia de Luna, Manuel Henríquez, and Manuel Bautista Pérez—will serve as entrées into colonial cultural politics. All three were called Portuguese and "New Christian" (converts of Jewish or Moorish ancestry); all three were charged with being secret Jews in one of the largest and most momentous autos-da-fé Spain ever produced. While their histories tell us much about the centuries-long legacy of European anti-Semitism, they also suggest much about the pivotal historical processes then transforming the globe.

These trials are our first-look introduction to the Inquisition, entitled "Three Accused Heretics." My hope is that the experiences of Doña Mencia de Luna, Manuel Henríquez, and Manuel Bautista Pérez will return some flesh and feeling to the abstractions of history. These are chronicles of terror and despair, reminding us all too well that social processes have human roots and human effects. These trials, along with others, also show the inquisitors—mortals with seemingly godlike powers—as the bureaucrats they were. They are seen to be human beings—replete with foibles, strengths, and shortcomings—who act in ways not always predictable or anticipated. We read about disputes, errors, missed chances, and disastrous calculations; we read tales of human strength and courage, about moments of extraordinary valor and acts of profound dignity; and sometimes we can even find flashes of humor. The cases should also help you judge, for yourselves, the lessons I have drawn.[55]

It was the fusion of bureaucratic rule and race that Arendt found so dangerous, and it was "state magic" that helped make race thinking so powerful, ubiquitous, and illusory. Our next two chapters, devoted to questions of bureaucracy and the mysteries of state, are intended to help us imagine which of those qualities attached to bureaucratic rule could have made race thinking such a menacing component of Western history.

First, in "Inquisition as Bureaucracy," a look into the Inquisition's bureaucratic side: at the standards and rules that inquisitors were supposed to follow, in the spirit of reason and equity, as they deliberated the truth of colonial subjects. Bureaucracies always serve larger political systems, and the Inquisition was profoundly shaped by the dictates of an emerging absolutist state. The bureaucratic arrogance that Arendt criticized in nineteenth-century England was rooted in the ethos of colonial administration, a form of government that held colonial officials accountable to London and not to the people whose lives they made decisions over. The political order of seventeenth-century Peru—at least in terms of political representation and accountability—was not all that dissimilar.[56] Although we will not be analyzing the dynamic between institutions and Spanish absolutism, a slant toward the bureaucratic side of things does lead to surprising insights into the execution of power. We witness, à la Kafka, some of the absurd consequences of following the rules, and we witness bureaucracy doing what it is supposed to do: namely, create a fair(er) playing field through procedures that, among other things, limit the authority of individual officeholders. We also get a snapshot of how bureaucrats were made, of how they acquired the extraordinary arrogance to make such extraordinary decisions over other peoples' lives.

Inquisitors were party to "state magic,"[57] and the next chapter, "Mysteries of State," attempts to pierce its illusions. Tribunal records, opening bureaucracy to inspection, suggest how inquisitors, immersed in their bureaucratic practices, might have contributed to the dawning modern concept that the state was an entity apart—separate from dynastic history—with its own logic, its own needs, and its own "reasons." These records help us imagine how the "state" could be perceived as if it were a concrete, material thing—how it could become both a fetish and part of our social selves. They help us imagine how the "state," as a concept through which we apprehend the world, could impede our ability to envision power in any other way. And they help us imagine how the state's mysteries could be unraveled.

Mysteries of state spilled over into mysteries of race, and state bureaucracies gave race their blessing: they institutionalized race thinking as a way of organizing power and as a way of organizing life. In other words, they made race part of the body politic. Then race, absorbing the state's aura, mimed its fetishism: "race" joined "state" as a concept that shrouded the political relations at its core. The remaining chapters in this book, beginning with "Globalization and Guinea Pigs," explore some of the Andean consequences.

During the seventeenth century, priests went out to the Peruvian countryside with homilies in hand; as they were to discover, though, preaching the Lord was not a simple affair. Preaching the Lord also meant preaching colonialism's new cultural order. These sermons, among other ecclesiastic instruction manuals, let us see, in rare focus, an official version of race thinking. Missionaries, believing it their duty to explain all of human history, including political hierarchy, took on the globe—and in the process dealt with the slippery field of nation-states, color, religion, peoplehood, racial capacities, political rights, and what they saw as the "natural order" of things. Father Francisco de Avila and Father Fernando de Avendaño, with the natural order of things in mind taught lessons about race, color, and globalization. And they used that Andean favorite, the guinea pig, to do it.

Avila and Avendaño's "natural order" was calibrated by the peculiar race-thinking notion that blood carried stains, and that stains could determine character traits, intelligence, political rights, and economic possibilities. The notion of blood purity was first elaborated in Europe, and the chapter "States and Stains" looks at what happened when that notion was transported to the Americas.

Inquisitors, like other state officials, were obliged to indicate the race and blood purity of everyone brought before them, and the records give us a ringside view of the New Christian dilemma in the New World. With debates spinning about the nature of blood stains (were they indelible? could baptism override them? could New Christians of Jewish descent ever lose their stain?), authorities in the Americas were vexed by a flood tide of blood-related questions. Were all New Christians alike? Was the blood stain of Europe's New Christians the same as that of Indians or blacks? Were all stains equal? When inquisitors and their colleagues responded to these issues as they went about their daily chores of statecraft, they were helping make race into a calculable thing. They were also imbuing race with very modern, often state-related, confusions: nation and religion, culture and genes, color and ability.

In the Andes, confusions could often surface as breathtaking conspiracies involving New Christians, Portuguese, merchants, witches, Indians, and blacks. Inquisitors, at different times, lumped together various of the above groups as colluding traitors against Church and State. The next three chapters ("New Christians and New World Fears," "The Inca's Witches," and "Becoming Indian") take on three, interacting colonial confusions: the "Jewish problem," the "woman/witchcraft problem," and the "Indian problem." As we'll see, magistrates inevitably brought race thinking to bear on their judgments just as they inevitably appealed to reasons of state to justify them.

Debates over the character of Portuguese New Christians—baptized women and men of Jewish or Moorish ancestry—were debates that linked questions about the new mercantile economy and colonial world order with concerns about race and Spain's emerging sense of nation. The supporters of purity-of-blood laws believed that religious conversion could not erase the stains of a heretical religious past, and inquisitors, who arrested New Christians on the assumption they were insidious Portuguese-Jewish merchants, were making the case for a "racially" pure Spanish nation and for a "racially" pure definition of "Spanishness." They were also participating in a vision of the world reminiscent of what we today call "racial profiling."

Most inquisitors were dubious about the commitment of New Christians to Spain or to Catholicism—loyalty, after all, was in the blood—and their doubt became alarm in Peru, where magistrates were convinced that New Christians, viz. internationalist merchants, were establishing subversive ties not only with indios and negros but with Spain's enemies abroad. The chapter "New Christians and New World Fears" delves into the conditions behind the cultural blaming, the circumstances facilitating the tribunal's transformation of New Christians into the hub of a great conspiracy of oppressed colonial malcontents and foreign interests.

New Christians were not the only ones to be accused of conspiratorial acts. In "The Inca's Witches" we look at a new set of heretics whose treachery was attached to colonial racial politics. During the seventeenth century, when New Christians were sparking tribunal concerns, some non-Indian women were being arrested for heretically colluding with Peruvian natives. These women (heresy wore a gendered face) were charged with secretly practicing witchcraft, and one of their black arts' most dangerous aspects had to do with Indians. By the middle of the seventeenth century, Peru's sorceresses were censured for going out to the countryside to learn Indian lore: employing coca leaf in their conjures, exhorting the Inca queen with Quechua words, and soliciting the Inca for help in their diabolic acts. Non-Indian "witches" were charged with practicing an Inca-centered, nativist—possibly even an anticolonial and antiracialist—form of sorcery. "The Inca's Witches" looks into how these women, construing a miraculous Inca Indian, were reinforcing colonial categories of rule but, like good witches, were also turning them upside down.[58]

"Indian," we must remember, was not a native concept and had no bearing on how Andeans conceived of themselves before the Spanish conquest. "Indian" was part of the new colonial world order. Nevertheless, by the seventeenth century some native Peruvians were calling themselves "Indian"—and that paradox is the subject of our next-to-the-last chapter, "Becoming Indian."

The world of the seventeenth century was a religious world, and native Peruvians constructed an array of religious stances: some became devout Catholics; others, consciously or unconsciously, took from both cultural traditions; and some from Peru's central sierra deliberately rejected the Spanish religion and became "Indian"—their version of Indian. They refused to eat Spanish food, refused to wear Spanish dress, and refused to allow women to be contaminated by Spanish sex. This anti-Spanish idiom had a decades-long history. And even though "Indian"—as category or identity—had played no part in earlier anti-Spanish movements, by the seventeenth century "Indianness" was at the center of an indigenous political critique. We shall see how "Indian," originating as a formal term of colonial state-making, could enter the broader cultural milieu and, to Spanish chagrin, take on (within limits) a life of its own.[59]

The fears inspired by "witches" who worshiped the Inca and by New Christian merchants who carried on with indios and negros were elaborated at the same time that some of Peru's native peoples were suspected of abandoning Catholicism for ancestral idolatries. This was the stuff of conspiracy: the "woman/witchcraft problem," the "Jewish problem," and the "Indian problem" were mutually reinforcing, swelling the authorities' anxieties over the brittleness of the social and political fabric (i.e., the cultural hierarchy) of the Spanish colonial state. Seventeenth-century Peru provides an extraordinary example of how such fears could coalesce, develop, and ultimately balloon into absurd theories of cultural blame. Securing European state-making to its moorings in global expansion helps explain the irrationalities that have accompanied the development of the modern age. This book, addressing the deep social contradictions of a world-in-the-making, shows how some Spaniards, notably Peru's mid-seventeenth-century inquisitors, were confronted by lifeways so profoundly different—morally, culturally, economically, and politically —from their perception of what was right that they felt their very survival—and that of a world worth living in—was at stake.

Spanish colonialism and the Spanish Inquisition leave us with questions and, perforce, a critique. In Anglo-American eyes, both of these phenomena are remnants of Europe's premodern past, examples of Spain's marginality to progress, signs of the enormous gulf between Spain and the true dawning of modern life. *Modern Inquisitions* argues the opposite: that both Spanish colonialism and the Spanish Inquisition attended civilization's birth. If this interpretation holds, we have to ask, why the disjuncture between the past and our common knowledge of it? Why the effort at historical distortion (after all, this canard goes back to the Black Legend of the late sixteenth century)? What, moreover, does this misrepresentation say about ourselves—about our claim to the mantle of progress, so crucial to defining and justifying who we are?

Modern Inquisitions, tracking Arendt's path back to the beginnings of modern experience, tries to locate the "submerged," darker currents of Western civilization, which are as essential to any definition of the modern world as our more lofty, civilizing goals. It tries to locate the "subterranean stream of Western history" that Arendt identified on the road to making sense of the morally insensible.

THREE ACCUSED HERETICS

Lima: Capital of the Kingdom of the Indies,
where the Viceroy, the Archbishop, and the Sr. Inquisitor live.
From Felipe Guaman Poma de Ayala,
El primer nueva corónica y buen gobierno (1613?).

There is no document of civilization which is not at the same time a document of barbarism. —WALTER BENJAMIN, "Theses on the Philosophy of History"[1]

B Y WAY OF CONFRONTING and understanding the human reality of the Inquisition, we shall consider in the following pages brief transcriptions from the trials that doomed two men and one woman who were accused of secretly practicing Judaism.[2] Doña Mencia de Luna, Manuel Henríquez, and Manuel Bautista Pérez—called Judaizers, or Portuguese or New Christians—were seized by the Lima Inquisition when nearly a hundred people were rounded up in connection with the 1635–39 *complicidad grande*, or "Great Jewish Conspiracy" to commit heresy and treason. Those convicted were punished in a dramatic and lavish auto-da-fé, or rite of final judgment. It was Peru's bloodiest. Manuel Bautista Pérez plus ten others were tied to the stake and burned alive; fifty-two accused Judaizers were exiled, whipped, and publicly shamed. Doña Mencia de Luna and Manuel Henríquez were arrested with the so-called conspirators and remained in jail for decades until exasperated inquisitors determined there was enough evidence for their cases to go forward.

The Spanish Inquisition was founded at the end of the fifteenth century to defend the Spanish realm against perceived threats to security and religious integrity. Its first target was "hidden Jews," but, with time, the Inquisition's charge broadened to include all sorts of heresies. Some trace the tribunal's roots to the century before, a dark period in Spanish history when popular and official anti-Semitism coalesced into mob violence. Hundreds of Jews were murdered and hundreds more were terrorized into baptism and conversion.[3] Spain's "New Christian" community was born out of these forced conversions and, from the beginning, "Old Christian" members of elite and popular classes looked on New Christians as a fifth column, as the "enemy within."[4]

As the enemy within the Christian polity, New Christians were frequently mistaken for practicing Jews. This misconception was reinforced by a racialized view of religion, a view born at the same time as the Inquisition itself. According to its dictates, baptized men and women of Jewish (or Muslim) descent were considered stained by ancestral heresies, regardless of conversion to Christianity or commitment to the faith. Purity-of-blood statutes, enacted by local municipalities and by the Crown, codified this belief; consequently, New Christians, carriers of "stained blood" (unlike Old Christians, carriers of "pure blood"), were officially barred from professions, university, or public office.[5]

Spain's emerging sense of nationalism, forged in the name of militant Catholicism, would brook no heresy or heretics, and the Inquisition sat in judgment over all manner of sins (witchcraft, blasphemy, adultery, priest solicitation in the confessional). Still, it was the menace of other organized religions—first Judaism, but then Protestantism and Islam—that bore the brunt of inquisitorial wrath. In the Peninsula, all three were targets, but in Peru (like other colonies), hidden Judaizers were uniquely feared and uniquely punished.[6] In time, inquisitors would be linking the Jewish threat to the global relations of economy and power—to the markets and colonies—of the emerging modern world.

By the seventeenth century, however, New Christians had acquired another moniker: they were also called Portuguese. So why were New Christians assumed to be Portuguese? And why was the Portuguese connection so explosive? To answer, we have to look at the consequences of the 1492 Act of Expulsion which forced around a hundred thousand Jews into exile. Some estimate that at least fifty thousand—half of all who left Spain—crossed the border into neighboring Portugal. By some estimates, this migration swelled the percentage of Jews living in Portugal to one-fifth of the country's inhabitants.[7] In 1497 these immigrants had to face yet another order to convert or be expelled. Most converted en masse, giving Portugal a coherent block of New Christians—some of whom followed Christ, while others retained their Jewish beliefs and secretly practiced Jewish rites.[8]

One hundred years later, when the Portuguese Inquisition launched vicious attacks against assumed Judaizers, many New Christians felt compelled to leave their homes once more. But this time they emigrated back to Spain. A substantial number of these emigrants were involved in global trade, creating a notable Portuguese–New Christian presence in the expanding area of transatlantic commerce.[9] It was this return migration that spurred the burgeoning Castilian stereotype, shared and promulgated by many inquisitors, that all New Christians were Portuguese, were merchants, were Jews.[10] Spanish inquisitors' concerns about a Jewish peril—

now attached to concerns about mercantilism and Iberian politics—exploded.

With "Portuguese" added to "New Christian" and "Jew," migrants to the Americas were now judged against the backdrop of Spain's foreign affairs and, in particular, Castile's often-ambiguous relationship with Portugal. King Felipe II of Castile assumed the Portuguese crown in 1580, and while Castile relished the new kingdom added to its rule, many Portuguese believed Felipe had usurped the throne. Tensions between Madrid and Lisbon ran high: many Castilians not only questioned the loyalty of Portuguese subjects but were disturbed by the growing involvement of Portuguese merchants in imperial commerce; many Portuguese, on the other hand, chafing at Spanish attempts to impose a Hispanic model of monopoly trade on their more liberal traditions, saw life under Spanish rule as a kind of bondage.[11] The fact that the majority of New Christians arrested (and executed) by the Spanish Inquisition were born in Portugal, or had parents who had been, only worsened frictions. Ancestry damned these women and men twice over: as Portuguese, they were mistrusted for their fidelity to Lisbon; as New Christians, they were mistrusted for their fidelity to Judaism.

These suspicions were further compounded in Peru by the 1624 Dutch victory over Castile in the battle for Northeast Brazil. A Portuguese colony since the fifteenth century, Brazil came under the jurisdiction of the Spanish monarchy when Felipe II assumed the Portuguese throne. Along with the throne, Felipe inherited Portugal's decades-long skirmish with the Dutch. The Dutch were Spain's principal rivals for control over South America, and during the first half of the seventeenth century Dutch forces not only were wreaking havoc with Spanish trade, but they were trying to establish footholds on both South American coasts.[12] It was a Castilian commonplace that Portuguese New Christians were secret allies of the Dutch, and many Spaniards, including the playwright Lope de Vega, blamed seditious Portuguese for Castile's defeats in Brazil: Bahia in 1624 (recaptured in 1625) and Pernambuco six years later.

For Peru's inquisitors, a Dutch colony on the border represented a serious threat.[13] Since victims of Spanish intolerance could practice Judaism in Dutch territories, the inquisitors feared that a vibrant Jewish community in Brazil would only facilitate the enemy's political goals. Of course, they worried equally that Bahians might encourage their recently arrived New Christian kin to cross the Amazon and settle in Peru.[14]

Although the Inquisition has become so familiar to us that its existence—along with its fanatical anti-Semitism—seem a given of Spanish life, we can't lose sight of the fact that many, including members of the elite, did not share its anti-Portuguese, anti–New Christian sentiments.

Throughout the Spanish realms, debates flared over the New Christian character and over tribunal justice. It should come as no surprise that Peru was a theater of conflicting attitudes and policies as well.

New Christians attained their greatest influence under the regime of the Count-Duke of Olivares (1621–43), who was Felipe IV's court favorite and perhaps the most powerful man in the kingdom. The duke supported New Christians, as did Felipe IV's confessor, the inquisitor general no less, in large part because they wanted to take advantage of the "Portuguese's" fiscal and commercial skills.[15] Following Olivares's general spirit of tolerance, men of Jewish ancestry were sought after for positions in government and became significant players in the world of Iberian finance—something Lima's accused heretics were well aware of.[16] Colonial Lima, like the rest of the empire under Olivares's tenure, saw New Christian merchants enjoying prosperity and esteem. Some were even on the verge of becoming a new aristocracy.

Nevertheless, in the sea of anti-Semitic feelings, resentment of New Christians and fear of their treacheries were never far from the surface. Lima's inquisitors—particularly when under the sway of Juan de Mañozca, one of the masterminds behind the Great Jewish Conspiracy—were distrustful of Olivares and the Portuguese presence. Under Mañozca's aegis, the tribunal's mission was to delineate and fight the battle for civilization; and, for most magistrates, Castile vs. Portugal, Old Christian vs. New Christian, True Christian vs. Jew were one and the same struggle.

The Lima office gathered its most comprehensive files in the names of Doña Mencia de Luna, Manuel Henríquez, and Manuel Bautista Pérez, and their dossiers give us a two-sided view of the tribunal's proceedings. Because inquisitors, respecting bureaucratic process, wanted to capture the testimony in detail, we have a particularly sharp view of the bureaucracy in action—gathering evidence, justifying arrests, reaching verdicts. And because the testimony is so detailed, we come as close as we ever can, perhaps, to the words and feelings of the accused. We find out about their pasts and we hear their pained cries.

Most of all, we recognize human beings: victims and bureaucrats alike. We see bureaucrats at work and we see bureaucrats being made. And with the disbelief—and curiosity—that comes with reading about terrible acts, we hear the despair and the heroism of survivors. No narrative can match their words.

Doña Mencia de Luna

It took just an accusation and an apple, according to Father Fernando de Montesinos, the official chronicler of Lima's 1639 auto-da-fé, to spark the discovery of the viceroyalty's Great Jewish Conspiracy. The apple because it introduced suspicion of Antonio Cordero's eating habits; the accusation because it eventually provoked Cordero to testify about the religious practices of enemies, friends, neighbors, and kin.

Antonio Cordero—twenty-four years old, Portuguese, and an agent for a transnational merchant—aroused suspicions one Friday evening during a verbal exchange with a client over food and ancestry: "and [Cordero] was eating a piece of bread and an apple for dinner, and [a client] said . . . wouldn't it be better to eat a rasher of bacon? And he replied, 'Am I to eat what my parents and grandparents would not eat?'"[17] The client relayed this information to the Holy Office, and the Holy Office, recognizing that the evidence was weak, decided to start a file but to do little else. Several magistrates, however, feared this evidence was the tip of a secret Jewish conspiracy and, concerned they would lose a golden opportunity, went to the "experts" for advice on how to proceed. When the experts gave them the go-ahead, inquisitors secretly detained Cordero. That was in April 1635. After a month in jail, Cordero requested a new hearing and set off an avalanche of confessions. Like most avalanches, its beginnings were small. Cordero began with three names: Antonio de Acuna, his boss; Diego López de Fonseca, a friend; and Manuel de la Rosa, the latter's employer. Within a month, the trio was arrested. Like the other two, Antonio de Acuna denied any wrongdoing at first, but after time in jail and excruciating turns on the rack, Acuna cracked. Confessing to heresy, he started to finger partners: among them were Henrique Núñez, Doña Mencia's husband; Rodrigo Báez, her niece's husband; and Jorge de Silva, a family friend whom Doña Mencia had nursed to health. It didn't take long—just three months—before Doña Mencia, her sister, and her niece were apprehended.[18]

Doña Mencia de Luna was one of Lima's new rich, a beneficiary of the wealth furnished by the seventeenth century's global economy. She was a Lima notable, no doubt dressing in silks and laces, hosting soirées, making her dedication to the Church evident by fervent worship and generous donations to its many charities. Like the other extravagantly successful merchant families, Doña Mencia's was well on its way to becoming part of a colonial aristocracy. With her husband and her niece's husband already imprisoned, Doña Mencia must have anticipated her arrest; but she most likely did not anticipate that the society whose rules she claimed to have lived by would turn her into a pariah.

One of the Inquisition's cruelest ironies was that pressures to confess could push women and men to do the unthinkable: to endanger those they most wanted to protect. Eventually, Doña Mencia's husband, her sister, her niece, her niece's husband, and two of her husband's business associates swore they saw her participate in illicit, Judaizing acts. Jorge de Silva, one of these colleagues—the man whom Doña Mencia took into her home and cared for—was one of the first to testify against her. But Jorge de Silva, like all the other witnesses, not only attested to Doña Mencia's heresies, he later denied them.

Jorge de Silva, a bachelor born in Portugal, fiercely denied committing any heresy with anyone—until November 17.[19] Then he did an about-face and requested an audience to "testif[y] against others including Doña Mencia de Luna."[20] Silva first described secret gatherings held at the home of Doña Mencia's sister (Doña Mayor), brother-in-law (Captain Antonio Morón), and niece (Doña Isabel):

> [Silva] remembers he declared to Captain Morón, to his wife and to his daughter that he observed the Law of Moses . . . and Doña Mencia de Luna was also present; and [Silva] observed its ceremonies and rites, keeping Saturday as a holy day, wearing clean shirts and clothing, . . . observing the fast for Queen Esther, which they celebrated in the month of September for three days straight . . . and not eat[ing] bacon or fish without scales in accordance with the Law of Moses which he believed would save him.[21]

In this round of testimony, Silva depicted his long convalescence at Doña Mencia's home as an opportunity for them to discuss Jewish things with ease.[22] Over the next several hearings, Silva's list of accomplices and heretical activities grew.[23]

Silva's transcript goes blank for a year and a half, until May 16, 1637, when he requested another hearing. This time, however, Silva did not elaborate on his previous confession; he completely repudiated it: "everything he had confessed to having done and said regarding the Law of Moses were lies," including "testimony [against] the people he had denounced."[24] Silva felt compelled to revoke the charges, he explained to an angry tribunal, in order to relieve his conscience.

Eight months later, Lima's inquisitors—Licenciado Juan de Mañozca, Licenciado Andrés Juan Gaytán, and Don Antonio de Castro y del Castillo—along with a consultant, Licenciado Don Juan de Cabrera, reached a decision of somber consequence to Jorge de Silva and to the complicidad grande. Exasperated by Silva's contradictory testimony, they determined to torture him into telling the truth: "[Silva] was taken to the torture chamber and belted to the rack . . . and the first turn was ordered . . . and he began testifying against many people, including against Doña Mencia de Luna."[25] The magistrates read Silva his confession recorded the day before, and "being of sound mind [Silva] ratified [it]."[26] Signatures were required, but sometimes torture got in the way: "and [Silva] could not sign his name because his arms had been injured. . . . An inquisitor signed for him."[27]

Henrique Núñez, Doña Mencia de Luna's husband, had appeared before the tribunal's bench nine and a half years earlier, and because Núñez refused to confess, even under torture, the tribunal "suspended" his case.[28] "Suspendido," however, was a dangerous status; in 1635, when accusations of Judaizing were festering, Henrique Núñez was arraigned again.

As in 1624, Henrique Núñez insisted he was innocent and was tortured, but this time Núñez could not endure the pain. Forced to suffer even more torture because, as the inquisitors explained in a letter to Madrid, they were convinced Núñez was still shielding conspirators,[29] a broken Núñez eventually named his wife.[30] Meeting the tribunal's expectations, Henrique Núñez acknowledged that he, along with his intimate family, formed a coterie of hidden Jews.[31]

The Inquisition arraigned Doña Mencia, her sister Doña Mayor, and her niece Doña Isabel on the same day—November 26, 1635. All three truculently denied practicing Jewish ritual; all three remained steadfast, even when confronted with a swelling number of witnesses against them.[32] Only torture caused them to break.[33]

The tribunal asked everyone brought before it a series of questions. These questions interrogated more than faith; they were used to reconstruct a certain kind of life history, one built on a predefined set of variables. In other words, the inquisitors were generating statistics: social status (single, married, widowed); age; social status in the Church (baptized, confirmed, baptismal church, knowledge of creed); religious ancestry (Old Christian or New Christian, baptized or pagan); race (español, mestizo, mulato, negro, indio); nationality; place of birth; genealogy (parents, grandparents, aunts, uncles, sisters, brothers, their spouses and children); godparents; occupation (of the accused and of family members); general narrative of life history—a trajectory from birth to present, including all places of residence, travel, and major life events.

Doña Mencia's life was forced into these categories and, to the chagrin of the inquisitors, there was no easy fit. Doña Mencia and her tormentors parried gravely over her position in the categorical scheme of things: "[Doña Mencia] said that all [her ancestors] are Old Christians and they are intermixed, Castilians and Portuguese."[34] But the prosecutor would have none of it. He called her a perjurer for saying that she and her relatives were Old Christians, "when the opposite is true and their New Christian status is very well known."[35] Doña Mencia refused to accept this version of her past: "it is just a lie. . . . she is an Old Christian, like her parents, grandparents, and great-grandparents."[36] And she denounced the tribunal for arresting innocents, who were suspect not because of what they had done but because of their genealogy or kin.[37]

The prosecuting attorney pressed on, confident because of the ample, eyewitness testimony of family members, friends, and acquaintances. Doña Mencia and her family—all of the same "caste and lineage"[38]— were prominent members of the viceroyalty's Jewish community (or so the prosecutor would have it) and her house was the site of frequent gatherings during the day and night, "and it can be presumed that the house is and has been a synagogue where the Law of Moses is learned and taught."[39] In addition to this exceptional sin, Doña Mencia was excoriated for concealing accomplices. In sum, Doña Mencia was considered a hostile witness, a liar who was reluctant or even adverse "to declare the truth when so commanded by the tribunal."[40]

Doña Mencia denied each of the charges made against her, point by point. She disavowed any knowledge of Judaizing reunions or synagogues, of fasting during the three days of Queen Esther's holiday, of observing Saturdays, of concealing co-conspirators, of ridiculing Christianity or, as we have already seen, of having a suspicious ancestry or belonging to a questionable "caste." Following procedure, witnesses were confronted with Doña Mencia's extensive denials and, just as firmly, clung to their version of the truth.[41] Doña Mencia, told about their testimony, still maintained her innocence. How to account for such extensive, eyewitness testimony? Much of the nonsense, Doña Mencia argued, was the product of torture or the threat of torture: the culprits were those who induced otherwise honest people to lie.[42]

"Your excellencies are the knife," Doña Mencia told the tribunal, "and [I] the sheep."[43]

And now Doña Mencia, who for nearly three years refused to acknowledge any of the charges made against her, was going to be tortured, as inquisitors, in search of the truth, unanimously sentenced her to the rack. Inquisitors meticulously kept to protocol. Before the sentence was carried out, they offered Doña Mencia the opportunity to retract her claims of innocence, and they read the increasingly elaborate and detailed testimony against her. As always, the charges were scrupulously precise, noting the specific acts, dates, frequencies, and locales of her descent to Judaism.[44] But Doña Mencia remained "negativa," and the inquisitors declared they had no choice but to submit her to torture.

After notifying Doña Mencia of her fate, an inquisitor, following standard procedure, read the famous disclaimer of responsibility: "that if she were to die during the torture session, or be wounded, or spill blood, or if one of her limbs were mutilated, it would be her fault and responsibility and not [the Inquisition's], because she did not want to tell the truth."[45] The inquisitors then ordered state specialists to prepare Doña Mencia for torture since, as representatives of the Church, they were forbidden to inflict corporal punishment or cause the death of a human being. Doña Mencia was told to undress and was put on the rack: "her toes were tied and a cord bound her toes and shins, and her arms and calves were put in the cinch."[46] As instruments of torture were placed on her body (with position and effect duly noted), Doña Mencia restated her innocence. She bluntly responded to the inquisitors' remarkable disclaimer with a salvo of her own: "if, being unable to bear the torture, she were to say anything, it would be worth nothing, would not be valid, because she would have said it owing to her fear of the aforementioned torture."[47] And then, as the cords were being tightened, "[Doña Mencia] said, 'I am Jewish, I am Jewish.'"[48]

But the inquisitors wanted more: they wanted the history of her heresies and, most anxiously, they wanted the names. Asked "how she is Jewish, who taught her and when," Doña Mencia replied that "she was taught to be Jewish in Seville and she was told to fast on Tuesdays and not eat anything and that her mother and sister are Jewish." Doña Mencia was told to be more precise: "what were the names of her mother and sister who she claims are Jewish? . . . how did her mother and sister Judaize?"[49]

At this point Doña Mencia found the torture unbearable ("and she said, 'O Jesus, I am dying, look how much blood I am losing because I have light blood'"), and she cried out, "[W]rite down whatever you want to."[50] This, of course, was not a legitimate reply by any tribunal measure. The inquisitors again cautioned Doña Mencia "to tell the truth, so that they would not have to order that [torture] be resumed and have to tighten the [cord] for the second time." And again Doña Mencia gave a nonanswer, "What am I supposed to say, I don't know anything."[51] So the inquisitors directed the torturers to take up their duties at the rack, "and as it was being tightened she began to complain, crying out *ay, ay*."[52] These were to be Doña Mencia's last words. The notary recorded: "and in this state, it would have been around ten o'clock in the morning, she fainted . . . and she was given a little water . . . and she did not regain consciousness . . . and torture was suspended."[53] Doña Mencia was dead.

But not quite, neither for the inquisitors, nor for her sister and niece, nor for her descendants. The tribunal still had to determine her standing in the Church. That finding would resolve Doña Mencia's future: if she could be buried in sacred ground, if her descendants would be allowed certain opportunities in the Spanish world, if her honor would be celebrated, or if she would be condemned and her body burned into oblivion.

The prosecutor held his course, his arsenal bolstered by the testimonies of Doña Mayor and Doña Isabel Antonia, who, under torture, condemned Doña Mencia after her death. The prosecutor condemned Doña Mencia as "a Judaizer, a heretic, an apostate, turning from the faith in derision and contempt of our savior Jesus Christ . . . and observing the discredited Law of Moses . . . with great danger and condemnation to her soul and dishonor to faithful Christians. [H]er days have ended. [H]er memory and reputation should not remain among the living and, in outrage at such a great evil, her name should be removed from the face of the earth."[54]

Doña Mencia was entitled to a defense in death as in life. The tribunal appointed Sr. Sarmiento, a deputy of the Holy Office, to fill that function as "the [legal] defender of the memory and reputation of Doña Mencia de Luna, deceased."[55] Sarmiento made a strong case for Doña Mencia's innocence, rebutting the charge that she died a heretic and apostate. His argument: "[S]he was never guilty of the charges against her. [R]ather, she died as she should have, defending the truth, . . . not giving false testimony against herself nor against anyone else . . . except for fear of torture."[56] And Sarmiento petitioned the tribunal to give Doña Mencia every right enjoyed by faithful members of the Catholic Church, including the right to be buried with true Christians in consecrated land.

Doña Mencia's fate was put to a vote. Weighing the evidence and merits of the case, the inquisitors, along with several outside evaluators, made the following determination: "Sres. Mañozca, Castro, a secular clergyman, and the consultants [to the tribunal] said she should be burned, in effigy, at the stake . . . ," but "the inquisitor Gaytán voted to 'suspend' the case."[57] Because of the mixed verdict, Doña Mencia remained in limbo for over twenty years. Not until 1664 did the sitting tribunal, determined to process all of the unresolved cases clogging the docket, settle her future: Doña Mencia was burned in effigy.[58]

Manuel Henríquez

The November day that Doña Mencia was indicted by the Lima tribunal, Manuel Henríquez was selling merchandize in Cuzco, worried that he would have a similar fate. His brother-in-law—Antonio Gómez de Acosta—had been seized three months earlier, and Henríquez was Gómez de Acosta's agent. Henríquez was unaware that his name appeared alongside Doña Mencia's in the writ of indictment.

Manuel Henríquez was brought before the tribunal one month later, on December 14, 1635. The magistrates wanted to know his life story, and Henríquez obliged: thirty-four years old, born in Portugal, married to a "doña" and the father of one daughter. Henríquez, like men on both sides of his family, made a living in the expanding world of commerce. By the age of eighteen he left Portugal to sell linens throughout Castile, and by the time he was thirty-two he had shipped out to Cartagena to enter the service of Antonio Gómez de Acosta. When the chief inquisitor asked Henríquez about his ancestry and "caste," Henríquez did not hesitate: "New Christian, and his parents, grandparents and the rest of his transversal and collateral kin were as well." Then came the next standard question: "if anyone in his family had ever been arrested or penaced by the Holy Office."[59] Henríquez said no. That statement would return to haunt him.

Henríquez claimed innocence; he wanted the magistrates to know that he was a devout, confirmed, and churchgoing Christian.[60] But the magistrates thought otherwise, and when Henríquez insisted, they parried with the retort heard by anyone who ever pleaded not guilty: "that they [were] not in the habit of arresting anyone without sufficient evidence."[61] Henríquez was then reminded of the advantages to an early confession: "his case would be expedited with all the speed and mercy it warranted." And he was reminded of the disadvantages: if Henríquez were to demur, "justice would be done." Henríquez responded, it seems, with great confidence: "[M]y lords, look at my case with justice, because I am innocent."[62]

On March 27, 1636, Henríquez changed his plea and admitted to having lied about the past: in fact, he and two siblings had been captured and punished before by the Inquisition, in Coimbra, Portugal. Henríquez's older brother had been the first to be apprehended, and Manuel was arrested soon after.[63] But, Henríquez went on to explain, he and his siblings renounced their old faith in prison and, with the help of Coimbra's inquisitors, rekindled their devotion to Catholicism. The three were reconciled to the Church in a public auto-da-fé and were made to wear a *sanbenito*, the special tunic marking them as former Judaizers. This auto, Henríquez recounted, took place in 1617 or 1618.

Henríquez's March confession was motivated by fear, fear that the past had made him vulnerable to heresy charges in the present. First of all, because in their frenzy to denounce others, accused Judaizers would brand anyone already in jail as an accomplice.[64] Second, because his previous run-in with the tribunal would make him an easy target.

Soon after, Manuel Henríquez requested another hearing, whose purpose was "to tell the whole truth . . . trusting in the tribunal's mercy." The "whole truth" meant a second flirtation with Judaism: that not only "as a boy . . . had [he been] deceived by the persuasiveness of his older brother," but as an adult he had been "deceived by Don Simón Osorio, a gentleman (*caballero*)."[65] Thus began a long story, told over four months and filled with spectacular charges against dozens of Judaizing accomplices.

In the course of this confession, Manuel Henríquez tantalized the court with detailed, eyewitness accounts of heresy.[66] Repeatedly asking for hearings, Henríquez named more names and itemized, with precision—and with the encouragement and guidance of the inquisitors—suspect exchanges between himself and other merchants. By the end of this mammoth testimony, all of it ratified, Henríquez had provided eyewitness accusations against more than forty souls.

At the end of July 1636, the prosecutor combined Henríquez's self-recriminations with the accusations of other witnesses and charged Henríquez with eighteen counts of heresy.[67] Henríquez, the prosecutor marveled, had cut a wide swath, "communicat[ing] about the Law of Moses . . . in many places in Portugal, in Spain, Madrid, Valladolid, Murcia, Seville, Cartagena, Panama and Peru, Huancavelica, Cuzco and the City of Kings [Lima]."[68]

Four months later, on February 4, Henríquez's testimony took an astonishing turn. Henríquez repudiated nearly all of the confessions he had made and ratified over the previous nine months. Switching pleas again, he now claimed to be a long-term practicing Christian, and that any admission on his part to have followed the Law of Moses was a plain lie. This was the first step in an extraordinary disclosure: A scheme was afloat—in the very bowels of the Inquisition—to fix testimony. The inquisitors thought themselves clever for having uncovered a vast conspiracy to resurrect the Law of Moses in the viceroyalty of Peru. Now they had exposed another one: a conspiracy to falsely confess to Judaizing so that there would appear to be a vast conspiracy of Judaizers in the viceroyalty of Peru. Henríquez was one of the first to come forward, but others, including most of the witnesses against him, eventually did the same.

According to Henríquez's version of things, the real culprit in these wrongdoings was Antonio de Acuna.[69] Acuna had persuaded Henríquez that he would never be able to survive the damning accusations made against him, particularly testimony in Panama that had reached the Lima tribunal,[70] just as Acuna had persuaded others that if they did not say what the court wanted to hear, they would either be tortured into confessing or burned at the stake. Faced with mounting evidence and constantly goaded by Acuna, Henríquez (like others) said that fear had driven him to acknowledge crimes he now claimed never to have committed: "since everyone was going to testify against him and they [the inquisitors] would have to burn him if he did not confess, . . . he confessed to what he had not done and spoke falsely against many."[71]

Henríquez told the court that there was an additional dimension to Acuna's schemes, one that played on the empire's confusions of nationality, race, and religion. Acuna had advised everyone "to give false testimony against Castilians [Old Christians]." And, why? "[B]ecause then it would be obvious . . . that all these testimonies were false," that the accusations against New Christians had no basis in fact. For then the magistrates would realize that they were going by stereotype, not by evidence, and that "whenever they arrest someone who is Portuguese, they accuse [that person] of being Jewish," regardless of the information against him.[72]

Remarkably, the perjury clique managed to convince at least one Old Christian, the muleteer Juan Ramos, to confess. Henríquez, Juan de Acevedo, and Juan Ramos were together in a cell, Henríquez testified, when Acevedo asked Ramos if he knew why he was in prison. When Ramos said he did not, Acevedo replied, "[B]rother (*hermano*), you are in jail for being a practicing Jew." And then Acevedo gave Ramos the solution to his dilemma: "[A]ll you have to do is to ask for a hearing and confess that you are Jewish." When Ramos skeptically pointed out that not only was he innocent, but ignorant ("brothers, I have not Judaized nor do I know how"), Acevedo's quick response was: "[G]o on, you don't have to say any more than that you observed Saturday and lighted the candle."[73]

Henríquez tried to explain why he had revoked testimony and, breaking a jailhouse bond, revealed the confession conspiracy to the tribunal. Full of grief and shame, Henríquez told the magistrates that "whatever he said against people for observing . . . the Law of Moses is false, because they have never done so in this kingdom, or anywhere on earth."[74] Henríquez was disgusted with himself for being so willing to lie, horrified at his readiness to betray wife and daughter to save his own skin. He was desolate; he could no longer speak the lies that had condemned so many. Night after night, Henríquez told the court, he would be overcome by this thought: "[O] my soul what have you done? You are burning in hell."[75] He had to make amends, affirm the truth.

The prosecutor brought a second series of charges against Henríquez, and Henríquez responded to them point by point.[76] As before, Henríquez acknowledged his arrest by the Coimbra Inquisition.[77] He also reiterated his part in schemes to deceive the tribunal. But he adamantly insisted on his innocence: in spite of all the deceptions and fabricated admissions of guilt, "he had never conversed with anyone about the Law of Moses, not in any store, not anywhere."[78]

Henríquez told the court that he and his jailmates had conspired to present false testimony because they hoped, in this way, to expedite the proceedings and avoid being tortured. Unfortunately for all those imprisoned, the current round of retractions—heard by the tribunal week after week, witness after witness—produced what they most feared. For as the confusions mounted, so did the Inquisition's use of torture—the tribunal's ultimate strategy to uncover the truth.

When Henríquez heard the directive, he begged, "I can't bear being tortured, I would rather die." Overcome, Henríquez was prepared to revoke all previous declarations of innocence. With words reminiscent of Doña Mencia's, Henríquez screamed, "[W]hatever I just swore to was a lie; . . . and . . . what I said about being Jewish is the truth."[79] But it wasn't enough. With the inquisitors' approval, Henríquez was taken to the torture chamber, where he promised to "tell the whole truth."[80]

Henríquez's whole truth was, no doubt, what the inquisitors hoped to hear, but their hopes had to be properly justified. In an instructive dialogue, they pointedly queried Henríquez about the basis of his Jewish faith. Asked about his apprenticeship into the world of Judaism, Henríquez explained that at age twelve, both parents began to teach him the essential ritual practices of fasting, observing holy days, and keeping a kosher diet.[81] This information, however, did not satisfy the inquisitors: they wanted to know more about Henríquez's command of the religion, and they wanted to know what prayers he had learned. In response, "[Henríquez] said that [his parents] did not teach him any prayers, only the fasts and Saturdays." The inquisitors were flabbergasted that Henríquez was so ignorant of Hebrew fundamentals, and they accused him of dissembling his religious past: "[T]hat [statement] could not be truthful (*verisímil*), [because] if [Henríquez] had observed the Law of Moses since he was twelve years old, how could he not know any [prayers] to speak to God and Moses."[82]

Henríquez retorted that he was not taught any prayers because his mother had died when he was twelve years old. The inquisitors again accused him of "not being truthful." They remained suspicious because, went the rejoinder, even though he was not Christian, he was clearly quite familiar with Christian prayers. They pressed: "if [Henríquez] were able to learn [Christian prayers] even when he did not follow the Law of Christ, how was it possible that he never learned any [Jewish] prayers."[83]

Henríquez had been tortured for nearly four hours. The tribunal entered this assessment into the record: "and at 1:15 he was returned to his cell, and he appears to be sound, without any lesions, except for the burn marks from twisting the cords on his arms."[84] After the requisite twenty-four hours between torture and ratification, the inquisitors read Henríquez's statement and asked him to confirm its truthfulness. His testimony, like that of so many of the witnesses in the "complicidad grande," was a pattern of grand denial and retraction: proclaim innocence; declare guilt; proclaim innocence once more (after denouncing the perjury plot); declare guilt once more (under the shadow of torture).

The inquisitors also determined that they needed to verify Henríquez's previous run-in with the Coimbra Inquisition for their case to proceed in a judicious manner, and they dispatched a request for the trial transcript.[85] No matter that it took months, even years, before transcripts would cross the ocean. This request saved Henríquez from the immediate fate of his fellow conspirators. So, years later, in February 1641, the Lima tribunal had a certificate of Henríquez's first trial in their hands.[86] By 1641, though, Henríquez had begun to crack. Forced, yet one more time, to listen to his jumbled confessions from the last seven years, Henríquez began "to talk nonsense." Henríquez's lawyer, following court regulations protecting the mentally ill from prosecution, called a halt to the proceedings; the inquisitors, on the other hand, warned Henríquez not to fake insanity.[87]

Five years later Henríquez was in despair: "and for nine years and so many months I have been suffering many arduous and taxing ordeals, giving me filth to eat, and lime, and fat, and dogs . . . and many others."[88] Rambling, he swayed between blaming himself for these horrors and defending, even if in an unconsidered way, a portion of his convictions. Sometimes, he did so with impudence: "and [my fellow] prisoners told me that [the inquisitor] Señor Don Juan de Mañozca had been sanctioned by the Royal Court in Quito where he was charged with being a drunk . . . and once when [Mañozca] entered the cells, [Henríquez] had said [out loud], 'Look, look, look at the drunk' . . . and this must have produced the suit against him."[89] Sometimes he did so with a cry that, in its desperation, recognized the magistrates' godlike powers, yet scoffed at their audacity: "Let the esteemed inquisitors sentence him as they wish, because he is already dead; and whatever they tell him to do, he will follow, as if they were God."[90]

On June 14, 1646, the prosecutor restated his case against Manuel Henríquez: "As a fraudulent, lying, obstinate Jew, Henríquez deserved to be put to death."[91] The tribunal unanimously agreed.[92]

Henríquez asked for paper to write a testimonial on his own behalf. First, he put the inquisitors in their place: "You, Gentlemen, are the judges of this lawsuit with respect to my death sentence (*relaxación*),[93] in accordance with my confession and testimony; but not [the judges] of anything else." Then followed the testimonial:

Very Noble and Illustrious Gentlemen,

I present this memorial and declaration to you so you can help me in this purgatory . . . where my soul wanders, and I ask you on the honor and passion of our lord Jesus Christ to show me the mercy of this tribunal and the mercy in you. . . . And I, Gentlemen, am in full agreement with the will of God, bearing my travails with patience because I am illuminated by God. . . . And thus, as God gives me burdens, he also gives me comfort with his divine sight and gifts of lemons and fragrance and houses and rosaries and bells and instruments . . . and you should know, Gentlemen, that I also have revelations from God so that I can be patient in the face of my destiny . . . and also I ask, Lord, how can I pay back the debts I owe in Spain, if I am in this purgatory[94] . . . and now I affirm the truth . . . dealing with my salvation in truth and not lies . . . so that I can write this declaration to you, esteemed Gentlemen . . . and I see that I was condemned to redeem my travails, . . . something I cannot do without toil and martyrdom . . . and for You Gentlemen to know about my low (*miserable*) standing, that I used to go around with my father and brother to holiday fairs held on saints' days in the countryside, selling cloth, and when those saints' days arrive, I see myself destined to be in those fairs, selling, as if I were there, and I know when each saint's day falls and then I have a feeling as my wandering soul has for other, destined things, and God explains all these matters . . . and I tell you this, Gentlemen, so you don't think I am deranged . . .

Manuel Henríquez[95] [signature]

Manuel Henríquez again figured on the Inquisition rolls in the 1650–51 summary of cases pending before the tribunal. According to the record, he remained in prison because the Lima Inquisition did not have the money to mount a public auto-da-fé, the only appropriate venue for the execution of heretics.[96]

Eight years later, on August 21, 1659, the Supreme Council dispatched an order to its Lima office. Madrid had read Henríquez's testimonials and doubted his sanity. In the interests of judicial fairness and in conformity with tribunal regulations, headquarters enjoined its subordinates to evaluate Henríquez's mental capacities. Madrid's instructions:

[D]octors should see this prisoner on different days and at different times to judge his mental state, to see if it is real or fabricated. . . . And the assessors (*calificadores*) should do the same thing, and the tribunal should convene special hearings to judge his sanity; and on the basis of these evaluations [by the doctors, assessors, and magistrates] the tribunal should meet again and vote and, being in accord, execute his sentence.[97]

José Toribio Medina, the great chronicler of the Spanish Inquisition in the New World, could find no resolution to Henríquez's case. He guessed that Henríquez was judged insane, watched over in jail, and never executed—like his fellow prisoner Enrique Jorge Tavares.[98] If Medina had discovered the 1664 case summary, he would have known that Manuel Henríquez and Doña Mencia de Luna shared a similar fate: the Lima Inquisition determined that both were unrepentant, vile heretics whose memory should be forever erased from the earth. But it was Doña Mencia's effigy that was set aflame on January 23, 1664; Manuel Henríquez was burned at the stake.[99]

Manuel Bautista Pérez

Of all the suspects caught in the August 1635 dragnet, none produced as much astonishment, concern, and scandal as Manuel Bautista Pérez. For Manuel Bautista Pérez was one of the world's most powerful men in international commerce, and when his arrest disrupted the extensive and far-flung trading networks under his domain, all of Spain's mercantile establishment suffered. It was the testimony of Antonio de Acuna—the man Manuel Henríquez denounced for masterminding the perjury conspiracy—that was responsible for snaring him.

This was not the first time that Pérez stood in front of the tribunal. He had been accused of Judaizing fifteen years earlier, arrested when a broadsheet proclaiming him to be one of the city's premier teachers of Judaism was found posted in Lima's main square.[100] But that was eleven years ago, with a different political climate and a different set of inquisitors. Nonetheless, as Pérez would never forget, the fact of his arrest lingered, both in the public mind and in the bureaucratic record.

Lima magistrates were well aware of their weakness in the Great Jewish Conspiracy trials, and they were very well aware that, given Pérez's prominence, no weakness would be more glaring or more investigated than in his case. Regardless, the inquisitors marched ahead and wasted little time.[101] On August 11, 1635, Manuel Bautista Pérez was locked in a cell; as Manuel Henríquez predicted and as the inquisitors counted on, the bank of witnesses against Pérez grew once a startling number of Peru's "Portuguese" community found themselves in jail.

The prosecuting attorney had over twenty witnesses against Manuel Bautista Pérez by the time he formally pressed charges. Most of the testimony against Pérez was provided by the same witnesses who testified against Manuel Henríquez and Doña Mencia de Luna, so the well-worn pattern of denial and accusation plagued Pérez's case as well. The same questions about evidence that previously gnawed at the tribunal's juridical footing surfaced here, too. And they did so with a vengeance, in part, no doubt, because of Pérez's extraordinary position in the viceroyalty and his allegedly extraordinary position in Peru's Portuguese/New Christian/Judaizing community. Pérez was called the "oráculo" (oracle, revered leader) of Peru's secret Jews by witnesses and by inquisitors alike.[102] "One of the most esteemed men in the kingdom [of Peru]" because of his "vast fortune,"[103] Pérez was also one of the most esteemed men among Peru's hidden Jews because of his vast knowledge. In the words of Bartolomé de León, a nineteen-year-old bachelor and colleague of Henrique Núñez (Doña Mencia's husband), Pérez was simply "the most learned (*el más ladino*)."[104]

So, for the second time in his life, Manuel Bautista Pérez found himself in front of a panel of inquisitors. Pérez declared his innocence, avowing he was a Christian, baptized and confirmed, who regularly went to mass, made confession, and took communion.[105] Asked to give his genealogy, he described a New Christian family with roots in Spain and Portugal, but whose sons and daughters were scattered over the world—in South Asia, Africa, and the Americas. Most of the men were involved in international commerce, and many of the women were married to merchants.[106] He swore that his profession never took him to "any kingdom not part of the Spanish realm" (i.e., not to those dangerous parts of Europe and the Middle East where Judaism could be freely practiced).[107] And no one in his family had been imprisoned by the Holy Office, except for Diego Rodríguez de Lisboa, his mother's first cousin, who had been arrested in Lisbon three years before but was released a free man.

Manuel Bautista Pérez cautioned the tribunal about the possibility of witnesses testifying against him for reasons of jealousy or retaliation: "two or three hundred people might have some kind of quarrel to pick with him over the sale of goods . . . or the amount needed to pay back a loan."[108] And Pérez then gave the court examples of likely candidates—like Domingo Montes, one of Pérez's *mayordomos*, who "went around telling everyone that [Pérez and his brother-in-law] were Jew-dogs" because they threatened to have him punished for beating an African slave to death; or Henrique Núñez (Doña Mencia's husband) and Antonio de Acuna, "upstarts and social climbers" who Pérez refused to have anything to do with.[109] Over the course of hearings from September 1635 to February 1636, Manuel Bautista Pérez provided the tribunal with a long list of enemies.

The Inquisition's prosecuting attorney, with testimony from over twenty witnesses, formally charged Manuel Bautista Pérez on thirty-four counts of "Judaizing." These accusations cover familiar ground: the perceived successes and advantages of "Jews" in Peru's mercantile economy ("as a Jew and with the love and affection [Pérez] carries for those who observe the Law of Moses, he has favored [Jews] in business activities");[110] his leadership role in the Jewish community ("rabbi" or "Great Captain"); and the conversion of his home into a grand synagogue.[111] The prosecutor also described a variety of heretical rites practiced by Pérez, and while these encompassed the standard litany of "Jewish" customs,[112] they included some rather curious ones as well. One involved tobacco ("[Pérez] would lift up some [tobacco] . . . and blow on it, a ritual gesture of sacrifice and libation that matches many descriptions found in the Old Testament");[113] or he would have a drink prepared from the cola nut "so he and all the other members of his caste and lineage (*casta y generación*) could talk about the Law of Moses in these extraordinary (*trasordinario*) languages without being understood by others."[114]

Manuel Bautista Pérez insisted on his innocence. He swore fidelity to Christianity, was incensed that his profound devotion to Catholic rites and charities could be construed as subterfuge, denied being a "Great Captain" of Judaism, and rejected any suggestion that he practiced Jewish rituals. He explained that several hundred people—"Castilians and Portuguese," business associates, family, friends, religious advisers—were in and out of his house every day; that he had many books in his library and not one referred to the Law of Moses; that a lengthy discussion in his library had prompted the brother of a Jesuit priest to write a short treatise on the dimensions of the sun, a treatise dedicated to Pérez; and that his enemies called him "Great Captain" (among other things) behind his back to mock and defame him. As for insinuations that he kept a "kosher" kitchen (draining blood; not eating bacon, shellfish, or the hindquarters of meat), Pérez asked the inquisitors to interrogate the cooks in order to find out about the meals he and his family consumed.[115] Also accused of stashing large sums of money, jewels, and luxury items to keep his wealth out of the hands of the tribunal, Pérez retorted that "had he wanted to, he would have had plenty of time to dispose of his wealth and hide more than 140,000 pesos." He went on to explain that, on the contrary, "he always lived with a great sense of security, like anyone who hadn't broken the law and who had nothing to fear . . . like a person who followed the Law of Jesus in good conscience."[116]

In similar fashion, Pérez countered the more unusual charges. It was preposterous to think that taking tobacco or drinking cola had anything whatsoever to do with ritual subversion. His testimony had this to say regarding cola: "in 1635 . . . when [Pérez] was first in prison . . . the warden even asked him for some [cola nuts], two times," and "any number of people, Castilians and Portuguese, knew about this fruit and would ask him for some."[117] He added that surely "el Señor Inquisitor Juan de Mañozca should be familiar with [cola] because it is a very popular beverage in Cartagena," where Mañozca had served before coming to Lima.[118] As for tobacco, Pérez said he hated it, thought it indecent, and made fun of people who used it.[119]

On top of these charges, Pérez was accused of slander—of defaming no less an institution than the Inquisition. The prosecutor denounced him for spreading the unfounded story that the tribunal hounded New Christians and arrested them without evidence. Pérez denied this, insisting on the contrary that he was a great defender of the Inquisition and praising it for, in essence, meeting the standards of any bureaucracy worthy of the name. Not only was the Holy Office "a very holy and just court," he argued, but "it is administered by disinterested people." As proof, he put forward an experience close to his heart: "[Y]ou can find someone being freed from jail every day," like his cousin Diego Rodríguez de Lisboa, like Pérez himself a decade before and, as he must have desperately hoped, like he would be soon.[120]

Like Doña Mayor de Luna and Manuel Henríquez, Manuel Bautista Pérez was caught communicating with fellow inmates and with family on the outside. During one session, the prosecutor handed him three sheets of paper, scribbled in code, and demanded that Pérez decipher them. All had something to do with forbidden acts. The first, written by Diego Rodríguez de Lisboa and smuggled into the cells with the help of bribery, warned that a group plotting to fix testimony had denounced Pérez in a very coordinated fashion.[121] The second was written by Pérez's brother-in-law and fellow inmate, Sebastián Duarte. It reported an exchange between Duarte and Manuel Henríquez, in which Henríquez wrote down bits of prison news: most ominously that he, Henríquez, had voluntarily confessed his guilt to the tribunal and that he hoped his testimony would not put Pérez and Sebastián Duarte in jeopardy.[122]

The third encoded letter was from Manuel Bautista Pérez to his brother-in-law, and its meaning, open to debate, was the source of bitter jousting between Pérez and the tribunal over Pérez's willingness to fabricate testimony.[123] The name of Manuel Bautista Pérez was not unblemished. On July 29, 1636, Pérez asked for an audience "to unburden his conscience" and confessed to perjury. The inquisitors' suspicions—but only some—were correct. For, indeed, Manuel Bautista Pérez had at one time counseled his brother-in-law to follow the path set by Acuna and company and confess to being a Jew. But Pérez had also repudiated his decision later.

With increasing despair, Pérez faced the reality that not only was evidence mounting—more and more witnesses were naming him the "Great Captain" of Peru's Jewish community—but his beloved brother-in-law Sebastián Duarte was also going to denounce him. Seeing no way out, he attempted suicide. Grabbing a knife hidden under his leggings, Manuel Bautista Pérez stabbed himself six times.[124] He then tried to explain to a doubting tribunal how he, a devout Catholic, could have committed such a sin. His testimony tells it all: "dazed by grief, he was not even aware of what he had done, for anguish had erased all judgment."[125]

In January 1638, after a year and a quarter had passed, Manuel Bautista Pérez was again formally charged with heresy.[126] Pérez responded to the second round of denunciations with continued pleas of innocence, pointing out that witnesses did not agree on the places, dates, and times when subversive activities were said to have happened and that many based their testimonies on pure hearsay or, worse, that many did not even know him. Pérez supported his claims with a careful discussion of his enduring effort to "pass," to remove any trace of "New Christianness" that might still cling to his person: "[Pérez] said that he never let it be known, either to people in his household or outside it, that he was a New Christian, . . . for he always tried to be taken for an Old Christian."[127] Precautions included a grand demonstration of piety through membership in sodalities, regular church attendance, and the performance of good works as well as a refusal to talk about "Portuguese" living in Flanders (where there were practicing Jews).[128] Manuel Bautista Pérez was proud to have (nearly) "passed." The magistrates, however, saw nothing but red flags—an admission to have covered up behavior or, worse, to have covered up "casta y generación."

Following procedure, witnesses were called in Pérez's defense. At least fourteen upstanding men, the great majority from the Castilian "casta y generación," provided depositions in his favor.[129] The most significant and influential witnesses were members of the clergy. A string of priests, mainly Jesuits, testified about the accused's fidelity to Church doctrine, his abiding affection for sermons (a popular medium of the day), his charitable gifts, and his impeccable reputation as a leading figure in the viceroyalty.[130]

All the same, the prosecutor remained unconvinced and once again restated Pérez's crimes. And once again Pérez spoke of his profound belief in Christianity, his desire to follow Christ, and his unshakable willingness to "give his life for our Holy Faith."[131] The tribunal responded that highly qualified people had gone over his case and found him guilty, and that since Pérez still refused to confess, it seemed to them that he should be tortured into revealing the whole truth. Pérez was escorted to the torture chamber:

> [After the first] turns, [Pérez] cried out to Jesus . . . recited the credo, and said he is a Christian . . . that "the truth is they want me to give false testimony. Christ of my soul, help me . . . I have so many witnesses against me, and so it is very just that they are torturing me, and I begin with contrition . . ." [After the fourth turn, Pérez] said, "They are killing me, they are killing me, Jesus who is the son of God, my suffering is not justified, for I know nothing . . . and I want to die like a soldier of Jesus Christ."[132]

Manuel Bautista Pérez was removed from the instruments of torture. In November 1638, the prosecutor repeated the allegations against him. With his lawyer present, Pérez admitted to one crime—that of communicating with fellow prisoners—and he repudiated the rest "even though the testimonies of twenty witnesses had been ratified under oath."[133] Pérez also told the tribunal that he understood why, given the evidence at their disposal, they might consider him guilty of heresy. But he would not budge, even after the damning testimonies of ten more witnesses. Manuel Bautista Pérez demanded justice.[134]

The tribunal declared the case closed and held a meeting "with learned and educated men with upright consciences" to discuss Pérez's fate. At his first trial, fourteen years earlier, fortitude in the face of torture had earned Pérez a reprieve; this time, all it garnered was reproach. After deliberating "in the presence of the viceroy, the Count of Chichón, the Royal Court and other advisers, assessors, and commissioners . . . all honest men," the inquisitors condemned Manuel Bautista Pérez to death.[135]

Pérez was as unyielding on the scaffold as he was in trial. Montesinos, who chronicled the execution, interpreted Pérez's final gestures as proof of his guilt—and of his honor:

> He gave signs of his depraved soul and his covert Judaism in the "kiss of peace" (*ósculo de paz*) he gave his brother-in-law, Sebastián Duarte, [also] standing on the scaffold . . . and by the way his eyes showed great anger toward anyone from his household and family who had confessed and repented. . . . [H]e heard his sentence with great dignity and majesty; he died unrepentant, telling the executioner to do his job.[136]

Two other letters were confiscated by the tribunal. Both were from Manuel Bautista Pérez's brother-in-law Simón Báez:[137]

I want to thank Our Lord one thousand times for his benevolence in allowing a letter with your signature to reach my hands, which put an end to the unfounded rumors spread by the common rabble that you had died, and some even swear they saw you being buried, and blessed be his mercy which has removed us from such confusion and let me know about your health . . . and blessed be our lord, Jesus Christ, who cleared this road. . . . [A]nd your son prays in front of the Virgin Mary and he says, "Please bring me back my *taita*[138] because I want so much to see him. . . ." Pancho is teaching Don Jaime with much care, he can read very well and he has just begun to write here in the house, and Juan is like a little lamb . . . and even though he can't really talk yet, he can say prayers to our beloved Jesus. . . . We have had mass after mass said, asking Our Lord to clarify this case and make it very evident that someone who would give a thousand lives for His Majesty should not be defamed as an infidel. . . . Your friends who are members of religious orders have stood by you and continuously ask . . . for your freedom . . . and I beg you to bear these blows with patience, trusting in His Majesty to declare the truth, and to disclose and eradicate those witnesses giving false testimony . . . and he will rectify this for his own honor and glory and so that you can return to your house with much honor and protect it, like a father. . . .

    Simón Vaz Henríquez [signature]

I received the second letter that you sent me with such pleasure, . . . a great comfort given us by Our Lord in the midst of so much travail. . . . [A]nd I gave the porter the 20 pesos and a bit more for him to give you . . . a pen and ink inside four sheets of paper. . . . Doña María Belásquez has been here two or three times with [our?] Jesuit *compañeros* . . . for it is important that our friends in this world aren't friends only when times are prosperous. . . . [T]he Porter should also be giving you some *quesadillas* that my sister [Pérez's wife] made, and she and Doña Isabel send two thousand embraces . . . and yesterday both were praying all day to the Virgin of Copacabana, an image that has only just been brought here by some Indians . . . and [they were praying] for her to help by means of her holy intervention . . . and receive our pleas and the sacrifices we offer her. May Our Lord watch over you and free you from the tribulations he has placed on [your shoulders].

    Simón Báez Enríquez[139] [signature]

Inquisition as Bureaucracy

PRINCIPALES
ADESERDESAMINADO

el buen prencipal sel etra y lengua sees panol q̃ sepa hazer
una peticion en te rrogatorio y pleyto y q̃ nosea borracho ni
coquero ni   jugador ni mentiroso en este reyno

Indian authorities should be literate in Spanish so
they can present petitions, interrogate witnesses, and go to court.
From Felipe Guaman Poma de Ayala,
El primer nueva corónica y buen gobierno (1613?).

Contrary to the image—still widely current—of inquisitors as small-minded clerics . . . fanatically dedicated to the extirpation of heresy, in the sixteenth and seventeenth centuries, the inquisitors were an elite bureaucracy . . . in principal a bureaucracy not of the Church but of the State.—HENRY KAMEN, *The Spanish Inquisition* [1]

W E IMAGINE THE Spanish Inquisition as an institution manned by ravenous, small-minded fanatics who would arrest people at will, sadistically apply torture, and then march their victims to the stake. But, if that was so, then how can we account for the tribunal record? How can we account for the fact that inquisitors mounted elaborate judicial proceedings, considered evidence before making arrests, insisted that testimony be recorded and ratified, consulted with superiors thousands of miles (and many months) away, released detainees held on insufficient grounds and, what is more astonishing, even returned confiscated goods?

We have been blinded by stereotype. Henry Kamen, preeminent English scholar of the Spanish Inquisition, cautions us to abandon this version of inquisitors as "small-minded clerics" and, instead, understand them as "an elite bureaucracy." To be sure, the Inquisition was an institution of the Spanish empire and thus was enmeshed in its national mission to impose Catholicism, root out heretical religions, expand political dominion, and enforce norms of cultural purity. Nonetheless, imperial ends were realized, first and foremost, through a modern bureaucracy which—like other Spanish bureaucracies of the day—was larded with procedures, protocols, and regulations. [2]

Like all bureaucrats, tribunal members were human beings, with biases and agendas, and as an up-and-coming elite, their ambition, self-interest, and self-righteousness could, at times, ooze from the records.[3] Yet, magistrates fundamentally believed that they were advancing society by defending the Spanish empire (and civilization) from evil and by bringing reason and impartiality to questions of civic order. In this chapter we look at some of the bureaucratic measures put into play to attain those civilizing goals: procedures meant to ensure dispassionate judgment and the attainment of truth. Armed with these rituals of rationality, inquisitors both served and created state reason. This was the logic of governing in the name of truth, the logic of judging subjects' truth in the name of the state.

Standards and Procedures

The ideal Lima inquisitor was, according to the highest tribunal authorities, "circumspect, judicious . . . not greedy or covetous, understanding, very charitable . . . and experienced and informed about life in the Americas"; he was "pacífico"—tranquil and unperturbed and not a hothead better suited to life as a swashbuckling conquistador.[4] The ideal inquisitor, thus bureaucratically disposed, was immersed in rules; and the tribunal seemed to have rules for everything from officeholders (each local tribunal had twenty—inquisitor, attorney general, defense attorney, notary, constable, office manager, accountant, pharmacist, porter, etc.)[5] to job descriptions and requirements (inquisitors had to be university graduates, preferably with a degree in law and with extensive professional experience).[6] There was even an ecclesiastic career ladder (e.g. inquisitor was higher than prosecuting attorney);[7] and most believed that an American posting was a rung on the ladder to bureaucratic success (through 1635, seven of nine Lima magistrates graduated to positions of higher authority, while the other two ruined their chances because of, shall we say, irregularities on the job.)[8]

While not precisely a court of law (the Inquisition was established to "meet a perceived national threat"),[9] the Inquisition had much in common with the secular and ecclesiastic courts of the day. In principle, its practices were guided by rules and regulations designed to promote equity and justice.[10] Inquisition manuals gave specific instructions about evidence needed for arrest and for conviction, methods for conducting interrogations, and criteria for determining sentences. And, as if to doubly check for fairness, tribunal decisions took account of the opinions of external consultants at every stage in the trial process—from indictment to penance.[11]

Like most European courts, the tribunal assumed that the accused were guilty unless shown otherwise. Yet, even though the burden of proof remained squarely on their shoulders, defendants were supported by several statutes: they were entitled to make use of a lawyer (appointed by the tribunal), to name corroborating witnesses, and to provide a list of enemies who might testify out of spite.[12] Procedures notwithstanding, assumptions of guilt, coupled with the (also regulated) use of torture, seemed to make the fight for freedom nearly impossible. It was to the prisoner's great advantage to admit heresy: the defendant's chances for benign treatment, as magistrates always pointed out, improved dramatically with confession. The tribunal's dependence on witness accounts (unlike Monty Python's version, there was no spy network), plus the incentive to denounce others, only encouraged indicted heretics to entrap acquaintances, family members, partners, enemies, and friends—and turn them into suspects.

Inquisitors were wedded to paper and pen and, in keeping with Spanish tradition, they were grand recordkeepers: the archives were engorged with correspondence flowing from one side of the Atlantic to the other. In addition to trial transcripts (sometimes summaries, sometimes full accounts), Lima inquisitors were obliged to send timely reports to Madrid, informing their superiors about the status of cases, about the tribunal's financial situation, about inventories of confiscated goods, and about any jurisdictional problems with other Church or civil authorities.[13] Secretaries in Madrid would copy all incoming letters and reports, forward them to the appropriate desk, and then send back advice and instructions via the semiannual journeys of the armada. Official procedure even covered, in surprising detail, how regional secretaries were to organize the paperwork: reports and other documents were arranged chronologically, with each case noted, alphabetically, in a designated ledger; the ledgers and other bound records were, by regulation, "indexed and titled" to facilitate use.[14]

Inquisitorial bureaucrats showed (perhaps surprising) regard for records and their integrity. Since witness accounts were the tribunal's principal source of evidence, official secretaries recorded testimony with remarkable precision—including howls of torture, registered as compulsively as any word.[15] Nor did inquisitors fudge records to support their arguments. Testimony was entered into the trial transcripts, whether it bolstered the tribunal's case or not;[16] in the same vein, officials highlighted or annotated sections, even if they undermined the prosecution's case.[17]

Paper Trails

Lima's inquisitors depended on and contributed to a growing, transatlantic paper trail. Because of their considerable recordkeeping, inquisitors were able to investigate religious activities over time and across continents, and they frequently turned to archives in order to verify testimony or to ferret out unsavory characters for further investigation. Accused heretics found that earlier convictions, once captured in writing, could develop into a decades-long plague. You have read how the archived transcript of Manuel Bautista Pérez's 1624 arrest was to play a critical role in his 1635 trial, and how transcripts of Manuel Henríquez's detention in Portugal loomed large in the evolution of his case. Joan Vicente's tribunal history, which I will briefly comment on now, is one more example of the paper trail's unrelenting grip and of its Kafkaesque results.

Joan Vicente was trailed for years. In 1595 Pedro Alonso appeared before the Inquisition's commissioner in Tucumán (Northwest Argentina), to report grave misgivings about a certain Portuguese named Joan Vicente. Alonso, newly arrived from the Continent, wanted the tribunal to recognize the kind of renegade who was calling the viceroyalty home, so he told them about the once-convicted Judaizer, Joan Vicente, who was now living in Tucumán. According to Alonso, Vicente had not only been imprisoned by the Evora Inquisition in Portugal but, in defiance of Church orders, had removed the sanbenito and hurled stones at it before fleeing for the New World.[18] Over the course of seven years, this accusation was repeated by several of Alonso's kinsmen, recorded by the Tucumán commissioner, and then sent to Lima where it joined other damning testimony.[19] Both Vicente and his wife, Isabel, confessed to backsliding, but they unwaveringly denied the charge that they had removed the tunics illegally or had stoned them.[20]

Testimony about what Joan Vicente and Isabel Báez did with their sanbenitos was contradictory, with the Alonso clan claiming desecration and the defendants claiming permission for removal. Seeking to resolve the question once and for all, the magistrates sent to Evora for a copy of Vicente's transcript. It took eight years to arrive.

In the interim, Isabel Báez died in custody, and the trial against her husband went forward. The case looked bad for Vicente: for one thing, many of his family members had been punished in Evora.[21] Worse, Lima inquisitors were busy gathering additional evidence: eyewitness accounts that Vicente was secretly practicing Judiasm in Peru.[22]

Joan Vicente languished in jail for four years before the inquisitors first decided to put his case to a vote. The verdict was split, with the inquisitor Ordóñez and two consultants voting for him to be burned at the stake and the inquisitor Verdugo and three consultants arguing for the case to be set aside "until the testimony and sentence from the Evora Inquisition arrived."[23] Three years later, on March 11, 1608, inquisitors and consultants met again to determine Joan Vicente's fate, deciding to deliberate without the Evora document in light of Vicente's extended stay in prison (seven years). Again a mixed vote.[24]

The transcript finally reached Lima on July 27, 1609. It was as clear as the document's penmanship that Vicente was telling the truth.[25]

Three months later, there was another vote, and another mixed verdict: on the basis of new evidence gathered in Peru, three judges determined Vicente was an unrepentant heretic. But, on June 17, 1612, Vicente's fortunes changed. Weighing the evidence, including the accuracy of Vicente's sanbenito account, inquisitors and consultants agreed that Vicente should once again be received into the bosom of the Church.[26] The inquisitors' compulsion to consult written evidence had kept Vicente in jail for nearly a decade; and although the Evora report helped save Vicente's life, it also turned a terrible event into a tragedy worthy of Kafka.

The extraordinary paper trail accompanying accused heretics of all stripes showed the Inquisition's extensive reach: testimony from hundreds of miles away could significantly influence the outcome of local trials.[27] The international scope of the Inquisition's bureaucracy added substance to the tribunal's stature and gravity to the evidence it could bring to bear. With the power to call on documents archived for decades and in far-flung locales, the Inquisition was able to assess testimony with the "objectivity"—and, hence, authority—that only written records could afford. The tribunal was deepening its "truths."

Bureaucratic Combat

Lima officials and Madrid headquarters were often locked in a duel, with Madrid trying to rein in an overexuberant and bureaucratically remiss regional office. This repartee was classic institutional, interrank squabbling: an attempt by superiors to retain control over a local office having its own agenda and the means (time and distance) to be derelict. In a kind of internal compromise, magistrates usually showed enough concern to meticulously inform headquarters of their doings, but not enough, say, to stop the doings altogether. Madrid officials, for their part, were of two hearts. Headquarters, for example, encouraged Lima magistrates to pursue their mission with great enthusiasm; yet, all the while, Madrid was wary of the tribunal's roughshod treatment of evidence and protocol. So, among its papers, the semiannual armada conveyed excuses (on the part of Lima magistrates) for why they had to skirt procedure, conveyed expressions of dismay (on the part of Madrid headquarters) that Lima had skirted procedure, and imparted directives (again from Madrid headquarters) on how Lima should redress its procedural wrongs. We will be looking at two cases of bureaucratic combat. The first has to do with evidence and indictments in the complicidad grande; the second, with purity-of-blood laws and Inquisition employees.

The Lima tribunal earned global infamy when, over a period of four years (1635–39), it arrested over one hundred men and women for plotting to secretly practice Judaism. The case against this cabal, the "complicidad grande," however, did not have an auspicious beginning, at least not in terms of evidence. Much sly and indignant discussion between Lima and Madrid centered on Peru's defiance of Inquisition standards in its rush to arrest and punish.

Inquisitors heard the first warning of a Jewish conspiracy in 1635, when one of Antonio Cordero's customers denounced him to the tribunal. The testimony against Cordero was weak by institution standards: only one eyewitness (the customer), who had had only one short conversation with the accused, and virtually no corroboration—one attestant able to confirm only part of the exchange and another unable to confirm anything because he was deaf. The prosecutor's brief was so flimsy, in fact, that the Lima tribunal decided to table any action. But after eight months passed and rumors about the Jewish menace swelled, magistrates grew concerned that an opportunity to stanch a clear and present danger to the empire would be irretrievably lost. So, the inquisitors decided to present their case to a panel of outside experts in ecclesiastic law, and let them determine if an arrest might be warranted. The consultants—weighing grounds and argument—apparently said yes. Cordero was promptly taken into custody, setting a precedent for the diminished standards to be used throughout the complicidad grande and setting in motion a wave of terror.

The Cordero indictment established the tone for slack procedure. Manuel Henríquez, for example, was arrested on the basis of two witnesses' accounts: one person, an eyewitness, claimed to have seen Henríquez indulge in questionable acts; the other, a less convincing, hearsay witness, repeated to the court what the eyewitness had told him the day before. Evidence was sparse and evidence was flimsy—suggestive at best. The eyewitness testified he heard Henríquez make suspicious statements (like preferring fish to pork), but at no time, he had to admit, did he observe Henríquez swear fealty to the Law of Moses or perform an unequivocally Jewish rite. Equally debased standards peppered other cases brought to the tribunal during the complicidad grande, including the suit against Lima's biggest catch, Manuel Bautista Pérez. Magistrates knew they had stretched, even disregarded, the rules and were genuinely concerned about Madrid's response; and, as good bureaucrats, they knew they had to make amends and they knew the right language in which to do so.

There was a pattern. The Lima crew would begin their letters to Madrid with a note of contrition, an expression of their discomfort at having ignored tribunal standards. They would point out, however, that even though they had disregarded some procedures, they had made use of others and that, in the end, the purpose of the regulations had been achieved: that is to say, not a single arrest was made without the support of independent, credentialed experts from outside institutions and, most important, the extraordinary number of eyewitnesses that testified after arrests were made more than compensated for the weak evidence at the start.[28] Then magistrates would lay out the rationale for the procedural breach, arguing that the special circumstances surrounding the complicidad grande more than warranted a rupture of protocol. Inquisitors contended that suspects like Cordero and Henríquez would otherwise have had the chance to escape; and, with that, the possibility of demolishing the biggest religious conspiracy in viceregal history would have vanished.

The inquisitors' trump, however, was one that bureaucrats have been turning to—and hiding behind—for hundreds of years: national security. Lima's tribunal correctly gauged the ability of "reasons of state" to cover breaches in legality, fairness, and morality. Inquisitors portrayed a Peru facing a serious threat: Portuguese-Judaizing-usurious-sabotaging spies lurked everywhere, ready to seduce Indians and blacks to their cause. In light of this kind of menace, niceties of Inquisition law—including standards of evidence and the ratification of testimony—could be legitimately ignored.[29]

The Madrid Suprema oversaw the complicidad grande cases with particular vigilance, and it sent a response to the Lima tribunal soon after receiving the first report of detentions. Exchanges between the two offices continued at an accelerated (for the 1630s) rate for years—even after the climactic auto was celebrated. The Suprema admonished the Lima tribunal "not to go forward with arrests without a substantial basis for doing so." Headquarters was rightly concerned about the complicidad grande turning into a New Christian witch hunt. They were equally concerned, however, that false testimony was leading to the mistaken arrest of Old Christians, and they cautioned Lima about "the unfounded testimony made against Old Christians by those of the Hebrew nation."[30]

Headquarters was stunned by news of the 1639 auto-da-fé, and it retorted with a memo expressing deep reservations about "an auto of such magnitude." The inquisitor general must also have been stunned by the cheekiness of his Lima subordinates, since, according to the rules, no auto-da-fé could be performed without Madrid's consent. By the time headquarters found out about the auto and wrote a strong rebuke in reply, it was too late: prisoners had already been either punished or executed.[31] But even though it could no longer determine the outcome, Madrid was dead set on ferreting out how such a breach occurred. Headquarters demanded that each tribunal member account for his actions in separate affidavits, which were to be transported by the next armada.[32] Madrid was determined, in other words, to assert the precedence of rules and procedures, to assert its dominance.[33]

Another (surprising) arena of conflict between Madrid and Lima had to do with Spain's infamous purity-of-blood laws. These statutes forbade descendants of New Christians to hold office or enter the professions, and the Inquisition was the state institution responsible for enforcement. Despite their renown and notoriety, though, Spain's purity laws could run aground—even in the tribunal's backyard—when they came up against the exigencies of daily life and local government.

Lima's magistrates, like others in the Americas, felt overwhelmed by the territory under their watch, and they frequently complained to Madrid about the need for more personnel.[34] Postulants for offices were subject to background checks, including blood purity, and the research and paperwork involved were quite time-consuming (especially since the investigation often had to span continents). Ironically, some of Lima's inquisitors tried to get around the statutes. Some of their best job candidates, it turns out, refused to submit to the certification process.

Recognizing Lima's staffing problems, headquarters authorized the office to proceed as best they could for the time being. One way Lima avoided lengthy investigations was to appoint individuals who were "[generally] held in high esteem."[35] When "the time being" turned into two decades, however, the Suprema reprimanded Peru for overextending a temporary solution, and it ordered Lima's inquisitors to once again fully research all candidates.[36] Over time, the Suprema and the tribunal reached a compromise or, better said, a modus vivendi. The Suprema allowed candidates for some functions—e.g., consultants and assessors—to take office on an "acting" basis until investigations were completed. But certain posts—e.g., that of defense attorney—had to be filled for the tribunal to conduct business at all, and, in resolving this dilemma, the Suprema had to soften its own stance on the rules. First, they determined that defense lawyers, like other high-ranking legal advisors, would have to undergo complete background checks; then they determined that if no one meeting the requirements could be found, "the defense of prisoners [should] be worked out in such a way that [the prisoners] not end up without a defender."[37]

Some in Lima, favoring function over regulation, simply took advantage of their physical and political distance from Madrid to appoint candidates regardless of procedure; and various commissioners—as well as helpers, doctors, notaries, and constables (along with their wives)—were never subjected to the requisite purity investigations.[38] Such total rule-bending, however, was scandalous in some eyes. Juan de Mañozca, who was named a Lima inquisitor in 1628, was furious to learn that many government employees would not display their insignia of office. Why? To avoid drawing attention to the fact that they either had never been investigated or were of questionable ancestry.[39] Mañozca, an aristocrat with metropolitan leanings, was horrified that men of impure pasts could so easily hold positions of importance in the Inquisition—let alone the viceroyalty.[40] We will return to his fury.

Verdicts Foretold

The great Colombian novelist Gabriel García Márquez was troubled by the deceptions of history—by our perception of it as an inevitable chain of events, a preordained resolution of fate. In *Chronicle of a Death Foretold*, García Márquez undermined this vision by telling two stories: one, an account of a murder that seemed destined; the second, an account of the same murder, but portrayed as the decisions made by individuals in light of the possibilities that circumstance had offered. García Márquez's lesson was that history, even when it seems most "inevitable," never is so; rather, history is made by human beings, making choices with the resources that the past has bestowed. Historical accounts make history appear "foretold"; but lived experience is engaged through a range of possibilities, no matter how limited and torturous. Life is messier than the story.

What of the Spanish Inquisition? Were its verdicts preordained? They appear to be—both because of our stories and because inquisitors condemned accused heretics in overwhelming numbers. But we have seen the paper trails, and we know they roil with arguments and disputes; we know that magistrates bickered among themselves over their subjects' truths. We know that while alternatives were narrow and arduous, tribunal acts were not a chronicle foretold. Procedural requirements—particularly standards of evidence and defendant rights—might, on occasion, stymie inquisitors who would be inclined to go forward in cases that, in their judgment, had the odor of clear-cut apostasy. Suits against two women accused of (among other things) faking holiness illustrate just how the rules and regulations could, albeit not always, get in the way.

One of Peru's most infamous *beatas* (sainted women who had visions and charismatic powers) was María Pizarro, known throughout the vice-royalty as a spokeswoman for angels and saints. There were many stories, and long ones, surrounding this case, but the dilemma that over time led her to the Inquisition's door was the equivocal identity of María Pizarro's voices. Were they diabolic or holy? The battle over the voices engaged Peru's most eminent religious institutions, and magistrates hoped Pizarro's trial would be an opportunity to showcase the tribunal and demonstrate, early on, its powers as an arm of state. The desired victory, however, was elusive because the inquisitors, as you will see, got caught by the rules.

The imbroglio began when three Dominicans and two Jesuits went, as exorcists, to expel the devil from María Pizarro's body. As time passed, the priests came to share their patient's belief that her interlocutor was not the devil, but either a guardian angel or San Gabriel. Eventually one of the Dominicans, who had in the interim become the prior of Quito, changed his mind and sent a memo saying as much to the newly established Lima tribunal. Inquisitors were delighted: they couldn't get involved in María Pizarro's case until there was evidence against her, and this letter provided them with an opening.

María Pizarro had become something of a cult figure by then, and among those who supported her view of things were men of considerable authority: one of her exorcists was the Jesuit provincial; another, the Dominican friar Francisco Santa Cruz, had quite a following of his own. The struggle over María Pizarro's voices had become a struggle between powerful institutions within the Church over the control of the conditions of truth-making.[41]

María Pizarro died in 1572, and it was decided to bury her secretly in the Mercedarian monastery. However, the question of her standing in the Church, "of her memory and reputation," remained. This was normally a matter for the Inquisition to pursue. But Lima officers were ensnared in a predicament: in their efforts to push the case forward, these most modern bureaucrats had "forgotten" one of the tribunal's cardinal rules: all minors had to be represented by a legal guardian, and the guardian had to be present at all interrogations.[42] After much hand-wringing, the magistrates decided that their best tactic was to confess their lapse and ask Madrid for guidance:

> We have not gone ahead with the proceedings against [Doña María Pizarro's] memory and reputation because, since she was never formally accused, she was not provided with a legal guardian, so neither [was she interrogated?] with his authority nor were the ratifications of her confessions signed in front of him . . . and in light of all this, it

seems that we should not continue until we report this to Your Lordship, so you can tell us what is to be done.[43]

The case was stalled, apparently, forever.

The "beata problem" emerged again, and in force, during the early 1620s, when inquisitors wrote to Madrid about the "growing danger created by these worthless women (*mujercillas*) with their feigned holiness."[44] In a situation paralleling the Pizarro case, institutional rules kept Lima magistrates from obtaining Luisa Melgarejo's much sought-after indictment (Melgarejo, notwithstanding her godly talents, had so scandalized Lima society by "living in sin" that secular authorities forced her to get married). Her claims to sanctity—"receiving visions and favors from on high" and knowing "when souls left purgatory and were on the road to salvation"—along with her popularity troubled inquisitors for more than a decade: "For over twelve years . . . some [have been saying] she is a saint," and she is frequently consulted by "imprudent, libidinous women" about "weddings, jobs, and journeys." But, worse, admitted the inquisitor Andrés Gaytán, she was "commonly revered and thought to be authentic, even among those of good judgment." Gaytán lamented how difficult it had been to develop a case, for, even though "learned men would grumble about her, it wasn't until July of 1622 that anyone would actually come forth and condemn her to the Inquisition."[45] So, in spite of Luisa Melgarejo's infamy and her challenge to inquisitorial authority, the tribunal had to follow regulations: they had to wait for someone to formally testify before they could begin to collect evidence and pursue an indictment.

Melgarejo's case was further complicated by the fact that, like Pizarro's, it was a prize in a struggle between powerful institutions. The Jesuits were Melgarejo's greatest devotees, so committed to her saintliness that they were willing to bowdlerize her fifty-nine journals—containing all manner of visions and prophesies—in order to thwart possible heresy charges. Lima magistrates were at a loss about how to go forward, for the battle for truth not only involved a "beata" but a very powerful religious order (the Inquisition's nemesis at the time). So Gaytán appealed to headquarters, explaining that not just Melgarejo but Jesuits "were all guilty," and he asked his superiors to examine the emended journals "for directives on how best to proceed."[46] This time (not always, as you know) Lima's magistrates were good bureaucrats and, keeping to procedure, waited for the Suprema's response before taking on Melgarejo (and ignoring the Jesuits).

The complicidad grande—site of many bureaucratic battles between Lima and Madrid—acquired global renown as an example of Inquisition savagery and was condemned for self-interested verdicts, disregard of evidence, and neglect of basic norms of justice and rationality.[47] Of the eighty-one men and women ultimately tried for Judaizing in the 1639 auto-da-fé, a significant majority were condemned: sixty-three were either penanced, exiled, or burned at the stake.[48] But eighteen were released, either because verdicts couldn't be reached or because there was not sufficient evidence for conviction or because it was clear that indictments had been based on perjured testimony.[49] We have to consider that even an event as tremendous as the auto of 1639 was not foretold.

Let's look again at the squabbles, at the dynamics behind decisions. One inquisitor, Sr. Gaytán, maintained doubts, throughout the deliberations, about the guilt of many of those indicted. Eventually, he changed his mind, clearing the way for the auto-da-fé to take place. The Suprema wanted to know why ("to explain in good conscience his opinion about the sentences [given to] those who were burned at the stake in the auto-da-fé held on January 23, 1639"). Gaytán replied, with palpable resignation, that he was the lone dissenter, every time and in every case; that he had simply caved in to the pressure of the majority.[50] What if he hadn't?

And what about the men and women who were deeply suspect, yet never apprehended. I am thinking here of people such as Doña Guiomar Enríquez, Manuel Bautista Pérez's wife, and Pérez's brother-in-law Simón Báez. Like family members who had been arrested, tried, and penanced, they too had been denounced by several witnesses; they, too, bore the dual stigma of "Portuguese" and "New Christian." And certainly their wealth would have filled the inquisitor's coffers just as heartily as had their kinsmen's. Yet, they were never brought to trial.

Another member of the New World–New Christian community who was never arrested, but who was eyed by inquisitors with suspicion and even greater desire was Don Diego López de Lisboa. Diego López was a thorn in the tribunal's side for decades. New Christian, Portuguese by birth, a renowned and wealthy merchant, López renounced the secular life and entered the clergy after the death of his wife. As a priest, López enjoyed a meteoric ascent. By the 1630s López de Lisboa was one of the archbishop's chief aides, serving as his confessor and mayordomo. He even had the honor of carrying the archbishop's train.[51]

The Lima tribunal compiled testimony against López de Lisboa over thirty-two years, but the biggest threat to his safety occurred during the complicidad grande, when Mañozca and Gaytán, discovering common cause, decided to go after López in earnest. One witness, a Portuguese women "of pure blood and from the nobility," testified that López and his family were rumored to be Judaizers, that his father, uncle, aunt, and father-in-law had been burned at the stake in Lisbon, that López escaped the Peninsula by fleeing to the viceroyalty, and that López "was suspected of doing evil things."[52] One dubious witness (himself in the royal prison on charges of "a calumny")[53] claimed he overheard López whip a sacred image and say "spiteful things about our lord Jesus Christ."[54] On October 6, 1638, Dr. Don Fernando de Guzmán, a priest in the cathedral, claimed he heard Don Diego López speak some words in Hebrew and, pressing the guilt-by-association line, pointed out that Don Diego enjoyed very close ties with several men already imprisoned for Judaizing, like Manuel Bautista Pérez; he added that the bond between these New Christians was so tight that "[Diego López] had even baptized several of [Manuel Bautista Pérez's] sons."[55] Some of López's suspect activities must have been particularly piquing to the magistrates, since they stepped so resoundingly on tribunal toes: López had purchased false papers certifying him to be an Old Christian; even more humiliating, he went over inquisitorial heads—to the king, no less—to get permission to travel to the New World.[56]

That was the crux of the testimony against Diego López. Inquisitors, however, added another, anecdotal dimension to their case: the reaction of "the *vulgo*," the general public, to Don Diego López's robust presence in Lima's ecclesiastic life. They pointed to the shameful consequences of the relationship between López and the archbishop in the public imagination. The vulgo, wrote the magistrates, outraged that someone like López could be so intimately linked to the viceregal religious hierarchy, would, just at the sight of him, "clamor and shout, 'Let that Jew López de Lisboa come over here'"; and at evening prayer, people would stand underneath the archbishop's windows and holler, "Your Lordship, kick that Jew out of your house." To the great embarrassment and shame of López and the archbishop, even Lima's clowns made a mockery of the situation: one, named Burguillos, used to call out to López, "No matter how hard you hold on to that tail [referring to the archbishop's train], the Inquisition is going to get you."[57]

But Madrid remained wary. In 1647 Lima magistrates wrote again with grave concern, since López's son, Don Diego de León, had won the competition for a university chair in canon law and would be in charge of interpreting "sacred canons and ecclesiastic material and the sacraments." They were troubled that "someone from such infected and suspicious origins (*raíz tan infecta*) . . . would administer poison rather than good doctrine" to university students. Commitment to the faith, inquisitors claimed, obliged them to notify the Supreme Council who, they hoped, would in turn notify the Council of the Indies, the principal governing board of Spain's overseas empire. To support their case, the magistrates included a transcript of the testimony compiled years before against Diego

López, Don Diego de León's now deceased father. But their efforts fell on deaf ears. After weighing the long-standing Mañozca–Gaytán effort, Madrid told the Lima magistrates to back off.[58]

Why was Manuel Bautista Pérez arraigned and López de Lisboa not? Both were powerful men; both were under scrutiny; both had a suspect history; both were extremely wealthy. Was it the vagaries of circumstance? Pérez, arrested early in the complicidad—before the Supreme Council could intervene—was, by 1637, damned by more than a score of witnesses; López, with a suspect past but no prior arrest, wasn't testified against until 1637, thereby avoiding the deluge of charges brought about by the "conspiracy." Timing was critical: the Lima tribunal could take advantage of the transatlantic communication gap during the first round of arrests; they wouldn't have so much leeway two years later. Or was it power? Was Diego López—well enough connected to petition the king with success—simply untouchable as the archbishop's minion? No doubt many factors were at play: from the mechanics of bureaucratic decision-making, to the strictures of judicial protocol, to the parochial interests of seventeenth-century Lima, to the sweep of possibilities cast by colonial politics. But can we envision a scenario in which Manuel Bautista Pérez would have avoided the prison cells, or Diego López not? I think so.

Torture and Truth

No act painted the Spanish Inquisition with greater infamy than torture. Yet, like its peer institutions throughout Europe, the Inquisition believed torture was a means to the truth—albeit, in the Spanish case, a means that was used reluctantly. Contrary to stereotype, torture was more supervised and less likely to be practiced in Spain than in other nations we associate with Western civilization.[59] Spain's bureaucratic bent supplied torture with a goodly number of rules, rules which were supposed to keep regional offices in check and ensure the humanity (if we can call it that) of its use.

Local magistrates were exhorted to use torture "following law, reason, and good conscience" and were cautioned "[to] take great care that the sentence of torture is justified and follows precedent."[60] Torture was never—according to the governing instructions—a punishment, but was, rather, a last resort to ease confession.[61] Regulations clarified, with some precision, when torture could be employed, how long sessions could last, which instruments could be used, and what would constitute physical abuse.[62]

Torture sessions were witnessed. A representative of the bishop as well as a physician were present. A court secretary recorded in astonishing detail the torture process itself, putting to paper the victim's words, gestures, and despair.

It is a devastating irony that inquisitors employed torture to get to the truth while, at the same time, doubting the truth of confessions obtained by torture. Magistrates believed "voluntary" confessions were more reliable than coerced ones, and trial transcripts nearly always indicated if confessions were freely given or not.[63] One way inquisitors tried to safeguard the validity of torture-induced evidence was through ratification. Secretaries wrote down everything said or moaned during torture sessions, and prisoners were asked to certify that their confessions had been truthful. By tribunal regulation, all testimony had to be confirmed; but, in acknowledgment of torture's lingering effects, torture testimony was not ratified on the day the torture was administered. Rather, ratification was done the following day, when magistrates had torture victims promise that "[they] would say the same thing once more" and that "none of this [was said] out of fear."[64] When it came to torture, the Inquisition paid little attention to the nature, origin, or status of accused heretics. Just as anyone—regardless of social condition, social standing, gender, or race—could be arrested by the Inquisition, so too could anyone be tortured into telling the truth. At times, though, inquisitors might delay torture for gender considerations (compare the inquisitors' treatment of Doña Mencia and Doña Mayor de Luna with that of their kinsmen).[65] But, in general, women and men, nobles and slaves, wealthy and impoverished, "negro," "mestizo," "español," "mulato," and "sambo"—and all the gradients in between—were charged, arrested, and tortured by the Holy Office. The Inquisition's judicial mandate promoted a kind of equality under the law attained by few other courts of the day.

Across the board and throughout the empire, torture was employed in a minority of cases reaching the bench; most detainees, accused of relatively insignificant heresies (like bigamy, cursing the name of God) did not suffer this anguish. But torture's weight cannot be judged by these statistics alone because, while not resorted to frequently, torture was applied selectively and fiercely: the bulk of its victims were Judaizers, Protestants, and *moriscos* (converted Muslims of Moorish ancestry). In Peru, most victims were Judaizers. According to Henry Kamen's estimates, over three-quarters of all accused Judaizers in late seventeenth-century Spain were tortured. And the figures for the Viceroyalty of Peru are similar.[66]

In light of the torture chamber's visible horrors (the rack, ties suspending suspects from their fingers, whipping devices, etc.), some tribunal regulations appear rather self-serving and hypocritical.[67] Ecclesiastic rule forbade churchmen to spill blood, so unrepentant Judaizers were "relaxed" to the secular court for execution; by the same regulation, secular henchmen—not Church officials—carried out the tribunal's torture decrees.[68] Prisoners were carefully examined to ensure that their skin remained intact—that no blood was visible to stain tribunal conscience. (I imagine it was with some relief that the attending notary could enter into Manuel Henríquez's dossier that "he appears to be without any lesions, except for the burn marks from twisting the cords," since Henríquez had been tortured for more than four hours and not the one hour stipulated in the rule book.[69] We also marvel at the Inquisition's disclaimer of responsibility for harm—or even death—inflicted during torture sessions. Doña Mencia de Luna, like all torture candidates, was warned that "if she were to die during the torture session, or be wounded, or spill blood, or if one of her limbs were mutilated, it would be her fault and responsibility and not [the Inquisition's] because she did not want to tell the truth."[70]

Torture, not surprisingly, produced results. Inquisitors usually got what they were after—confessions and names.

Doña Mencia de Luna knew torture's power. Bluntly and candidly, she rebuked the tribunal for feigning that it was an avenue to truth. Torture was a monster of distortion, a caricature of legitimate means to uncover human actions and beliefs. In response to the charges against her—buttressed by the testimony of many supposed eyewitnesses—Doña Mencia could only explain that "they must have been tortured and talking nonsense."[71] And when ordered to the rack, Doña Mencia made it abruptly clear that she would be "talking nonsense" like the many "eyewitnesses" to her crimes. Any confessions from her lips, statements of guilt, details of life as a Jew, names of teachers and fellow travelers, would be the words of torture.[72]

Perhaps the rack's most noteworthy success was its ability to spur victims to recall and name accomplices—real or fictitious. The Lima tribunal never would have been able to construct a complicidad grande, let alone a case against the conspirators, if not for the effect that hours in the chamber had on loosening tongues and the imagination. When Antonio Cordero, the complicidad's first suspect, was brought before the bench, he confessed to Judaizing but refused to incriminate any of his compatriots. It was only after a turn on the rack that Cordero promised to cooperate and "say the truth . . . that Antonio de Acuna, his boss, Diego López de Fonseca, a friend, and Manuel de la Rosa, an employee of the latter, were Jews."[73] In like fashion, it was only after the rack that Manuel de la Rosa confirmed Acuna, Cordero, and Fonseca as partners in crime; and it was only after the rack that Antonio de Acuna provided a list of fellow conspirators so extensive that it enabled the tribunal to characterize the phenomenon as a "complicidad grande."[74]

But the real conspiracy of the great Jewish conspiracy was the manipulation of guilty pleas for the sake of life. The scheme to fix testimony was based on a compelling argument: once there was evidence against you, once the tribunal suspected you were guilty, the only way to leave the cells relatively intact, let alone alive, was to tell the inquisitors what they wanted to hear. And as Manuel Henríquez, Juan de Acevedo, Jorge de Acuna, and the rest knew from the start, the more confessions, the more likelihood their names would figure in testimony; the more testimony against them, the stronger the inquisitors' case; the stronger the case, the greater the inquisitors' justification to torture them into telling "the truth."[75] The copiousness of confessions was, in no small measure, an homage to torture.

Thus, torture produced results to the tribunal's liking. But it also produced lies and terrible confusion. Accused heretic after accused heretic changed their testimony from innocent to guilty either while suffering torture or under its threat. Many then refused to ratify their earlier testimony or later revoked it—only to confess again when torture returned. The problem, from the bureaucratic point of view, was what to do about those who reclaimed their innocence—only to become guilty again and innocent again and guilty again. The complicidad grande's orchestration of confessions is a casebook on how torture could provoke anything but truth; how, in fact, it inspired criminal activity as defined by the state— perjury, false testimony, and "revocations." Consider, for example, the history of Jorge de Espinosa: 1) March 1635, arrested for Judaizing, claimed innocence; 2) June 16, 1636, admitted heresy after hearing formal charges against him; 3) June 17, 1636, ratified confession; 4) November 19, 1636, retracted confession; 5) December 1, 1636, ratified retraction of confession; 6) December 6, 1636, retracted his retraction and admitted heresy in torture chamber; 7) December 12, 1636, ratified retraction of retraction.[76]

The inquisitors named a crime for this pattern of seesawing testimony. An accused heretic who pronounced innocence then guilt, then innocence then guilt (and so on) was a *revocante*. "Revocation" was serious. If condemned for the offense, a prisoner could count on harsh discipline, usually an additional punishment to add to an already onerous sentence.[77] Not surprisingly, many condemned to burn at the stake had "revocante" added to their list of crimes. Of those so convicted, Juan de Acevedo most provoked the inquisitors' ire. All of Acevedo's crimes were associated with false testimony in one form or another: the elaborate perjury, recounted so deceptively that it could fool seasoned magistrates; then his multiple retractions and revocations.

> [H]e confessed to being Jewish during the second audience we had with him, and he asked for mercy, describing such an expanse of rites and ceremonies . . . that it was a cause for amazement, our hearings lasting for entire days at a time; he denounced many, and gave false testimony against many . . . and there was no part [of the world] free of people he had testified against, neither Spain, nor Portugal, nor Guinea, nor Cartagena, nor other parts of the Indies . . . and he was condemned to be [burned at the stake] for being inconsistent, *revocante*, and for his many false testimonies.[78]

Inquisitors, as you might imagine, were absolutely furious when they realized what was going on. Not only were they getting confused, they were getting duped. For a sense of how much, you first have to read their joyous report to the Suprema in which they describe the roundup of nearly one hundred crypto-Jews, brag about the riches recovered ("[wealth accrued] is added proof of the special favors that God has bestowed upon the Holy Office"), vaunt their success in obtaining testimony, and herald the prospects of procuring more.[79] Compare this with their deflated assessment at the time of Juan de Acevedo's execution, that "he had presented [those declarations] with such fidelity that he even induced the most vigilant and experienced judge to believe they were true."[80]

Some collaborators in the confession conspiracy couldn't abide their sins. They couldn't bear the anguish they felt from falsely accusing friends and family, betraying neighbors, colleagues, or even enemies; or from persuading others, whether Portuguese or Castilians, to confess to being the heretics they were not. Juan de Acevedo, with self-reproach, requested a hearing to confess that "he testified against many who were honorable persons, illustrious people in this republic."[81] Tomás de Lima was full of remorse at having convinced Manuel Alvarez, a devout Christian and a New Christian, who had sworn that he preferred to be tortured rather than to lie about his faith, i.e., to falsely testify that he was a practicing Jew.[82] Manuel Henríquez was appalled at his willingness to finger Old Christians and, worse, "even [to give] false testimony against his wife and daughter."[83] And Manuel Bautista Pérez was so aggrieved that he had considered perjury and counseled his brother-in-law to lie and say Pérez was a Jew that he tried to stab himself to death.[84]

Max Weber defined the modern state in terms of its monopoly over the legitimate control of violent means, and thus recognized its latent savagery. The right to physically brutalize citizens was part of that equation, and torture has played a role in the development of modern institutions of government. Although the Inquisition has been pilloried as an institution of torture run amok, its use of torture as a legitimate means to get "the truth"—it bears repeating—was shared by nations we are more likely to call civilized (like England, France, and Holland). Torture, then, was party to both state control over violence and to state control over truthfulness. The history of the West, in its origins and global dominance, teaches us that torture, bestowed with legitimacy by state institutions, was intrinsic to our civilization. It also teaches something else we will be returning to: that the horrors of torture can be written away in bureaucratic language and practice.

All manner of bureaucratic activities come to light in the transatlantic exchanges between Lima and Madrid: discussions about evaluating evidence, the rationale for arrests, the fairness of sentencing, the importance of archives. We find appeals for assistance and demands for information from other tribunal offices; we find concerns about procedure and attempts to circumvent procedure; we find inquisitors exasperated at having to conform to standards; and we find inquisitors exasperated that standards have not been followed. We find a local tribunal, enjoying the autonomy of distance—thousands of miles and sometimes more than a year away—but still, remarkably, under the Supreme Council's command. We get a close-up of inquisitorial "petty politics," and we get a long shot of its direction as a global, imperial institution. We understand the unpredictability—within bounds—of bureaucratic decision making. Tribunal correspondence, plus archives stocked with indexed and annotated trial records, tell a story of the newly modern world's forays into state-making. They tell a story of the effect institutional process had on Inquisition justice. On a more intimate level, they tell a story of how human beings, made bureaucrats, used bureaucratic procedures in their quest to determine the "truth" of imperial subjects, i.e., the state truths that were party to civilization's violence.

MYSTERIES OF STATE

Good Government: Royal Court and Officials.
From Felipe Guaman Poma de Ayala,
El primer nueva corónica y buen gobierno (1613?).

You may object that it is not a trial at all; you are quite right, for it is only a trial if I recognize it as such. —FRANZ KAFKA, *The Trial*[1]

T HE SOCIAL RELATIONS of political dominion have a way of disappearing before the naked eye, argued Philip Abrams. Some would call this "state magic."[2] Abrams would add that we are its unwitting accomplices: we talk about the "state" as if it were a tangible, physical being, and appeals to its "reasons" have assured our compliance in all manner of brutal acts. But the state, Abrams contended, is ideology: a deeply rooted communal belief which cloaks concrete relations of power.

Just because the state is a part of our collective imagination doesn't mean that the state doesn't have real effects; for its ideological core, its "insubstantiality," is powerful, coercive, and driving—as real to human experience as any corporeal presence. The state's "ghostly power," Michael Taussig claimed, is akin to the "commodity," another spectral force of modern times. He explained that we give commodities life—we turn them into fetishes—because in our daily living we dissociate commodities from the social relations that produced them; we imagine commodities as if they were independent things or even beings, existing apart from their human creation. And the experience of living in a state, Taussig argued, presents an analogous dilemma.[3] Think about it. We most often grasp state systems abstractly (as the public good), or concretely (birth certificates, licenses), or as rules (pay taxes, get drafted), or as an ineffable presence. Yet, this very mode of understanding shuts out the social relations and political forces determining the state.

Inquisition magistrates and their targets played, for the most part, unsuspecting roles in the broad cultural work of state-making, in construing the mysteries of state. For, as part of the tribunal's bureaucratic enterprise, they were making the state—as governing system, concept, and mythology. In dialogue, they were forging both the modern social relations of state and the very means through which we apprehend living in a state. They were inventing the ideology enclosing its construction in time and the thicket of human relations at its core. How is it that the state could appear to be what it was not: autonomous, unified, and even godlike? How could bureaucrats appear to be what they were not: a godlike aristocracy? How could state subjects appear to be what they were not: abstract ciphers in a dossier of statistics?[4]

The Disappearing State

State magic is cultural sleight of hand. Corrigan and Sayer even called state-making a cultural revolution. They insisted that to understand the depth of state incursions into our lives—to see all the blinders—we must take the state's cultural work seriously. This effort calls for heeding the forms the organization of power takes, along with the ways in which meanings are effected and broadcast; heeding, in their words, "the routines and rituals of rule."

The political rituals of baroque statecraft—autos-da-fé being a preeminent example—were pedagogical displays on a mammoth scale. The inquisitors say as much: the autos would school the public in civic values, in morality, and in the implacability of Spanish Catholicism.[5] An indelible reminder of the tribunal's command over life and death, autos would also propagate the mysteries of state, transforming magistrates into gods and the Inquisition into a force—a being—of its own. Autos-da-fé were momentous events, sparking a deluge of emotions—fear, awe, respect, even love (or so it was hoped)—and the auto celebrated in 1639 was the most grandiose, perhaps most infamous, that Lima ever witnessed.

The day after the auto was publicly announced, tailors and carpenters went to work: they had seven weeks to prepare the paraphernalia (insignia, tunics, crowns) to be worn by the prisoners; seven weeks to prepare an elaborate stage, "sumptuous and grand" (forty-seven yards long, thirteen wide, fifteen tall); seven weeks to prepare stands to accommodate the public. The stands were divided into sections for commoners and for the colony's distinguished officials—the viceroy (and the *virreina*), the Royal Court, the captain of the royal guard, and high Church authorities.[6] Unlike commoners, who packed the wooden stands as well as the balconies and doorways en route, dignitaries sat in the plush comfort of pillows, protected from the elements—cosmological and human.

The procession winding its way from the tribunal to the scaffolding must have been an extraordinary sight. It began with clergy carrying crosses, draped in black cloth as a sign of mourning, from every one of Lima's churches; the clergy were followed by nearly seventy penitents, lined up in order of the severity of their crimes. The eleven to be turned over to secular authorities for burning were found at the very end, "wearing crowns and tunics, embossed with flames and devils in various guises as serpents and dragons."[7] Lima's dignitaries—in the dozens—accompanied the procession, in order of rank, dressed in the opulence reserved for their class. All the while, two royal squadrons stood guard, one in the Inquisition's plaza and the other in Lima's principal square.

These were transcendent rites of power, overwhelming rites—the kind that Durkheim would have argued imprint society's force onto unknowing individuals; the kind that Corrigan and Sayer, transporting Durkheim's insights, would argue imprinted the State onto unknowing individuals. And they were the kind that some of the Inquisition's victims would argue performed blasphemy, by making mortal judges into beings similar to God.

The autos-da-fé performed the tribunal's illusions of unity on a grand scale; and their less spectacular rites did so on a smaller one, but no less effectively. An example: magistrates were careful that accused heretics never saw beyond a façade of perfect agreement, never guessed that officials disputed among themselves about the justification of arrests or the solidity of evidence. Remember, when Manuel Henríquez claimed not to know the reason for his arrest, the inquisitors, in one voice, replied that "they were not in the habit of arresting anyone without sufficient evidence."[8] They did the same with Manuel Bautista Pérez and all the others who dared protest their innocence.[9] Through modest rites as well as the more dazzling, inquisitors were promoting an institutional persona: Inquisition as a unified and autonomous, just and rational political being, an institution of State.

The cultural routines of rule—the government technologies (to use the coin of Foucault) that habituate subjects to a particular political order— are not as obvious as the rites of state, and perhaps, for that reason, are that much more pernicious. They have similar effects, but, enacted in the day-to-day of state activities (judicial, educational, policing, or revenue-collecting), they appear unexceptional, commonplace. We could say, following Hannah Arendt, that state routines make the state's godlike powers as banal as following the rules.[10]

Taken together, elaborate rites and mundane routines are the cultural practices that urge us to imagine power in certain ways: that make state categories (like race thinking) and the classifications we use to make sense of our world one and the same; that make the history of the state disappear from social awareness; and that facilitate transformation of the state into an independent, quasi-divine force. These are the habits that, by dominating our social vision and our social bodies, impede us from conceptualizing political experience in any other way.[11]

Making State Subjects: Gods and Statistics

Swearing in arraigned subjects; standing the accused before the bench; recording testimony, ratifying testimony; censuring writing material, sneaking in quills and ink; buying false documents from Europe, sending to Europe for archived transcripts; obeying the Supreme Council, sidestepping the Supreme Council; debating verdicts with experts, appointing defense attorneys; registering financial assets, forfeiting property; taking bribes, giving bribes; demanding information about birth, status and caste, providing information about birth, status and caste— these were some of the mundane practices of state-making recorded in Inquisition archives. Contrary to appearances, these procedures were social accomplishments and expressed a history of socialized authority; for the immediate nexus of inquisitor and accused was part of a chain of political relations that traversed continents and spanned decades.

Colonial subjects and colonial bureaucrats emerged from these procedure-clad relations as they engaged one another in the rites and routines of state. In other words, bureaucrats, like subjects—or subjects, like bureaucrats—made themselves and one another in the process of state-making. But while our theories have easily placed the state's beleaguered subjects—the mass recipients of state discipline—in the throes of history, our attention has sidestepped the plight of bureaucrats.[12] We tend to forget that state functionaries also constitute the "people," are also habituated to living in state systems. Bureaucrats were not outsiders, insinuating discipline into their subjects' being; bureaucrats were also constituted in the dialectic of state-making.[13]

Inquisitors were bureaucrats with a mission. Their job was to safeguard God's new chosen people—Spaniards and their empire—from heretical incursions.[14] Magistrates must have drawn the strength (and arrogance) to make inordinate decisions over others from what they believed to be their divine charge. Tribunal work, however, was carried out by means of bureaucratic practices, and bureaucratic practices also provided a divinelike grounding to the commission of otherwise unthinkable acts. This connection is our focus.

Standards, rules, protocol—that was the stuff of statedom and bureaucracy; and tribunal members, like their counterparts around the globe, were immersed in them. Peru's inquisitors took their vow to follow the rules seriously: they maintained steady contact with Madrid in spite of what would seem to be preposterous obstacles, and they made a show of respect for protocol, even in the breach.[15] But nowhere was the inquisitors' attachment to procedure more evident than in the fervor to find (and make) the truth. When Antonio de Acuna, arrested early in the 1639 conspiracy, begged for an audience to confess his (and others') heresies, an inquisitor, forgoing sleep, remained at Acuna's side from dusk until dawn.[16] The same thing happened in the case of Juan de Acevedo. Inquisitors took pride in their efforts, even when these efforts were for naught (like spending hours writing down perjured testimony).[17] For inquisitors, the prize was not just the outcome or the evidence, but the social practices themselves.

These social practices, at the crux of state rationality, brought a flavor of invincibility to truth-finding. Followed carefully and virtuously (in bureaucrats' eyes), these practices could promote a sense that truth was somehow immanent in the process, that it was an institutional property—beyond the decisions of mere mortals. Appeals to the credentialing process—like appeals to the "experts"—encouraged these feelings. So did the Inquisition's remarkable written record.

The Lima tribunal, with access to documents from decades past and across oceans, exuded omnipotence. Its arms and eyes seemingly everywhere, the tribunal could be experienced—by those in its clutches, by those in its ken, and by the magistrates themselves—as an all-powerful, all-embracing institution. It was like a force transcending individual limits of time and space, able to reach into the past to judge the present and, through present judgments, able to prescribe the future. Magistrates must have perceived themselves as an elect's elect, as a temporal embodiment of transcendent historical forces that were making the Spanish the rulers of the world. And inquisitors, in their language and practice, in their discourse and rituals, encouraged this perception in the populace at large and, most decidedly, in themselves.

In the dialectic of state-making, godlike inquisitor bureaucrats transformed human beings into "its"—fragments of humanity reworked by "state science" into statistics. Neither bureaucracies nor statistics are inherently evil, so the argument goes: they are necessary. How else to administer polities of such size and complexity? But regardless of the ends to which they are put, statistics, like the bureaucratic institutions in which they thrive, mold human understandings.[18] Statistics shape our sense of the makeup of society, of the structure of political life, of the significance and morality of human practices, of the rights of state managers and state subjects—of the appropriate way to represent and investigate the world.

The inquisitors collected all kinds of information about the men and women under their purview. Interrogations—and you are now familiar with some—read like a modern census form: age, place of birth, education, residence, family, caste. Inquisitors were nowhere more godlike, however, than when they used violence in the name of state reason, and the most disturbing use of "state-talk" was in the documentation of torture.[19]

In the seventeenth century, state torture was neither formally illegal nor a source of shame or scandal; and, never doubting the legitimacy of torture, inquisitors made records in abundance. Their very existence documents a significant modern practice of state-making: the objectification of experience, the transformation of social relations into recordable or legible form.[20] This particular set of "statistics" is egregious, mutating, as it does, relations of power and pain into a digestible flatness. We find descriptions—think of the torture accounts early on in this book—but no set of words can translate the defilement of a human being's very humanness.

The bureaucratization of torture: records expose what can be unleashed in the name of public welfare; not only the physical terror, but structures of thinking and feeling built on an abstraction of life. State abstractions seem to remove horrific acts from the realm of accountability, and they do so by dismembering humanness: abuse is splintered into columns of an account ledger, torture is fragmented into events and responses, horror is objectified into smaller and smaller components. Perhaps intentionally—but most probably not—the breakdown of human existence into fragments makes a whole life easier to discard. This is the pornography of bureaucratic rendering, which deafens the perpetrators and us readers to torture's cries—and which distracts us from the web of social relations, from the power, that lies behind what the bureaucrat registers as truth.[21]

Spain's state horrors have entered the public record because bureaucrats met their obligation to register them. As a result, at the very least we have the evidence in hand—evidence that can shame us all.[22]

Fallibility and the Bureaucratic Paradox

Yet, however divine their pretensions, however elegant their presentation as unified state beings, inquisitors were caught by a bureaucratic paradox. They had to publicly acknowledge that they were both mortal and fallible; they had to show that they responded to reason in the service of the state.

In spite of the fact that magistrates did not "make arrests without evidence," they could—as we know—arrest the wrong people. Some accused heretics had cases too tenuous to pursue. Others created doubts by "conquering torture,"[23] and others had their cases dismissed because of something like our double jeopardy.[24] Some men arrested under the shadow of the conspiración grande were reprieved with "suspended sentences" and "absolved for the moment." Others, like seven Old Christians fingered during the perjury scheme, were completely acquitted—an uncommon outcome prompted, according to the chronicler Fernando de Montesinos, by the gravity and infamy of the occasion.[25]

Inquisitors staged an elaborate rite of exoneration to publicly demonstrate the purity of these slandered men—as well as to publicly demonstrate their own commitment to standards, evidence, and truth. Marching in the auto-da-fé's great procession, the seven were paraded through Lima's streets on horseback, carrying palm fronds, bedecked in exquisite clothing, and accompanied by some of Lima's finest citizens. To give you the flavor of their newly found grandeur, here is a description of Alfonso Sánchez Chaparro's acquittal dress: "[on] this day [of the auto] . . . he was wearing a black suit, very costly, with gold buttons, gold chains, a very expensive small ribbon of diamonds, holding a palm frond, on a white horse, beautifully adorned, taken out by six well-disposed livery slaves in expensive uniforms of Florentine cloth, light blue in color, with black adornments, orange colored capes, silk hose; [and Sánchez Chaparro was accompanied by] his sponsors (*padrinos*), who were also beautifully adorned."[26]

Again the paradox: magistrates spun an illusion of omnipotence; but their position in the modern state rested on the obligation to respect evidence and standards; and that mandate could force magistrates (albeit rarely) to admit error, to admit their own fallibility. So, the tribunal might have assumed a "totalizing" mask, but their honored standing, built on an openness to evaluation and a respect for rules (built, in other words, on a bureaucratic ethic), exposed that mask for what it was. The Inquisition was not an all-powerful institution directed by divinelike magistrates; it was manned by fallible human beings.

The Knife and the Sheep

Women and men who appeared before the tribunal were party to a relatively novel way of organizing power: via institutions of state. And because the Inquisition was newfound (established in Peru in 1570), prisoners were especially attentive to its boundaries, its claims, and its authenticity as an instrument of justice. Behind prison doors, most assessments—and measures of defiance—came in the form of words: words expressing doubts about the institution's legitimacy, words of mockery. Victims had little else. Their courageous criticisms and obvious disdain went straight to the heart of the institution's flaws and debilities.[27] When victims derided either individual judges or the proceedings in general, they laid bare the tribunal's failings and its mythology; they showed it to be a man-made, historical institution. Nowhere is this show of contempt more remarkable than when men and women, rendered virtually powerless—whose fates, whose lives, were in the hands of the tribunal—dared to confront magistrates head on.

Doña Mencia de Luna denigrated the inquisitors—unforgettably—for using intimidation, imprisonment, and torture as a means to truth: "[Y]our excellencies are the knife and [I] the sheep."[28] What did torture produce? she asked. And she answered her own question: exactly what the inquisitors wanted to hear ("write down whatever you want to"; "what am I supposed to say, I don't know anything").[29] If inquisitors wanted a guilty plea, they would get it; if they wanted names, they would get names. But, she persisted, what kind of truth would this be? What would be the value of words provoked by physical intimidation? What would be the merit of a religious court whose testimonies were built on coercion?

Manuel Henríquez knew bureaucratic mandates well: his Lima trial was suspended until court records arrived from Portugal; he was kept in jail so the tribunal could determine if he was capable of reason; his sentencing was postponed because the Inquisition didn't have the funds to mount a proper auto-da-fé. Henríquez's disputes with Inquisition officials reflected a marked ambivalence toward the institution and toward state bureaucracies in general—a combination of respect, profound distrust, perhaps faith, and certainly hatred. Some of the challenges he levied at the tribunal were couched in bureaucratic rhetoric and aimed at the gap between standards and practice; others went straight to issues of legitimacy, of the right of an institution to make such claims on its subjects.

Henríquez accused the tribunal of not heeding protocol. He disputed the validity of the procedures used to regulate torture, challenged the tribunal over the appropriateness of his arrest, and argued he had never received the judicial representation due him as a subject of the Crown.[30] Savvy that state institutions were legally bound to official standards, Henríquez knew that a charge of procedural violation could work on his behalf. Henríquez was "bureaucracy literate"; he knew enough to accuse the inquisitors of not carrying out the rules. Yet, by calling on procedure as a legal strategy, Henríquez also recognized bureaucratic virtues: rules were instruments capable of achieving justice.

Regardless, the Inquisition destroyed Manuel Henríquez, and his death contributed to the political processes making mortal functionaries into something godlike. Henríquez had his own words to describe this metamorphosis: "Let the esteemed inquisitors sentence him as they wish, because he is already dead; and whatever they tell him to do, he will follow, as if they were God."[31] Henríquez thereby gave voice to a shattering insight into civilization's underside: he recognized that the apotheosis of state bureaucrats called forth the death of state subjects.

But, then, perhaps Henríquez's words also formed a language of burlesque—mocking the inquisitors' despotism and rebuking their arrogance for assuming a prerogative that could belong only to God. Henríquez had more than once expressed his disdain toward the inquisitors. Hadn't he cut the inquisitor Juan de Mañozca down to size, calling him a drunk in front of his peers? Hadn't he disputed the tribunal's neutrality and disinterest: "Inquisitors are [both] the enemies and judges of the accused."[32] And didn't Henríquez boldly spell out to the court what their jurisdiction over him could be: they had the right to sentence him, but no more. They were officeholders with precisely defined and limited authority over the fate of other human beings; they were not all-powerful: "You, Gentlemen, are the judges of this lawsuit with respect to my death sentence (*relaxación*), in accordance with my confession and testimony, but not [the judges] of anything else."[33]

Of the three, Manuel Bautista Pérez appeared to be most convinced by the virtues of the emerging state: the impersonal nature of its institutions, the objectivity of its actions, its disinterested protocols, its embodiment of universal interests. Pérez believed in the nation's underlying fairness. The Inquisition, Pérez swore, was an exemplar of how the reason of law should operate; justice was not at risk, because the tribunal was staffed by prototypical bureaucrats—by "disinterested people," in Pérez's words.[34] Pérez vaunted great confidence in Peruvian jurisprudence: "[If you] hadn't broken the law [you] had nothing to fear,"[35] reminding his interrogators that had he thought otherwise he would have hidden his enormous wealth.

That is what Pérez claimed. Perhaps, he, like Henríquez, had pounced on a rhetorical strategy—an appeal to an already well-planted institutional ideology. But Pérez, up to this point, had every reason to believe in state virtue. As he told the court, the Inquisition in Peru and Lisbon had proved its commitment to disinterested judgment: he, after all, had been arrested by the Inquisition and released; his cousin had been arrested and released; his competitor Núñez had been arrested and released.

Neither state institutions nor functionaries seemed to have mystified Pérez, who was in no way intimidated by Mañozca and felt little qualm reproaching the inquisitor for letting stand the absurd ideas about the role of tobacco and cola in Jewish rites.[36] Perhaps his wealth and neo-noble expectations—combined with a history of manipulating state institutions

(Pérez was not above forging documents or lying to officials)[37]—helped cast bureaucrats in a very human light.

We won't ever know Pérez's heart or creed. But I would contend that his terrible tragedy, at least in part, was that he believed in the system that had made him one of the elite. Pérez, like many of us, had faith in the institutions that claim to be impersonal and dispassionate; he believed that in the end justice would prevail. At one point Pérez actually conceded the difficulty of his case: even if all the standards and rules guaranteeing impartiality had been met, he admitted, he still would have trouble proving his innocence. The weight of testimony, the overwhelming number of witnesses, and the experts' impeccable credentials worked against him. Pérez's suicide attempt was prompted by his great despair, but also by a profound sense of justice betrayed by the treachery of a state in which he had placed both hope and trust. Perhaps it was Pérez's abiding belief that he had been wronged by state functionaries—and not by the principles on which the Inquisition rested—that gave him the inner strength to tell the henchman to do his duty as he was tying Pérez to the stake.

Mystery and Legitimacy

The tribunal, like other bureaucracies, projected two images: on the one hand, it was an independent, irrefutable force of state; and on the other, a human organization made up of magistrates both upright and despicable. It was seen as a legitimate institution, an unquestionable institution—and a sham. It inspired dynamic, ambivalent, and incompatible sentiments: deep faith and trust, gratitude and hope, skepticism and hatred, terror and awe.

An anonymous chronicler had this to say: "Here is the [Lima] Inquisition, so detested and feared by all of the peoples [living there]."[38] The Inquisition cultivated fear and aroused raw horror: you can feel it in the testimonies, in the despair after the arrest of friends, family members, or business partners; it jumps at you during the roundup of the Lucena-Rodríguez-López family early in the sixteenth century,[39] as it does during the dragnets of the 1630s. Fright, and perhaps a reluctant acceptance of Inquisition authority, pushed women like Catalina de Baena and two of her cohorts to run to the Potosí commissioner and denounce themselves for witchcraft;[40] as it did Doña María de Aguilar and three of her companions, first in 1597 and then again thirty years later.[41]

Menacing, threatening, prompting dread and hopelessness, the tribunal compelled submission.[42] Intimidation had snowballing effects: eroding bonds of trust, sabotaging social relations, augmenting isolation and feelings of vulnerability. And as fear wore down social relations, it must have enhanced the Inquisition's perception as a force in its own right. The Inquisition seemed to be everywhere and see everything: Pedro Báez, a witness in Manuel Henríquez's trial, supposedly said in wonderment that "he did not know how the inquisitors could possibly know about all these things."[43] This aura was no doubt nurtured by the tribunal's magisterial autos-da-fé, but it was also inflamed by rumors: the stories about the Inquisition's attainments, about its reach and, ultimately, about its irrationality.

In the dialectic of perceptions about the tribunal's character, presumptions of suprahumanity were never far from the most vulgar of human attributes. It was not uncommon to hear the Inquisition called an unconscionable institution, whose magistrates were no more than greedy hypocrites. Women and men caught in the Lima dragnets expressed this outrage: from Francisco Rodríguez, who in 1595 claimed that the Lima office "arrested people without blame," to members of the conspiración grande, thirty-five years later, who denounced the inquisitors' "avarice," to Francisco Botello, on trial at the end of the century, who said they were "pilferers."[44] Lima's magistrates heard themselves called "cruel" and "barbaric"—for their savage executions—or "just thieves," for their selfishness and sanctimony.[45] As an institution proclaiming moral authority, the tribunal was ripe for charges that it didn't live up to its mission: in addition to cupidity, magistrates were accused of being womanizers and drunkards.[46] All of these challenges chipped away at the institution's feet of clay.

While many indicted by the tribunal believed that the entire institution was rotten, some defended it and supported its goals but were skeptical of individual magistrates. Manuel Bautista Pérez was one of the latter group, as were followers of "sainted women," or beatas, whom the Inquisition had imprisoned on charges of fraud and diabolic deception (it was up to the tribunal to determine if prophesies and visions were authentic or the work of Satan).[47] Nuns from Lima's Convent of the Incarnation, for example, were staunch Catholics, respectful of Church hierarchy and respectful of the colonial state. But they found themselves at odds with the Inquisition when magistrates indicted Doña Inéz de Jesús for heresy. The sisters believed she was a saint, a visionary wrongly punished, and they were angry enough to exhort their peers to fight the tribunal's injustices, "pray[ing] to God because a great servant of God was in grave need, suffering without any cause."[48]

Yet in spite of these suspicions and stabs of cynicism, the Inquisition undoubtedly enjoyed the support of the public at large.[49] Most Spanish subjects living in the viceroyalty—or anywhere in the empire for that matter—believed that the tribunal served the general good, even if it did act excessively at times or, on occasion, punish the innocent. The great majority of colonials saw the Inquisition as a bulwark of civic order.

Look at the crowds. During the dragnet of 1635, swarms of young men stood by the tribunal's doors to cheer on the noblemen bringing in suspected Judaizers.[50] And throngs attended the autos-da-fé. Bystanders might have been there for a host of reasons—because they were supposed to be or because it was a form of local entertainment—but they expressed, nonetheless, a sturdy desire for the tribunal to carry out its duties.[51] This is how one observer described the audience-crowd at a seventeenth-century auto: "an infinite number of onlookers" from all parts of Lima and beyond, crammed into available windows, terraces, balconies and scaffolds, jostling for space, spending the night in bleachers (the elite got reserved cushions with tickets from the deputy inquisitor), and overwhelming guards with their numbers and enthusiasm.[52] When Angela de Carranza, a beloved and believed-in beata, was finally condemned by the Inquisition, "the people" (at least according to the magistrates) expressed their deepest gratitude: "the people's censure was the severest ever seen to date . . . overwhelmed [as they were] to see someone punished whom they expected to adore forever, glad to find themselves free of the contaminations and delusions, righteously angered by the enormity of the crimes and grateful to the Inquisition . . . for having uncovered and destroyed . . . this monster."[53]

The Inquisition represented itself as it was perceived by many: as the defender of the colony's religious and civic order. Its job was to protect the viceroyalty from enemies within, from the heretics—fraudulent beatas, witches, blasphemers, bigamists, adulterers, and hidden Jews—who would undermine the Spanish empire and civilization, one and the same. Its purview was religious crime; but, as the Inquisition explained to everyone—to the Supreme Council, to the viceroy, to the king, and to the people—its mission was unmistakably political. The Inquisition was the centurion of national security. Inquisitors appealed to reasons of state to justify their disregard for bureaucratic mandates; and they also appealed to reasons of state to make a case for their preeminence as a state institution. In a world as violent, as uncertain, and as extraordinary as seventeenth-century Peru (a modern world-in-the-making), the Inquisition stood for surety, stability, and public order. Listen to the crowds. The tribunal captured the public imagination by answering its needs, and thus did the tribunal hasten its journey as an autonomous political being.

Although native Peruvians were not under the Inquisition's domain, they were certainly aware of its presence. One of the most extraordinary statements of tribunal support was penned by Felipe Guaman Poma de Ayala, a descendant of the indigenous nobility who addressed a thousand-page critique of colonial society to King Felipe III. *The Chronicle of Good Government*, Guaman Poma's masterwork, was a message to the king, and to the world, about the almost incomprehensible destruction induced by Spanish colonialism. Although Guaman Poma severely criticized colonial rule, he was a loyal subject and a devoted Christian; and he blamed the degeneration of indigenous life on a lack of "good government," on the incompetence and perversion of colonial officials, rather than on the structure of Spanish rule. He spared no one for stunting the moral promise of Christianity, and he understood the Inquisition to be an ally in that mission, willing to defend Christian ideals and punish the wicked regardless of their social standing. Guaman Poma judged the tribunal to be the one Spanish institution having the integrity, power, and interest to rein in colonial officials, whether sinning priests or transgressing governors. He praised the tribunal as a fierce standard-bearer of public order in a colonial world run amok.[54]

Guaman Poma made his general case to the Crown through a comparison of Andean life under the Incas and under the Spanish. Though not Christians, the Incas built a well-ordered society that, he claimed, worked for the benefit of all; on the other hand, the Spaniards, nominally Christian, were corrupt, took advantage of their positions of authority, and fashioned a government anchored in self-interest and partisanship. One way Guaman Poma heightened the contrast between Christian, colonial "bad rule" and non-Christian, Inca "good rule" was to point out facets of Inca governance that resembled what Catholic absolutism was supposed to be. The Incas, in Guaman Poma's rendition, had an Inquisition-like way of maintaining moral order.

Guaman Poma, describing the punishments enforced by Cuzco "[to uphold] the justice they had in this kingdom and for the punishment of bad people," presented a hierarchy of offenses and a hierarchy of reprimands that sounded very inquisitorial. The first punishment on his list, for example, was *zancay* (life imprisonment), which, in his words, denoted "jails for traitors and major crimes, like the Inquisition [has]."[55] Other Inca disciplinary tactics echoed the Inquisition's as well: prisoners were housed so that "they could not talk with anyone"; punishments included "execution, whippings, exile." The Incas also used "torture . . . to make people confess."[56]

Guaman Poma held that the tribunal's greatest contribution to public welfare lay in its power to castigate fellow bureaucrats who were not conforming to the norms of good government. One of his principal targets was the clergy, and many illicit priestly activities found their way into Guaman Poma's account. Clergy were charged with exploiting Indian labor in mines and small textile factories (*obrajes*) or with forcing parishioners to work for free as domestic help. Their most egregious crimes, however, were associated with sex, and Guaman Poma harped relentlessly on the theme of priests who, under the cover of various pretexts, forced women, particularly Indian women, to have sexual relations. The Inquisition was his front line of attack—with good reason, since the tribunal, recognizing the problem, included many of these clerical transgressions in its yearly edict of faith, heard in every parish throughout the viceroyalty.

What was Guaman Poma's solution to Peru's bad priests, who were "prideful, completely unrestrained, who fear neither God nor justice?"[57] In his words, "the priest who is bad-tempered and cruel and has committed other sins, should be punished by this kingdom's Holy Inquisition";[58] or, again, "it was not enough for them to be punished, [their sins] should be made known to the Holy Inquisition."[59] In this way, Guaman Poma explained, "a good example will be set for the faithful, [for] Christians . . . throughout the world and in this kingdom."[60]

In addition to Inca comparisons, Guaman Poma devoted a hefty section of his report to a description of the institutions that ought to constitute colonial government. And the Inquisition figured prominently. He called the entire staff, from honored inquisitor to commissioners, familiars, prosecutors, and bailiffs "good Christians" (a strong compliment in light of what he usually called Spaniards). He also remarked on the tribunal's exemplary structure and the great respect it merited, and he singled out two of his contemporaries, the inquisitors Pedro Ordoñez Flores and Juan Ruiz de Prado for their "charity," "generosity," and "good works in the service of God and Crown."[61] Assessing the often embattled institutions that made up the colony, Guaman Poma praised the Holy Office—the organization and its magistrates—as the best that Spanish rule had to offer the viceroyalty. In Guaman Poma's calculus, the Holy Office was the exemplar of "good [colonial] government," an institution necessary for Peru's well-being. Unlike other state offices, he argued, the Inquisition did not shy away from punishing Peru's rich and powerful: the Inquisition was mindful that all, regardless of caste or class, were equal before God.

The Spanish Inquisition—infamous and famous, an outpost of hypocrisy and a rampart of social order—provoked a melee of passionately held opinions regarding its authority, legitimacy, and function. The Inquisition had effects, however, that went beyond its official and tumultuous role as arbiter of heresy; like other state institutions, the Inquisition also habituated its subjects to the structures of modern power, to the bureaucratic ways and manners of modern political life. Bureaucratic expectations and bureaucratic worldviews, we find, were insinuating themselves into colonial souls—sometimes in unsuspected ways.

The Inquisition was a premier licensing institution of the Spanish world. It had jurisdiction over travel outside the realm or overseas, and during much of the period we are exploring, anyone going to Spain's colonies was officially required to get the tribunal's permission. According to the street smart, a false travel permit was almost as easy to get as a real one; nonetheless, some travelers felt obliged to petition the Inquisition for a license. A few lived to regret it.

Duarte Méndez was one of the early unfortunates. In 1595 he went to the Lima office to get a travel permit. Following procedure, the tribunal investigated Duarte Méndez once they got his request and, unluckily for him, found a substantial file of incriminating material. With file in hand, magistrates rushed to put him in jail.[62] Similarly, Antonio Morón, Doña Mencia de Luna's brother-in-law, asked the Lima tribunal for a license to go to Panama; and Morón, too, ended up in jail (even though the evidence against him was minuscule).[63] Both Duarte Méndez and Antonio Morón petitioned for travel permits under what, in hindsight, were risky conditions: both had several family members and friends sitting in prison cells. Why would they have risked arrest by going to the tribunal for a travel permit which, given the reality of the day, could have been purchased on the black market? Were the two just foolhardy? Duarte and Morón must have believed in the "system" and its commitment to fairness—at least enough not to fear going to the Lima office. Perhaps they had become sufficiently modern to believe (consciously? implicitly?) that they had an obligation to follow state regulations. Or sufficiently modern to not even think about *not* obeying them.[64]

The tribunal's licencing authority also received an unusual salute from three men brought before the bench on charges of witchcraft (the only three men so charged, as far as I can tell). All three, testifying decades apart, claimed that the Inquisition had given them a licence to go on with their activities; in other words, that the tribunal was an institution in the business of giving out certificates for competence in sorcery. In every case, witnesses testified that the witches bragged about their special credentials. In 1615, Miguel Cabalí swore to a client that "a commissioner had granted him a permit to use his [skills] . . . to find where there was gold and other hidden things";[65] Gonzalo de Navarreta, three years later, vowed that "inquisitors from Granada had given him a licence to discover stolen goods and treasures";[66] and, finally, nearly sixty years later, Pedro de Marmolejo, "who went all over curing [people] with herbs and other things," alleged that he too "got a licence from the Holy Office," once he passed an exam.[67]

Inquisitors were outraged, as you might imagine. They were not running any sort of degree-granting institution. Yet the three "witches" and their clients shared the belief (albeit heretical) that a tribunal licence added luster and authority to their curing and fortune-telling practice. (Women accused of witchcraft didn't ask for the state's imprimatur—already inured, perhaps, to the gendered twist of state-sanctioned knowledge?) In any case, the requisite that expertise and knowledge be certified by government was imprinted in the viceroyalty's increasingly modern, cultural landscape—even if in unexpected places.

A view of the Inquisition as an irreproachable institution of government was, by the seventeenth century, appearing to dominate the viceroyalty's cultural politics, and the Inquisition's inescapable presence surely contributed to making the state an intimate part of a colonial "modern self." State ideologies made the Inquisition into an entity larger than life, and its institutional being appeared to be increasingly anchored in the viceregal way of living in and imagining the world. Yet, at the same time, men and women experienced the Inquisition through sensibilities that cast doubt—in various ways and in various degrees—on its grandeur. The Inquisition did not completely commandeer the beliefs and feelings of colonial subjects, perhaps not even those of one of its greatest supporters. You can judge. Let's take another look at Montesinos's account of the 1639 auto and at his story of a bond forged between God and a heretic Judaizer, condemned by the inquisitors to die at the stake.

Francisco Maldonado de Silva, who renamed himself "Elí el Nazareno [the Nazarene], unworthy servant of God," spent thirteen years in prison before he was executed. There was never a question about Silva's beliefs: Silva circumcised himself in jail, refused to eat meat so as not to break kosher rules, defended Judaism in public debates with Catholic theologians, and wrote long discourses in praise of Judaism from his prison cell.[68]

Montesinos showed little more than contempt for other doomed prisoners, but Silva won his respect. Not only was Montesinos affected by

Silva's sharp intelligence, he was deeply touched by Silva's determination to proselytize, even from the impossible conditions of an Inquisition cell. Silva was clever, the priest was forced to admit, overcoming hardships through an alchemy of old papers, charcoal, and a hen's bone to pen critical tracts (dedicated to the inquisitors, no less), "written in a hand so fine it looked like print."[69] But it was the extraordinary event that took place on the auto's stage of executions that captured Montesinos's—and the public's—imagination. Silva's final moments were astonishing:

> It is worthwhile noting that after the summary of charges against those condemned to death (*relajados*) had been read, a wind arose, so intense, that the oldest residents of the city claimed they had never seen anything so severe in many, many years. [The wind], with piercing violence, ripped apart the cover that had been shading the platform—at the exact place where the condemned man [Silva] was standing.

> [And, at that moment, Silva] said, looking up at the sky, "The God of Israel has arranged for this [to happen] so [he] can see me face to face from the heavens."[70]

By calling attention to God's act and recording it for the present and future, Montesinos transformed a windy January day into something imbued with cosmic significance. The seventeenth century was a time when extraordinary events were understood to be signs of providential will, and the violent winds, along with Silva's implied dialogue with God, must have carried grave meanings, portentous enough in Montesinos's view of things, to merit comment. Was it possible that God was ready to receive into his bosom a declared heretic, a man condemned by the very institution entrusted with carrying out God's will? Montesinos gave us this description, and nothing more. Still, it is extraordinary, given that Montesinos was so trusted by the inquisitors that they chose him to write the official version of the 1639 auto. Could Montesinos have been both a devoted supporter of the Inquisition and an unwitting purveyor of suspicions about tribunal justice and tribunal pretensions?

Perhaps this was the work of an angel of history, a clarion of concealed injustice (a figure coined by Hannah Arendt's great friend, the social critic Walter Benjamin, writing as fascism tightened its grip). An angel of history, for all one knows, may have been bestowing all Lima—and Montesinos's readers—with a flash of understanding about the inequities of an age.[71]

The Inquisition held a special place in Spanish statecraft. It was the one state institution found throughout the realm, on the Peninsula and in the colonies; it was an arbiter of religious orthodoxy in a country that defined religion as nationalism; and it was a bureaucracy responsible for the empire's cultural (i.e., national) security. It was, in fact, an institution of state that defined what nationhood meant, fixing internal cultural boundaries in tandem with Spain's position in an increasingly global world. As such, the Inquisition held an advantaged position in one of state magic's most prodigious feats: constructing a "nation" as if it were autonomous and self-directing when, in fact, it was neither.

The Inquisition's mission would appear to be an internal affair; but, to the contrary, concerns about Catholic preeminence had everything to do with political and ideological battles that crossed state borders. The history of Islam on the Iberian Peninsula was tied to victories of North African caliphates over Spain's Gothic lords; Spain's thriving Jewish communities of the fifteenth century were made up not only of victims of the Roman diaspora, but of Jews expelled from medieval England and France. But, most significant, the Spanish Inquisition was consolidated as an institution during a period of extended warfare on two fronts: war with the Muslim Ottomans and war with Protestant Europe—political conflicts that were also religious wars.

Throughout the seventeenth century, the Inquisition contributed mightily to defining the boundaries of political and religious orthodoxy in Spain, boundaries it feared were being permeated by the ideas and ships of Protestant and Muslim enemies. Vigilance, the tribunal declared, was required both at home and in the vast stretch of territories—in the Americas, Asia, and Africa—that formed Spain's colonial possessions. Threats internal to Catholic Spain were inseparable, then, from the broader theater of European hostilities, an arena now global in scope. The Inquisition, that most Spanish of institutions, was concocted in the cauldron of modern global politics.

The very notion of a closed and bounded, autonomous state—Abrams's reified state, Coronil's occidentalist state, the modern state—was spawned in the midst of world politics. And state-making's own cultural work was such that it shrouded the state's international, colonial, and race-thinking makeup from view. Working for the benefit of the state, bureaucratic practices put blinders on officeholders, clients, and subjects alike. Thus our attentions became focused on the state as an independent being, with its own, autonomous rationale. We now recognize that the modern state is not quite so independent. Many believe that the modern state began its international journey only decades ago, with the advent of global production, or only one and a half centuries ago, with northern European colonialism. Students of the Spanish empire know better.

What knowledge have we lost by detaching the modern state from its more than five-centuries-deep global roots? We have lost our origins in colonialism; we have lost our origins in race thinking. The hidden hands fashioning "state" and "race" have been working together for years, as partners building the West's "subterranean stream." For state-making's magical act not only institutionalized race thinking and gave it legitimacy; it made race thinking part of the body politic.

GLOBALIZATION AND
GUINEA PIGS

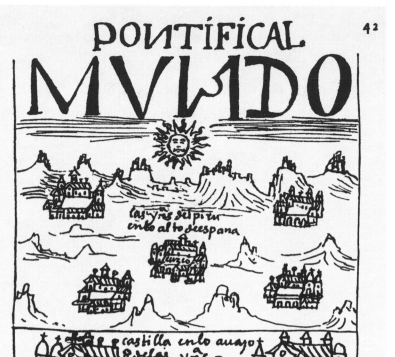

The World: The Indies of Peru are above Spain;
Castille is below the Indies.
From Felipe Guaman Poma de Ayala,
El primer nueva corónica y buen gobierno (1613?).

Haven't female guinea pigs that are all white produced litters with guinea piglets that are black, brown and white? . . . Likewise, in this way, our first fathers . . . [were] white, and their descendants, some are brown, others black, and others white. — FR. FRANCISCO DE AVILA, *Tratado de los evangelios* [1]

[E]veryone in the world, whites, blacks, and people of . . . color. — FR. FERNANDO DE AVENDAÑO, *Sermones de los misterios de nuestra santa fe católica* [2]

FATHERS FRANCISCO DE AVILA and Fernando de Avendaño reckoned they knew native understandings (and misunderstandings) well enough to publish, in 1648, the bilingual sermons they had preached over the course of their decades-long careers. Avila, by this time a canon in Lima's cathedral, and Avendaño, an advisor to the Inquisition and professor of theology, were warmly praised by fellow clerics — who were well aware that the native ignorance of Christianity they so conspicuously bemoaned was, in no small measure, a product of their inability to communicate God's word in Quechua. With these two volumes, pastors could at least sermonize in a language that was intelligible to Indian ears.

In keeping with Christian tradition, the sermons highlighted signposts in the sacred calendar, related the travails of saints and sinners, and narrated Christ's sojourn on earth. But the sermons were much more. They were a social practice, an early form of mass media, whereby Spaniards presented to Indians a Spanish idea of the emerging modern world and the role each group had in its making. However, to be in any way convincing, Avila and Avendaño were compelled to account for the Spanish conquest and the extraordinary transformations it caused in natives' lives. They had to make sense of great devastation to human life, to crops, and to herds; they had to make sense of terrible losses of family and community; they had to explain why their religion (as opposed to the Incas') would not tolerate any trace of indigenous beliefs. To do so, Avila and Avendaño appealed to nothing less than world history: to the history of Rome and Spain; to the history of Jews, Moors, and Incas. Said another way, they had to articulate the new global and social relations—those of empire and nation—that had so changed Andean life. Both men lectured about the relations we call class, race, and caste; both preached about nationalism and religious purity; and both gave the Incas' descendants a place in the new, transnational world order.

Like most homilies, Avila's and Avendaño's were directed at others, but spoke reams about themselves, and about their grasp of the early modern world. They give us a rare and articulate view of the initial meanings of race thinking: we see the entanglement of race, religion, and nation; we pick up long-standing disputes over innate character versus belief. We hear them transport the notion of "stained blood" to the Americas; and we watch them juggle the related enigma of how a just God could consider all human beings equal, yet allow such hellish distinctions between human beings on earth.

Preaching Hierarchy

Avila and Avendaño preached hierarchy in their sermons. First, they turned to the ancients to clarify God's basic, hierarchical order of society—of rulers and ruled, of rich and poor.[3] But Avila's and Avendaño's primary task in Peru was to turn this Old World wisdom into lessons of colonial cultural politics: they had to revamp the old hierarchy of Europe to contain the new, modern hierarchies of colonialism and nation; they had to explain why differences of wealth and power were experienced in racialized form.

The modern world was of much greater complexity than the world of the ancients, the priests explained to their flock and to themselves: the premoderns were unaware of the global dimension to God's work and, consequently, did not recognize that God had sheathed his economic and political divisions in a casing of caste and race. "Spanish," "black," and "Indian" —in the modern scheme of things—were other words for one's lot in life. According to the Avila-Avendaño calculus, blacks were the principal example of God-created servants, born to "serve . . . or learn trades, or work or plant fields."[4] Indians were to be "drafted to work in the mines." For God, they continued, "[had] created some men to be kings . . . and rule over others." Spaniards, of course, were the kings and rulers.[5]

Then came the vicious comparisons. "If you [Indians] purchased a black slave," Avila asked his Indian flock, "who is better, you or your '*ne-gro*' . . . ?" And, the obvious answer: "[O]f course it is you, because they [blacks] don't do more than obey your orders."[6] Going up a rank in the global ladder, Avila asked his congregants to weigh the worth of Indians and Spaniards. No surprise who came out on top: "Hadn't Pizarro, with only one hundred and sixty men, defeated the Inca Atahuallpa, who had . . . over forty thousand well-armed soldiers? Didn't the Spanish—with God's help—conquer Peru's natives and force them to perform all manner of onerous tasks?"[7] And hadn't Indians noticed how many of their kin and family had died, hadn't they noticed how few of them were left? Hadn't they realized how unproductive they were, and how hungry, how they, "with all [their] idolatries were barely capable of harvesting twenty *fanegas* of wheat a year, while Spaniards managed two or three thousand."[8] This was God's will. Softening his harangue with appeals to God's equity, Avila told his audience that if Spaniards displeased the Lord, they too would suffer all the devastations inflicted on Andeans. But for the present, he cautioned, it was God's will that the only place Indians would "find respite from labor in the mines" was in heaven.[9]

Common Origins

Priests, furthering colonialism's cultural work, addressed hierarchies of power and wealth as God-given possibilities, distributed along an axis of racial castes. This modern vision, however, collided with another—that all men were equal in God's eyes. And so we have a familiar modern dilemma. Although Christian ideology accepted racial disparities in life, it nurtured propositions—and dreams—of human equality; it taught that human beings were one in God's eyes and that human beings shared one origin in God. Evangelists not only had to account for God's contradictory and selective implementation of equality, but they had to explain how racial differences, so starkly experienced by "New Christian" natives, could be sanctioned by a divine source who so loved common origins and human unity.

The idea that human beings shared a common genesis did not sit well with Peru's natives. Indians, traditionally, did not believe that Indians themselves shared the same ancestors—let alone Spaniards and Indians.[10] By the mid-seventeenth century, some Indians were giving credence to a novel, two-god pantheon: one set of ancestors for Indians, another for Spaniards.[11] Indios, Avila discovered, were beginning to understand their tragedy as a sign of divine displeasure on the part of native gods, who were furious that Andeans seemed to prefer an alien, Christian god over them.

Avila told his parishioners he knew that the abrupt and terrifying changes brought by colonialism might prompt some natives to abandon Christ and return to idolatry, and he used his sermons as a platform to acknowledge the Indian argument (and heresy): viz., that the Christian god "won't do for us Indians"; "we are not like *españoles*"; "we *indios* have a different origin and appearance and, being thus, we are not of God's flock nor is the Spaniards' god our own."[12]

To dispel indigenous beliefs in the separate ancestry of Spaniards and Indians, the preachers went back to Adam and Eve. Avila was characteristically (and self-servingly) blunt: Andeans had "ridiculous [origin] stories and fables," the notions of a "people without reason," and it was his mission to argue for the truth held by a people with reason, i.e., the biblical story of Genesis. "What is certain," he preached, "is what the Holy Book says about mankind's beginnings." And the Bible's message is that all of humanity "sprang from one man, named Adam, and one woman, named Eve."[13] In order to account for human oneness, though, Avendaño and Avila had to account for the human distinctions that would seem to belie it. They had to make sense of color.

The Problem of Color

On the fourth Sunday of Lent, Avila preached a sermon meant to reveal the biblical lesson of creation and the shared beginnings of all humanity. His goal was to tackle the basic Andean proposition that since native peoples looked different from Spaniards—and especially since they had a different skin color—they must have originated in different gods. To make his case, Avila had to account for what natives perceived to be two gaping contradictions in terms: that progenitors of one color could produce offspring of different colors and, specifically, that white Adam and white Eve (of course) could have begotten the world's multicolored peoples.[14] The evangelist turned to examples that native Andeans would find very familiar.

The first problem was to illustrate how ancestors of one color could have produced multicolored descendants. Avila turned to sheep. He asked his audience to estimate how many there were in Peru (sheep were legion). Avila then explained their genesis: ewes and rams, unknown before the Spanish invasion, crossed the Atlantic with the first band of conquistadors. Avila reminded his parishioners that an extraordinarily large number of sheep had been produced by the fifty original; he also reminded them of the sheep's remarkable range of colors: "some black, others white, some brown." Then the human comparison: in like manner, "we [humans] have multiplied . . . [and] spread throughout the world: whites, blonds, browns, blacks."[15]

To account for how white Adam and white Eve could make many-colored young, Avila called on the example of native species—corn and guinea pigs. He had his audience look at a large ear of corn with white kernels, and then at another that was predominately white, but with some darker kernels. The moral: out of white kernels, other colors grow. Next, Avila turned to guinea pigs and underscored what was again obvious to Andeans: "[H]aven't female guinea pigs that are all white produced litters with guinea piglets that are black, brown, and white"?[16] Thus Avila concluded, when it came to skin color, human beings underwent the same process as some of Peru's most important indigenous plants and animals: "Likewise, in this way, our first fathers . . . [were] white, and their descendants, some are brown, others black and others white."[17] Avila had resolved the riddle of phenotype and genotype, by arguing that all of God's children, from crops to man, started out white—but then some changed color over time.[18]

A World Historical View: Moors, Jews, and Indians

Avila and Avendaño plumbed history—particularly the tortuous events linking Spain with *moros* (literally, Moors) and Jews[19]—for lessons of relevance to their Andean mission. Preachers turned these harrowing pages from Spanish history into cautionary tales about fidelity and Christian supremacy. Other, perhaps less-obvious, morals were drawn as well—about descent, religion, achievement, and nation. The first business, however, was to teach about the Jewish and Muslim devils—a duo Andeans would join if they didn't forswear their idolatries.

First, the fire and brimstone. Moors, Jews, and idol worshipers were the world's principal heretics and, as such, would be subject to God's terrible wrath ("He who does not love the God of the Christians . . . will go to hell . . . and that is why idolators will go to hell, [as well as] those who are called Moors, and the Jews").[20] But a hellish future was not all that was in store. Idol worshipers (i.e., Indians), reduced to the same pitiful status as Moors and Jews, would, like them, also be punished in this world, and in inquisitorial fashion. They would die horrible deaths; they would go to the stake; they would be, to repeat Avila's warnings, "burned alive."[21]

Moros had become such renowned heretics in Andean circles that some native Peruvians commonly used "moro" as a synonym for "heresy in general." Avendaño made clever use of this linguistic detail in a homily designed to introduce Indians to other "moros" equally menacing to Spain's spiritual quest and political ascendancy. He asked Indians to make a list of the people who would fit the "moro" category and then expressed concern that one group in particular—whose "evil" presence was increasingly felt in the Americas—had not surfaced on their register. Avendaño was thinking about the Protestant English, "those who come by sea to rob [us], . . . [those people] called Englishmen."[22] Indeed, the English were harrying Spanish trade, battling Spain for control over territory in the Caribbean, and harassing settlements along the Pacific coast. Moors were one political bane of Castile's existence, and Protestant England was another. Avendaño's sermon had transformed a world history lesson, the story of Moorish perfidy in the Mediterranean, into a lesson in current Peruvian events.

Los moros, los moriscos (Christians of Moorish descent), and *los turcos* (Ottomans) were often confused in missionary sermons. The Ottoman empire had the strength and means to challenge Spain, and the morisco debates, on both sides of the Atlantic, were taking place as Spain was battling the Ottomans for dominion in the Mediterranean. It was not uncommon for Spaniards to mix up domestic enemies and external rivals, and the kind of conspiratorial worldview that, as we will see, could make New Christians of Jewish ancestry into global plotters also merged these three very different, Islam-connected groups. History belied this Spanish stereotype: the Ottomans and North African caliphates (Moors) were sometimes allies, but not always; and although some "moriscos," like other New Christians, remained faithful to the religion of their ancestors, others became loyal Christians. Preachers, then, in their confusion, were preaching a very modern convention to their Andean flock—that shared religion made for shared politics; or, a variant, that nation and religion are one.[23]

Spain also fought "los turcos" on the spiritual battlefield. Catholic liturgy, as preached in Peru, singled out turcos as a hoped-for target of God's wrath, and Avila and Avendaño forcefully encouraged natives to pray for their destruction.[24] Spain's continual battles with "los moros" mirrored Spain's continual battles with America's idolatrous natives, and surely Avila's and Avendaño's pleas for the Ottoman empire's downfall embraced as well their desire to dominate idol-worshiping Indians, who were forever backsliding or, as was the case along the viceroyalty's frontier, impossible to conquer.

Conflicts with idolatrous Indians resonated with Spain's other internal enemy, the Jews, albeit in a different register. Jews played a special role in the morality tales transported to Peru. Our evangelists attached much fire and brimstone to Jewish perfidy; and that was because the Jewish experience was cast as history's exemplar for Indian missteps and Indian misfortunes.

Jews, like Indians, refused to accept God's word, and both bore—in Avila's and Avendaño's world history—the terrible outcomes. God, out of profound love for humanity, had sent messengers to Jerusalem and to the Andes. To the one he sent Jesus; to the other, Spaniards. But neither Jews nor Andeans would accept God's word: Jews refused to believe in Christ's divinity; Andeans returned to the idolatry of their ancestors. Both the Jews and the Incas, Avila and Avendaño harangued, had been, at one time, the lords of the land, had been their regions' most prestigious and powerful "naciones." Now they were the most despised. Jews and Indians alike had sorely felt God's wrath: Rome conquered Jerusalem; Spain conquered Peru. The Jews were banished from their land, exiled to Babylon; the Indians watched others take their land, as loved ones died.[25] The sermon:

> Don't you see how these Jews condemned themselves? . . . And forty years after [Jesus's crucifixion], the Romans came with countless armed men and demolished [Jerusalem], destroying it all, and burning down the temple and killing everyone. . . . Look how God lets nothing [sinful] transpire without punishment. . . . [A]nd now we will speak a bit about your land and your ancestors and your kings, the Incas. . . . [During their reign] the entire land was boiling in sin, principally idolatry . . . and God wanted to enlighten the land . . . and just as God sent Captain Titus from Rome to Jerusalem . . . he sent Francisco Pizarro. . . . [A]nd then more Spaniards went to Cuzco and they destroyed the temple where the Incas worshiped . . . and today there is no longer the [quantity of] Indians that there used to be; the towns are desolate; the homes are falling apart. . . . [D]on't you recognize you had the same [fate] as the Jews?[26]

The Jewish diaspora was a good evangelical lesson for missionaries eager to convince Andeans of the need to stay converted. However, the "Jewish problem" was not only a story of the first century, but one of the seventeenth; and that made the comparison, as well as the link, between Indians and Jews that much more intimate, urgent, and compelling.

The history of Spain, the Moors, and the Jews, however, was just as much a lesson for the missionaries as it was for the Indians. Missionaries sent to indigenous communities perceived their efforts in light of Spain's tumultuous religious past, understanding early Church strategies to convert "pagan" gentiles, and especially later attempts to convert Moors and Jews, as rehearsals for ventures in the Americas. When "extirpators of idolatry" assessed their mission in Peru, they were sobered by difficult and, in the case of Moors and Jews, apparently unsuccessful evangelizing campaigns in Spain. As Father Pablo José de Arriaga wrote in his handbook *The Extirpation of Idolatry in Peru*, "[I]t has scarcely been possible to extirpate so evil a seed [Judaizing] even in so clean a land [Spain], where the Gospel has been so continuously . . . and thoroughly preached and where the Most Righteous Tribunal of the Holy Office has been so diligently and solicitously vigilant."[27] And "the problem of setting aright and causing to be forgotten errors of belief learned at a mother's breast and inherited from father to son can readily be seen in the recent example we have had . . . in the expulsion of Moors from Spain."[28] If the task of "rooting out" the hidden evils of Judaism and Islam in Spain was so monumental and difficult, though, what might the New World have in store for the guardians of the faith in Indian country? Fortunately, Arriaga assured his readers, "the disease of the Indians" (i.e., their reluctance to denounce native religions for Catholicism) was not "so deeply rooted a cancer as that of the Moors and Jews."[29]

Still, the question remained: How to explain the persistent treachery? How to explain why the viceroyalty's Indians, like its Jews and Moors, refused to abandon their ancient faith? The answer was that Indians, like Jews and Moors, carried "stained blood."

Stained Blood

In the colonial confusions over race and religion, the connection of Jews with Indians played a particularly significant role. That linkage was front and center in dilemmas over conversion: Did baptism erase sins and character flaws, or were sins and character flaws part and parcel of stained blood? The question here is how that linkage affected missionary judgments; how evangelists, whose vision was stamped by the New Christian experience, understood newly baptized Christians in the New World. Avila called Jews the "mala casta" (the evil caste), damned, it would seem, forever.[30] But what about the Indians? Would baptism and patient teaching be able to transform Indian instincts, or did stained blood always leave its mark?

Indians were called many things by the colonizers—brutish, inept, dullwitted, etc.—reflecting the general Spanish feeling that Andeans had "limited capacities." Avila and Avendaño preached that belief from the pulpit ("you [Indians] have meager understanding"),[31] and both were concerned about the difficulties novice missionaries might face when they tried to convey the Gospel to a backward people.[32] They were worried that Indians, with their restricted capabilities, would neither be able to understand the basic text nor be able to participate in the new, modern confession. (As modified by the reform-conscious, institution-rationalizing Council of Trent, sins were to be counted, not just recited; and in the eyes of *doctrineros*, the teachers of Christian doctrine, most Indians, "because they were so stupid and dim-witted, do not know how to add them up.")[33]

Indian character was marked by other chief qualities, or deficiencies: Indians were not to be trusted, Indians were cowardly, Indians were lazy. Indians were typed as thieves and liars, people "of little truth"; accordingly, the telling equation: the testimony of six Indians was equivalent to that of one Spaniard.[34] Indians were said to be fearful, gutless, "notoriously pusillanimous," and so craven that "trembling, [they] would do whatever was commanded [of them]."[35] And Indians were said to be so slothful that they had to be "habituated to work by His Majesty." These assessments, according to Quito's renowned bishop and author of a guidebook for missionaries, Alonso de la Pena Montenegro, were well grounded since they were based on the published accounts of at least ten highly respected experts.[36]

But then real life intervened to complicate matters. Spaniards, as sensitive to social hierarchy as the next person, recognized that there were pronounced differences within Andean communities (as well as between them). In fact, Spaniards had encountered native men and women who seemed remarkably like Spaniards: they dressed like Spaniards, ate like Spaniards, wrote like Spaniards. Some could even be richer than Spaniards. These were the viceroyalty's "indios ladinos."

The term *ladino*, with etymological roots in "Latin" (*latino*) encompassed the indigenous elite, those few members of Indian communities who, besides enjoying other privileges, were sent to school. The greatest skill they acquired was the ability to read, and that ability set them apart from most Peruvians of any category, giving them an exceptional advantage in a society increasingly dependent on bureaucracy and contracts. Like the Incas before them, the Spanish took advantage of stratification within native polities, using local headmen, the ladino *curacas*, as intermediaries with native commoners. Under colonial mandate, curacas acted as the point men for state institutions—organizing tribute and labor services, overseeing religious activities. In the main, European functionaries had dealings with these "indios españolados,"[37] who, in turn, had much to gain (although, on some occasions, much to lose) from maintaining their Spanishlike personas.[38]

Evangelists, probably most comfortable with Indians who were most like themselves, gave ladinos high marks. Avendaño came to the conclusion that certain differences within native communities could even be used to evangelical advantage: ladinos could serve as models of good Christian living for other, less acculturated natives. In one sermon, Avendaño pointed out that "good Spaniards and many *indios ladinos*" went to confession throughout the year, not just at Eastertime; in another, he (perhaps mistakenly) prized "ladinos," in contrast to Indian commoners, for abandoning, even mocking, the old beliefs in ancestors and idols.[39] Quito's bishop also bestowed ladinos with qualities usually associated with Spaniards. Thinking about the relative worth of native testimony, Pena Montenegro was forced to admit that "although the great majority of Indians are not trustworthy, some are *ladinos*, virtuous, and full of reason."[40]

Not only was the good bishop sensitive to the status differences within indigenous groups, he was also aware of the ways that status—by severely framing life's possibilities—could contribute to behavior understood by many of his colleagues to be innate. Pena Montenegro was not reluctant to describe Indians as cowardly and timid; this we know. Nevertheless, at times he did recognize that cowardice could be a child of circumstance; that Indian peasants, relatively powerless, were vulnerable to the whims of those who controlled their livelihood. This vulnerability might express itself in gestures of fear, such as "trembling," or in anxiety to "do whatever was commanded [of them]." Or it might affect the willingness of parishioners to meet their moral obligations: Indians, for good reason, would be less likely to challenge Spaniards whom they overheard plotting venal sins. So it was that Pena Montenegro, who deprecated Indian character, could also write that missionaries "should pay attention to people's [relative] equality, for if they are not of equal [standing], fear and cowardice could very much affect [their conduct]."[41]

Thus, even though evangelists, like most critics of native life, launched grand declarations about a fundamental Indian nature and, with ease, projected the opinion that character traits were built into their caste, they also saw that the lived reality was a perpetual, if unacknowledged, challenge. These men especially, who spent time in the countryside trying to convert souls, could not entirely ignore the inequities of circumstance thrown up by colonial life; nor could they ignore gross differences among Indians, between commoners and ladinos. Facing their indigenous followers and faced with their own experiences, Avendaño, Avila, Pena Montenegro, and others had to qualify the stereotypes: all Indians weren't poor, all Indians weren't liars, all Indians weren't mentally deficient.

Working with Indians made missionaries confront their own deficiencies. In fact, many shamed the Church by not living up to their side of the Indian–Catholic bargain—and I'm not referring here to clerical escapades having to do with women and money, but to defaults on their obligation to teach and proselytize. Some authorities recognized that what many of their associates had deemed mental limitations were actually a consequence of Indians having been "little instructed."[42] Churchmen like Father José de Acosta, cited by Pena Montenegro as an expert source, blamed their colleagues for the Indians' sorry state. Indians "are not beasts . . . they do not lack talent or wit."[43] Moreover: "If *indios* appear incapable it is not because they are animals, but because priests don't teach them; they [the priests] are the ones at fault, not [native] stupidity."[44]

Acosta, again seconded by Pena Montenegro, also believed in the importance of custom, arguing that Indians would think better if they lived better. Here, he was not only alluding to the need to appoint model missionaries—who spoke the native language and kept to their vows of poverty and chastity—but also to the need to create the right environment, to inculcate the habits of living in which reason could thrive. For Acosta, appropriate custom included cleanliness, especially when going to mass ("combed and washed"), remembering proper etiquette ("saying grace at meals and thank you when finished"), and using implements of civilization, like tables, beds, and chairs—things which would "promote and lead to a rational life."[45]

But, in their less optimistic moments, these priests saw the inculcation of reason as a more complicated process, where evil custom—seemingly passed on biologically from parents to children—would almost always impede native Peruvians from entering the full flower of civilization. Pena Montenegro, following Acosta, characterized the Peruvians as merely a middling group along a scale of civilization graded by level of rationality. Peruvians (along with Mexicans and Chileans) were somewhere in the middle—distinct, on the one hand, from the more polished natives of China and Japan and, on the other, from the savages who "run around naked in the jungle."[46] At the middle rank, Peruvians followed some principles of good government, albeit "all mixed up with . . . many errors and superstitions that darken the [already] diminished and weak light of reason that they possess."[47] An even more pessimistic Pena Montenegro (and Acosta) believed that baptism—that life-changing ritual—had little effect on their erroneous beliefs or habits: "[Peruvians]—both those who have already converted as well as those who still live in idolatry—are descendants of the same pagans"; that is, ". . . for the most part."[48]

So then, to return to the paramount issue: How to explain—in light of these ambiguities—the persistence of native heresies after so many years of evangelization? Our preachers found an answer in what we would call the inheritance of culture: "For these [Indians] are children of idolatry which they inherited with their ancestors' blood."[49] Pena Montenegro, overwhelmed by the size of the task ahead, would decry the fact that "so many Christian Indians, Indians who have been baptized" go live in the highlands or scrub where they never again see a priest, never have the opportunity to "have the [proper] moral and political teaching." Thus, he lamented, "baptized children are left to the education of their parents; suckling at the breast, they absorb the errors in [their mother's] milk."[50]

Avila gave a similar accounting: "they got the inclination [to commit idolatry] from their mother's womb." With artful ambiguity, he went on to say that this acquired inclination, plus deficits in learning, ensured that "they inherited the evil of their parents." Avila, Pena Montenegro, and the other missionaries certainly recognized the importance of instruction (or what would be the need for evangelists?), and they admitted that some Indians might learn. "Por milagro" (miraculously), in Avila's telling, some had abandoned their fathers' ways. Nonetheless, the doctrineros firmly believed that their flock was plagued by a burden of culture inheritance: the sinful habits of the ancestors weighed heavily on the present. What medium, then, was transmitting this "evil of their parents"? Avila summed it up with these words: "their stained blood."[51]

"Sangre manchada," as with the descendants of Moors and Jews. "Sangre manchada," a curse to New Christians and a curse to Indians and blacks. Pena Montenegro even constructed a hierarchy of truth-telling according to the degree of stain (i.e., "mas o menos manchada"): españoles were more trustworthy than indios, who were more trustworthy than negros.[52] It was in the blood, ranked blood. Avila, Pena Montenegro, and Avendaño were men of their colonial times. Thus, with all the instruction in the world, "indios" and "negros"—indelibly stained—would still be lesser beings in a colonized earth ". . . for the most part."

Conflicting ideologies, conflicting practices. The inconsistencies in Pena Montenegro's guide and in the doctrineros' sermons reflect the murky basis of colonialism itself, the irrationality of using race thinking—and a kind of cultural race thinking at that—to divide up the world.

Global Lessons

Spaniards believed that knowledge of the planetary nature of human existence was a mark of cultural progress. And so the inverse: Indians, woefully unaware of the world, of the true extent of God's creations, were just plain backward. Part of preaching Christianity, then, was to awaken native subjects to their ignorance and to instruct them about their place in the world. To account for human diversity and our common descent from Adam and Eve, to account for God's hierarchy of good government and the corresponding functions of blacks, Spaniards, and Indians, evangelists were compelled to describe humanity's global reach.

First, missionaries had to explain that the world was round. Using his hand as a model, Avila asked Indians to envision his middle finger as an axis around which God created ocean and land, to imagine that "the earth is [like] my hand, surrounded by the sea."[53] Chiding them ("you Indians don't know anything about this") and assuring them ("I will tell you [about it] now"), Avila wanted his flock to consider not only the earth's shape but the real miracle—"just how many [different] peoples there are in this whole wide world."[54]

Avila began by tracing out coastal towns and the peoples controlling them, starting with Panama and going toward Peru:

Darién, . . . Quito, . . . Chimu,[55] which is Trujillo, and we arrive here and from here we go to Chile and from Chile to the Strait of Magellan, and then [we] go around to Brazil, and [continuing along] the same coast [we come to] the Amazon River, and continuing [we come to] Cartagena and we arrive again at Panama.[56]

This, Avila emphasized, was just the beginning. For while the South American coastline "was full of peoples and towns," so was the continent's interior. To further dazzle his audience, Avila named many of these and, flaunting his worldly and Andean knowledge, emphasized polities that were part of the Inca empire: "Popoyán,[57] . . . Cuzco, Collao, Omasuyo, Qquechua, Ccana, Canchi, Aymara, Sora, Rucana, Guamanga, Huanca, . . . Potosí and Tucumán."[58] And this was only one continent, South America. What of the rest of the world?

It was an opportunity to enlighten. Mexico was the starting point for Avila's rest-of-the-world and, after noting Mexico's "innumerable amount of people," Avila traced, more or less, the Pacific route plied by Iberian merchant ships and missionaries: the Philippines(?) ("Islas, Archipiélago"), Indonesia, then "India, China, Japan" followed by a quick tour of central Asia and the Middle East ("Persia, Tartary, Constantinople"). Continuing West to Europe, Avila divided the continent into the "nations" of "Italy, Germany, France, and Spain." His lecture ended with "Africa"—the one continent he did not subdivide into ethnicities or nations.[59]

This global tour was a physical and political map of the world, an outline of continents plus their major polities, and these very broad markers were then further refined. Here is Avendaño's more subtle vision of God's creations—and it is a jumble:

all kinds of men, white, black, and from any *nación* living in the entire world, the Christians and the Moors and the Turks, the idol worshipers[60]; Indians, no matter what community [*ayllu* in the Quechua text] they are from, the Chinese, the Japanese and the Mexicans.[61]

To which he added

[men] brown in color, Spaniards, French, Chiriguanias, Ccollas, Aymaraes, Ingas, Qquechuas [native Andean groups], . . . and all the rest.[62]

Black, white, brown, indio, negro, español, Castile, France, Italy, China, Turks, England, Spain, Jews, Japan, Moors, idol worshipers, Collaguas, Aymara, Africa—these were the categories evangelists used as they subdivided and made sense of the globe. Pena Montenegro, Avila, and Avendaño saw the world as a riot of religions, cultures, incipient nations, places, peoples of color, colonizers, and colonized.

Yet, to provide some order to what Avila called "all this . . . beyond calculation," preachers turned to race thinking. Underneath all of this extraordinary diversity of God's languages, religions, towns, peoples, nations, and empires we find two related patterns. In the words of the doctrineros: 1) "here is all mankind, some white, some brown, others black"; and 2) "God is the creator of all men, Indians, blacks, and Spaniards."[63] Missionaries made sense of the seventeenth century's vast and incalculable diversity by tracing racialized divides—divides enmeshed in colonialism—over the multitude of God's creations. The social categories ordering power at home and abroad were entangled from birth, and race thinking was the ordering principle of this emerging, complex world.

A Colored Globe

Pena Montenegro, Avendaño, and Avila often spoke of humanity as if it were a troika of peoples: español, indio, negro.[64] Colonialism first produced these new classes, built on ideologies of ancestral corporatism, political and economic function, and color. But by the mid-seventeenth century, color could, in effect, stand in for corporatism: Avila's creation triad was also marked black, brown, and white. The rhetorical dilemma was to account for the global hierarchy, created by the colonial process in general, that transformed Europeans into world rulers, Indians into subjects, and Africans into slaves.[65]

The doctrineros engaged a cultural milieu in which there was a precedent for making color into a significant dimension of social difference: viz. the use of "black" (*negro*) to refer to African slaves. I imagine that this color-coded representation of what were global social, economic, and political relations opened the way for others. So when Avila, sermonizing about humanity's common origin, wanted to make clear that there were Europeans in this world besides Spaniards, he preached about "other nations of white men."[66] Or when Avendaño wanted to stress that Adam's and Eve's descendants were found throughout the globe, regardless of nation or ethnicity, he divided them by color: "everyone in the *world*, whites, blacks, and people of . . . color."[67] Categories and colors could be interchangeable: Avila and Avendaño sometimes used color and caste in one breath. When Avila warned his native audience of their obligation to receive Jesus's love, Avila clarified that he was speaking of "not only you Indians, but . . . [all] the peoples (*naciones*) of the world, white, black, and brown."[68] When Avila wanted to assure his parishioners that the devil deceived humankind in an impartial manner, he said that "[the devil] was adored by whites, along with blacks, and Indians."[69] Note how easily Spanish, Indian, and black slipped into white, brown, and black.[70] In these short passages, Avila, like Avendaño, articulated a very modern slant on the world's diversity: one built around phenotypical differences, structured by the frame of colonial cultural politics.

Magical Race Thinking

The rich complex of human relations that was squeezed into "color" was not accidental. The color trio that so easily trips off our tongues today was, from its inception, intimately connected with the modern world's colonial and state-making origins. White, black, and brown are abridged, abstracted versions of colonizer, slave, and colonized. But the modern world's broad abstractions are of a special character: negro, indio, and español present themselves in discourse as if they were a self-evident given of human experience. These big abstractions would have us think that black people or white people existed independently from colonial social relations—as if blacks, whites, or browns existed separately from Spain and Spanishness; as if whites, browns, blacks, Spaniards, and Indians could have existed one without the other; and as if the abstractions themselves were not part of human history.

Race thinking facilitates this chimera, by "disappearing" the social relations that are intrinsic to it. Race thinking, in league with the state, is as magical as the state.

STATES AND STAINS

The doctrineros' mestizo offspring are carted off to Lima.
From Felipe Guaman Poma de Ayala,
El primer nueva corónica y buen gobierno (1613?).

Spaniards in this kingdom should carry their [stain]-identity cards . . . wherever they go. [And these would indicate] if he is a peasant, or nobleman . . . or Jew or Moor or *mestizo* or *mulato* or *negro*. . . . How else would we know if someone is stained by a little Jewish, Moorish, Turkish, or English [blood]?—FELIPE GUAMAN POMA DE AYALA, *El primer nueva corónica y buen gobierno*[1]

ON FEBRUARY 4, 1637, Manuel Henríquez requested an audience with the inquisitors. He told them about a scheme, concocted in the cells, to get New Christians out of jail. This New Christian conspiracy, however, had little to do with religion and everything to do with lies. In league with Jorge de Acuna, Juan de Acevedo and others rounded up in the 1635 dragnet, Henríquez was advising fellow inmates to "give false testimony against Castilians." Why? ". . . because then it would be obvious . . . that all these testimonies were false," i.e., that the hundreds of accusations made against Portuguese women and men for Judaizing were as groundless as the accusations made against Old Christians. The hope was that when inquisitors were faced with a deluge of perjured testimony against Castilians—whose innocence was never in doubt—they would "realize that whenever they arrest anyone Portuguese, they [automatically] accuse them of being Jewish."[2]

Henríquez and company's plan made perfect sense in light of the confusions of the times: the modern confusions of "nation" with religion, of religion with ancestry, and of ancestry with political loyalty. The plotters' idea was to lay bare these irrational assumptions by turning them upside down: if inquisitors, king, and council could find the absurdity in making blanket charges against Old Christians, they might find a similar absurdity in making blanket charges against New Christians. Henríquez, Acuna, and all the others who, most likely, confessed in order to live harbored the belief, and the trust, that the authorities responsible for their predicament would spot the mistake and correct its consequences. They would recognize the cultural fallacy of conflating Portuguese, New Christian, and Jew—and of infusing all with characteristics of race.

In this chapter we are concerned with the dynamics of state building and race thinking—with the practices making "government in the name of truth" into a bureaucratic mandate to fix the racial essence of state subjects. Inquisitors adopted two race-thinking designs as they went about the business of state. One, at the root of the Henríquez plot, racialized culture through purity-of-blood laws but expanded its course to the nation-state (Portuguese) and to economic function (merchant or landowner-military). The other, the colonial frame, racialized global geopolitics, infusing imperialism into a caste structure and attaching color to both political and economic privilege (negro = slave; indio = brown = tribute-payer; español = white = exempt from tribute). Some scholars have thought of these designs in a linear fashion: e.g., purity-of-blood statutes as a precedent for race thinking; "ethnicity" or "culture" as a nascent form of race thinking in contemporary life.[3] But a careful look at Peruvian history also suggests that race thinking took several, coeval shapes and that race thinking's duplicity lay in the ways its different manifestations went unrecognized and became intertwined.

The Spanish Inquisition—though only one of several state bureaucracies—was a significant player in the arena where social categories were made into racial truths.[4] Nowhere is this more evident than in the murky areas of New Christian/Portuguese/Castilian/Spanish and Spanish/black/Indian/mestizo/mulato personhood. Tribunal court records—along with a legal compendium, a manual for missionaries, and a native chronicle-critique of the Crown—are the principal sources helping us imagine the vision underlying the inquisitors' judgments, a vision of humanity that magistrates were working to create and re-create. Those sources also help us understand the ideologies, conceptions, and commitments that the magistrates found so dangerous.[5] To explore the political culture that would have nurtured Henríquez and company's confession conspiracy, then, we will focus on the entanglements of Peru's double race thinking: the confusions of "casta y generación"; the contrary meanings of New Christian in the New World; the complications of blood purity; and, finally, the dialectic behind Spanish preeminence.

Just What Is "Casta y Generación"?

All women and men brought before the tribunal were asked to locate themselves in the global and social order of things. That meant defining themselves in terms of the formal categories of state—name, age, place of birth, marital status, and social standing—as well as casta y generación, or caste and lineage. In seventeenth-century colonial courts, casta y generación usually referred to indio, negro, and español, as moderated by mestizo, mulato, and sambo—the "mixed breeds" who didn't fit the original colonial plan. Españoles and partly Spanish mestizos and mulatos were also required to specify the nature of their "Spanish" ancestry: to declare if they were Old Christians, and therefore taintless, or if they were descendants of one of the New Christian subcastes of Jews and Moors.

Casta y generación should be a straightforward concept. However, it was anything but: Europeans born in Spain or in its colonies were not always considered "Spanish";[6] being Portuguese could have as much to do with religion as with nationality; being a Jew or a Moor could have as much to do with kin as with belief; being mestizo could have as much to do with legitimacy as with ancestry; and being indio could have as much to do with dress as with descent. Casta y generación was at its most confusing, though, when it came to the category "New Christian."

Were All New Christians Alike?

In early modern Europe, Spanish jurists and theologians were sparring seriously over the New Christian character; however, the Spanish conquest brought added complications to these debates about ancestry and faith. For, with colonization, Spaniards began channeling pagan natives into the same, New Christian state-of-being, and the viceroyalty's thousands of new converts were triggering fresh challenges to peninsular disputes. Did descent tarnish the religious capabilities of every novice, or did it just affect certain ones? Or did descent affect certain novices to different degrees? Now, then, tied to the big question—Could New Christians ever be good Christians?—we find the colonial sequel: Were all New Christians alike?

First, the official view. Jurists, like Juan de Solórzano Pereira, the editor of the seventeenth century's premier compendium of laws governing the Americas, resolved the New Christian problem by deciding that New Christians were not all alike. Of course, New Christians were *somewhat* alike: there was never any doubt that the colonial caste system's subordinate groups, Indians and blacks, were infected with corrupt blood like their Portuguese counterparts. But Indians and blacks, Solórzano argued, became New Christians under different circumstances and, therefore, were subject to different ordinances. For example, although peninsular law excluded Jews and Moors from government office, professions, and the nobility, there was nothing to suggest that blacks and Indians should suffer similar restrictions.[7] Blacks and Indians, according to this reasoning, were of superior mettle, and so, by comparison, carried stains that were easier to bleach.[8] This considered opinion was linked to another comparative judgment: Solórzano calculated that it would take the descendants of Moors and Jews two hundred years to become like Old Christians, but it would take Indians and blacks only four generations.[9]

This tally represented a major shift in official judgment. Bureaucrats specializing in human nature used to give Europe's New Christians four generations, too.[10] But that was before the conquest, the rigors of state-making, and the necessities of colonization brought their own dialectic to bear on questions of personhood. The result, on the official page, made it clear that race thinking in the Spanish empire took different forms and, in addition, that these forms were in dialogue. The result, in practice, was a twin lesson in how political necessity infused political principle: ideological requirements—in this case, the formal responsibility of colonial regimes to colonial subjects—could trump "color" (Indians and blacks were better than the "Portuguese"); nonetheless, these ideological requirements were being systematically contradicted in colonial practice, and nowhere more heartily than in the Viceroyalty of Peru.[11]

Colonial Stains and Colonial Possibilities

So, according to experts, Portuguese New Christians were stained. Stains blackened their character; and it was the state's responsibility to stop them from holding public office. Peru's blacks and Indians also carried polluted blood. How would that pollution affect their possibilities in public life, in a colonial world? Missionaries sent to evangelize Andean natives could hardly avoid these race matters, and Pena Montenegro's guidebook for missionaries casts a telling light on how Peru's governing class made sense out of the irrationality of race. Pena Montenegro had to decide concrete and prickly issues: Could competent Indians and blacks be shut out of a religious calling because of impure blood? Were they capable of preaching anywhere and to anybody, or should their efforts be restricted to people of the same "casta y generación"? The dilemma pitting blood against ability was simmering in the Americas, and Pena Montenegro's guide was one attempt to resolve this quandary of imperial cultural geopolitics.

Pena Montenegro combed the existing literature—the mounting royal *cédulas*, the papal decrees, the legal compilations. But his findings were ambiguous: the experts' opinions on "stains"—stains derived from Indian blood, black blood (enslaved and free), and mixed blood—supported both sides of the debate. Sorting through this theological chaos, Pena Montenegro, whose leanings were "pro-ability," sided with the underclasses ("the

Church of God . . . regularly admits everyone who is apt, virtuous, and appropriate, without exception"; "Indians [and blacks] do not forfeit the right to be ordained on account of . . . their origin and nature").[12] Men of all colonial backgrounds, whether mestizos, indios, or negros, could enter the priesthood, in his judgment, so long as they met the Church's standards: they had to be competent and knowledgeable, moral and upright, and legitimate.[13] Ever the preacher, he made his point about the Church's openness with a case steeped in another sort of tainted blood. He reminded his audience of the Church's early days when a bishop had been famously reprimanded for not accepting a converted Jew into the priesthood. With antiquity as a precedent (and admonisher?), Pena Montenegro argued that Peru's recently converted should be allowed to follow the same path as those of ancient Rome.[14]

Peru's race-tinged prejudice, however, was an unavoidable presence, and Pena Montenegro was forced to admit that the ordination of blacks would bring added complications to colonial realities. The colonial caste system making negros into slaves posed a particular set of problems: first of all, Spaniards considered slavery to be a venal, "indecent," honorless condition; second, the slave was subject to his master's will and, in principle, could be stopped from carrying out his spiritual duties. But the really vexing issue was the awkwardness of color in a color-conscious world. Could blacks—at the lowest rung in colonial society—minister to whites, at the highest? Some experts argued that blacks should not, "because it would cause great horror to see a black person step to the altar to say mass for *naciones blancas*" (literally "white peoples"). Other authorities, Pena Montenegro assured all concerned, "very weighty ones" at that, claimed the opposite: "*Negros* should become priests without hindrance" because "in these parts where there are so many [blacks], with some holding the rank of captain and other military offices, [a black priest] would not cause any revulsion."[15] Nonetheless, he had to acknowledge he was on weak ground, for he found much less support in royal decrees, in ecclesiastic orders, or among the experts for Africans, or their descendants, to go out into the world and preach.[16]

Finally, what about the "expulsos"—kin to women and men expelled from Spain? Only when discussing the question of black ordination, did Pena Montenegro ask about the standing of New Christians. Why here? Perhaps because of the great weight of impurities that negros and New Christians alike were presumed to carry. Unfortunately, Pena Montenegro was not very expansive in his discussion of the arguments pro and con; nevertheless, with his tendency to value ability over stain, he formally came out in favor of the *expulsos*.[17]

Pena Montenegro's manual outlines a template of possible outcomes with respect to these dilemmas of race, faith, and ability. But how and if the bishop's arguments were used to guide decision making in specific cases, how and if they shaped the lived experience of colonial women and men—that's something else. At least his words were heard in the ideological climate of the times. Did they help precipitate the ordination of indios and negros? Perhaps, but we need more studies like Kathryn Burns's monograph on Cuzco's Santa Clara convent to give us a flavor of racial politics on the inside.[18] Nevertheless, Pena Montenegro's abstracted ideal of colonial racial equality—where pulpits would be open to qualified men regardless of casta y generación—remained, for the most part, an ideal. Notable exceptions were to be found, however, among the viceroyalty's well-placed, educated, up-and-coming New Christians.[19]

A Theory of Race Fractions

As the seventeenth century progressed, state officials attempted to build ever more precise categorical boxes in which to place their ever more racially confounded subjects. The world has witnessed various solutions to the conundrum of "mixed race," and official Spain devised a different one for each of her two race problems. Inquisitors followed something like the "one drop of blood" rule in their dealings with New Christians: in the end, New Christians remained New Christians, regardless of their Old Christian forebears. Bureaucrats came up with a more subtle solution, however, to the colonial order's racial paradox: subcategories based on percentages of tainted blood. In both cases, though, whether race was cut into pieces or used as whole cloth, race thinking was never in doubt. Taken together, Peru's race-thinking designs helped expand and stabilize the experience of living in a race-phrased universe.

Race fractions brought unexpected predicaments to a range of ecclesiastic issues. One such issue involved marriage dispensations. Missionaries, who preached the sanctity of wedlock, had to confront problems with respect to marriages between baptized natives and their uncivilized fellows. Would an Indian with a spouse who refused to convert be allowed to divorce in order to marry a Christian?[20] Here the answer was easy: yes. But race fractions turned an apparently simple problem into a thorny dilemma: Would the same dispensation be applied to a mestizo? Yes, but this was the seventeenth century, and racial mixing didn't stop with mestizos.[21] "Degrees" had multiplied, and Pena Montenegro had to work out a solution for "the quadroons (*cuarterones*)," or offspring with one-quarter Indian blood, and, more troublesome, for the "children of Spaniards with quadroons; and, then again, for children of Spaniards with octoroons (*pu-chuela*)."[22]

Trying to sort all this out, Pena Montenegro eventually had to confront the most bedeviling issue of all. Could someone with Indian ancestry ever become a Spaniard? Was there any point at which the amount of "stained blood" became so negligible that it no longer counted?[23] So, should quadroons or octoroons (or beyond) be granted the special dispensations allowed Indians and mestizos, or not? Pena Montenegro drew his line at the offspring of Spaniards and octoroons: 1/16 percent Indian blood was so minuscule an amount, he contended, that it disappeared. Here Pena Montenegro turned to a host of experts from throughout the colonies—the Philippines, Peru, New Spain, New Granada, Quito—along with the weight of public opinion (which played a particularly significant role in this case) to find an appraisal matching his own. Pena Montenegro we should note, ended up reaching the same conclusion as the legal scholar Solórzano: it would take four generations to rid a body of Indian stains.[24]

Pena Montenegro argued that mulatos were subject to similar principles, so that the continual admixture of European blood could eventually whiten a lineage and overcome its black ancestry: "they would have so little [Ethiopian in them] and so much European that they would not be taken for [blacks] . . . [and thus,] following public opinion, the portion [of them] that is . . . Ethiopian begins to disappear."[25] The "European-izing process," then, would appear to be equally applicable to "Indian" and "black" blood; but that was not always the case in Pena Montenegro's equations.

For, in other contexts, Pena Montenegro ranked indios and negros along a scale of stain. Not that either mestizos or mulatos were blessed with blood purity; both had pollutions coursing through their veins. However, black stains were the blackest. Pena Montenegro noted this distinction when he asked who should be sent to minister to the countryside if there were a choice between a mulato and a mestizo. The mestizo, of course. Even though both bloodlines were polluted, the mulato blood, in his words, "had an uglier stain (*una mancha mas fea*)."[26]

Calculating Practices

Pena Montenegro's calculations became part of the official race ledger of the era, and in spite of a tilt toward capacity over descent, they reinforced the fundamental racial logic at the heart of the colonial state. Inquisitors never employed a calculus as precise as Pena Montenegro's. They did, however, give flesh to abstract categories, by marking human boundaries in racial terms and by inscribing "percentages" into the identity of colonial prisoners. Accused heretics of all stripes found that admitting "stain" was not enough. New Christians and mestizos and mulatos had to declare exactly how much stain flowed in their blood. They had to become fluent in race fractions.

Colonial statecraft articulated, with some refinement, the "racial mix" of its colonial subjects. The smallest mix commonly found in tribunal records was "quadroon," and magistrates applied it to black as well as Indian stains. Women accused of witchcraft were made into Indian quadroons: for example, Doña Luisa de Vargas (a.k.a. *la cuarterona*) and Doña Bernarda Cerbantes, who "heard she had a *mestizo* grandfather on her mother's side."[27] And women accused of witchcraft were made into black quadroons: Ana de Castañeda, quarter mulata; Juana de Morales, quarter mulata; and Ana María de Ulloa, quarter mulata.[28] Magistrates also recorded a "metis" category for those with black and Indian ancestry, although the common term was "samba." Thus, Francisca de la Pena was "a *mulata samba*," and María de Castro Barreto was said to be "of *samba* color because she is the daughter of a *mestizo* and a *negra*."[29]

Are we witnessing the beginnings of a typology of looks—like using "*samba* color" to reinforce María de Castro's racial place? Men and women would sometimes make a stab at identifying heretics by means of physical characteristics: "He said he was the son of Spaniards, but he looks *mestizo*"; or "she looked like she had *mulata* [in her]"; or "[the accomplice] was *morena* in color"; or "he looks to be Spanish"; or, in reference to an accused Judaizer, "he looks *mestizo*."[30] "Looks," shades of color, carried an awful potential that was beginning to be realized—to be transformed into an "objective" scale of humanness, into a measure of real distinctions among human beings.

Peru's Portuguese community was subject to a similar—if less articulate—calculus of pollution. As with the colonial caste system, inquisitors demanded that accused Judaizers provide the details of Old Christian–New Christian mixes: exactly which parents, grandparents, and collateral kin were tainted and which were not. Here are a few of the ways they responded. Juan Rodríguez Mesa confessed to being a descendant of "the Hebrew nation" but, when pressed, reckoned one exception: his grandmother on his mother's side, "who he took to be an Old Christian."[31] Henrique J. Tavares, Portuguese, declared he was Old Christian "on the part of his paternal grandfather."[32] In one breath, Francisco Rodríguez asserted he "was from the caste and lineage of Jews"; in another, he declared his father was Old Christian.[33] The infamous Bachiller Francisco de Silva, the confessed Jew who not only evangelized in prison but saw God face to face, confirmed that his father's entire lineage was "de Judíos" but that his mother's was Old Christian.[34] And the unrelated Bartolomé de Silva, who initially claimed that "his parents were Old Christians," later decided "that his parents had something of New Christian [in them]."[35]

The Lima Inquisition required indicted Judaizers to name their New Christian and Old Christian ancestors, but unlike the calculations for men and women "de color," the New Christian scale was a descriptive one: inquisitors did not attach a precise stain fraction to New Christian identities.[36] Perhaps this was because percentages didn't mean much. Having an Old Christian grandfather or an Old Christian mother did little to alter the New Christian stigma: it didn't seem to matter how much New Christian pollution was circulating through the prisoner's body, or how much Old Christian honor. New Christians were equally suspect whether tainted by one grandfather or an entire line of kin.

Nonetheless, whether calculated as percentages or as totalities, whether mocked, questioned, or seen as God's truth, race thinking—that irrational melange of race, nation, ancestry, and culture—had gripped Peruvian imaginations,[37] albeit in different ways and with different confusions.

Alternative Understandings and Basic Agreements

But although Peruvians—across caste and class—appeared to see the world increasingly in terms of race-based looks and race fractions, Peruvians also made fun of such notions—to the great consternation of secular and episcopal authorities. These countercultural activities were audacious enough to alarm officials, who were concerned that Peruvians (particularly indios) were able to change caste as easily as they changed clothes.[38] Here are just a few examples of race sneering found in the tribunal archives: Angela de Figueroa, Gabriela Colmenares, and Doña Francisca de Bustos—accused witches all—troubled magistrates by dressing "Indian style"; Doña Inés de la Peñaililo warned one client never to say that a Spanish woman had given her love charms "but, rather, an Indian," since the Inquisition did not have jurisdiction over natives; Doña Luisa de Vargas—who told inquisitors she carried one-quarter Indian blood and sometimes went by the nickname "la cuarterona"—also called herself—and was known by others as—Luisa Blanca (Luisa White).[39] Alvarez Enríquez and his brother Vasco de Xerez flaunted their "new" origins by dressing in the velvets and silks that only Old Christians were supposed to wear; Juan de Acevedo became Don Juan de Acevedo in Peru; Manuel Bautista Pérez, consciously acting and talking like a Castilian, tried to remove any palpable traces of his Portuguese origin; Luis de Valencia and his son, Juan de Acosta, insisted "they were taken to be noblemen"; Don Simón Osario and Antonio Leal (among others) bought Old Christian ancestry with false documents; and, the most grievous mockery of all, Manuel Henríquez and his co-conspirators accused Old Christians and Castilians of being Jews.[40]

Of course, Portuguese New Christians and native "New Christians" had their own ideas about the meaning of New Christian, the significance of race, and what it would take to become an Old Christian. Perhaps not surprisingly, they agreed on a few basics: for one, the child of a New Christian was an Old Christian. Hernán Jorge, asked to categorize his ancestry, claimed his parents were "New Christian descendants of Jews" but that he, on the contrary, was a "baptized Christian . . . an Old Christian."[41] Like Hernán Jorge, Francisco de Silva gave "New Christian" a one-generation shelf life: he was both an "Old Christian" and "the grandson of Portuguese."[42] Guaman Poma de Ayala, the Andean nobleman and critic of colonial life, shared in this understanding: "the children of baptized Christians" were Old Christians.[43] New Christians, Guaman Poma said, were just that: the recently converted, Peru's indios and negros.[44]

Guaman Poma and Hernán Jorge would have agreed as well that to be Christian meant to join the faithful, to worship Christ, and to be a member in good standing with the Church. Christianity, for both "New Christians," was a question of belief and practice, not ancestry. With that understanding, Guaman Poma berated Spaniards for not behaving in Christian fashion and made his case that, in Peru, Indians newly converted to Christ's ways were better Christians than Spaniards: "[Greedy Spaniards] say that Indians are barbarians and not Christian. It is the opposite."[45] He also reminded Europeans that there was a time when they, like Indians, had been ignorant of Christ's ways and that Spaniards had become Christians the same way Andeans were becoming Christian—by desire and learning, not by descent.[46] Portuguese echoed these sentiments, pointing out in moving testimony that there were New Christians who worshiped Christ with a passion not always matched by Old Christians. Some even argued that Portuguese were better Christians, or at least more honorable ones.[47]

But Portuguese and natives did not always have the same opinions.

Guaman Poma's Global Design: Andean Race Thinking

Guaman Poma—like many of his Portuguese peers—was at odds with himself when it came to questions of belief and culture, race and nation. He insisted that faith was a question of action and not ancestry.[48] Yet he shared the inquisitors' skepticism about the true faith of Iberia's

New Christians. Guaman Poma strongly believed in Christianity's bedrock equality ("Christ died for everyone, whether Moor, Jew, black"), but he seemed reluctant to consider that the descendants of Jews and Moors could be Christians, too. In his long letter of protest to the Crown, Guaman Poma never distinguished between a New Christian past and present; he never talked about "New Christians" or "Portuguese"—just about Jews and Moors.[49] Only natives were given the benefit of the doubt. So while Guaman Poma wrote pages and pages demanding that the faith of native Peruvians be judged by their actions and their ideas, he froze Portuguese "New Christians" in the faith of their ancestors.

Guaman Poma was an unrelenting supporter of, in his words, "blood and lineage"—the cornerstone, in his opinion, of good government. His design for a just and well-ordered colonial society was built squarely on notions of purity, both of caste (Spaniard, Indian, or black) and of status (nobility or commoner-peasant). In homage to the racial and caste divisions of the modern colonial world, he partitioned all humans into three undefiled races: "[T]o be a worthy creature of God, son of Adam and of his wife Eve [requires] . . . pure Spanish, pure Indian, pure black."[50] And each pure caste was to be ruled by a member of its own nobility (i.e., someone like Guaman Poma should govern Peru) who, in turn, would owe allegiance to the king of Castile. Guaman Poma's vision—predating Avila's by decades—joined race, government, territory, and sovereignty in broad, global strokes: "[T]hus, Castile belongs to Spaniards, and the Indies belong to Indians, and Guinea belongs to blacks. . . . Each are the legitimate owners, possessors, not by virtue of the king, but by virtue of God and his justice."[51]

Guaman Poma argued that a successful colonial government ultimately depended on preserving strict boundaries between society's constituent groups. He was as concerned about the lower orders *within* castes trying to become what they were not born to ("[F]rom peasant they want to become lord, and from poor lineage, king" or "from Indian tribute-payer to Indian nobility")[52] as he was about caste members trying to pass for what they were not.[53] Combining both concerns—and an obsession to construct a native nobility—Guaman Poma urged Andeans to marry their social equivalents, and he pressed curacas—members of the colonial indigenous elite—to be sure that "they do not give their daughters in marriage to either Indian peasants (*mitayos*) or to Spaniards, but rather to their equals, so that a good caste (*buena casta*) is produced in this kingdom."[54]

If marriage between unequals in rank menaced good government, marriage outside of race and caste, Guaman Poma charged, would bring its demise. Facing the stunning decline of native populations and the unbearable erosion of community life, Guaman Poma turned to *mestizaje*, or "racial mixing," as their principal cause.[55] He wrote apocalyptically about the proliferation of Peru's "malas castas," the stained, illegitimate "mixed breeds"—mostly mestizos, but also mulatos and sambaigos (Indian and black unions)—whose scandalous lives seemed to him to feed colonial disorder.[56]

Colonial caste mixtures were a ready target of Guaman Poma's scorn, but so was New Christian blood. So, on top of mestizaje, he railed against the depravity of Jewish stains—calculating them to be more denigrating than the also despicable, bastard stains carried by mestizos. This is what he had to say about marriage between Old Christians and Jews: "If the [husband] branded by the stain . . . were from the lower orders or a Jew, and the wife from a line of *caballeros* and Old Christian, she loses everything. . . . [T]heir [children] are of a ruined caste, worse than *mestizo*."[57] And, in this context (as opposed to writings in which Guaman Poma berates Spaniards for their un-Christianlike behavior), he gave "Old Christian" a similar meaning as the inquisitors. Old Christian represented an overlap of descent, nation, and status; it meant Castilian, honorable, pure-blooded, and noble and, by implication, everything Jews were not.[58]

Guaman Poma took the español-indio-negro triad seriously, so seriously that his take on Spanishness could be curiously at odds with the Spanish one. Spaniards understood their racial vigor to reflect an absence of Jewish and Moorish pollution—a sentiment we know Guaman Poma supported with vehemence—but when Guaman Poma was immersed in this global race system, he supported with equal vehemence the opposite view. Arguing that the "mala casta blanca" (evil white caste) was still the "casta blanca" (i.e., Jews, Moors, and their descendants were full-blooded, white Spaniards), Guaman Poma expounded on the virtues of Spanish endogamy, including the intermarriage of Spaniards with Jews and Moors: "[H]ow good this law [of racial endogamy] would be, because one Spaniard vis-à-vis another Spaniard—even if he were a Jew or a Moor—is a Spaniard." Spaniards, "would not mix with any other people (*nación*) except Spaniards."[59] And, in this, as you will see, Guaman Poma came close to the philosophy of those New Christians, like Doña Mencia de Luna or Manuel Bautista Pérez, who believed themselves as Spanish as any Old Christian.

Coupling Spanish imperial race theory with his own designs for indirect rule, Guaman Poma argued that Spaniards—whether Old Christians or Moors or Jews—would always be foreigners in Peru. In his schema of racialized nationalism, the "nation" as a whole trumped any internal differences of wealth, status, or even "tainted blood." And in line with imperialist requirements, membership in that nation was congruent with ancestry, with casta y generación—not with residence or place of birth. Guaman Poma's version of indirect rule argued that even if Spaniards were to come to Peru, hold important positions, and prosper, they were always outsiders: "Castile belongs to Spaniards, the Indies belong to Indians." The Indies might owe allegiance to Castile, but Spaniards were forever alien in the Americas, whether born in Lima or born in Madrid.[60]

Guaman Poma ardently defended his global race triad; at the same time, he just as ardently recognized that his global race triad was inadequate. For one thing, it papered over internal differences in rank, something that Guaman Poma, with his noble pretensions, was acutely sensitive to. (In one rendering of colonial order, Guaman Poma actually put "Indian noble" in the same category as "Spaniard," and "Spanish peasant" in the same category as "Indian.")[61] Guaman Poma also berated Spaniards for lumping Indians together as if they were one people: "[Spaniards] called [the Americas] Indies, because it meant land in the daytime [i.e., *en días*] and not because the natives called themselves Indians. . . . And thus [Spaniards] call them Indians, even to this day; and it hurts." But he was also aware—from sermons, books, discussions, and experience—that *viracochacuna*, the Quechua term which most Andeans gave to Spaniards (and sometimes to Europeans in general) were not all the same, either. Viracochacuna were divided by their political and cultural histories, just like Indians. To be fair, Guaman Poma berated Indians for engaging in the same kind of stereotyping as Spaniards: "Indians also call [all Europeans or Spaniards] *viracocha*, [even though] each group has its own name," whether "Castilian, foreigner, Jew, Moor, Turk, Englishman, [or] Frenchman."[62] Some of Guaman Poma's "groups," by the way—like Englishmen—could also inherit stains in the blood.[63]

Guaman Poma had a practical strategy to ensure that purity of race (and class) would prevail. Having absorbed Spanish civic lessons, he had a healthy respect for documents in general, and for lineage certificates in particular, and his scheme for enforcing racial boundaries was an exemplar of modern state practice. Guaman Poma simply said that everyone in the viceroyalty should carry blood-purity identification. Now, Guaman Poma was not naive. He was well aware of Peru's black market for phony documents: "[Here] everyone is a *caballero*. In exchange for 4 *reales* they have a certificate of proof."[64] But, in spite of that bourgeoning trade, Guaman Poma was convinced that stain-verification certificates, carried in the breast pocket, would be the best, if not the only, way to approach the problem of "passing." For "how . . . can we know if someone carries the stain of . . . Jewish [blood], or Moorish, or Turkish, or English"[65] or "if he is a peasant . . . [or] a nobleman," or if he is a Jew or a Moor or a mestizo, mulato, or negro.[66] Without a certificate, race was too confusing.

More Race Thinking

Our modern world-in-the-making was ridden by slips and incongruities that showed race thinking for what it was. The Henríquez-Acuna confession conspiracy—skewering the idea that New Christian, Jew, and Portuguese could metamorphose into a racial being—was a telling, and ultimately tragic, example. We end this chapter by returning to the issue that first provoked it: the damning equation of New Christian = Portuguese = Jew. Plus, we add "español" to the mix.

The inquisitors practiced a kind of racial profiling in their efforts to uncover the truth. This profiling attached guilt (or its overwhelming possibility) to a specific class of human beings; and it was not a great leap from possibility to near certainty to stereotype, as the victims of tribunal justice were well aware. In their pursuit of New Christian ancestry, magistrates showed that their judgments were beholden to stereotypes—and that those stereotypes could create their own kind of truth, a truth which could, in a twisted way, create a kind of reality among the living.

In seventeenth-century Peru, New Christian = Jew = Portuguese was the currency of the day. Not just inquisitors, but viceroys, slaves, the general populace, and even the accused themselves regularly used "Portuguese" or "New Christian" when they meant "Jew." Inquisitors wrote letters to the Crown complaining about the "Portuguese" presence;[67] Father Vázquez de Espinosa, in his description of the Indies, talked about the New Christians who ("praise God") had been punished by the tribunal; so did Antonio Suardo, writing in his diary about arrests made during the "complicidad grande."[68] Castilians in the Lima cathedral, listening to sermons with a strong anti-Jewish message, thought they were "directed at the Portuguese" parishioners;[69] a slave swore to the tribunal that his owner, Jorge Paz, was a Judaizer because "whenever a Portuguese came to talk to [Paz], he would close the door."[70] Portuguese = Jew was in the cultural air.

New Christians might have been born in cities as noble as Seville or Madrid, but that made little difference to the inquisitors. When determining "casta y generación" they invariably linked New Christians with Portugal. Most often, the court would record a New Christian's place of birth, but then emend it to reinforce the Portuguese connection.[71] Thus, Felipa López, although born in Seville, was from the "casta y generación de judíos portugueses"; Diego López de Fonseca, who shared the terrible scaffold with Manuel Bautista Pérez, was born in Badajoz, but "decended from Portuguese."[72] And Sr. Castro y Castillo, the tribunal secretary, used this same shorthand in case summaries sent to Madrid: Juan de Ortega, Portuguese, born in Bordeaux, France; Diego Gómez, Portuguese, born in Seville; Manuel Alvarez Despinosa, Portuguese, born in Madrid; Antonio Fernández, Portuguese, born in Valladolid.[73]

Even indicted Judaizers confounded "Portuguese" with "Jew," and so participated in—and accelerated—the confusions between religion, nation, and race. Padre Manuel Núñez Magro was said to have worshiped in Venice's famous synagogue "with all the rest of the Portuguese";[74] Joan Vicente talked about confessing his Jewish beliefs to fellow Portuguese.[75] Indicted heretics were routinely accused of buying goods from or residing with or visiting "Portuguese with whom they shared *casta y generación*."[76] Inmates active in the "confession conspiracy" called Manuel Bautista Pérez the captain or rabbi of the Portuguese;[77] even Manuel Henríquez swore, "[C]ursed be the Law of Moses and damned if I have anything more to do with the Portuguese."[78]

The prosecutor's charges played on a stock assumption that Portuguese would inherently make common cause, that the mere fact of being from the same "caste and lineage" would compel New Christians to conspire. This premise appeared again and again in the prosecutor's indictments. In the 1627 broadsheet denouncing Pérez as a rabbi, "[Pérez's] name was followed by [others], all of the same *casta y generación*";[79] an associate of a well-known merchant, who had been taunted and called a "Jew" in public, felt compelled to defend him because "the Castilians cannot stand anyone from his *casta y generación*";[80] Pérez was accused by the prosecutor of giving incomplete testimony to "conceal . . . the names of conspirators who were of his *casta y generación*."[81] Again and again we see the racialized nature of "truth."

But the contradictions embedded in this muddle of descent, faith, and nation were insurmountable, and so they inevitably came to the surface. It should not be surprising, then, that witnesses themselves voiced the impossibility of such a cultural melange, even as they were calling one another Portuguese and accusing one another of Judaizing. Some detainees pointed out the irrationality of the equation when they were questioned about their wives—with whom, of course, they shared "casta y generación." When Antonio Cordero was asked if his wife was "Castilian or Portuguese," he insisted she was a devout Christian, although the "daughter of Portuguese";[82] so insisted Sebastián Duarte, although his wife—Manuel Bautista Pérez's sister-in-law—was known to have Portuguese–New Christian ancestry;[83] and so did Alvaro Méndez, although his wife was a member of "the Hebrew nation."[84] And in these cases, the inquisitors agreed with the accused—in spite of their wives' questionable backgrounds and their suspect marriages. Even inquisitors could have doubts that all Portuguese were New Christians were Jews.

Contrary to stereotype, all Portuguese were not the same. Inquisitors (on some level) knew this and so, of course, did the accused Judaizers. Witnesses opened up the Portuguese box for inspection and revealed that Portuguese came in different stripes. Some were Judaizers, others were not; some were wealthy, others were not; some were New Christians, others were not; some were merchants, others were not.[85]

One accused heretic, Jorge Rodríguez Tavares, decided to take the inquisitors' profiling head-on. Rodríguez was "not well thought of by [the Portuguese] in this town."[86] Economics seemed to play a part, for Rodríguez claimed to be desperately poor, but with enough pride not to want Manuel Bautista Pérez to think his visits were a pretext for handouts.[87] Miserable, excluded, and definitely not a beneficiary of Portuguese largesse, Rodríguez was riled by the idea that the Portuguese could be viewed as a homogeneous, united community—so riled that he squarely confronted tribunal members with their prejudice.

Inquisitors saw themselves as modern and impartial state servants and, accordingly, above the common misperceptions of the day. The magistrates didn't want to appear to be blinded by stereotypes. They were deeply offended by Rodríguez's suggestion that the tribunal was, in fact, condemning Portuguese out of hand: "[W]hat did Rodríguez mean by . . . 'You [inquisitors] think all Portuguese are alike'?"[88] Nevertheless, in spite of all the thundering declarations of the importance of evidence, the magistrates consistently made New Christian ancestry into proof of sin and Portuguese birth into proof of guilt. Like many of us caught between the incongruity of race thinking's stereotypes and the reality of social practices, the inquisitors did—and occasionally did not—believe that New Christians were Portuguese were Jews.[89]

We must remember that state bureaucrats did not always agree about official definitions of personhood, and the way inquisitors defined "Portuguese" could, at times, be at odds with the regulations set by others. A good example was when the viceroyalty, strapped for cash, decided to levy a tax on all "foreigners." In order to tax foreigners, royal officials had to first define what being a "foreigner" (including a Portuguese) meant, and Lima's royal authorities determined that "nationality" was fixed by place of birth. With this understanding in mind, Manuel Bautista Pérez, born in Portugal and desperate to avoid what would have been a hefty tax payment, went in search of a document to certify he was a native of the realm. Miraculously, Pérez's elderly aunt somehow "found" just such a document—a baptismal certificate archived in one of Seville's distinguished parishes. Circumstance had much to do with how state institutions defined their subjects; and Manuel Bautista Pérez, who worked so hard to appear "Old Christian," often passed (or had the money to pass). But in these momentous times of the complicidad grande, Pérez, like the majority of indicted Judaizers, was nothing but a Portuguese.

Limited Critiques

New Christians were severe critics—not of colonial hierarchies, which they never questioned, but of the inquisitorial bent to racialize Spanishness into Old Christian purity. The Manuel Henríquez-Acuna-Acevedo conspiracy expressed one critique of race thinking's inherent illogic, challenging the notion that ancestry determined religious belief and nationalist loyalties.[90] Other accused Judaizers challenged the concept of casta y generación in different ways. Some claimed ignorance (Diego López "didn't know if he was an Old Christian or a New Christian");[91] some refused to equate Portuguese with caste (Henrique Tavares didn't know what "[his ancestors'] *casta y generación* was, but [he did know] that they were Portuguese").[92] Doña Mencia de Luna's background was cloudy, too: her husband, Henrique Núñez, admitted he was New Christian, but then added that "truthfully, he did not know if he was a New Christian or Old"; Doña Mencia's older sister, Doña Mayor, said that she didn't know her casta y generación, but that "her parents were taken to be Old Christian"; Doña Mayor's daughter Doña Isabel Antonia said "she was the daughter of Portuguese" but couldn't say what her caste was either.[93] It was Doña Mencia, however, who voiced the most stunning rejection of all.

Doña Mencia de Luna's riveting testimony conveyed another challenge to the New Christian = Jew = Portuguese equation, one that, in its way, also went to the truth of race. Curiously and ironically, Doña Mencia was accused of being the Jewish community's most stalwart defender of New Christian endogamy,[94] but that accusation flew in the face of what Doña Mencia had to say about her ancestry, about the nature of Portuguese–Castilian relations, about the makeup of the colonial elite, and about the meanings of Old Christian and Jew. When asked by the prosecutor to name her "casta y generación," Doña Mencia said "that all [her ancestors] are Old Christians" and "they are intermixed, Castilian and Portuguese."[95]

The prosecuting attorney called this response perjury. He had Doña Mencia pegged as a closet New Christian and Jew in search of a cover-up.[96] But the prosecutor's prim, unmoving truth was not Doña Mencia's. The inquisitors recorded her statement: "it is just a lie, that [she] is a New Christian, which she is not; rather, [Doña Mencia] is an Old Christian, like her parents, grandparents, and great-grandparents."[97]

We could—as the inquisitors did—dismiss Doña Mencia as a liar trying to dupe the court (and save herself). But there is another way of looking at Doña Mencia's defiant refutation. Perhaps she didn't agree with the choices, did not accept the categorical terms through which the prosecutor (and much of Spanish society) understood human difference. In the prosecution's judgment, Doña Mencia was declaring the impossible: no one could claim to be both Old Christian and New Christian at the same time; or, looking at Doña Mencia's more subtle version of kinship, no one could claim to be both Old Christian and "intermixed, Castilian and Portuguese" at the same time.

Doña Mencia had a different understanding of what the modern world's emerging distinctions should look like. In her eyes, ancestry was irrelevant to social distinctions based on religion, and in the colonies, place of birth was irrelevant to caste: even full-blooded New Christians could become Old Christian, and even men and women born in Portugal could become Spaniards. Doña Mencia and her tormentors parried gravely over her position in the categorical scheme of things; their dispute, after all, went to the heart of who she was as opposed to what the inquisitorial bureaucracy would define her to be.

Doña Mencia, along with other New Christians (more on them in the next chapter), refused to countenance the wizardry that was turning religious belief into a caste, and nation into a racelike snare of social being. But only to a point. Doña Mencia's concern was to remap *español* so that Castilian and Portuguese, Old Christian and New Christian could share a place in the evolving modern scheme of things. Still, I imagine she drew a line separating español from the rest, and I doubt she would have extended her philosophy of racial boundaries to indios and negros. So Doña Mencia, who wouldn't consent to certain ancestral calculations, was, like most of us, blind to the nature of other racial designs. She did not (could not) see that the same conflicting, overlapping ideologies and social relations at the heart of *portugués* and *castellano* were also at the heart of negro, indio, mulato, mestizo, and sambo.

Español and the Two Racial Designs

Portugués and castellano, on the one hand, and negro, indio, mulato, mestizo, and sambo, on the other: these were the two racial designs of state-making and colonialism. Español, as social relation and social category, was the bridge between the two—the bridge that Doña Mencia could not see.

Doña Mencia's contention that Castilians and Portuguese were Spanish was part of a broader debate about the relationship between Castile and "Spain." The ambiguities of that relationship, although directed at questions of peninsular authority and its representation, could not avoid the politics or culture of colonial entanglements. At issue were the confusions embedded in español. Español could equivocally—and concurrently—refer to a territory, a political ideal, and a colonial relation. The view from Peru will be instructive.

To repeat, Spain as such did not exist in the seventeenth century; rather, it was composed of separate principalities under the domain of the Castilian king. Although not an integrated, sovereign nation, the idea of Spain had nonetheless already captured minds. Spain (or Spanish) represented a unitary ideal, able to override the regional enmities dividing the Peninsula.[98] It also, however, referred to a colonial relation, and this significance evolved as imperial government took form. Peru's first conquistadors called themselves "Christians," ready to do battle with natives who worshiped in "mosques" like the Muslim infidels; it took decades, and the emerging institutions of the colonial state, before Peru's Iberian immigrants were to call themselves Spaniards.[99] Critically, "Spain's" two referents—national ideal and colonial power—developed in tandem.

The dialogue between "Spain" and "Castille," then, took an eye-opening turn in the colonies—something well conveyed in the sermons of the doctrineros Francisco de Avila and Fernando de Avendaño. References to Castile and Spain, or to Castilian and Spanish, are peppered throughout those remarkable homilies, which set out to tackle the history of the globe. As might be expected, Avila and Avendaño chose "Castile" whenever they wanted to distinguish among the different regions inside Iberia: "the devil was powerful in Castile and in the other places [on the Peninsula] where Spaniards lived."[100] And, in line with the focus of much early modern cultural history, Castile entered the scene whenever Avila or Avendaño spoke about the actual physical embodiment of power. If the king was involved, they named "Castile." So when Avila wanted to give Indians an idea of the glory of Rome, he compared Caesar with "King Felipe who is in Castile,"[101] and when Avila wanted to convey that even the most powerful kings were humble before God, he began with "the grandest" of all, "the great king who resides in Castile."[102]

Sometimes, however, the choices were not so clear. There were moments when preachers used Castile and Spain interchangeably: when Avila proclaimed the devil was as likely to seduce Europeans as he was Indians, he wrote "Spaniards" in the Romance version of his sermon and "Castilians" in the Quechua;[103] And, when Avila and Avendaño described the nations of the globe, there were times when they named "Castilla" and times when they named "España."[104]

The curiosities, however, have to do with colonialism. The king governed Peru in the name of Castile; nonetheless, the doctrineros, writing one hundred years after the conquest, identified the conquistadores as "espanoles" (even though the conquistadores would have called themselves "cristianos") and they chose "España" to indicate where they came from. When Avila or Avendaño talked about the Andes or the Inca empire as colonies, they spoke of them in relation to "Spain."[105] It was said that the Inca foresaw his empire destroyed by foreigners; in Avendaño's hands, the prophesy became a sermon about the Spanish defeat of the Inca army.[106] God sent "españoles" to Peru, preached Avila, and those españoles were led by "the Marqués Don Francisco Pizarro."[107] In his description of Pizarro's route to victory from the coast to the Inca capital, Avila wrote: "[T]hen the *españoles* went to Cuzco . . . where they killed many, many [Indians] . . . and today Spaniards continue to live here, and to go to and from Spain."[108] By the seventeenth century, Spain was the country that Pizarro—who was from Castile and conquered the Incas in the name of Castile—either lived in or returned to. Pizarro had become a Spaniard.

Spain and Spaniard connoted two things—an ideal of nationhood and a global role, roughly that of "colonizer"—which, although separable, were inevitably intertwined. At the same time that Avila wrote about Pizarro's return to "Spain," he wrote about the españoles and their role within the racialized framework of colonial Peru; at the same time "Spanish" was drawing on a sense of commonality that was not yet—but had a potential to be—the cultural matrix for a rising nation, "Spanish" was understood as a political relation of colonial rule. The terms shaping political life on the Peninsula were locked, in counterpoint, with their colonial analogues. As a result, colonial experience enforced Spain's protonationalist appeal.

"Spanish" was a category of humanness that, following Castile's victories, traversed the globe; and, as such, it united an extraordinarily diverse set of people: men and women from different regions, speaking different dialects (or even languages) and from different social classes. It was the colonial category par excellence: a global relation that, on the one hand, constructed an international ruling elite and, on the other, muted the profound internal divisions constituting Spanish society on the Continent and abroad. It was a global relation, in other words, that could generate a taste for "national community."

The concept of "national community," however, was part of a roiling controversy in the seventeenth-century Spanish world, not least because it was colored by the Portuguese = Jew equation.[109] That was the "New Christian" problem trapping Doña Mencia and all the rest captured during the Great Conspiracy. Sometimes español included Portuguese; but, in most circumstances, español suggested a banner of nationalism with a racialized religious twist. Under this banner, as Manuel Bautista Pérez discovered, one's Spanish birthplace was worth little.[110] It could never expunge the stink of the "mala casta blanca," the white caste whose evil was inherited and whose destiny was an eternity in hell.

The shield guarding Spain's two racial designs was purity of blood. It could ensure that the "mala casta blanca" did not stain "authentic" Spaniards, and it could be called on to justify the special privileges and rights enjoyed by españoles in the colonies.[111] Autos-da-fé made that distinction very public: accused witches of "pure" Iberian descent were spared the humiliation of the lash and seminudity, but their sisters "of color"—regardless of how little stain tainted their blood—were paraded through the streets of Lima with breasts bared and backs whipped;[112] accused Judaizers, suffering grisly punishments on the auto's stage, became a spectacular lesson in the boundaries that separated the "true" Spaniard from his inauthentic look-alike. Colonial and New Christian race thinking, then, came together in the figure of "untainted" Spaniards—the "nación" especially chosen by God to lead the conquest of the Americas. For blood purity was by no means incidental to Spain's divine charge. As the jurist Solorzano reminded his readers, God had selected Spaniards to take his mission to the New World—and not any other people—because it was Spaniards who bore the purist blood.[113]

The empire's two racial designs (as well as the rival views) worked in a dialectic, as modern history wed relations of state-making to colony-building. Transported to the Americas, the New Christian syndrome, with its language of stains and its obsession with blood purity, was injected into the blood of indios and negros (now they, too, were judged by *sangre manchada*), intensifying the racial bent of colonial geopolitics.[114] In turn, the racial logic of colonialism, increasingly concerned about human mixtures and race fractions, made its obsessions felt by all "españoles," who were now accountable to state officials for the finer details of tainted descent. Race thinking's two dimensions were bound in counterpoint: together they confused nation, culture, and caste; together they celebrated an illusion of purity; together they sharpened the divide between Spaniards and everyone else; together they made social categories into racial truths. Together, as accused Judaizers and accused witches were to find out, they constituted a new idea of what it meant to be human.

NEW CHRISTIANS
AND NEW WORLD FEARS

Christian Spaniards.
From Felipe Guaman Poma de Ayala,
El primer nueva corónica y buen gobierno (1613?).

It is no longer possible to isolate the Jewish question or the antisemitic ideology from issues that are actually almost completely unrelated to the realities of modern Jewish history. —HANNAH ARENDT, *The Origins of Totalitarianism* [1]

CASTILIANS AGAINST PORTUGUESE; Old Christians against New Christians; "los católicos" against the "nación ebrea"; authentic Spaniard against the "mala casta blanca"—the battle lines were drawn.[2] We have touched on some of the conditions that made these hostilities possible and on some of the burgeoning notions—around descent, religion, nation and, most decidedly, race—that shaped their seventeenth-century character. To get a still deeper purchase on these antagonisms—along with their racialized, Lima twists—we will now examine "social blame" and its role in forging the race-thinking divisions of colonial power. Our entrée will be the threatening ways in which "New Christians/Portuguese/Jews" grabbed colonial imaginations: the fears they provoked, the societal dangers they embodied, and the cultural boundaries they challenged.[3]

Stereotypes of commercial advantage, perfidy, hatred of Christians, and extraordinary manipulation of language were anti-Semitism's building blocks, but in 1620s–30s Lima they took on a particular cast: New Christians usurped trade and merchandising to the detriment of Castilians; New Christians, because of their international ties, were not loyal to the Spanish empire; New Christians were plotting treachery with Spain's rivals for control of South America; New Christians were plotting with the potentially subversive groups within the colony (indios and negros); finally, New Christians were able to ally themselves with these "enemies within" because of a remarkable ability to conspire in secret languages. The viceroyalty's understanding of the Jewish menace thus elaborated a familiar set of anti-Semitic charges, but with a twist appropriate to the world's new colonial conditions. Seventeenth-century accusations of Jewish conspiracies had a long history; but in Peru they were embroidered on the geopolitics of empire and race thinking.

Modern Imaginations and Economic Threats

In the early decades of the seventeenth century, the Lima office was abuzz with stories about Peru's growing community of crypto-Jews.[4] Letters warning of "this plague which, so dispersed and spread out, has been thriving in many parts [of the viceroyalty]" presented a litany of well-worn treasons;[5] yet they also expressed fears rooted in the new mercantile age—fears that the emerging global economy was opening the door to unthought of subversions. Merchants were the enemy, went one memo sent to Madrid, for merchants were little more than spies. And merchants, of course, were indistinguishable from New Christians, or Portuguese, or Jews. Merchants, according to the memo's author, had global trading networks and outlets in Holland, Lisbon, Brazil, and Spain, and they were using them to orchestrate not just the destruction of the Spanish empire, but that of the entire Christian world.[6]

The source of this memo, a ship's captain, supported his case with several claims. He argued that one measure of Jewish sabotage was the fact that Jews had a controlling interest in the Dutch West Indies Company—a commonplace notion of the time, but one contradicted by the company's records.[7] Additional "evidence" turned on the seditious behavior of two "Dutch/Portuguese" Jews. One, Antonio Váez Henríques, a.k.a. Mosen Coen, was said to have orchestrated the Dutch capture of Pernambuco, Brazil.[8] Another, Diego Peixotto, also alias Mosen Coen, was said to have plotted treachery among his workers, forcing the crew "who are *negros* . . . to come to them [the Dutch/Portuguese Jews] to learn the language."[9] As you can see, this letter said very little about heretical "practices" but a lot about the mystique surrounding Portuguese Jews, global geopolitics, and the new mercantilist economy.

Rumors abounded. Portuguese New Christians were monopolizing most, if not all, sectors of mercantile activity; Portuguese New Christians were cornering finance and controlling credit; and Portuguese New Christians were dominating the distribution, retail, and trade of every and all manner of goods. Colonial prejudice explained the success of Portuguese merchants as being a result of their one-sided control over markets, and that axiom, in turn, inflamed the raw sentiment that Portuguese achievements were gained at Old Christians' expense: "[Portuguese] had built up an entire merchant marine along with a system of credit, with their agents scattered throughout the land" and, as a result, "a Castilian of pure stock doesn't have a ghost of a chance."[10]

Although New Christians were considered to be threats from the Inquisition's beginning, the content and force of anti-Semitic discourse changed as political tensions, coupled with a growing mercantile economy, increasingly charted colonial life. Stereotypes about Jews' extraordinary abilities to acquire wealth scarcely figured in the tribunal's early decades. During these years, men and women were charged with performing the rituals of Judaism: keeping the Sabbath, wearing festive clothing on Saturday, "fasting on the day of the Great Fast [Day of Atonement] and on the holiday of Queen Esther, and say[ing] prayers, in 'Romance'"[11] because, in the testimony of Felipa López, "[the Law of Moses] was good for the salvation of her soul."[12] In the Lima office's first years, being Jewish was not a ticket to material wealth but a step toward salvation.

By 1615, however, accusations took a mercantile turn: wealth or financial acumen entered the record as evidence of heresy. It was in that year that Jorge de Paz, a merchant who moved to Peru after sojourns in Seville and Brazil, was brought before the tribunal. He was denounced by a prosecution witness for secretly worshiping the Law of Moses, and one proof of his heretical activities was that "he was very successful in acquiring money."[13] Getting rich, then, was becoming a diagnostic for Judaizing practices.

As the sentiment tying Jews with money pervaded the Andean region, its correlate—that Jews would help each other in financial matters to the detriment of Old Christians—was gaining currency as well. Francisco de Vita Barahona is a good example. Born in Galicia (Spain), forty-three years old, arrested in 1623 for Judaizing—Vita Barahona emigrated to the Indies to work as a merchant. At first, he refused to admit to any heretical practices, but after a year in prison and confronted with the lengthy and detailed charges against him, Vita Barahona confessed that

> once when in dire straits, Juan Núñez Saravia, my cousin, . . . gave me . . . 1,000 *reales* to take to Lisbon for a fair and I gave him a promissory note of 300 *reales* more than the amount loaned to me and, after four months passed by, Juan Núñez Saravia called me over and returned the 300 *reales*, explaining that his uncle told him to return it . . . because his uncle is a man of good conscience and because according to the Law of Moses a Jew is not permitted to charge another Jew interest.[14]

Again, special treatment between cousins (if it ever happened) became a credible proof of Judaizing. The strongest expressions of Jewish economic intrigue, however, appear in the testimonies of the men and women arrested in the Great Jewish Conspiracy. We have only to look at the cases of Manuel Henríquez and Manuel Bautista Pérez.

After Manuel Henríquez confessed, he was ordered by the tribunal to explain his decision to turn from Christianity to heresy. The practice of Judaism, it seems, was as much a survival strategy as a road to salvation. Poor and defenseless in South America, Manuel Henríquez would have had to face the New World's hazards and opportunities alone. Becoming a Jew, he claimed, not only ensured his basic needs would be met but provided an entrée into the world of commerce—and guaranteed his success. As a Christian, Manuel Henríquez would "remain lost, poor, and in need like others who were in the Indies and didn't have anyone to lend them a hand."[15] As a Jew, Henríquez would have networks: Simón Osorio would feed him and supply credit; Antonio Ferrerin would sell him merchandise "cheaper than anyone else"; Sebastián Cutino would give him whatever he needed; Antonio and Jorge de Espinosa would "buy up whatever he brought over."[16]

Many witnesses accounted for Manuel Bautista Pérez's extraordinary wealth by simply pointing to his "Jewishness." Jews, it seems, were God's chosen people, particularly in the arena of commerce: "*Compadre*," Pérez supposedly said to Diego Ovalle, "*things are going well because God has enacted many favors on our behalf, because we observe the Law*" (underscored by the tribunal in the original).[17]

Jewish successes, as reported in the confession conspiracy, were especially noticeable in the colonies: "[Peru is] a good land, where God will grant you a thousand favors."[18] Or, in the words of Bartolomé de León, also caught in the dragnet of 1635: "[I]f you observed the Law of Moses, all you needed to do in order to return to Spain a rich man was go to the Indies."[19] Correspondingly, many witnesses testified that Judaism could be practiced more easily in the New World than in the Old. As Juan de Acevedo supposedly told Manuel Henríquez, "[T]his land was good for [practicing Judaism] because no one prevented you from observing [it]."[20]

Magistrates were ever ready to suspect New Christian achievements in trade and finance, because, they claimed, such successes could only have been obtained at Old Christian expense. Unfortunately, witnesses, testifying wildly against one another in the confession conspiracy, gave body to their fears. On the one hand, inquisitors impugned Diego López de Fonseca, executed in the auto-da-fé of 1639, for privileging Jews in trade;[21] on the other, they impugned Luis de Valencia for unfairly benefiting from them: "it is sufficient that we are all one (*todos unos*) in order to help each other . . . and [we] should go and help the weakest [Luis de Valencia] . . . since we all observe the Law of Moses."[22] Innumerable charges were brought against Pérez for offering to assist his fellow Jews: "with the love and affection he carries for those who observe the Law of Moses, he favors them in business matters . . ."[23] (i.e., favors those who, in Rodríguez Tavares's words, were "one of us").[24] And, following the rhetoric of the times, helping "one of us" inevitably thwarted "one of them,"[25] for "a Castilian of pure stock doesn't have a ghost of a chance."[26]

Lima magistrates pointed out this threat when trying to appease Madrid's concerns about the tribunal's maverick activities. Writing about the "Jewish plague" and its devastating stranglehold on commerce, they explained:

> Since about six or eight years ago, the number of Portuguese who have entered the Kingdom of Peru (where many had been living before) has been very large. . . . [Lima] has been overwhelmed by [them]. They have been turning themselves into the Lords (*Señores*) of Commerce: the street called the "Street of Merchants" was practically theirs and theirs alone, so was the entire alleyway; and the large [warehousing] containers even more so . . . and they ruled over trade and commerce in such a way that from gold brocade to sackcloth, and from diamonds to cuminseed, [from the lowest slave of Guinea to the most precious pearl][27]—all passes through their hands.[28]

The letter then went on to specify New Christians' unfair business practices. Credit issues loomed. Portuguese were able to finance substantial commercial projects by means of credit agreements among themselves: "one commandeered an entire flotilla largely based on the credit [Portuguese merchants] had extended to one another";[29] in the course of expanding their mercantile domain, "these Portuguese" punctually paid off the interest on their loans, while leaving the principal standing.[30] (The latter practice may be common enough in today's credit card world, but in the seventeenth century it was an apparently unorthodox approach to financial management.) Mañozca and company reminded their superiors that the Portuguese were so clever, astute, and crafty at manipulating finances that they were "able to dupe even the most knowledgeable."[31] And these abilities, the magistrates added, were just reflections of the Portuguese's conniving (and inherited) character.

Inquisitors were troubled by the extended networks of Peru's Portuguese agents, the lords of a vibrant and growing system of international trade. With bases in European mercantile centers as well as in the new colonial entrepôts, New Christians could gain access to and distribute goods from around the world.[32] To inquisitors that meant even into the farthest reaches of the empire, including Indian territory, "tierra adentro," where Spain's institutional powers were at their weakest. It also meant trading with other members of their "nación" who lived in places like Venice, Rome, Bordeaux, or Amsterdam, where Judaism could be openly practiced.[33] It also meant dominating the slave trade and creating a special allegiance with Africans in bondage. International trade was intrinsic to anti-Semitic fears.[34]

Once again, the popular ideology about entangling economic interests gave international networks a strong odor of heresy: Judaism was practiced—and could be learned—in the dangerous places beyond Spain's grasp. It is not surprising that confessions delivered during the "confession conspiracy" played on these fears. Where did Simón Osorio, the man who purportedly cajoled Manuel Henríquez into becoming Jewish, learn how to decipher his elaborate Hebrew calendar? In France. Where did Manuel Henríquez's friend Jacinto Henríquez learn to observe the Law of Moses? In France.[35] Where did Luis de Valencia discover Jewish ritual? In Italy. And that is precisely the reason why Pérez refused to talk publicly about Portuguese living outside the Spanish realm, and why he cautioned his brother-in-law, Luis de Vega, to be silent about the months spent in Flanders.[36]

The international thrust of New Christian trade—so dangerous to Peru's spiritual integrity—endangered the empire's spacial integrity as well. This was the inquisitors' argument and they knew that, at the end of the day, it was their trump card. Magistrates pointed out how Portuguese were circumventing Spanish commercial law, underwriting a booming black market, and—perhaps worst of all—not paying tariffs owed to the Crown. With family and compatriots in places like Amsterdam, Italy, and France, they argued, New Christians were sending earnings to places outside the imperial orbit—further undermining Spain's often fragile economy.[37] Unlike authentic aristocrats who conquered with swords, New Christians, Peru's new seigneurs, were simply conquering with money, as the inquisitors Mañozca, Gaytán, and Castro y del Castillo reported to headquarters: "[The Portuguese] are the lords of the land, consuming, spending, and *vanquishing*" (emphasis mine).[38]

Colonial Conspiracies

Shocked and dismayed at the magnitude, reach, and severity of the 1639 auto-da-fé, the Madrid office demanded that each inquisitor provide an explanation, or rationale, for his decision. The inquisitor Castro y del Castillo's response was a familiar one: he supported the auto because the crypto-Jewish threat was actually part of a larger, more insidious challenge to the Spanish empire. The Great Jewish Conspiracy, he wrote, had also been a conspiracy to commit treason. The same Portuguese merchants who met their fate on the auto's scaffold had been orchestrating a plan to hand Peru over to the Dutch:

> and it was not just a conspiracy to Judaize, but to commit hostilities and [engage in] criminal machinations . . . and one morning it was discovered that someone had been making a hole in the strong and thick street wall of the warehouse where gunpowder was being stored . . . and the [gunpowder] was to blow up the city, and [Lima's New Christians] had been in communication with the Dutch and were waiting for them.[39]

Heresies had turned into conspiracies had turned into reasons of state.

It was a commonplace of the times that New Christians were secret allies of the Dutch, an anxiety that was only magnified by the Dutch presence in Brazil.[40] The threat of the "Dutch enemy," however, was intensified by other colonial misgivings, compounded by fears that New Christians were also conspiring with Peru's enemies within, the blacks and Indians.

Inquisitors (and others) believed that the Portuguese used a variety of tactics to get indios and negros to do their subversive bidding, and one of the most insidious was religious sabotage: turning Peru's fledgling Christians away from Christianity. This concern was an old one. As far back as 1602, a royal decree sent to Peru warned that New Christians were corrupting the beliefs of natives recently converted to Catholicism, and local authorities were ordered to be on the alert "so that no error or evil sect is sown among the Indians, who are barely secure . . . in our faith and are vulnerable to any novelty."[41] Solórzano, several decades later, wrote about similar dangers to the faith of Peru's "simple people."[42] Inquisitors, as you might imagine, were equally uneasy, and in their 1636 report to Madrid they noted with alarm that "this perfidious [Hebrew] *nación* was taking root in just a few years' time and in such a way that, like a weed, it would strangle the new Christianity [of indios and negros]."[43]

Heresy was a first step on the slippery slope to treason, argued the inquisitors. And imperial stereotypes intensified the fears attached to any tie between indios, negros, and New Christians. As prejudice about New Christians found its match in prejudice about Indians and blacks, links between Indians, blacks, and New Christians took on more menace. Spanish prejudice demeaned indios and negros as either "gente simple"—simple-minded folk, easily led astray—or as inherently vicious, on the edge of violence. Both sets of attributes—opposing but mirroring—made blacks and Indians innately susceptible to Judaizers' corrupting influence and, accordingly, ever on the verge of rebellion. (It should not surprise us that viceregal authorities feared rebellion. The Spaniards knew that they were unpopular and outnumbered; and, by this time, Indians and blacks had, in various ways, defied colonial rule.)[44]

If Spaniards feared the ability of New Christians to seduce barely Christian souls, it was merchandising—a New Christian "trait"—that presumably gave these New Christians the opportunity to do so. Where did New Christians communicate their heresies to one another, express their hatred of Christianity, as well as turn "simple peoples" away from the faith? In the thriving mercantile spaces of colonial life, of course. In testimony after testimony, witnesses pointed to the hubs, routes, and outposts of colonial mercantilism as the places where treachery ruled: in the slave markets of Portobello (Panama) and the entrepôts of Angola, Guinea, and Cartagena (where Manuel Henríquez and Manuel Bautista Pérez were said to have learned and communicated their heresy); along the peddling routes stretching from Lima into the Andean highlands (routes taken by Manuel Henríquez); in the offices of Lima's major merchants, in Lima's bustling market streets, in the market stalls of the plaza, and in the slave warehouses in Lima's San Lázaro parish (where we find Manuel Bautista Pérez). Commerce gave traders, agents of the big Lima merchants, the ability to spread their networks into the outer reaches of the viceroyalty, far from the eyes of government officials or prelates.

There was an old, anti-Semitic canard that New Christians had extraordinary linguistic skills, and in Peru, this talent included the ability to talk to slaves in a common tongue. Not only did Portuguese speak a remarkable language, ripe for "conspiracies and heresies" ("a secret language, [spoken] right in front of Old Christians who just heard normal words, not that out-of-the-ordinary language"),[45] but they shared linguistic codes with blacks. Inquisitors were concerned about exchanges between prisoners and negros, since slaves were in a unique position to pass on valuable information, secretly deliver letters, or bring in such prohibited goods as paper and pens. Magistrates tried to prevent communication between prisoners and slaves and only employed "negros bozales" (wild, born in Africa), who spoke no Portuguese or Spanish, to work in the cells. But New Christian linguistic genius inevitably prevailed, since, in spite of precautions, New Christians found out about the tribunal's secret plans—including the date of the 1639 auto.[46] For slaves, the risks were high. But collaboration brought promises and hope: Antonio from Angola, Manuel Bautista Pérez's slave, explained simply: "[Pérez] promised me my freedom."[47]

Jews and Indians, according to seventeenth-century lore, had their own special ties. Since the first encounters between Europe and the Americas, theological questions were raised about the Semitic heritage of the New World's native peoples. Distinguished clerics, philosophers, and jurists from all the colonizing countries and from many of their colonies debated the question of common ancestry; and for those who believed that indigenous peoples were descended from the Lost Tribes, Jews and Indians became natural allies.[48] Two proponents were the well-known priest-chroniclers Fray Buenaventura de Salinas and Antonio Vázquez de Espinosa (who wrote about the glories of the Lima tribunal). Buenaventura de Salinas found a certain likeness of temperament between Indians and Jews: "cowardly, ungrateful, lazy, superstitious, crafty, liars."[49] Vázquez de Espinosa, however, was convinced that a shared ancestry helped account for similarities not only in character and physique, but in religious practices and beliefs: "Indians are alike in every respect to the Hebrews from whom they derive . . . in physique and temperament and in other characteristics, such as their customs, rites, ceremonies, superstitions, and idolatries."[50] These "customs, rites, ceremonies," remember, were roads to treason.

The potential damage of an alliance between New Christians and Indians was, to the inquisitors, nowhere more stunning than in the Portuguese ability to facilitate relations between internal and external enemies, to facilitate the complicities of Indians and the European rivals of Spain. The Lima tribunal, tracking the growing migration of New Christians to Peru, joined a chorus of letters to Madrid warning that Indians were supporting the Dutch in Valdivia and in the "isla de quince grados."[51] Indeed, in the early 1630s indios rose up against the Spanish in Northwest Argentina—the very region where magistrates believed Portuguese/Judaizers were settling en masse.[52] And later in that decade, Peru's viceroy wrote about a similar eventful confederation between native peoples and "Portuguese" —now doubly suspect owing to the growing rift between Spain and Portugal and the Dutch presence in Brazil.[53] But, as inquisitors were never tired of reminding their superiors, they were the vanguard troops, stanching the overlapping assault of New Christians, foreign enemies, and Indians that threatened to unravel Spain's colonial order. They insisted that Madrid "recognize how the Holy Office of the Inquisition not only served to extirpate heresies, but also, in large part, [served to maintain] the temporal tranquillity of the kingdom."[54]

One curious development in the mix of colonial ideologies of blame was that Jewish immorality was being constructed in black and Indian terms; in other words, Spanish conspiracy theories were transforming Andean

and African customs into heretical Judaic practices. Manuel Bautista Pérez
—whose enterprise stretched from the Peruvian highlands to Angola—
was at the center of this intriguing metamorphosis.[55] He was accused by
several witnesses of practicing some rather exotic Jewish rituals. One was
with tobacco: "[Pérez], taking [the tobacco] in his fingers and then pressing it to his nostrils, would say, 'Señor compadre, this tobacco is very
good,' and he would scatter it [on the ground] or blow on it."[56] Another
was with cola: "Then, at other times, he [Diego de Ovalle] would say
to [Pérez], 'Do you have any *colilla* to drink with water?' (a root or fruit
from Guinea which is brought from Cartagena, and by drinking water
after putting it in the mouth, it becomes sweet) [this definition is part of
the recorded testimony], and Manuel would order [his servants] to bring
some."[57] As if to reinforce the "Jewish" derivation of taking tobacco and
drinking colilla, one witness added, "[Diego de] Ovalle and Manuel Bautista would speak to each other in a language only understood among
themselves, talking about the Law of Moses."[58]

Later, when the inquisitors compiled formal charges against Manuel
Bautista Pérez, they condensed these testimonies into the following
charge: "[R]itual offerings (*sacrificios*) were made in the prisoner's house;
[when] the prisoner was asked for tobacco . . . he scattered it and blew
on it, a gesture appropriate for libation and ritual offering, as is associated
with many places in . . . the Old Testament."[59] The charge continued: [A]t
other times, with the same intent, when the prisoner was with a certain
person . . . he was asked for cola . . . and, drinking it, this certain person
spoke with the prisoner . . . in an extraordinary (*trasordinario*) language
. . . so that the prisoner and the rest of his *casta y generación* could speak
of [Judaizing] . . . without being understood by others."[60]

Manuel Bautista Pérez emphatically denied these allegations. He
strongly objected to charges that he made ritual offerings to the God of
the Old Testament, let alone with cultural artifacts from South America
and Africa. Pérez reminded Mañozca, who had come to Peru after heading
the Inquisition in Cartagena, that "he should have heard of [cola] because
it was so common in Cartagena."[61] Furthermore, not only "did everyone
there [use] it," but cola was quite a normal and accepted drink throughout
the colonies. So if anyone were to "ask for some sweet water in his house,"
it would be served "without anything else being implied."[62] Regarding
tobacco, Pérez countered that he didn't even like it.[63]

Far from having an Old World origin and, therefore, far from being a
possible component of traditional Jewish ceremony, tobacco was first cultivated in South America. The accounts of tobacco's role in "ritual offerings"—blowing on it or scattering it—describe Andean tradition much

more accurately than they describe any Hebraic tradition.[64] Andeans believed tobacco had sacred and curative properties, and *sayri* (the Quechua word for tobacco) was a name associated with Inca royalty.[65] Nevertheless, the presumption that Jews and Indians shared ritual practices was not limited to Mañozca's court. As we have seen, Antonio Vázquez de Espinosa, a cleric with no direct ties to the Inquisition, believed that the common origin of Jews and Indians explained the similarity of their "rites" and "ceremonies."

Nor did drinking cola resonate with Judaic ritual. A popular African plant and beverage, cola was brought to the New World with the slave trade. No doubt, as Manuel Bautista Pérez claimed, it was well known in Cartagena, one of the Spanish empire's principal slave depots. And, no doubt, Mañozca was well aware of its origins.

Transforming the drinking of cola and the sniffing of tobacco into heretical Jewish practices seemed as fanciful to Manuel Bautista Pérez as it does to us. However, the intellectual and emotional climate of the colonial Spanish community—where currents of anti-Semitism merged with fears of indios and negros—most likely rendered this ideological distortion into a rhetoric that fit. At the very least, the infusion of heretical Judaizing with Andean and African traits made cultural sense.

How striking that goods associated with processes at the heart of Spain's colonial endeavor—the conquest of indios and the expansion of the African slave trade—were conflated with the practices of Judaism. Global commerce and cheap labor anchored Spain's colonial enterprise, and "New Christians" (Jews) and Indians and blacks were key figures in this equation. At least according to stereotype, New Christians dominated international trade; indios and negros embodied the colony's sources of cheap labor. Both groups were needed for the success of Spain's global endeavors, and both were distrusted. New Christian merchants, slaves, and colonized Indian subjects were outside the traditional institutions that had structured life in the Iberian Peninsula before colonialism began to change the rules. In different cultural and economic ways, each signaled the novel social relations of the emerging modern world. The cultural finger-pointing described above hints at the tensions that animated the new economy and new politics—as well as the cultural order on which they rest.

The Promised Land

For many Spaniards, Peru was a land of opportunities unattainable in Europe. The New World, distant from metropolitan vigilance, held out a promise to loosen or turn a blind eye to some of the constraints that hobbled social mobility in the Peninsula.[66] In the colonies, where trade and commerce fostered wealth, merchants especially savored these possibilities, and "Portuguese" merchants were no exception. "Peru was a good land," said Luis de Vega; for God was going to grant Jews "a thousand favors" in the New World. Some even said that the Lima tribunal was less severe than others: in contrast to the cruel and irrational Lisbon office, arresting Portuguese at whim, this was a "new kingdom, and . . . its rulers would not want to burn . . . anyone at the stake."[67] Perhaps Luis de Lima, born in Portugal and executed with Manuel Bautista Pérez, best expressed the hopes and expectations placed in colonial Peru by merchants and would-be aristocrats: "[T]he land of Peru was for the Portuguese the promised one, finding there riches, honor and esteem; [it was also] the permissive one because men there care more about money than they do about [people with] different, foreign ways of living (*vidas agenas*)."[68]

In Peru, transformations of social position went beyond the status that money could buy. New Christian men and women told tales of rebirth in the New World—baptized anew, as some would have it. Many changed their names; others claimed not to know anything about their ancestry; others transformed themselves into Old Christians.[69] There were practical reasons to adopt aliases or to bury New Christian descent—as we are painfully aware. However, when Dr. Pinero, Antonio Núñez, and Doña Mayor de Luna declared that "they were taken to be Old Christian," I imagine they believed, or nearly, that they were.[70] And when Hernán Jorge testified that his parents were "New Christians, descended from Jews," while he was a "baptized Christian and an Old Christian," I doubt he was dissembling.[71] The New World, with its relative openness, offered an extraordinary gift to Portuguese who could get to its shores. Immigrants could remake themselves; they could pass.

Some discovered an aristocratic heritage, even descent from Spain's most illustrious lineages. Don Simón Osorio, overseer of the Duke of Lerma's obrajes, apparently became a "caballero gallego" when he landed in Quito; Don Antonio de Lorenzana, relator of the Royal Court, became a "caballero," said one witness, in order to shed his New Christian origins; Don Jorge Cuello, another New Christian cohort of Manuel Henríquez, used to brag that everyone believed he was a "caballero" in Cuzco; and Jacinto del Pino, yet another, claimed he was known as an Old Christian in the remote mining town of Caylloma and that if the inquisitors were to ask, he would say the same.[72]

No one defended noble standing more steadfastly than Luis de Valencia, and no one could have had a more checkered past or curious ancestry (from the inquisitor's point of view). Luis de Valencia, captured in Panama, was sixty when brought before the tribunal. He was born in Lisbon, thrived as a merchant, and had an array of family members who either married into the nobility or were members of the court. According to his uncles (Valencia never knew his father, who died in a shipwreck off the coast of Goa), "he and his parents were always taken to be noble"; "[his paternal grandfather] had married a noblewoman"; his aunt "married a physician to the king's armada"; one of his cousins, on his father's side, "married Juan Gutiérrez in Lisbon, a servant (*criado*) of the Cardinal Prince"; one of his mother's brothers "was married to Doña María de Mineses, the archbishop's niece"; the other, who was a royal agent, died in a battle with the British.[73] Not surprisingly, son echoed father: Juan de Acosta declared that he was "taken as a noble man [whose] parents and grandparents [were] clean of any stain of Moorish or Jewish blood."[74] Was Luis de Valencia, "always . . . taken as a noble," truly "clean of any stain"?

When the inquisitors asked Luis de Valencia about his genealogy, he claimed to have three siblings, and the inquisitors believed him. I think he had two more, Francisco Núñez de Olivera and Feliciano de Valencia. At the turn of the century these two men, "de casta y generación de judíos," were brought before the tribunal for Judaizing: both were penanced in a 1600 auto held in Lima, and both singled out their older brother, Luis de Valencia, as the one responsible for persuading them to leave the Church. Francisco Núñez, a merchant and the younger of the two, was circumcised: "he understood that he was circumcised, . . . and it must have been done when he was a little boy, although his parents always denied it."[75] There is no record of Bachiller Feliciano de Valencia undergoing a similar examination. He was not a merchant but a lawyer, who had studied at Spain's most prestigious university (Salamanca), taught in Portugal (Coimbra), and had planned to join the Jesuit order—until dissuaded by his elder brother, Luis. A man with impeccable credentials in the modern world of letters, Feliciano told the court that his parents, as members of the Count of Benavente's retinue, also held prestigious positions in sixteenth-century Portugal. Arrested in Ica, Feliciano confessed immediately to practicing Judaism as best he could.[76]

So what do we make of Luis de Valencia's testimony? Was he of noble birth? Or was he a descendant of Jews? If Francisco Núñez and Feliciano de Valencia were indeed his younger brothers, Luis was stained by Jewish blood as well as by siblings who had been publicly penanced by the tribunal. But even without this evidence, inquisitors—having weighed the accusations of six witnesses, along with reports by four physicians that Luis's misshapen foreskin was not the product of venereal disease (as alleged) but of circumcision—remained unconvinced.[77] But there is another tack to understanding Luis de Valencia's audacity and befuddlement: perhaps like Doña Mencia de Luna, Luis had a different vision of what it meant to be an authentic Christian and an authentic Spaniard; perhaps, like her, he preferred a different measure of nobility, one more attuned to the paths of success in a modern world than to paths of racial descent.

Luis de Valencia's conception of modern hierarchy was mirrored in the Henríquez-Acevedo plan to obtain the release of New Christians. Their strategy to lay bare the folly of racial profiling was bolstered by a kind of categorical turnabout with respect to the visible number of New Christians in positions of power. If New Christians were Jews, then the inquisitors, Suprema, and court would have to account for the fact that so many "Jews" were in exalted posts at the center of government. Antonio de Acuna and Manuel Henríquez listed several who were remarkably close to the king's ear: the policy experts (*asentistas*, or "politilogues" in Foucault's theories) advising the court and council on the major issues of the day. Acuna's testimony, in all likelihood, reflected the actual efforts in Felipe IV's court to open up the realm to New Christians. At the same time, Acuna was also taking aim at the tribunal's most preposterous ideas. Could all these important men—known to be New Christians/Portuguese—actually be Jews in disguise, betraying king and council? Or were these New Christians/Portuguese, really Christians, loyal to Spain? If they were really Christians, they could not be Jews, nor could their blood be stained. Or, from the other side, as caballeros, noblemen, university graduates, professionals, priests, and monks, Jews could be Old Christians.[78] In the face of these conundrums, how could magistrates possibly assume that all Portuguese/New Christians were Jews? Or so went their thinking. How could rational men—as the inquisitors were fond of calling themselves—make decisions based on a faulty premise that Judaizing was carried in the blood or that New Christians were a race.

By claiming noble pretensions, Luis de Valencia was saying something similar. He and his kinsmen—successful members of Spanish society—going to the finest schools, taking significant posts, even dying for the Crown—were, in essence, nobility; they were not tainted New Christians, they were Christians, ennobled by the possibilities of a new modern age.[79]

The wealthiest merchants, regardless of casta, forged what we could call a colonial aristocracy, living in a style matched by their material success. No *limeño* better exemplified this New World elite than Manuel Bautista Pérez. Pérez, who had erased any vestige of Portuguese from his language, any sign of "New Christian" from his way of life, adopted all the behaviors and conventions of a prosperous nobleman. He was a member of Lima's most prestigious religious brotherhood, the Holy Sacrament; he was generous, hosting feasts and elaborate gatherings; he performed good works, by helping those in need, lavishly supporting charitable causes, and soliciting alms for the San Andrés hospital for indigent Spaniards; he dressed in the finery of aristocrats; he was a much sought-after patron. Reciprocally, as befit one of such noble demeanor, Lima society treated Manuel Bautista Pérez like a patrician: books of literature and philosophy were dedicated to him, praising his contributions and talents.[80]

As one of Lima's most notable patrons, Manuel Bautista Pérez's home was always full: with aristocrats and aspiring aristocrats, with merchants and gentry, with guests from the Church, university, and Lima's artistic circles. Descriptions of Pérez's famous gatherings, or "juntas," help us imagine how his home became one of the viceroyalty's most prestigious salons. By Pérez's account, several hundred people were in and out every day, and although many were there for business, others were there to take part in his salon's vibrant intellectual life. Witnesses, like Pérez's brother-in-law, Luis de Vega, testified about the great debates that would take place there, debates about the theological world—the Incarnation and the Holy Trinity—as well as the natural one—the sun, chaos, and the hemisphere.[81] As a result of one encounter, Jusep de Paz, the brother of a Jesuit priest, wrote a small treatise on the sun's magnitude, which he dedicated to his host, Manuel Bautista Pérez.[82] Pérez, in turn, vigorously defended these intellectual gatherings, denying they had anything to do with Judaizing heresies.[83]

Pérez was also proud of another sign of elite standing, his library, which, according to his antagonists, housed the books needed to support Jewish rituals and beliefs. According to the inventory taken after his arrest, Pérez's library contained a wide range of books: from accounting manuals and commercial guides to grammars, dictionaries (one was Latin-Italian-French-Spanish), and spelling primers; from the classics (including Pliny, Cicero, and Seneca) to contemporary literature (Lope de Vega and Cervantes); and from Catholic religious texts to Pérez's favorite subject, history—including biographies of Seneca and Santa Teresa, chronicles of Portuguese, Gothic, and Spanish kings, studies of Flanders, Africa and Asia, of Lima and Guatemala, and of the world. There were no heretical texts.[84]

In addition to hosting lavish gatherings, Manuel Bautista Pérez's aristocratic demeanor was accented by the finery he wore—including, no doubt, velvets, silks, brocade, and silver-plated sword. Wardrobe, however, could be a delicate subject in the Viceroyalty of Peru. After all, what you wore was supposed to say much about who you—inherently—were. But in

Peru, where new social selves were in the making and social boundaries were more easily trespassed, clothing, in some eyes, epitomized everything that was wrong in colonial society. Just as inquisitors were to complain about Spanish women wearing Indian clothes, they were equally perturbed by the spectacle of pseudoaristocrats wearing elite garb, especially if they had tainted blood.

For certain metropolitans, the commercial enterprise of colonialism, where suspect Portuguese played such visible roles, was a troubling project.[85] According to royal decree, aristocratic privilege was withdrawn from anyone punished for Judaizing, and it was a penalty that extended over generations. Inquisitors were outraged that condemned Jews, as well as their children—infected as they were—could enjoy the finery of elite society. And Inquisitors were equally affronted, or even more so, when they discovered "Judaizers," only recently penanced, brandishing the trappings of nobility. Francisco de Vitoria Barahona, sentenced in 1625 for Judaizing, was again punished in 1631 when he was caught with a "gold-plated sword and dagger at his belt, wearing silk and riding a horse."[86]

What Is a Spaniard?

Yet some Spanish metropolitans, like Peru's inquisitors, harbored a broader, if not as precise, exasperation. We have listened to their misgivings about indios, negros, women, and "Judaizers"; and, indeed, most cultural finger-pointing was directed at these "problems." But another gnawing concern volleyed with these more prominent suspicions: Spaniards were not behaving like Spaniards, or at least as Spaniards should. Inquisitors and other observers of the viceroyalty noted that Peru simply encouraged "greed," and Spaniards were not immune to its appeal.[87]

But greed is never simple; and what Mañozco, Gaytán, and company decried, what they saw as the perfidious influence of Judaism, was embedded in the social relations of colonialism itself, in the social relations of the modern world. Colonialism didn't just provide fresh opportunities for moneymaking; it did so in ways constrained and encouraged by the novel forms of living born out of Europe's state-making and colonizing ventures. The terms of colonialism, the forms of social intercourse structuring it, incited all Spaniards, regardless of social standing, to understand themselves as having the inherent right to dominate colonialism's subordinate peoples; in the process, they jettisoned the traditional hierarchies that had stratified them as Spaniards in Europe. Church and secular authorities were aghast at the arrogance of Spanish immigrants, who were notorious for believing that "when they come to these lands, all [Spaniards] can be equal and noblemen."[88] In the words of another metropolitan, "Once they have crossed the sea, they think the most despicable Spaniard is like the noblest *caballero*, and all come decorated with the belief that they will be served by Indians."[89] Or, as our anonymous Portuguese chronicler wrote of Peruvian criollos: "[T]hey do not like to work very much, they are very vain when it comes to questions of nobility. . . . [T]here isn't one, no matter how poor he might be, who does not have a silver piece and a slave in his service."[90] Or, again, as the treasurer of the Potosí mines wrote to the king:

> Things in these kingdoms, Your Majesty, are different from what reason understands they should be. . . . [W]e are amazed . . . and we have to consider and make sense of the fidelity [i.e., the loyalty of servant to master] shown by Castilians in Castile, and the pride and insolence they have in Peru; the humility of workers in Spain and their haughtiness and pride in these kingdoms; the humble and mundane thoughts that many have in [Spain] and the elevated and exalted desires they have here. . . . [A]nd should they return . . . , they want to be no less than the richest and best of their village and, if not, [they want to] be the lord of an estate.[91]

Colonial relations, facilitated by merchant capitalism's untold wealth and promise, had turned the Peruvian Spaniard into an upside-down version of his European cousin. Peru's inquisitors distrusted the viceroyalty's new kind of wealth or, better said, the colonial relations that gave it such prominence. So they wrote to Madrid about the viceroyalty's stricture-free atmosphere, about the "libertad" in which Portuguese/Jewish/New Christian merchants took shelter.[92] They also described an ugly world being born, where self-interest reigned, where money was the goal of life, and where, as a result, the "Jewish perfidy" made inroads not only among those new to Christianity, but among Old Christians as well: "like a weed, it would strangle the new Christianity [of indios and negros]; and inflict great outrage on the Old, because in these parts the ultimate aim of those living here . . . is self-interest, not anything else . . . and that is what they all aspire to . . . and they believe one is a man only to the degree to which he knows how to acquire goods."[93]

Lima's inquisitors—Mañozca, Gaytán, and company—writing of their concerns about the colonial world around them, harbored one view of what "Spaniard" should be, a vision rooted in a Europe of the century past and in a racialized colonial culture. The sea change in social relations and possibilities produced by colonialism tinted "the Jew" with the pollutants, the dangers, of the emerging modern world. Lima's New Christian/Portuguese merchants—with their global networks and mercantile (as opposed to landed) wealth, their neoaristocratic lifestyles, and their presumed special ties with the colony's feared, yet needed, subordinates— were beacons of peril. But some perils, like the ambiguous category español, were indispensable in these evolving modern times.

Manuel Bautista Pérez, Luis de Valencia, and Doña Mencia de Luna vaunted a different "Spaniard"—one that entitled merchants and aristocrats in equal manner; one that, within the borders of Spanishness, credited accomplishment along with ancestry. And it is tempting to think of Doña Mencia, Manuel Bautista Pérez, and Manuel Henríquez as harbingers of a new kind of elite, an elite whose interests and imaginations were founded in the rhythms of the new world, of the modern colony-driven world.

THE INCA'S WITCHES

Christian Blacks.
From Felipe Guaman Poma de Ayala,
El primer nueva corónica y buen gobierno (1613?).

Coca kintucha, hoja redonda, coca kintucha hoja redonda
¿por que delito padesco tanto?

O my perfect coca leaf, round leaf, O my perfect coca leaf, round leaf,
What have I done to suffer so?—TRADITIONAL QUECHUA SONG

MAGISTRATES PURSUING THE Great Jewish Conspiracy were appalled by another failing running deep in the viceregal character: its attraction to Indian things.[1] Creoles, they discovered, were fascinated by native ways—an attraction especially dangerous because of its consequence for women. For witches, by and large, were women, or so inquisators presumed, and native lore, native cures, and native herbs were becoming increasingly prominent in their repertoire.[2] In tribunal eyes, "witches" had joined hidden Jews as culprits in the subversion of Peru's moral fabric and political stability.

A novel edict of faith posted on church doors during Lent in 1629 tells much of the story. Following inquisitorial tradition, this edict—a statement of the heresies and immoral habits that Catholics were obliged to report to the Holy Office—was read in Peru's churches and publicly displayed on church doors. The Peruvian version, however, was different in one respect from every other edict read in any church throughout the Spanish empire. Like the others, it contained the standard warnings about hidden Jews, Muslims, Protestants, bigamists, fornicators, and priests soliciting sexual favors. But the Peruvian edict also had this warning, directed to the particular problem of

weak women, given to superstitions . . . who do not doubt . . . their adoration of the devil. . . . [T]hey invoke and adore him . . . and wait for images . . . of what they want [to know], for which the aforesaid women . . . go to the countryside and . . . drink certain potions of herbs and roots, called *achuma* and *chamico*, and *coca*, with which they deceive and stupefy the senses, and the illusions and fantastic representations that they have they judge and proclaim afterwards to be revelations or to be a sure sign of what will happen in the future.[3]

This preoccupation with the dangers of witchcraft, however, was highly unusual in the Spanish realm. In the eyes of most historians, the Spanish Inquisition tended to minimize the perils of witchcraft, not emphasize them. What stands out in this edict, as well as in letters of concern sent to Madrid, is the inquisitors' anxiety over the allure of Indian customs, Indian dress, Indian remedies, even Indian language, for women who were not Indian.[4]

How to make sense out of both the bewitchment of Indian customs and the inquisitor's chagrin? One way would be to place both in the broader swirl of Spain's imperial and state-making designs.[5] This focus is not, of course, the only way to look at the trials or even, perhaps, the best way, but it is an illuminating one. Keeping to the path already charted, we will explore the Peruvian witches' brew as an element in the cultural wrangles of Spanish colonial rule.

Tagging witches, like tagging hidden Jews, was part of the Inquisition's efforts to assign cultural blame, and the cases against accused witches give us the broad strokes of a tableau of social fear. But they also provide a window into the subtler domains of the colony's cultural arguments and tell us something about the unintended consequences of Spain's cultural work. Witches' testimonies reveal much about the vagaries, the seesawing, of hegemony-building. For even as some testimonies expose the failures of imperial teachings, they also show the tenacious hold that colonial categories of humanness exerted on Spain's Peruvian subjects. Yes, colonial witches who saw power in Indian herbs and Indian mountains, and even, as we shall see, in the vanquished Inca, might have been arguing, in their way, about the legitimacy of Spanish rule, about its limits and impossibilities. Even so, their political critique was built on a scaffold of colonial ideology: the racialized categories of colonial rule framed their understandings of the world, of nature, and of the inhabitants of viceregal Peru. The witches' illegal, if rich, montage of cultural makings was part of an appraisal that drew its force—and inspired fear—precisely because of colonialism's contradictions and pervasive cultural designs.[6]

We know about witchcraft accusations through trial testimonies; but we do not know, with anything approaching certainty, what these women actually did in their life to merit the charges. The inquisitors imposed their definition of witchcraft on testimony that could have been coerced or fantasized, and these depositions, like those made by supposed Judaizers, must be examined with great analytical care. Nonetheless, I still believe we can—albeit in a limited and provisional way—unravel some of their mysteries. Although the question "Were these women witches" doesn't make much analytical sense, I think we can talk sense about some of the language of witchcraft and its transformations—in large part because the discourse is so varied, so exceptional, and so outside the stereotype. (Where else do we find Inca sorcery?) Our story, moreover, was developing over decades and over a broad region—spanning more than one set of inquisitors, one set of local commissioners, or one cabal of women. Let's delve now into a curious cultural history that, over the course of seven decades (1590s through the 1660s), saw colonial subjects who did not fit the moral imperatives of their race: non-Indian, coca-chewing, mountain-worshiping, Inca-loving "witches."

Witch Hunts: The Early Years

The seventeenth-century Church embraced a flock who believed in the magical nature of the world; it also, as part of its Counterreformation efforts, strove to eradicate some of these notions—now defined as heretical. When Spanish inquisitors came to Peru, they sought out evidence of these superstitions and fables, many associated with witchcraft, and the edict of faith is a good source for what they expected to find:

[I]n order to know and divine the future or unknown things from the past . . . they practice the art of Necromancy, Geomancy, Hydromancy . . . using spells, sorcery, witchcraft . . . invoking demons, having an express or, at the minimum, a tacit pact with them . . . in order to find stolen goods . . . discover places where there are hidden treasures . . . and predict . . . the people and merchandise arriving on [the armadas] . . . and they declare [this] by reading palms . . . and dreams . . . and they throw lots with beans, wheat, and corn . . . mixing sacred things with the profane: like the Gospels, [prayers], altar stone, [and] Holy Water . . . with magnetic rocks, hair, . . . powders and other similar charms . . . understanding that with them . . . they will have good fortune in battles . . . and in business dealings and . . . in bringing together men with women and women with the men they desire. . . . [A]nd for these and similar effects, they say certain meaningless and superstitious orations, invoking God, or Our Lord, or the Holy Virgin . . . mixed with other indecent and disrespectful invocations.[7]

This litany of spells, bewitchments, pacts, and prognostications would have sounded familiar to inquisitors from anywhere in the empire, and Peru's witchcraft trials are full of charges that could have been taken right from this list. In the tribunal's earlier years (the 1590s), witches were accused of the same unholy practices as their peninsular sisters; however, unlike them, Peru's accused witches came from a host of backgrounds that reflected their New World homes. Some were españolas, either born on the Continent or in the swelling American cities of Lima or Potosí; others were mestizas, with Indian mothers; others were mulatas whose mothers came from Africa. Although a few were married and some had aristocratic pretensions, most were single, widowed, had husbands only on paper, and were involved in unconventional (but not uncommon) arrangements with lovers, or "galanes."[8] We know these things about their ancestry, love life, and occupation because even the early records were attentive to race, ancestry, and marital standing.

Inquisitors noticed that Lima's witches were especially fond of "mixing sacred things with the profane." They would conjure charms reciting the Lord's Prayer, the Ave Maria, or the credo; they would cast spells making appeals to Saint Martha, the Holy Trinity, or Saint Erasmus. And in a similar vein, they would steal the Church's sacred accouterments to use in their sacrilegious endeavors, placing special store in items from Catholic ritual such as ara (scrapings of altar stone), holy water, and chrism (the consecrated oil used in baptism, confirmation, and ordination). Thus, "sacred things" could be made into powders, mixed with beverages, and given to fickle men to make their hearts true—or compounded for other, similarly profane, ends.[9]

In this early period, some of the accused flirted with more dangerous sources, turning to the imputed "powers" of Catholic Iberia's first enemies within. In the 1590s, Jewish symbols and morisca insights were not uncommon ingredients in devilish brews, where they joined a myriad of saints, sacred relics, stars, and items from nature.[10] Ten accused women from the "Potosí conspiracy," residing in Bolivia and in Cuzco at the time of their arrest, were led by a Sevillan, Doña Francisca Maldonado, in a series of chants in which Jewish themes did—but not always—appear. They included the "Prayer and Incantation to Santa Marta" (Our lady Saint Martha, . . . loved by the queen of the angels . . . with the sea and the sand and the sky and the stars and the Eucharist from the altar, and the Holy Trinity . . .); the "Incantation to Saint Erasmus" (. . . with the moon and with the sun, with the Mountains of Zion, with the seven tribes of Israel, . . . with the seven Missals, with the seven Easter candles, with the chrism); and the "Incantation of the Lights" (. . . with the Holy Trinity,

. . . with the sacred Eucharist . . . and with the altar stone, and with the priest . . . and with the Tablets of Moses).[11]

One member of the Potosí conspiracy (cited as Witness no. 3), taught by the mestiza Francisca Despinosa, told the inquisitors she was disturbed by the references to Jewish things:[12] "since the Tablets of Moses and Israel are named in this incantation, the witness told [Despinosa] that it could not be a very good thing."[13] But Francisca Despinosa held the opposite view: "[I]ndeed it was [a good thing] . . . since it was said with the faith of God."[14] All of these women claimed innocence and ignorance; or, in the case of Doña Francisca Maldonado: "[W]hen she said [these prayers] she didn't know they were evil" and, when she found out the contrary, she "went right away to the bishop of Potosí and denounced herself."[15] I believe her and I believe the others. None of them had any intention of blaspheming the Church; for these women thought they had "the faith of God" behind them—even if they invoked the "Mountains of Zion," the "seven tribes of Israel," or the "Tablets of Moses." It was the Church that made them blasphemous.

Living in the colonies opened up a Pandora's box of knowledge—herbal cures, divining tricks, and potions for love and power—rooted in the wisdom of three continents. The same women who were accused of conjuring with the Tablets of Moses and the tribes of Israel were also experimenting with indigenous lore, using it as a complement to their own traditions. Doña María de Aguilar, a well-heeled mestiza from Cochabamba, married to Potosí's chief fiscal agent, was condemned on two "Indian-related" counts. She was said to "speak in Indian" with some of her cohorts; and, more damaging, she was charged with actively seeking native "hechiceras" to assist in "sorcery" sessions.[16] Francisca Gómez, mestiza, married to a Spaniard, and not part of the Potosí conspiracy, was also rumored to be lured by Indian doings. In fact, her attachment to native religious life was what got her in trouble. Two Cuzqueñans denounced her to the tribunal for running off to join native pilgrimages for the purpose of learning "Indian witchcraft."[17] By the mid-1590s, seeking out the knowledge of Indian women was a suspicious act. It was the "Indianness" that was so disquieting, as inquisitors (along with their objects of investigation) found themselves increasingly drawn to the dangers of native wisdom.[18]

More Indian Brews and the Infamous Tapadas

Ana de Castaneda, "the color of a quarter *mulata*," appeared twice before the inquisitors: once in Cartagena in 1592 and again in Lima twenty years later. Her case is fascinating on two counts: we find out that over the course of those twenty years, she, like other "witches," was incorporating more and more indigenous lore into her repertoire; also, we get to meet her renowned clients, the *tapadas*, Lima's infamous veiled ladies, whose reputation must have contributed to the tribunal's distrust of witches.

At her first arrest, in Cartagena, Ana de Castaneda was penanced for "invoking demons and for mixing the sacred with the profane."[19] These charges followed Ana to Lima when, two decades later, she faced several more accusations: invoking demons, saints, and God for magical ends; mixing potions to make men love women (including "a priest whom she made leave his parish and go around crazy [with desire]");[20] and using a covered glass filled with water to read the future (whether a pregnant *"doncella"* would end up marrying the father of the baby, whether a distraught woman's husband would be arriving on the flotilla from Panama, and whether a young woman would remain single).[21]

As you might gather, Ana de Castaneda's special skills were in the arena of love.[22] She was taught several love cures by indigenous women, and the native seed called *palla palla* was one that Castaneda was especially fond of. "Palla" is the Quechua word for noblewoman, and "palla palla" means double strength in Quechua syntax. This antidote had a prized place in colonial Andean gender wars: it was said to have singular abilities to calm down angry husbands and stop them from beating their wives.[23]

Ana de Castaneda's talents attracted an extensive following, and women "of all social conditions and ranks," the inquisitors noted, would seek her out for a variety of love cures.[24] Who were these women? Why were their diverse backgrounds—cutting across Peru's social and cultural ladders— of such intense interest to the tribunal? And, in any case, how could a society whose "ideal" woman stayed behind closed doors have produced such a substantial number able to freely walk city streets and freely consult a "witch" under suspicion? Witnesses identified these women as "atapadas" (= *tapadas*, or "covered," "veiled"),[25] women who would, without apparent shame or concern, promenade around the city, go to its public plazas, or flirt from balconies—masked by very carefully and seductively draped veils. Lima's tapadas were notorious and, according to one historian, "were so visible and ubiquitous that they became, in the popular imagination, symbols and prototypes of women's life in colonial Peru."[26] Their lifestyle, shall we call it, entered the public record in several venues; they were the object of royal denunciations, they were censured by the Church, and they were serenaded in poetry.[27]

Martín del Barco Centenera, in 1602, wrote an epic poem about South America's wonders and peculiarities and, when he came to the theme of colonial Lima, he praised the tapadas as examples of both. Taken by the duality of their existence—scorned by authorities, yet a vital presence in the city—Barco Centenera wrote about their charming, but untoward, accessibility, as well as about the attempts of the Third Lima Council (convened at the end of the sixteenth century to set directions for the Catholic faith) to condemn them.[28] Not surprisingly, the council was concerned that tapadas, able to traverse the city incognito, were enjoying improper liberty, promoting public scandal, and "distract[ing] people from the cult of God." So they ordered that "no women should walk the street or be seen at their windows with their face covered."[29] The viceroyalty's bishops were trying to stem a tide, for they felt that the tapada's ranks had actually grown since Viceroy Francisco de Toledo called attention to them a decade and a half earlier. With this, the council initiated a pattern that was to repeat itself over three centuries: authorities would make pronouncements, and women would keep on wearing veils.

Peru's viceroys fared no better than the bishops. The Marquis Guadalcázar published an edict in 1624, "The Decree of the Tapadas," in another attempt to bring some propriety to Limeñan customs. The Decree reads nearly like the Lima council's, "probibit[ing] women regardless of status, quality, or rank from wearing veils in the streets, or on Lima's public promenades." The royal authority's concern targeted the veil's ability to obscure the markings of social standing so crucial to colonial order: "rather [the tapadas] should all reveal their faces so that they can be seen and recognized and esteemed and held for who they are."[30] Punishments were stiff, and varied according to the offender's status, but the bans were rarely enforced. During the seventeenth century the viceroys continued their attack on the immorality—the potential for social disorder—that tapadas seemed to encourage. In 1634 civic authorities actually placed some tapadas under arrest; nevertheless, three years later, another ban on veils was proclaimed, suggesting yet again the hollowness of royal edicts.[31]

Tapadas found themselves to be the object of bans in Spain as well as in Lima, for as scramblers of social hierarchy and, in their way, protestors of ruling politics and norms, tapadas were everywhere seen as a potential threat by authorities.[32] It was in the colonial capital, however, where they were perceived to be most dangerous, and the hazards they presented to civilized living seemed to grow (at least symbolically) with the complexity of colonial politics and culture. Ana de Castaneda's tapada accomplices appear repeatedly in colonial witchcraft trials throughout the century.

Even if unable (or, ultimately, unwilling) to stop women from going "tapada," secular and religious authorities judged them to be grievously mocking the political, gender, and racial hierarchies at the heart of the colonial enterprise. It should not be surprising, then, that "hechizos" involving tapadas could get blamed for inciting all kinds of political havoc. When the mining center of Potosí was jolted by riots between Spanish nationals (Basques vs. Castilians), Ana de Castaneda was accused of being a ringleader: it was said that she had turned "the whole city upside down . . . with her sorcery, tricks, and lies, and that even the convents of friars and nuns were not safe."[33]

Ana had a different view; she saw herself as deeply religious. When Ana de Castaneda appeared before the tribunal, the notary recorded that "she went about wearing the habit of Saint Francis"—identifying her as a beata, or holy woman, who spent her life in devotions. She also claimed to be "the wife of Fray Diego de Medina, a Dominican monk." (Yes, that's what the trial record says, two times!) And Ana de Castaneda's attorney repeated these declarations when he, unsuccessfully, asked the court for leniency on her behalf.[34] Like Doña Francisca de Maldonado and Francisco Despinosa before her, Ana de Castaneda never believed she had performed an evil act.[35]

More Witches and More Indians

As the decades passed, Indian objects were playing an increasing role in witchcraft paraphernalia, and by the time the 1629 edict of faith was being hung on church doors, their impact was palpable. The number of witches appearing before the tribunal was growing as well, for the edicts prompted women to turn themselves in or to denounce others. Again, witches' special skills addressed the daily stuff of life. Regarding questions of love, for example, they could supposedly foretell if husbands would be coming on the next fleet, if they would arrive married to others,[36] and if they would remain passionate and treat kinswomen well.[37] By now, witches were engaging questions of justice: it was said that they could stop royal officers from carrying out a sentence, or even stop inquisitors from pursuing a case.[38]

Catalina de Baena was one of nearly a dozen women chastised in the years after the edict's first appearance. Born in Jerez de la Frontera, Spain, and living in Potosí, Catalina's was a hybrid lore, drawing on Christian items (special masses, prayers) and on Indian ones (native herbs and poultices). There was another native object on her list, one that must have ratcheted up the perils of Indian "hechizos." Catalina was accused of searching old Indian burials, or guacas, for the bones of *gentiles*—native peoples who, never baptized, had not been touched by the Christian world.[39] Robbing pre-Columbian graves for "hechizos"—this, indeed, was a formidable turn in Andean witchcraft.

In keeping with the cross-ethnic character of Andean witchcraft, Catalina de Baena was guided by two Indians, had a black accomplice, and was schooled by a mulata. In her words, she "went to some *guacas* in the company of an Indian man and woman . . . and brought back a sack full [of bones] . . . and left them in the home of a '*negra*,' Isabel . . . who then told the *mulata*, Francisca, who was supposed to prepare them as she had promised."[40] All who testified against Catalina agreed that she had brought back "bones and the skulls of two bodies" from the Indian burial grounds, around twelve miles away.[41] Two witnesses swore they had seen her cache, which was eventually turned over to Potosí's commissioner.

But the women attending this "coven" were more than grave robbers; they were students of native traditions. One witness testified that "in order to take the bones from the tombs, [Catalina] had put some cloth with gold, chambray, pearls, and taffeta inside the [burials]."[42] This last point was subject to dispute: Catalina de Baena denied leaving an offering like that, but confirmed, regardless, her trek to get native bones.[43] In any case, either Catalina or the witness (an accomplice and client), or both, knew enough about native custom to confess they had left several items of worth behind in a gesture of "ayni," the bedrock Andean principle of reciprocity. No matter who did or said what, *peruanas* were becoming fluent in distinctly Indian ways.

Like the other accused witches, Catalina de Baena denied ever making a pact with the devil, adding that "she didn't know what that was and . . . this thing about pacts seemed like Latin to her."[44] She described saying special prayers in church—like reciting thirty-three "Hail Marys" and thirty-three "Our Fathers" (a gesture still employed for good fortune)—and she confessed to a written conjure found in her possession, but insisted that she would never use Indian bones for maleficent ends. But that's not how witnesses saw it or, better said, how they declared it. They claimed that Catalina had unearthed bones for an evil deed, "to bewitch a woman named Doña Isabel de Mendia"; and, according to several witnesses, "[she] was desperately ill in bed as a result."[45] Regardless of its intended purpose, Indian magic had developed a reputation that was to follow it throughout the century: Indian magic was dangerous magic.[46]

Race thinking framed Peruvian culture, and it showed its hidden ambiguities in Catalina de Baena's witchcraft trial. Over the course of her confessions, Catalina not only declared Francisca, the mulata, to be the region's preeminent witch, but affirmed that it was Francisca who had "ordered her" to bring the Indian bones to Potosí. In the occult realms, Catalina de Baena, an española, a member of the superior caste, could be commandeered by a mulata, Francisca, whose official standing was so inferior that her last name wasn't even recorded by the tribunal. The colonial racial hierarchy cut both ways: it gave dominance to españoles in the realm of official politics, but when it came to the subterranean powers of shamans and witches—a realm, as Frantz Fanon reminded us, of projected fears of the powerful—it put authority in the hands of Peru's subordinates.[47] If we take Catalina at her word, Catalina believed in the magic of Indian bones and in the knowledge of a *mulata hechicera*. Yet, she also believed in Spanish imperial law and in the assumptions about humanity on which it rested. Catalina appealed to the tribunal for leniency on official racial and gender grounds: she was an honorable Old Christian whose "bad companions had made her disgrace her lineage"; at the same time, she was merely a simpleminded woman (as opposed to a rational, complex-minded man) and, albeit "well born," "acted out of necessity and foolishness like the rest of her gender."[48]

The tribunal listened sympathetically to Catalina's pleas, attentive to her standing and sex. Magistrates showed themselves to be rational men as well as men of their culture. They doubted Catalina's reputed powers, holding that "Doña Isabel de Mendia's illness was due to burning fevers and not magical spells," while attributing Catalina's superstitious beliefs to women's inherent weaknesses.[49] And they strictly adhered to a racial rationale when meting out punishments: the inquisitors penanced Catalina de Baena with a four-year exile from Potosí, but never had her suffer the humiliation of public whipping—a discipline regularly assigned to her caste inferiors.

Catalina de Baena would run afoul of Inquisition authorities once again: she was accused of breaking the tribunal's vow of silence by letting one of her slaves give writing material to a fellow inmate. Catalina demurred again to a personal weakness, but of a different kind. She claimed that a renowned witch, a mulata, had severely intimidated her, and that Catalina, the honorable, Old Christian española, had lost all will once in the mulata's powerful sway. The renowned witch was named María Martínez; and, with further testimony, we find out that she and Catalina de Baena knew each other well, having enjoyed a considerable history of conjuring together.

María Martínez, born in Portugal and the daughter of her village priest and Andresa Martínez, from Guinea, had a fierce reputation for straightening out questions of passion and justice. Martínez was *zahori*, "she could see everyone as if they were made of glass, and could see right into people's insides,"[50] and because of her gifts, she was sought after by Spaniards, "doñas", free blacks, and slaves alike.[51] One witness saw many women—"with cloaked faces"—visiting Martínez at night "to do witchcraft business."[52] Even when under tribunal guard and imprisoned in the tribunal cells, María Martínez was able to create a stir. Pedro Bermúdez, the bailiff, said that one night more than fourteen women tried to seek her out, causing such an outcry that even the prisoners began to shout in protest.[53]

The inquisitors took her talents seriously, too, indicting María Martínez with the harshest counts of any brought against an accused witch in Peru: "she believed that the devil was omnipotent, which could be judged as heretical blasphemy; . . . [had] an explicit pact with the devil, more than just invoking him; . . . and is suspected of being the devil's succubus."[54]

María Martínez represented another kind of sorceress making her way into colonial records: the zahori. During this time, as slave labor was becoming increasingly important to the Peruvian workforce, so were the divining gifts of women, and of a few men, forcibly taken to Peru from Africa.[55] Martínez's acute diabolism reflected the revelatory powers ascribed to the viceroyalty's "negros"; it reflected her sexuality as well.

Doña Antonia de Figueroa, a twenty-three-year-old widow and a client of María Martínez, accused Martínez of wanting to "visit because she had fallen in love with her."[56] Doña Antonia elaborated on her accusation, adding that the "prisoner said that she had not [carnally] known a man for over seven years because she had been dealing with the devil."[57] Martínez's sexual activities were never investigated directly by the Inquisition, but the declaration that she had not had sex with a man for years certainly made Martínez vulnerable to two of the most damning charges against her: that she had been the devil's paramour and that she had entered into an explicit pact with the devil, since sex was the way the devil initiated his followers.

Speaking in her own defense, María Martínez denied ever having engaged in heretical acts. Like all of the women interrogated by Inquisition courts, Martínez was very much a participant in orthodox Catholicism. She was, first of all, "a baptized Christian" who regularly went to confession and regularly took communion; she had studied the catechism more than most, had been confirmed, and was very conversant in the fundamentals of the Catholic faith.[58] (Perhaps too well versed: she used to recite the communion words, "corpus meum" in her love prayers.)[59] In jail at the same time as Elí, el Nazareno (Francisco de Silva), María Martínez was so angry at him for deprecating the cross around her neck that she ran to tell the tribunal.[60]

Nonetheless, Martínez's zahori skills were not sufficient (either by her lights or by the reigning discourse pairing witchcraft abilities and race) to effect the darkest of hechizos. For this she needed Indian lore, considered the most dangerous and the most deadly of all. Even Martínez admitted she had tried, through a native intermediary, to track down an "indio hechicero" in order to kill a man who had testified against her.[61] In the end, María Martínez decided not to pursue her vendetta. But the courts dealt with Martínez harshly, parading her through the streets, whipping her 200 times and then exiling her from her New World home for ten years.

The arrest and punishment of these suspects—following the 1629 edicts directing attention to women and their use of Indian "hechizos" that were first posted on church doors—was an attempt to stop the "plague of women" that seemed so threatening to colonial order.[62] Indian herbs like coca and palla, Indian "bones" and "gentile" burials, even Indian "witches" (and some zahori) continued to mark colonial witchcraft in the years to follow.[63] So did the contradictory tangle of colonial relationships, which, on the one hand, would bring together women from a variety of ranks and races for collective healing and divining and, on the other, would mark divisions between them grounded in both the official and in the magical powers of race.

By midcentury, trials against non-Indians accused of witchcraft—whether Spanish, mulata, mestiza, or negra, free or slave—show a remarkable turn in "Indianness." Coca was becoming the centerpiece of witches' collective rites, but paired with a new group of notables from the colonial "hechizo" repertoire. Now we find the Inca, and sometimes the Coya, or Inca queen, hobnobbing with saints and singing credos. As often as not, they appear in tandem with a set of special "diablos"—the devils representing colonial "offices" or "professions."[64]

Cuzco royalty first appear in the trial of Ana María de Contreras, penanced by the Inquisition in the Gran Auto of 1639 and brought up again on charges, seven years later.[65] The mulata slave explained that the great numbers of women who sought her out, lavishing money and food, pushed her to return to old "deceits and tricks." Ana María's "deceits and tricks" included "having worshiped the mountain peaks and rocks in memory and signification of the Inca and his wife."[66] Mountain peaks and rocks were the soul of the native sacred landscape and the scourge of priests sent to extirpate Indian idolatries in the countryside. However, outside Cuzco, they rarely embodied the Inca or his wife, but stood for local and regional divinities. Ana María's Inca of the mountains was a seventeenth-century creation, giving voice not to a pre-Columbian but to a nascent, colonial version of the meaning of peaks and rocks.

In 1655, one of the charges against Doña María de Córdoba, a Limeñan since birth, was that she envisioned a magnificent Inca during sorcery periods; another was that she invoked several "professional" diablos, tied to markets and commerce; and another was that she used coca in the process. The daughter of a viceroy (the Marqués de Guadalcázar) and Doña Inéz de Córdoba (or so it was said; it was also rumored that her father was an eminent clergyman) and the mother (according to hearsay) of the current viceroy's child, Doña María appeared to be on firmer financial footing than most of the other accused witches. Doña María de Córdoba, the owner of much finery, including a coach, was found chewing coca with another woman at the time of her arrest, and the inquisitors ended up arresting both. Seven women and one man (four eyewitnesses and four hearsay) testified about her healing and divining sessions, which were always conducted in groups, with several friends, "maestras" (teachers or mentors), and relatives of the person to be healed. The readings were built around images made from wads of coca leaf, spit into a porcelain bowl that was filled with wine.[67]

Several figures were said to appear in Doña María's porcelain bowl, and the two that are of interest to us are the Inca and that company of devils. Although she denied ever praying to "the devil" or even seeing his figure in the porcelain bowl,[68] Doña María did admit (later revoked and then reaffirmed) chanting to a set of colonial "diablos," specialists in commerce and officialdom.[69] Like the Inca conjured along with them ("dressed in Indian clothing with a star in his forehead")[70] this cohort cut rather "stately," elite figures. But while the Inca was regal, the devils were tied to colonial trade, colonial markets, and colonial bureaucracies: "[W]ith this I entreat you . . . the fish market's *diablo*, the shopkeepers' *diablo*, the notary publics' *diablo*, and with those who trick the lawyers."[71] To encourage these figures to materialize, Doña María would chew coca leaf and chant songs like: "Coca, my mother, please do this, what I ask you to do, for the faith I have in you, for the one who sows your seed, for the one who cultivates you, for all who worship [idolatrize] you, for the Inca, for the Colla [Coya], for the sun and the moon that illuminated you in the earth where you were sown, and for the water with which you were irrigated."[72]

There is a curious ideological debut to be found in the depositions against Doña María de Córdoba. Several witnesses accused her of "taking down the cross over her bed" and putting it "face down in a box" whenever she started her coca sessions.[73] The ecclesiastic establishment always considered witches to be enemies, but this is the first time, in these records at any rate, when accused witches were said to perform a certain kind of anti-Christian ritual—removing the images of saints or turning holy images upside down—before the dark arts could be employed.[74] Hidden Jews were often said to do the same thing.

Befitting someone of renowned ancestry, Doña María de Córdoba was spared public shaming. Although the sentence was never carried out, she was supposed to receive 100 lashings, executed within the Inquisition's walls. The magistrates pronounced this unusually harsh sentence because Doña María had been caught doing other forbidden acts. To the inquisitors' chagrin, she seemed to have free run of the prison, unlocking cell doors, talking openly with prison mates, communicating to the outside, even managing to conduct a love affair with Rodrigo Dandrade, a supposed Judaizer.

Doña María de Córdoba was chewing coca with Doña Luisa de Vargas when the tribunal's bailiff knocked on her door. Doña Luisa, punished by secular authorities and then released by the Inquisition on grounds of double jeopardy, was the witch known by several, racially derived names. She was called both Doña Luisa "la cuarterona" and Luisa Blanca (white),[75] and the confusions in Vargas's aliases were reflected in the formal genealogy she presented to the tribunal. At her first hearing, Doña Luisa de Vargas claimed parents both "Old Christian and noble";[76] but when arrested again, ten years later, she was classed as a "cuarterona de mulata."[77] Like her sometime accomplice, Doña Luisa was expert in love matters: a specialist in "domesticating" (*amansar*) men, and occasionally in domesticating women—she was the preferred sorcerer of one of Lima's magistrates.[78] Doña Luisa, also schooled in more political conjures, was the witch who gave moral support to a friend about to appear before the inquisitors. "[H]ave womanly valor (*valor de muger*)," she told her *comadre*, and then she "taught her a special charm against inquisitors to give her strength to face the judges when called in front of the tribunal."[79]

Doña Luisa used a variety of ingredients in her ceremonies to fix love lives or to facilitate justice, including wine and the holy water from three churches and special "unguents for the shameful parts (*partes vergonzosas*),"[80] but at the core of this white/quadroon's recipes were Indian herbs, Indian drinks, and Indian chants. Coca was the centerpiece, chewed for its effects, for its secrets, and for its uncanny way of bringing together the ritual players; but other items, like *chicha* (Andean corn beer), palla palla, tobacco, and guinea pig were also part of Doña Luisa's mending kit.[81] Like so many of the accused, Doña Luisa intoned the common orations to Saint Martha and "would talk as if she were praying"; however, her sacred language was inspired by Quechua, with chants often "spoke[n] in the Indian language."[82]

How did Doña Luisa find out about these orations, plants, and cures? Doña Luisa told how she first learned about certain herbs and ointments for love magic from "una negra," about other plants from indios, about "*coca* and the drink Indians call '*chicha*' from a *negra*," and sacred altar stone from a *mulato* sacristan.[83] In turn, Doña Luisa would teach her knowledge to others. Sometimes she would even write out prayers and send them to acolytes—to the inquisitors' great surprise, since she claimed to be illiterate.[84] And Doña Luisa, like most of the accused, boasted a clientele as diverse as her teachers.

While coca was her principal conjuring instrument, the Inca was her principal object. Doña Luisa, at least according to the testimony of twenty-four witnesses, would appeal to several figures, but it was the Inca whom she ultimately implored to intervene in life's destinies. ("and blowing some tobacco smoke into the porcelain, and calling . . . the Inca (Inga), saying strength and vigor I give you, my Inca, so you reveal the future and the truth").[85] Doña Luisa called the Inca, "with all his vassals," sure that the Inca, the former Indian king, possessed all the power and authority that was royalty's due.[86]

The Inca, the Indian king ("el rei indio"), was also "el rei gentil," the pagan king, the king of Andeans before the Spanish conquest and the advent of Christianity.[87] The *rey gentil* had never been baptized; and Peru's clerics, very controversially, decided the Incas and their kin were fated for an eternity in hell. Doña Luisa and her colleagues, on the other hand, did not condemn the Inca; rather, they believed the Inca possessed special powers precisely because of his pagan state.

To Church consternation, Doña Luisa's ideological universe also gave her the authority to baptize others, to bring the Inca into her known, civilized world: "O my Inca, o my father, I baptize you with this wine, in exchange for the chrism and the water that you never had. . . . I drink to you and I call for your help and I call for your vassals' help." Continuing the chant, Doña Luisa appealed to a particular Inca: "and I ask for you, Don Melchor."[88] Don Melchor Carlos Inca, was the last known direct descendant in the male line of an Inca king.[89] Don Melchor has virtually disappeared from current writings on Andean colonial history; however, in the seventeenth century, the "last Inca king" was imbued by some—by non-Indian "witches" and by native Calchaquis (see below)—with a vital, even supernatural mystique. I doubt viceregal authorities were as sanguine, for calling on a known member of the Inca royalty must have seemed close to sedition.

Coca took on powers in these witches' hands that it did not have in indigenous ones. Coca was (and is) used for divining and curing in the indigenous Andes, but not in the life-altering ways described here. With a foot now in European and African traditions, coca was transformed into an instrument of *colonial* sorcery. Colonial authorities responded in kind, converting coca chewing, with no known addictive properties, into a "vice" or kind of depravity: "women who chew *coca* do not pray, do not commend themselves to God, do not say 'good day' to one another. . . . [T]hey do not cook, or clean, and sell everything they have in order to buy *coca*":[90] or as one inquisitor succinctly put it, *coca* was "the herb that should be banned."[91] Notwithstanding tribunal opinion, a growing sector of Peruvian non-Indians perceived coca as the key to a merging Indian/Inca domain, a domain constructed with colonial borders and infused with the magical powers that colonizers themselves had foisted on native experience.

From the late 1650s age of Doña Luisa Vargas and Doña María de Córdoba, and for decades to follow, a masterful Inca, beseeched by coca, dominated the so-called witches' rites. Their rituals continued the patterns set before: they were carried out in groups, were attended and overseen by women from all of Lima's social classes, and were peppered with Indian language, herbs, techniques, and consultants. One oration was attributed to María de Castro Barreto y Navarrete; described as being "color de samba," she was the daughter of a mestizo and a female slave of General Don Sebastián de Navarrete. In that oration, even the major deputies of colonial authority—priests, magistrates, and miners—were depicted as being in thrall to the Mama Coca/Inca queen.[92]

> Mama Coya [Inca queen], Mama Paya, my Lady, my beautiful one, I do not chew you out of vice nor to do harm to anyone, only so you give me good fortune . . . so that just as you are loved and beseeched by everyone, by friars and clergy, royal authorities, missionaries and miners, may I be so loved and esteemed. . . . [A]nd I implore you, Mama Coca, Señora, father, my only life, my only mother.[93]

While María de Castro implored coca and the Inca queen, Doña Inés de Peñailillo—española and, as was rarely the case, the widow of an Indian—beseeched the Inca. By reputation Lima's "master of superstitions,"[94] Doña Inés would beg for his assistance, and the Inca "would appear seated on an embroidered throne, surrounded by servants and vassals." Chewing coca, Doña Inés would also call out, by name, several Andean mountain peaks, including distant Ecuador's "Chumbaraso."[95] Chimborazo, hundreds of miles from Lima, was (and still is) revered by natives living great distances away—like the followers of the Taqui Onqoy, a mid-sixteenth-century millenarian movement.[96] Doña Inés knew her Andean cosmology; she also knew about Peru's race thinking and its official consequences. Doña Inés asked her clients not to tell anyone—and this, she specified, included priests at confession—that a Spanish woman had given them love charms. Since the tribunal did not have jurisdiction over native peoples,

Doña Inés thought she could save her skin if patrons would say their witch had been an Indian, "against whom the Inquisition could not initiate procedures."[97]

Doña Ana Ballejo, alias Doña Ana del Castillo, a Spaniard and a priest's daughter, chanted completely in "the Indian language" and, as a result, inquisitors had to have her orations translated before entering them into the record.[98] It was said that Doña Ana made her clients remove their rosaries before she worked her spells, although Doña Ana claimed she had nothing to do with the devil and that her orations were successful "by virtue of San Nicolás, Santa Marta, San Antón, and the *coca* leaf."[99] Doña Ana, who filled over seventy sheets of paper with stories of her successes, seemed taken by prayers emphasizing the mystique of pagan beliefs, the bewitchment of coca, and the powers of the Inca nobility: "I conjure you with the *palla* and with your ancestors and with the idols whom you believed in, my father, I drink to you with this wine [and] with this *coca* that you used in your sorcery."[100]

Whether seen as an instrument of wizardry, prophesy, or vice, coca chewing was bathed in an aura that was eminently Indian, which is to say, eminently colonial. Indian mystique was steeped in pre-Columbian religion, transformed into an underground, idolatrous force by the Church. It also absorbed the extraordinary powers bestowed by many Peruvians—including royal officials and churchmen—on the Inca king and his progenitors. Women's perceived abilities to threaten and disrupt public order only multiplied when draped in a shawl of Indianness.

Incas and Indianness

There were no "Indians" in the Andes before the Spanish conquest, just different ethnic polities, and none of these, except for the empire-builders from Cuzco, were Incas. Moreover, the Incas, although admired by some, were resented by the many who saw their autonomy compromised by Inca expansion. Yet, coca conjurers, in their rites and chants, limned a coherent and unified people called "Indian," and tied "Indianness" to the figure of the Inca monarch. This ideological union echoed a broader strain in the Andean milieu, one that had the Inca—now sporting "absolutist" garb—personify the keystone of colonial cultural fiction: namely, the Peruvian "Indian."

The Inca inspired ambivalent and contradictory feelings among Peru's non-Indian populations, and throughout the colonial period debates simmered about the nature of the empire and its political legitimacy. The royal position was that the Incas were tyrannical despots and therefore illegitimate rulers—a rather self-serving appraisal that would provide justification for Spain's own imperial enterprise. Opposing it were long-standing arguments that the Incas were utopian exemplars, presiding over an ideal and harmonious Andean kingdom.[101] By granting them unlimited authority, both postures, although ostensibly at loggerheads, shrouded the Incas in a mystique of power that they never possessed when alive.[102]

Fantasies of the Inca's unchecked authority were filled with the mystery and the powers of hellishness. By reigning seventeenth-century Church calculations, all nonbaptized Andeans were destined for hell. Religious authorities, echoing secular findings of Cuzco's despotism, declared the Inca, his family, and his ancestry to be partners in the devil's kingdom. Father Fernando de Avendaño, who we know as one of the century's renowned "extirpators of idolatry," made it clear in his sermons that deviltry and Inca political spuriousness were closely entwined: "Tell me children (*hijos*) . . . How many Inca kings have gone to hell? Everyone. How many Inca queens? All of them. Why?. . . . [B]ecause they worshiped the devil in *guacas*."[103]

Yet, while seventeenth-century colonial authorities believed Inca rule opened doors for the devil, they also perceived Inca rule as a kind of wonder of absolute authority. "Indians worked harder under the Incas than they do now under the Spanish," preached Avendaño, providing a lesson in supposed European benevolence touched with a hint of wishful thinking.[104] Avendaño, who used the Incas as hell-bent examples of idolatry's error, also presented them as powerful rulers, capable of inspiring the love, fear, and respect that were supposed to shape sentiments toward the Catholic spiritual realm.[105] Francisco de Avila mined the same vein, hoping that sermons about Inca power on earth would inspire Indian subjects to show comparable deference to Spanish kings and to the universal Christian God.[106]

Colonials marveled at Inca creations, along with the Inca power over their subjects that must have accompanied them. Take the impressions of our nameless Portuguese crypto-Jew, writing from Holland about his Andean travels: "[The Incas] were the most feared and respected and well served by their vassals of any we know about in the world." And as the most potent monarchs in human history, the Incas oversaw projects of a magnitude and sophistication unimaginable in Europe. "That's why," the anonymous chronicler judged, "they constructed works that seem *impossible* to mankind" (emphasis mine).[107] Looking with amazement on Inca ruins, Spaniards wondered at the kind of unconditional control over human beings that could have produced these artifacts, which were beyond European (or human) imagination.

Some members of the colonial elite, estate owners and royal authorities, were so dazzled by the Inca mystique that they fashioned themselves as Inca rulers. Guaman Poma de Ayala, the native chronicler and critic of the colonial regime, tells of *encomenderos* (holders of labor grants) who insisted on being carried around in Cuzco-style litters: "the aforesaid *encomenderos* and their wives have themselves transported in litters, as if they were saints in procession. They are received [and feted] with dances . . . and songs. Better said, they order themselves to be carried about like the Inca."[108] Guaman Poma furthered his critique of colonial officials—in particular, their ability to act with impunity—by striking another Inca comparison. This is how he characterized the priests, *corregidores* (magistrates), and lawyers who imposed their will on Indian populations without check. "They have all become 'Incas,'" he said with not a little irony.[109]

The colonial allure of Inca authority, with its promises of power over "natives," prompted one Andalusian gentleman to become an Inca, of sorts.[110] Don Pedro Bohorquez claimed that the Calchaquí Indians, thorns in the Spanish side on the colonial frontier, took him to be their ruler. According to Bohorquez, the Calchaquís believed he was no other than the last Inca king, Don Melchor Carlos Inca.[111] Bohorquez assured the viceroy that the Calchaquís, under his jurisdiction, would be willing to abandon their rebelliousness, to stop harassing Spaniards, to join the Catholic fold, and to embrace the authority of the Crown.

The Crown was willing to accept this unusual turn of events as a short-term modus vivendi. However, the entente collapsed when Bohorquez actually took on the accouterments and presumptions of an Inca king and, in the name of his Indian kingdom, mounted armed challenges to Spanish sovereignty.[112] But there never was an "Inca king of the Calchaquís." Living on the empire's southern border, the Calchaquís were sometimes allies of the Incas but were not colonized by them. So when Bohorquez declared himself king, he was wrapping himself in the colonial "Inca's" ideological force as well as in the universalist concept of Indian to which it was bound.

The ideological union of 'Indianness" and Incas, of native powers and an Indian king had a growing appeal to non-Indians living in Spain's Inca colony. The fantastic control over human beings and access to fortune that a colonial Inca seemed to promise sparked colonial imaginations. Nor can we overlook the gendered dimension of Inca attachments. For although encomenderos, carried in Inca-style litters, were deemed legitimate bearers of a colonial Inca custom, and although the "Inca andaluz" was accepted by colonial officials until he promoted sedition, colonial women, who sang to the Inca and sought out Indian herbs, were branded as witches and decried as a public menace. Even so, whether deemed legitimate or hellish, they all drew on a shared source of Inca allure and on the mystique of Inca power.

During the middle decades of the seventeenth century and in the years to follow—when the strength of Spanish imperial dominion was battered by internal dissension, economic downturns, and foreign challenges—the Inca's powers in love, luck, and government appeared to grow. Listen to Ana María de Ulloa who, while praying to fix the outcome of a civil trial, seemed to capture that sentiment perfectly: "O my *coca*, o my princess, o my Inca, since for you nothing was impossible."[113]

Accomplices and Conspiracies

For the non-Indian world, the apparent omnipotence of the Inca (and of Indianness) was a way to probe and take advantage of the weaknesses of Crown and Church. The vaunted political "stability" of the seventeenth century (the mature colonial state) covered up contradictions gnawing at Spain's colonial endeavor.[114] Bankruptcies and fiscal crises periodically shook seventeenth-century economies, particularly at midcentury.[115] The precipitous and continued decline in Peru's native population, whose labor in mines was crucial for state revenue, posed additional threats to the government's viability. And although colonial churchmen and authorities railed against the abuses suffered by natives, as well as the blatant inequities and skewed morality of fellow clergy, officials, and entrepreneurs, they seemed incapable of implementing meaningful reforms to combat either economic woes or moral delinquency.[116]

Spaniards had political enemies, too. In Spain's worst fears, those enemies were ever threatening to sabotage the colonial enterprise from without and within. We have already talked about the one clear advantage that colonial conditions put in the lap of foreign rivals: the ability to form allegiances with native peoples—whether still to be "pacified" (to use the Spanish term) or disgruntled with colonial rule. Royal energy was spent fighting constant frontier wars—with the Calchaquís, for example—as well as nipping seditious activities by Indians who, by seventeenth-century Spanish estimates, should have been loyal subjects. Foreign entanglements, then, only enhanced the cachet of the native "enemies within." And it is in this regard that public debates over the existence of idolatries and the subversive qualities attached to native religion take on relevance, especially for colonial witches who had turned to Indian heresies.

Native practices, as Doña Inés de Peñalillo reminded her clients, were not subject to the Inquisition's scrutiny.[117] We have already met "idolatry" inspectors, like Avila and Avendaño, who, under diocesan jurisdiction, were sent out to "visit" Indian communities and assess the depths of their pagan beliefs.[118] But in order to get the ecclesiastic and state support needed to mount campaigns equal to the task, colonial missionaries had to first convince potential sponsors that idolatries existed. Peru harbored a long tradition of naysayers, and Jesuit missionaries like Fernando de Avendaño, supported by regulars like Francisco de Avila, lobbied hard to convince colonial authorities of the pervasiveness of both idolatry and its twin heresy, Indian witchcraft.[119] They had even uncovered idolatries in Lima's Indian quarter, and if that was the case, the missionaries argued, wouldn't a civilizing presence be even more imperiled in the hinterlands?[120] Thus, it behooved royal government to support the missionary activities necessary to, in words now familiar, "extirpate . . . discover and remedy so hidden an evil."[121]

Both in clerical tracts and in the ecclesiastic trials in which native heretics were judged, idolatrous behavior was often paired with political dissension, even revolt. It was the idolatrous who tended to leave their state-mandated *reducciones* (settlements) to be closer to their gods;[122] it was the idolatrous who would promote disrespect toward local officials;[123] it was Indians abused and angered by colonial practices who would leave the company of Christians to join the infidels' ranks;[124] and it was the infidels who were fighting the wars of the frontier and exacting such a high price for Spain's colonial venture.[125] Idolatry (like Judaism) breathed sedition.

Idolatry was also twinned with witchcraft, and "extirpators," finding witchcraft in native religious practices, were quick to find native women doing the devil's work, especially at his most perverse.[126] Martín de Murúa, a notorious doctrinero, along with Father José de Acosta, who penned much of the work of the Third Lima Council, understood native women to be the most likely to use the black arts to cause death;[127] and, not surprisingly, extirpators sent to the Lima countryside uncovered plots that linked female sorcery to the death of officials, landowners, as well as amorous rivals.[128] *Indias*, assumed capable of the darkest magic, were accused of wreaking all kinds of havoc in love and in politics.[129] As gender stereotypes were ricocheting, missionaries and inquisitors came to share the opinion that when evil involved women, native and nonnative transgressions were cut from the same cloth. All the more reason for them to see non-Indian women turning to (deadly) Indian habits as a looming menace.

The colony was perceived to be threatened, of course, by another set of internal enemies with a history linked to Indians. Hidden Jews shared much with witches, and not only subversion. Both were specialists in magical arts, both worked in covenlike conspiracies, both directed their venom at Christendom by desecrating Christian icons. The "Indian disease" only magnified the anxieties provoked by Peru's New Christians and by Peru's Old Christians gone native.[130] Taken together, all this pointed to riveting tensions within colonial cultural politics: between "heresies" and legitimate cultural difference; between beliefs and the practices of daily living; between religious orthodoxy, ancestry, and gender; and between official policies that bounded "culture" in racialized boxes and the whirlwinds of colonial experience that belied those policies.

Cultural Branding and Cultural Critiques

Inquisitor anxieties over witchcraft and "Indianness"—posted on Peru's church doors—were concerns about the cultural work of Spanish hegemony. Colonial rule, inscribed in cultural terms and through cultural hierarchies, was threatened by witchcraft ideologies that reached into the political and cultural arenas of empire-building. The imagined threat of colonial witchcraft swelled as it absorbed fears surrounding idolatries, New Christians, women's disorderliness, native subversions, and the allegiances of slaves, foreign enemies, and Indian malcontents.

Colonial witches conjured "hechizos" that firmly placed them in the colonial world of seventeenth-century Peru. With remarkable gifts of cultural improvisation, they addressed the disappointments, failures, and hopes—in affairs of the heart and in issues of justice—of their contrary colonial circumstances. Non-Indians by any official calculus, they were drawn to "heresies" of the Incas and native lore. Yet, in spite of—or along with—heresies that crossed the boundaries of race and social standing, these women were in thrall to the categories of colonial rule. Colonial witches, coupling Inca and coca with "Indian," were making a stereotype of Peruvian "Indianness" (and an ideology of *indigenismo*) that is with us to this day. In like manner, their perception of the social universe was parsed by the very cultural divisions that the colonial state imposed. Doña Ana Ballejo would chant to "the three souls of Calvary, one of a *negro*, the other of an *indio*, the other of an *español*."[131] The colonial universe was conceptualized, even by witches, as a triumvirate of racial cultures.

Colonial witches might have been skeptical of the kind of authority over domestic life that the Church was attempting to establish. Nonetheless, even while dubious about aspects of orthodoxy, women, in their prayers and conjures, never doubted the efficacy of saints, of Catholic symbols or, interestingly, of certain features of state power. Many chanted to the diablos of colonial tradesmen, merchants, notaries, and bureaucrats—figures with the means to fix fortunes of love or to intervene when colonial institutions touched their lives. So, of course, could the Inca, who was increasingly described in a regal, absolutist form.

But while monarchy ruled, even in heresies, Inca monarchs pointed to the limits of colonial authority and to the illusions of colonial rule. At the very least, colonial witches, harboring Inca dreams and praying to Indian ancestors, glimpsed the fiction of cultural boundaries as they reconfigured the possibilities of their past.

And, perhaps, of their future. Andean witches, attempting to intervene in destiny, turned to the colonial Inca: the king of colonial Indians, born in the new America, and, perchance, a harbinger of the Creole age to come.

Becoming Indian

Christian Indians.
From Felipe Guaman Poma de Ayala,
El primer nueva corónica y buen gobierno (1613?).

Now, see, the world is upside down. . . . [W]e are persecuted and
in another time. — LUCÍA SUYO, Indianist minister [1]

IN THE MID-SEVENTEENTH CENTURY, around the time inquisitors
were voicing concerns about witches and Jewish conspiracies, Hernando Hacas Poma was accused by special envoys from the Lima
archbishop of engaging in and fomenting heretical behavior. Hacas Poma,
from the central highlands, was both a member of the native elite and
a local minister of native religion (in missionary words, "a dogmatizing
idolator"). Andean natives were preached one kind of "Indianness" by
priests like Francisco de Avila and Fernando de Avendaño, whose cultural
work was to ensure the viceroyalty had its measure of steadfastly Catholic Indian subjects. But Hernando Hacas Poma preached his own brand of
Indianness and, as Avila knew and recorded in his sermons (see "Globalization and Guinea Pigs," above), it was a version that resoundingly opposed the colonial spiritual (and temporal) establishment.[2] This is the sermonizing that got him in trouble:

> Indians, precisely because [we] are Indians, should worship [our]
> *malquis* [ancestors, lineage] since they are the ones who look out for
> the fertility of fields and the well-being of Indians; and only Spaniards
> should worship God and the painted saints which are in the church,
> since they are the gods of the Spanish.[3]

The fact that Andeans, as subjects of the Inca empire, had experienced
another sort of colony-building will be crucial to Peru's "Indian story."
Harboring a wide range of sentiments toward their former Inca masters
—from devotion to detestation—Andeans, at the time of the Spanish
conquest, reserved their strongest allegiances for their ethnic polities, or

ayllus. The puzzle I want to explore is the following: how some Andeans, after about one century of Spanish rule, began to see themselves (somewhat) as Inca descendants and as "Indians"; or, in other words, how Andeans, who had primarily identified themselves as members of ayllus, began, in addition, to conceive of themselves in the terms of political order imposed by their Spanish colonizers.

First, a caveat. Not all Andeans took up Hacas Poma's dictum and—as we might expect, given the fault lines of ethnicity, rank, region, and locale (urban–rural)—indigenous Peruvians construed an array of religious stands.[4] Some, adoring the Spanish God, contributed to a vibrant Andean Catholicism.[5] But many or most Indians—deliberately and not—seized on both cultural traditions. Within the first decades of colonialism, Andeans took Santiago, the Spanish god of conquest, to be one of their mountain gods, and even the most bitter anti-Christians incorporated Christian elements into their Indianism.[6] Regardless of Avila's ranting, it would be difficult, if not impossible, to estimate how many Indians shared Hacas Poma's vitriol;[7] or how many, of those who didn't share his vitriol, still believed in the spiritual power of the ancestors; or how many believed in Christ *and* in Andean ways. What we do know is that Andean religion had been fastened to Christianity since the beginning of colonialism; and my hunch is that when and where campaigns to extirpate idolatry were virulent, some Indians were seized by their "Indianness" to respond with a virulence of their own.[8]

This chapter turns on the processes intimated by Hacas Poma's pleas and by the extirpators' indictments; that is to say, on the politics of identity-making, on the broad contests over definitions of humanness that were at the heart of the colonial enterprise. After a hundred years, some Andeans, beginning to take "Indian" to heart, found their imaginations haunted by Spanish categories; yet their self-understandings—along with the novel ways of engaging the world that a sense of Indianness inspired—were surely at odds with Spanish designs. We delve here into a piece of Peru's unintended cultural history, when Spaniards tried to make Indians out of Andeans.

Inca Histories

Andean Indianness was a product of Spanish colonialism, yet its meanings were bound to the experiences of a century before. Spanish colonizers arrived on the heels of the great Inca expansion, and Andeans' understanding of European rule, including its eventual expression as a sense of common Indianness, was colored by memories of the Inca past. The Incas consolidated their Andean reign about a hundred years before the conquistadors set foot on Peruvian soil; and Inca dominion, like all attempts at state control, was worn down by conflict as the lords of Cuzco (like the lords of Madrid) demanded concessions in labor, power, and faith.

The Incas created units of "other" as an administrative tool, freezing conquered polities into subordinate ethnic units.[9] Like the Spanish, they used cultural markings to define and order social categories; but unlike them, the Incas legitimated differences in belief and tradition. Although the lords of Cuzco, self-proclaimed descendants of the Sun and Moon, established devotion to the empire's ruling gods throughout the conquered Andes, their strategies of statecraft sanctioned provincial religious beliefs, including ayllu commitments to non-Inca ancestor heroes and heroines. The Inca system of indirect rule reinforced ayllu religious practices, including the complex, overlapping allegiances to gods and to mortals that marked regional faith and politics.

The Incas projected their own "civilizing mission" onto conquered ayllus, combining welfare politics, generosity to underlings, and astonishing environmental engineering. Vaunting a Pax Inca, Cuzco successfully contained internal strife, expanded areas under cultivation, and took on redistributive responsibilities in the face of crop failure or ecological disaster. Within the limits of imperial dictates, the Incas also assumed the norms and practices regulating hierarchical relations within the ayllu—the institutionalized generosity that bound chiefs to provide tools, seeds, and festivities during labor exchanges, denied them any rights over the peasantry's personal production, and required chiefs to sponsor lavish celebrations for communitywide benefit.

Local chiefs became Cuzco's administrators and, in keeping with Andean standards, they were generously rewarded. These curacas were granted special privileges: prizes of women, gold and silver objects, cloth and ceramics of Inca design, even grants of land for their extended family. Although the Incas, in some cases, confirmed prerogatives (like access to labor and land) that probably predated the conquest, many of the privileges were new, setting curacas off not only economically but culturally from their ayllu-mates. The Incas also recognized that these local middlemen might abuse their power and, therefore, in their role as the Andes' supreme benefactors, cast themselves as the defenders of Andean peasants against curaca mistreatment.[10]

The Inca vision of the Andes, one that incorporated Cuzco's dominance as integral to Andean welfare, had mixed receptions. People from Huarochirí, the region where Avila made his name as an idolatry extirpator, portrayed political relations in their origin myths and, no doubt to Cuzco's discomfort, ignored the Incas in many of their narratives: local heroes and heroines, the founders of ayllus and protectors of community welfare, were the principal figures transforming the geopolitical landscape. Huarochirians did present the Inca in some tales, but their accounts were filled with ambiguity. The Inca was both powerful and needy: unable to resolve political dilemmas without the assistance of Huarochirí's heroes—yet, at the same time, the dominator of people and gods, ruler of an empire. The Inca, then, was a force to be tolerated; even with all his bumbling, he could still be a force to reckon with.

Ayllus to the north confirmed an Inca presence of a different nature, one much more powerful and integral to local survival. They claimed, no doubt to Cuzco's delight, that the Incas were their very own ancestors, and that by commingling with local heroes and heroines, the lords of Cuzco were directly responsible for their community's well-being and prosperity.[11]

These histories—versions of political contests in which Incas do not appear, explicit recollections of pacts between Incas and local deities, more subtle encounters between Cuzco and the provinces—etched the collective memory of those people the Spanish called Indians. They formed understandings of subordination, including notions of legitimacy and strategies for living. They also became models against which Andeans could judge contemporary and future pacts with the powerful of Europe.

Intimations of Indianness

The transformation of what had been the Inca empire into a Spanish colony was a decades-long process. The Crown built on both the political hierarchy handed down by the Incas and the political transformations of sixteenth-century Spain to construct the institutional foundations of their colonial state. The Spanish, like the Incas before them, created new social categories of humans—new units of "others"—in the course of institutionalizing their rule.[12] Like the Incas, the Spanish derived their great wealth from institutions that tapped the labor of a colonially fashioned peasantry; like the Incas, they attempted to shape Andean senses of self and position—with varying degrees of success—by expanding an imperial religion. Like their Inca counterparts, Spanish instruments of government built on systems of indirect rule, promoting local elites as mediators in imperial bureaucracies.[13]

However, Spanish colonization—anchored in alien traditions of political economy, political morality, statecraft, and culture—unleashed forces that often proved devastating to Peru's native peoples. Tribute requirements, including labor drafts in Peru's rich mines, contributed mightily to Spain's coffers and, ultimately, to incipient capitalism, but they weighed heavily on peasant shoulders, belying Spain's avowed commitment to the material well-being of its subjects. Spanish religion, a militant Catholicism that expelled nonbelievers from its realms, tried to straitjacket Andean faith with bewildering demands for orthodoxy. Spanish gender norms decried women's participation in Andean public life and denounced their fatal attraction to Satan and heresy.[14]

Last, we find a significant contrast in the very categories of colonial relations: Inca government, elaborating long-standing habits of cultural difference in the Andes, inscribed ayllu or "ethnic" distinctions as units of empire. The practices of Inca state-making were particularist; and Andeans did not conceive their experience under Inca rule as a common one.[15] Spanish practice, on the other hand, building on the experiences of an emerging modern European state, imposed broad, universal classifications on its subjects: the infamous triumvirate of races. All natives of the "New World" were "Indian" subjects of Spain; all Spaniards, regardless of social distinctions, were privileged colonists; slaves, transported from Africa, were "blacks."[16] Spanish legal theory—fusing economic function, "ancestral purity," cultural difference, and political hierarchy—divided its free vassals into two "republics." And this uneasy fusion—stamped in law, economic policy, theology, and stereotype—established conditions of living that made Indianness (and Spanishness) a possibility.[17] Thus a new sense of common experience, interest, and destiny—transcending fault lines of internal privilege and ayllu—became a potential nourishment for Andeans' social selves.

Early hints of such colonial identities appear in the Andes three decades after Spanish rule, when the Taqui Onqoy ("Dancing and Singing Sickness"), a movement of nativist redemption, inspired women and men, curacas and peasants in Peru's central highlands.[18] Signaling both the despair attending European dominion and the hope of being able to abolish it, Andean gods began to take over Andean souls. Those possessed by the dancing sickness blamed the deteriorating condition of their lives (impossible labor demands and high mortality) on themselves and other natives for deserting *guacas* (deities, sacred places) for Christian gods.[19] To right the wrongs of this world, the Taqui Onqoy adherents argued, would require Andean peoples to return to their sacred traditions, to restore the sacred balance between guacas and mortals, and to renounce Christianity and all things Spanish—church attendance, catechism classes, Spanish clothing and food. Guacas might have been defeated by Christian gods once, but now the tables would be turned. And the promised victory would be a total one: Spanish gods, completely routed, would disappear from the Andes and from native life.[20]

Peter Worsley, a scholar of colonial millenarian movements, was struck by their capacity to provoke new loyalties and to mobilize alliances across traditional, often hostile political boundaries.[21] And, as Steve Stern has suggested, the Taqui Onqoy might mark the beginnings of a Pan-Andean consciousness, one that transcended the borders of ayllus and ethnicity.[22] But the Taqui Onqoy adherents were not yet "Indian," at least not quite. For this early nativist ideology refused to envision any Andean future (even an oppositional one) in a Spanish-dominated world. The Taqui On-qoy did not accept—at least in principle—a Spanish presence in the Andes; they would brook no compromise with colonialism (Christian gods would disappear). Nor would they be captured by colonial definitions of their humanness: unlike seventeenth-century nativists, the Taqui Onqoy adherents do not appear to call themselves by any name analogous to "indios," nor, interestingly, do Inca gods—with the exception of Huanacauri—appear in their pantheon.[23]

Nevertheless, even the Taqui Onqoy was steeped in colonial constraints and paradoxes, as its battle cries projected the confrontations of colonial rule onto the heavens. Guacas did not know how to possess souls until they were taught by Christianity. The movement's female champions, organized in Andean fashion into gender-specific religious groups, called themselves the "Sainted Marys." And with all the fears that the movement unleashed, Spaniards found no evidence that its ideological clarion had prompted natives to take up arms.[24] As an ideology of native position and possibility in the colonial world, however, it did set directions of understanding—directions that would be resurrected and transformed during the century to follow.

Becoming "Indian": Social and Political Practices

The Taqui Onqoy was one in a series of challenges to Iberian control that prompted Spanish authorities to tighten their grip on the Andean colonies. Spurred by such concerns, Viceroy Toledo set in motion a series of measures whose goal was to strengthen and consolidate Spain's institutional presence. These reorganizing efforts, initiated toward the end of the sixteenth century, ushered in what many historians have called the "mature colonial state"—that long seventeenth-century period of relative political stability. They also set the stage for the challenge of "Indianism" (my term).

Toledo's reforms, reflecting the growing interests of European absolutism, were an attempt to consolidate state power. The colonial bureaucracy was expanded and its powers increased; its officeholders exercised juridical authority over Indians and oversaw the collection of tribute and the allocation of native labor. As the protector of Indian subjects, the paternalist Spanish state guaranteed the corporate right of Indian communities to land and resources; it also—following Iberian models of municipal government—allowed them considerable autonomy with respect to local concerns.[25]

Spain's attempts to engage native living practices with the machinery of colonial rule were ultimately successful, but it was an achievement that varied dramatically by agenda and region. Plans to forcibly resettle Andeans into compact villages (reducciones) were notorious failures in Hacas Poma's region of the Andes.[26] And Toledo's efforts to remove curacas from ayllu government were met with such determined resistance that he was forced to abandon his plans.[27] Colonial state-building was a protracted compromise. For all its "maturity," the colonial state was not all-powerful; but it was hegemonic.

Spanish political ideologies and practices riddled Indian–Spanish relations with contradictions. Indians were demeaned by colonial institutions, official policy, and popular prejudice. But Spanish political theory paradoxically proclaimed their equality, or near equality: Indians, like Spaniards, were fully human, free vassals of the Crown. The Spanish state also defined Indians as social minors, and state paternalism provided Indians with certain guarantees. Indians were assured corporate rights to land and special court protections; and under Spanish law they could fight their very guardian, the state, concerning abusive labor and tribute demands. Thus, as Indians learned about the regime's benefits, they also became schooled in its weak points.

Catholicism, too, preached conflicting messages. For while they were instructing Indians in the morality of colonial hierarchies, clerics like Avendaño and Avila taught the equality of all mortals—Spaniards and Indians—before God. And while instructing natives in the quasi-holiness of priests, Catholicism also allowed churchgoers to sue abusive priests—as Father Avila was to find out and bewail.[28] The ringing question for natives was this: If Christian gods could protect Indians from an eternity in hell, why couldn't they guarantee Indian welfare in this world, as they seemed to be doing for Spaniards.

Seeing the colonial endeavor threatened by its own excesses, Spanish policymakers, beginning with Toledo, attempted to enforce a rigorous division between the Spanish and Indian republics.[29] Spaniards, however, also feared the cultural challenge that separation might—and did—encourage.[30] In the seventeenth century some Andeans did indeed challenge Spanish authority out of a renewed sense of collective rights and possibility. Working within the colonial frame as it existed, this movement took advantage of the promises of Spanish religion, the paternalistic guarantees of Spanish law, and the inconsistencies of Spanish ideology. It also drew on indigenous traditions. Nativism, following a logic foreshadowed in the Taqui Onqoy, exalted an ethics of native sovereignty and explained Andeans' degrading experiences in religious terms. Moreover, encouraged perhaps by Spanish preaching and by the respect of non-Indian "witches," nativism began to link reconstrued memories of the Inca past to new "Indian" critiques of the colonial present.

Becoming "Indian": Taking the Spanish at Their Categorical Word

"The reason why 'Indians' [are] dying," explained a respected community leader, also condemned as a "witch-dogmatist,"

> [is] because they no longer adore their *malquis* [ancestors] and *guacas* like their elders formerly did, which is why there used to be so many "Indians" who had more fields and clothing and who lived in greater tranquillity. It is because they adore the *guacas* of the Spanish people—nothing more than a few painted and gilded sticks—that "Indians" keep on dying and losing their lands. Spaniards' gods don't give "Indians" anything. "Indians" because we are "Indians" should adore our *guacas* and ancestors.[31]

Indianism verbalized the collective experience of Andean colonized subjects—high mortality, loss of lands, insufficient food or clothing, a harried and insecure existence—as a constant assault on life's fabric. And, as did the Taqui Onqoy, it fingered a continued commitment to Christian beliefs as the culprit. In their collective sinning, Andeans had abandoned their fundamental obligations to guacas; and, reciprocally, the guacas had turned their backs on them. The Spanish gods, governors, and saints had clearly betrayed *their* promise to protect Andeans' welfare.

During the seventeenth century's middle years, Indianism seemed to command a powerful grip on some Andean imaginings. Along with its promise to transcend ethnic borders, Indianism galvanized allegiances across lines of gender and privilege. It appealed to women and men—between whom colonial practices had driven a wedge over the issue of public legitimacy—by challenging colonial gender truths, even turning them upside down. And it called to the curacas and peasants by appealing to a sense of justice, to a long-standing ethic of obligation: to an Andean truth that while allegiances across divides of wealth and power might produce ayllu well-being, they could not be taken for granted.[32] Indianism must have been compelling in these difficult times, but it was also fragile. Competing ideologies and allegiances—to ayllus or curacas, or even to priests—might rip into its strength. Unfortunately, given the limitations of our sources, there is much about the movement that we will never know.

Indianism's language was structured by colonial categories: human beings were "Indians" or "Spaniards" in this imagining of life's prospects. This was a new, race-thinking way for Andeans to envision themselves and their social universe, and they put the new categories into nativism's service, as "Indian" caught some of the spirit of the Church militant and the modern state, spreading out beyond traditional ayllu boundaries. Still, seventeenth-century nativism—perhaps recognizing the limits of Andeans' real life possibilities—did not keep up the uncompromising militance of the century before. Indianism was willing to defy the Church, wrestle the state, and battle Spanish incursions into Andean ways—but increasingly it had to do so within colonial bounds. So, even though Indianism was deeply oppositional, in vision and in practice, refusing to acquiesce to being defined by colonial authorities and Spanish saints, it nevertheless deferred to Spain's presence. Spain's gods would remain on Andean soil. This significant shift away from the belligerency of the Taqui Onqoy should not be interpreted as evidence that Andeans were lacking in courage. Certainly they were courageous in their beliefs, beliefs for which many could be brutally whipped, made to labor in colonial sweatshops, or forced into permanent exile.[33] It does suggest, however, some important dimensions in the building of colonial hegemonies and colonial subjects.[34]

Nativist ideology insisted that guacas, the gods of the past, could be kept alive by worship, just as their now "Indian" descendants could be kept alive by returning to "Indian" traditions. Reconstituting the ethos of the past in the colonial present was, of course, an impossibility, but it was precisely the tension of impossibility that charged the critical spark on which Indianism thrived. And part of that history—the ethos of the past—entailed revitalized memories of Inca rule.[35]

Relations with Inca Masters in the Colonial Present

Incas appear in many seventeenth-century nativist understandings of self and place. Andean narratives of origins, hierarchy, and political legitimacy would now also draw on the Inca experience—on reconstrued memories of life as Inca subjects.[36] While it is difficult to determine the pervasiveness and depth of Inca attachments, Father Avendaño's fire-and-brimstone sermons, like the one asking "How Many Incas Reside in Hell?" hint not only at colonial fears concerning Inca memories, but at the broad net those memories cast.

Some ayllus envisioned their very existence to be tied to Inca powers, conceptualizing themselves as the descendants not only of local guacas, but of Inca goddesses and gods, Inca queens and kings. The lords of Cuzco were said to bring the very stuff of life to the provinces: corn, chili peppers, dwellings.[37] And as Inca ancestors were cherished well into the seventeenth century, so were rites commemorating Inca conquest and the attendant obligations between Cuzco and the colonized provinces.

The Incas consecrated political bonds between themselves and conquered peoples through elaborate rituals of human sacrifice. Usually an *aclla*, one of the empire's renowned "chosen women," would, as a representative of the newly conquered ayllu, be executed in ceremonies to the Inca and Sun. This imperial rite, which included deifying the victim in her regional pantheon, celebrated the political subordination of her people. One such aclla was Tanta Carhua from Peru's north-central highlands. She was feted by the Inca king in Cuzco, and then by her community, before being buried in royal lands adjoining her ayllu's territory. Tanta Carhua's death commemorated and institutionalized imperial relations between her homeland and Cuzco; for with Tanta Carhua's sacrifice, her father and his male descendants became middlemen in Inca administration.[38] Almost ninety years after the Spanish conquest, these ayllus were worshiping Tanta Carhua, and two generations after that, returning extirpators uncovered the same heresy.[39]

So it was that in seventeenth-century rituals colonial Andeans reenacted the creation of bonds between conquered ayllus and Cuzco, bonds pivoting around chaste women and "Incanized" curacas, bonds transforming Andeans into Cuzco's subjects. Ceremonial prominence was given both to native elites (as brokers to an imperial power) as well as to ayllu dependence on these men who were fluent in an alien, powerful culture. Colonial ayllus were not merely celebrating the Incas, the "past," but were memorializing specific qualities of the power relations that engaged them. The nature of those relations, then, could set the language of Andean expectations and judgments, and so, at least in some ayllus, become part of Indianism's critical charge.

By the middle of the seventeenth century, extirpators discovered that "Inca" had taken on new meanings. Native Andeans, notably accused "witches," had broadened "Inca" into "Indian." Ayllus throughout the highlands transformed the Spanish conquest into a yearly commemoration, reenacting the conquest as a ritualized battle. This "invented" tradition (still performed) staged a war between Spaniards and Incas, now symbols of the current political adversaries in the Andes. Through ceremony, ayllus that had never identified with Cuzco when under its rule were now equating the fundamental colonial hostility between Spanish and Indian as a struggle between Spaniards and Incas.[40]

The implications for Andean ways of knowing bear thinking about. "Inca," as a gloss for "Indian," was taking on greater discursive and critical prominence in the indigenous world, and "the Inca," as culture hero, was standing for that world. "Inca," then, enveloped a political morality: the image of a legitimate "Indian" kingdom whose sovereignty over the Andes had been usurped by Spain. This ethic might have presaged better-known, later dreams of an Inca utopia, so eloquently analyzed by Antonio Flores Galindo, in which the Inca's return to Peruvian soil would signal Spanish defeat and the coming age of "Indian" justice.[41]

Battles of Inca against Spaniard—utopian strands—as moving and provocative as they might prove to be, produced hopes and visions at a cost. Casting the Inca as culture hero set certain directions to Andean remembering. Cuzco's noblewomen, its queens and princesses, played a prominent role in the Inca empire,[42] and—if Avendaño's sermon is any guide ("Tell me children . . . How many Inca queens [have gone to hell]? All of them. How many Ñustas [princesses, noblewomen]?",[43] not to mention the incantations of witches—those women were still vital to Andean memories well into the seventeenth century. Coding Inca (Indian) history as a battleground of kings would weaken the imprint of Andean noblewomen, and that of women in general. It would also overshadow the battles fought between Incas and other Andean ayllus over political sovereignty, the intrusive demands of Inca empire-building, the ambiguous role of curacas, and the burdens Cuzco's lords placed on peasant shoulders. "Inca" suggested a common Andean-Indian ground, while, in reality, that ground was split apart by antagonisms of gender, ethnicity, and privilege. "Inca" might spark remembrances of Cuzco's paternalism, its notions of imperial obligation, which contrasted so sharply with Spanish practice; yet romancing Inca history would also leave in place a vision of social order in which Indian subjects presumed their social selves to be anchored in a benevolent and universally loved Inca king.

Compromising Rituals

Nativist religious practices, ebulliently anticolonial, were torn by compromise. In the hostile climate of the seventeenth century, Andean nativists—battered by extirpators—could ignore neither the weight of Spanish institutions nor their belligerence to Andean beliefs. Indianism had to be practiced with caution and strategy.

Nativist ministers tried to keep their worship pure. Anything Spanish was considered polluting, so whenever guacas were commemorated or ancestors honored, Indianists would ban the use of Spanish artifacts and the consumption of Spanish foods ("and during [native] confessions, they didn't eat any kind of meat except for llamas and guinea pig, because . . . mutton, pork, goat were an abomination"). Or, more dangerously, Andean nativism curbed attendance at church and at catechism classes ("and we were not to go inside the church because all our offerings and confessions would be soiled"). Even the choirmaster was forbidden entrance to the community during native religious celebrations, because his association with Christianity "had made him polluted."[44]

Andeans also tried to purify the dead. Whether baptized or not, the dead were ancestors and could not be left to suffocate in Christian cemeteries. So with great celebration kinsmen were removed from underground tombs and placed in caves where ancestors traditionally rested. Entire ayllus, led by underground priests and "elderly women," retraced the pathways worn by those who died; and during this pilgrimage "elderly women" would laud their existence in song, and at midnight "all the Indian women would go out and walk the streets, crying, spilling drops of llama blood and *chicha*, calling out to the dead."[45]

The dead could also assess the colonial experience. They, too, could encourage militancy. In the words of an accused dogmatist:

> Whenever a Christian Indian dies, they slaughter llamas and invite the entire pueblo, and they blow air into the lung and if there are spots, they say that [the dead person] is angry, and his relatives would offer more guinea pigs, *coca*, llama fat [and] corn . . . and [the local religious leaders] would say that [the Christian Indian] had died because he hadn't worshiped his ancestors properly nor his "idols" . . . nor had he kept the fasts and made confessions, as the *hechiceros* [= "witches"; Spanish term for local religious leaders] had commanded . . . and they would die very soon if they didn't . . . honor their ancestors and kin.[46]

Andeans expressed a keen awareness that in death, life is commemorated. For colonial Andeans, particularly those galvanized by nativist ideologies, that meant a way of life that defined itself by contending with Iberian attempts to exterminate it.

Indianists would worship their guacas under the cover of saints, and any Christian holiday became a time to celebrate the ancestors. As one

Indian admitted to her interrogator, "[E]very year they would celebrate their *guacas*, and in order to cover this up, they would make [these celebrations] on the holiest days of the Church, like Easter, Christmas, and Corpus Christi."[47] So throughout the village of Otuco, on Corpus Christi and Saint John's Eve, native priests would proclaim "that it was time to worship the *malquis* [ancestors] and would order [people] to fast according to the old customs."[48] And during the night "all the *ayllus* would go out, led by the priests and 'the elderly women' carrying their drums, playing them through all the streets, singing their songs . . . in their language, according to the old traditions, referring to the stories and histories of their ancestors, going inside the homes of those who headed the *cofradrías* [Christian brotherhoods] where they would drink and get drunk until dawn."[49]

Saints were blasphemed. When Andeans celebrated the feast day of Saint Peter, remarked one witness, Indian ministers would order the festival's sponsor to take the saint's image along with its banner to his or her home, "and they would give offerings of *coca*, guinea pigs, and *chicha* [to the idols and malquis], . . . all in front of [St. Peter's] banner."[50] As if to add insult to injury, native "witches," often under the protection of curacas, would ask the festival sponsor to give up the saint day's communal offerings; and the "witches" would take the collection to the ancient ritual centers, where they would worship the old gods with elaborate ceremony.[51] Wouldn't the extirpator Hernando de Avendaño have been furious to find out that Otuco's Indianists spat out his name and cursed him when they worshiped the charred remains of the guacas he thought he had destroyed twenty years before?[52]

Yet with all this blasphemy, guacas (or their creators) sensed how Christianity had bridled them. Ancestor heroes demanded appeasement for the contaminating ambience in which they were worshiped. Nativists had to supplicate them: "Our lords and fathers . . . Don't be angry, for we do not have these festivals for the Spaniards' god nor their saints, but for you."[53]

Some Christian rituals were difficult to avoid. Annual confession was one. Resigned (realistically) to the powers of the colonial state and the great importance attributed to yearly confession, Indians creatively discharged their duties. Curacas and nativist ministers, working in concert, told their ayllu-mates to confess "Catholic sins"—like eating meat on Friday, not going to mass, having premarital sex—to their parish priests. The joke was that these "offenses" were not sins in Andean eyes. Real sins were worshiping the Spanish god, not worshiping guacas, entering the church while fasting for Indian ceremonies, eating Spanish foods during Andean holy times and, the greatest transgression, confessing "idolatries" to Catholic priests: "because if they were to find out, they would take away our traditions."[54] Andean leaders were well aware of the aura of priests, the powers of the confessional, and the fragility of Indianism's borders.[55]

Depending on possibilities and circumstance, nativist strategies could be great or small.[56] Andeans were taught the virtues of deception and the tactics of cover-up in order to avert ancestral wrath and maintain nativist dignities. Indian souls were forgiven if compelled to violate Indianism's commandments; ministers simply instructed their followers "not to adore saints or receive the sacraments with your whole heart, but just to comply, because [Catholic rites] were just things to mock."[57] Other ayllus, managing to escape from their colonial settlements, had grander strategic possibilities.[58] The Nauis and Camas ayllus, for example, returned to their "pueblo de gentilidad," to the hilltop "towns of their paganism," in order to be closer to the gods. Their reasons expressed deeply felt spiritual needs. Indian identity compelled them to maintain sacred bonds with their ancestors as well as to preserve the communal integrity of land against colonial law: "because their idols and *malquis* are in [their old pueblos] . . . [and] they had greater freedom to worship and adore idols there"; "because in Mangas [where they were resettled in a "reducción"] they didn't have community and they had lawsuits."[59]

The idolatry campaigns bore on ayllus in different ways. Some had to face the impossibility of public worship. Ocros, for example, enacted measures to restrict common access to native gods. Their guacas had gone underground; now only Indianist priests could interpret their words: "[Once] the Spanish arrived . . . [the guacas] reached an accord and determined that it would not be propitious for their survival to give public responses to [every] Indian, but rather, they should hide . . . in such a way that they would stay concealed underground where only 'witches' go."[60]

Others, fearful that inspectors would discover their Indianist ways, retreated to a more private devotion. Lucía Suyo, a convicted minister, testified that Indians could no longer adore their gods as they used to, with public revelries of dance and song. They were afraid of giving themselves away. Nativists had to worship individually and in secret.[61] She also told how Indians, expressing sorrow, begged their guacas to understand: "Now, see, the world is upside down. . . . [W]e are persecuted and in another time."[62] The Indianist Lucia Suyo was speaking the millenarian language of seventeenth-century Europe.[63]

Nativist practices in the colonized Andes were gendered, in processes that played on Spanish "patriarchal" assumptions. In contrast to longstanding Andean traditions, Spanish law presumed that women were innately unsuited to holding public office. Another side to this attitude was that women were witches, a premise that colored the trials spearheaded by

Peru's inquisitors as well as by Peru's idolatry extirpators. We know that Spanish theology in the colonies, where fears about social order were inflamed by race thinking, targeted native women as the most likely consorts of God's enemies—Peru's devil guacas.[64]

Men played key roles in Andean nativism, and some who led nativist worship were even called "witches"; yet the idolatry trials abound with references to women witches and the "virgin" priestesses of "Indian" guacas.[65] Women like Juana Icha were accused of a full gamut of sorcery, from healing wounds to bewitching colonial bureaucrats, priests, and native tax collectors. Her fury was directed against indigenous and Spanish officials who had transgressed what she, and others, believed to be the legitimate bounds of authority. Juana Icha became an advocate for "Indian morality," and the standards she represented harkened to pre-Columbian understandings of social justice, of the obligations of those in power to their subordinates. Her support was ayllu-wide. Listen to the testimony of a local official who suffered her wrath:

> [A]nd Don Francisco Poma Condor, the mayor, apprehended Juana and then let her go . . . and then Don Pedro Yauri, an *indio principal* ["principal Indian," i.e. curaca or headman] of the village recaptured her, but she still escaped, and Pedro de Zarate, the priest, ordered her arrest, but to no avail . . . because the Indians of the village support her.[66]

In a similar fusion and countering of gender ideologies, Indianism merged the sexual purity of celibate women (and perhaps the political prestige associated with the aclla of Inca times) with efforts to preserve the "purity" of traditional Andean life.[67] Virgin women (often named María; remember the Taqui Onqoy), living as "Andean" and hidden a life as possible, were kept away from the immoralities, the contaminations, of Spanish civic offices, Spanish religious institutions, and Spanish men. The gendered institutions of Spanish colonialism systematically eroded the life possibilities of most Andean women; and in a colonial irony, those same institutions provided them with the instruments of challenge. In native eyes, witches and virgins—the devil-inspired subverters of colonial disorder and the pure, uncontaminated ministers of an ordered past—gained a kind of underground legitimacy as the champions of Indian traditions.

Native Views of Purity

Indianism was concerned with purity. Its ideological thrust was to keep Spanish and Andean things apart, especially during sacred moments. No mutton; no catechism; no church. It also celebrated racial chastity: Indianism's virgin priestesses, worshiping the ancient gods in the high tablelands and kept pure by living far from the reach of Spanish society, were also far from the reach of Spanish men. Indianism's purity centered on culture — on the customs and practices that distinguished Spaniards from Indians — but it, too, entered the divides of race.

This was another Spanish inheritance. Yes, the Incas prized the aclla's chastity and the Incas held rituals of social cleansing as well; but the celebration of virginity was part of the imperial rites of conquest, not a means to make an Inca "race," and the impurities swept by Cuzco's lords into Cuzco's rivers had been produced by, among others, the empire's rulers, not by a contaminated people.[68] These were the pollutions of power, not the pollutions of ancestry. That was a European passion—also absorbed, in its own way, by Indianism.

Spanish race thinking grabbed native understandings of the world in different ways. Cajatambo's Indians absorbed some of its exclusionary ideals; the indigenous chronicler Guaman Poma de Ayala, absorbed a fuller version. Let's revisit his ideas about race and purity. Guaman Poma's chronicle of good government, recall, included vigorous attacks against racial mixing: the colony's deterioration, notably the monumental decline in Indian population, could be laid at miscegenation's door. It was Indian women, however, who opened it.[69]

Guaman Poma was deeply troubled by the rapid decline in Peru's Indian population, a legacy of colonialism that was in full view throughout his years of highland travel. He believed the way to stanch it was through good colonial government, and good government had to rest on a political morality of honor, chastity, and unsullied blood. Iberian principles of purity appealed to Guaman Poma, and he clarified them as purity of race (Spaniard, indio, and negro) and purity of rank (nobility, commoner, peasant). Like Iberians, he found women's lascivious nature to be a threat to good government, particularly in the colonies, where strict boundaries between the races were crucial for public welfare. For Guaman Poma, only chastity before wedlock and same race, same status marriage could ensure the purity of lineage and rank necessary for Peru's social health.[70]

Guaman Poma hammered at these themes throughout his *Nueva corónica*, and he made his point by comparing the moral decadence of colonial society to the virtue of Andean "costumbres" before the Spanish invasion. With an irony that could not have been lost on Spanish colonizers, Guaman Poma took Christian ethics as his moral standard: although Andeans were not practicing Catholics before the Iberian onslaught, they did know how to govern well; that is to say, in a "Christian way"—not only with charity and justice, but with sexual restraint. Female virtue was intrinsic to Guaman Poma's "buen gobierno," and he described women's sexual practices before the Spanish conquest in this way: "[A]mong their women, they found no adulteresses, nor were there any whores. . . . [W]omen were virgins when they married, and they held this to be a [matter of] honor. . . . And thus [Andeans] multiplied greatly."[71] Although ambivalent about aspects of Inca rule, Guaman Poma believed that Cuzco's lords presided over a well-ordered society, i.e., one grounded in the means to secure female virtue: "The greatness that this New World of the Indies had, keeping women virgins until thirty-three years of age. . . . O what a beautiful law, not only of the land but of God. . . . [N]either the [Spanish] emperor nor any of the world's kings has known such a beautiful law."[72]

Guaman Poma linked the corruption of the social order to the corruption of women: it was their essential disloyalty and wanton sexual impulses that produced social decay, impure races, and muddy social boundaries. He explained that Indian women were prone to seek men outside their caste, preferring Spaniards to hardworking and honest Andeans. This was the india's insidious disgrace; worse, such indias had no honor, less even than negras who, as slaves, were at the bottom of honor's barrel. Calling Indian women "whores," women without virtue, Guaman Poma bemoaned their treachery and betrayal:

> Some [of these Indian women], since they have been cooks for the priest or *encomendero* or *corregidor*, or any Spaniard, [and] has been [*sic*] a servant, mistress, or had a child by him, or has fornicated with an *español, mestizo* or *negro, mulato*, these aforementioned Indian women end up being liars, thieves, great whores, lazy . . . and do not serve either God or His Majesty nor do they obey their authorities. . . . [N]ow, an [Indian woman] does not want to marry an Indian man, an Indian commoner. And these Indian women are worse than *negras*, and now they have no honor.[73]

Guaman Poma offered two solutions. The first was in line with Viceroy Toledo's policy of residential segregation. It maintained that all non-Indians—Spaniards, blacks, mulatos, and mestizos—be outlawed from Indian settlements. If, in spite of this ban, native women had children by non-Indians, both the woman and her offspring should be exiled from her pueblo and prohibited from taking residence in Indian villages.[74]

Guaman Poma's second solution argued for the right of parents (or the state) to intervene in women's marriage choices. Armed with this prerogative, Andean elders could pressure daughters to betroth Indian men of comparable standing. Guaman Poma looked to Inca statecraft as a model in this regard, and he credited Cuzco's reported control over marriage for the empire's notable social order and stability.[75] This remedy for colonial disorder, however, ran counter to ecclesiastic law, and Guaman Poma, who accompanied various clerics on their extirpating missions, must have known that. According to the seventeenth-century colonial Church, spouses had the right to marry of their own free will; and spousal choice had precedence over parental objections whenever they were in conflict.[76] Guaman Poma's resolve suggests the depths of his concern about indigenous survival as well as his conviction that "dishonorable" marriages were the cause of Andean decline.

Guaman Poma railed against the "malas castas": the stained, illegitimate "mixed breeds"—mostly mestizos, but also mulatos and sambaigos (Indian and negro unions)—whose scandalous lives, in his judgment, seemed to feed colonial disorder.[77] Guaman Poma's vision transformed Peru's mestizos into emblems of death—glaring evidence of native mortality and social degeneracy. His impassioned pleas for purity of rank and race—and for the need to surveil women's honor in the name of the public good—drew on the dominant rhetoric of these colonial times. Through it, he attempted to make moral and cognitive sense out of a threatening and deteriorating world.

Guaman Poma's chronicle of good government defended Andeans by defending their honor, i.e., by remaking pre-Columbian history into a utopia of social virtue, where women were chaste and social boundaries were fiercely guarded. Bound by this vision, he could eloquently denounce the plight of indigenous women under colonial rule,[78] even as he placed much blame for the collapse of social order at their feet. But native women were not the sole object of his piercing attacks. Spaniards—the entire colonial entourage (and priests in particular)—were chastised for bringing iniquity to the Andean world. Nevertheless, when Guaman Poma apportioned blame for the collapse of Indian pueblos—and of colonial order—he singled out women and their reeking shame: "[Indian women] have become shrews and whores. . . . It is because of women that men abandon [their pueblos] . . . [W]omen deserve to be punished more."[79] With Christian insight, Guaman Poma reminded his readers that "the first sin ever committed was by a woman";[80] and, mirroring the fears voiced by inquisitors hunting non-Indian witches and extirpators hunting Indianists, he added with scorn: "[T]hus you [women] created the first idolatry" and "served the devils."[81]

Guaman Poma elaborated one vision of past and present Andean worlds, drawing, in part, on a language of purity and women's disgrace. Other native Peruvians—Indianist men and women, headmen and commoners—drew on a similar discursive lattice, but came to different understandings. Extirpation campaigns exacted a steep cultural price, both on Indian deputies like Guaman Poma and on Indian targets. Re-creating the terrible climate of fear that strangled colonial Peru, extirpators, like inquisitors, deepened the fractures tearing at colonial life. The combined pressures of Christian militancy and colonial authority exacted a toll, even on the most resolute Indianists. You could hear it in their voices.

The Spanish in Indians

Although the language of Indianism was ferociously anti-Spanish, it was, at the same time, pervasively (if unconsciously) Hispanicized. Some guacas had acquired Hispanicized ways, wearing Hispanicized clothing and sporting Hispanicized beards. Colonization introduced Spanish figures to Andean idioms of collective sense; and Hispanicized, Christianized guacas participated in this uneasy ideological terrain that was shaping ideas of Indianness: of where "Indians" came from, who they were, and what their futures might be.

One example is the god Guari (also Huari), who in various narratives brought order, agriculture, and Andean civilization to ayllu life. An elderly woman, accused of witchcraft and dogmatism, told her young acolyte:

[B]efore there were Incas and *apos* [mountain gods; also people of rank or Spaniards], when Indians would kill one another in order to defend their fields, [Guari] appeared in the form of a Spaniard, an old man with a beard, and he distributed all their fields and irrigation canals to them, in every pueblo . . . and these are the same [fields] that are now sown, and it was Guari who gave Indians food and water.[82]

Extirpators found a similar story in Ocros, a community that remained aggressively anti-Christian despite several idolatry inspections. Ocros's founding deity, Huari Viracocha, had indigenous origins, yet he also had a European heart. Viracocha was the Quechua term used by colonial Andeans to mean Spaniard, and as befit his name, Huari Viracocha was a Spaniard, so powerful that he could turn local heroes into stone.[83]

The most ubiquitous, and startling, Hispanicized Indian deity in the colonial Andes was Santiago (Saint James).[84] Santiago was quintessentially Spanish. The "killer of Moors," Santiago led the Spanish charge to reconquer the Iberian peninsula from North African infidels, and Santiago, "the killer of Indians," led the Spanish charge to conquer the idolatrous Incas. Spaniards laid these victories at Santiago's feet, and deemed him so crucial for their Andean triumph, that they renamed Cuzco, the Inca capital, in his honor. Nonetheless, after several decades of colonization, Santiago had also become an Andean heresy. In the words of a horrified missionary:

> [T]hey made offerings of *medio reales* (coins), coca and *chicha* (maize beer) and called for the devil, naming him Santiago, and then a phantom appeared, mounted on a white horse. And chewing coca leaves they invoked him, "Come Santiago, *apu huayna*" (young lord; *apu* refers to both humans and to mountain gods); and hearing these words, the phantom would come down from the roof in great and shining splendor . . . and would respond, "I will help you as long as you don't confess, don't hear mass, don't pray in church, but just dedicate yourselves to my worship."[85]

Before the Spanish conquest, native peoples populated their landscape with deities who embodied notions of power. These deities were usually associated with the Andes' imposing mountains, and, in Andean imaginings, they were emblems of a political geography stretching from local subordinates to the commanding deities of Cuzco. Now fighting for Indians, Santiago joined forces with the mountain gods, and became their principal representative in the broader whirl of colonial celestial—and temporal—politics.

Santiago-mountain gods, Hispanicized and Indian, had their doubles on earth. Curacas were appointed by Spaniards to negotiate relations between colonial authorities and their native communities. Headmen were responsible for collecting tribute, mobilizing labor drafts, maintaining political order, and keeping their followers on a Christian path. In return, royal officials gave curacas special privileges, privileges that were reserved for Spaniards: curacas, unlike native peasants, could dress in European finery and eat from European dishes; curacas, unlike native peasants, could go to special schools to learn European languages and other fine points of civilization; curacas, unlike native peasants, could freely engage in commercial transactions, including buying and selling property. With one foot in an alien, Hispanicized universe, curacas, unlike native peasants, could acquire the skills and savvy to manipulate colonial institutions—just like Santiago.

The Spanish conquest of the Andes transformed the economic and political character of imperial rule. Colonial Peru, unlike Inca Peru, was an alien place, one that disregarded, for the most part, any substantive responsibility for the material welfare of Indian subjects. It was an alien place that declared Andeans to be of a different race than their masters;

and it was an alien place that increasing defined peasants and their production in mercantilist terms.

Mercantilism was unknown in the Andes before the Spanish arrived, and it spurred a metamorphosis in Andeans and in their gods. Hernando Hacas Poma, fearing the hungry mountain gods, knew that *chicha* (corn beer) and coca would no longer satiate them. Mountain god-Santiagos, riding glorious stallions with silver spurs, had more modern claims to make on their followers. Colonial mountain gods wanted money.

Andean imaginations transformed native gods into middlemen in the colonial political economy of race thinking and mercantilism. Indians understood that their celestial deities needed "*medio reales*" (money) in their pockets to negotiate with the powers-that-be. Mountain god-Santiagos demanded and captured the market's mystique, and, in this, they were not unlike their Hispanicized Indian counterparts, now property owners and merchants. Indianized Santiagos and Hispanicized curacas had mastered the exchange relations that were spreading throughout the countryside: they were the only native beings who could attain the market's magical fruits of profit and power.[86]

Perhaps Hispanicized "guaris" and Indianized Santiagos were nodding to Spain's apparent unyielding presence; perhaps they also voiced Indianism's inescapable dependency on the Spanish world. For an Indian space in the seventeenth century was increasingly dependent on the manipulation of Spanish institutions, on clever maneuvering around Spanish paternalism, laws, politics, religion, and economics. That world was brokered by Hispanicized curacas, fluent in both an imperial and a local milieu. Curaca-led victories in court, secretly abetted by the moral force of guacas, could ensure an ayllu's landholdings in the face of outside challenges, moderate forced labor obligations in the mines, curb the abusive behavior of Spanish bureaucrats, or inhibit the ability of priests to set up residence in the countryside.[87] Indianist triumphs on Spanish turf directly shaped the day-to-day terms of colonial living and helped guard the terrain where Indianists hoped to prosper.

As bonds to a money-loving, legalistic, mountain god tightened, Andeans' sense of their own redemption and of the new social order they might struggle to achieve increasingly engaged the colonial society their gods mimed. Unlike the enraged guacas of the Taqui Onqoy, Indianism's guacas were prepared to share the Andean heavens with Spanish gods. They also seemed willing to accept (up to a point) the colonial institutions that made "Andeans" into "Indian" subjects. Indigenous headmen and peasants prayed to their guacas that colonial labor obligations might be moderated, not abolished; that tribute demands might be eased, not abandoned; and that money (a Spanish introduction) might be forthcoming, not eliminated.[88] Indianist militants of the seventeenth century did not seem to question—at least not in entreaties to guacas and ancestors—the legitimacy of the Spanish regime to exact demands on them. They did, however, profoundly challenge the terms of those demands. Headmen and commoners did not accept Spanish colonial calculations of life's rules: Indianists were deeply concerned about the nature of Spanish exactions and the genuineness of Spanish commitments; they fought bitterly—in prayers, in court, and in blood—to ensure that the demands were just and that the obligations to Andeans were met.[89] Their militancy notwithstanding, nativists (implicitly?) understood themselves to be subjects in a larger world of social hierarchies on which their being and welfare depended. Spain, including its castelike and patriarchal understandings of cosmic order, was finding a place in "Indian" selves.

The Meanings of "Indian"

Contests over social selves, over potential ways of being human, lay at the heart of the colonial enterprise, as Crown and Church, in policy and prejudice, struggled to make Andeans—that varied swatch of peoples living under Inca rule—into "Indians." Colonial order turned on the sociological invention of "race," integral to the making of the modern world, and "New World" humanity was channeled into a hierarchy of españoles, negros, and indios. A hundred years after the Spanish incursions began, some Andeans started to define their lives, at least in part, by a new category, "Indian"; but, as I have tried to show, Indians mobilized by nativist beliefs bore little resemblance to the Indians that colonial policy and colonial religion intended to create.

Inspired by a resurgent nativism, men and women, curacas and peasants, living in different ayllus and worshiping different guacas, galvanized an Andean "common sense" of things into a sense of Indianness, into a critical, anticolonial ethos. What had been the practices of Andean living —the customary ways of burying the dead, praying to ancestors, preparing fields, roofing houses, getting married—became weapons of colonial critique. What had been the ritual practices brought by colonial masters—attending catechism classes, celebrating saints' days, going to confession—became instruments of ridicule. Praying to guacas for guidance and support, Indianist curacas would engage colonial institutions of government for Indianism's benefit. But colonialism's unyielding presence—its relative strength in relation to the ayllus' political weaknesses—along with its guarantees of Indian rights as a community of human beings, pervaded

Indianism's practices and Indianism's spirit. Indianism owed much of its character to the colony's structure of power, categories of rule, and entwined ideologies of racial hierarchy, state paternalism, militant Catholicism, and abiding gender differences.

Indianism set certain tones of knowing and could set certain tones of unknowing. Extirpation campaigns—forcing human beings into a polarity of either Christian or devil worshiper, and making all Incas into God's enemies—encouraged some Andeans to recast their histories of Inca dominion. Judging colonial predicaments in a new light, some even constructed a notion of Indian sovereignty and a resurrected Inca king—a notion that repressed memories of Cuzco's queens, women's participation in Andean public worlds, and Inca incursions into ayllu life. Or, turning Spanish gender norms inside out, Indianists made Andean "witches" into political vigilantes, and "virgins"—the emblem of Andean purity—into standards of social legitimacy. All the while, indigenous guacas, the standard-bearers of Indianism, began to take on Iberian-style beards and godlike powers. Indianist imaginings were fashioned in, but were not reducible to, the antagonisms of colonial life. These novel, sometimes jarring ways of picturing experience were construing paradoxical "Indian" senses of self and possibility in an intricate dynamic with the practices of Spanish hegemony and even, perhaps, with the other, non-Indian "witches" whose practices validated Indianist knowledge.

Indians still battled Spaniards in the seventeenth century, but now their fights were waged in courts, in small-scale acts of resistance, and principally on religious terrain. The extirpation campaigns, coming in waves throughout the century, seemed both to heighten Indianist resolve and to prove the danger and seriousness of Andean religious commitments. Nevertheless, Indianist movements, while winning significant cultural victories and some political gains, were ultimately bound by colonial terms of living: they did not directly challenge colonial power. Nativist ideologies, construing Indian senses of place and possibility, situated Indians within the confines of the hierarchic colonial world. Politically weak, Indianists were born into a world of necessary compromise; and no matter how contentious, fragile, or conditional their loyalties, seventeenth-century Indians were colonial subjects—at least in some part of their contradictory selves. We can see that the consequences (intended or not) of Indian vs. Spanish contests still left colonials in command. With all its demonstrated weaknesses, the colonial regime was able to successfully contain challenges to itself. That is what "hegemony" is all about.

By keeping the dance of race and state before us, we open our analysis to power's most intimate dynamics, to the ways in which the social relations of empire—grasped and framed through ideologies of race thinking—impinged on the making of colonial Andeans. Our analysis becomes more human, as we grasp how structures of power can claim souls and, in the process, limit life's possibilities as well as stifle social imaginings.

Indianism's simultaneous embrace and rejection of the colonial order charted courses of possibility for years to come. Throughout the next hundred years, Indian ideologies would galvanize political activities built on a growing conviction that the Inca was the rightful king of the Indian world. A profound sense of the illegitimacy of the colonial regime—not necessarily a rejection of the Crown—could join together ideological descendants of the seventeenth century's Indianist critics. But these were different times, with different possibilities, and different configurations of power. Nevertheless, the contradictions borne by Andeans in the 1780s—during the longest Indian rebellion in the Americas—harken to ambiguities of Indianness from the previous century: Indian allegiances were divided between royal forces and Tupac Amaru II, and rebel Indian forces were divided by conflicting ayllu loyalties, gender divisions, and contested elite prerogatives.

Finally, the experiences of Andean Indians should cause us to reflect on our own social imaginings. The past several decades have witnessed challenges to much of mainstream anthropology's common sense. And terms like "Indian"—an extraordinary catchall that mixes together (in various proportions) the juridical categories of states and colonizers, knowledge categories of the social sciences, popular stereotypes, and the identities of "indigenous" (for want of a better word) peoples—have come under scrutiny. James Clifford, among others, has pointedly reminded us of the term's woeful inadequacies.[90] "Indian" is not a fixed inventory of traits, a thing, making up a fixed identity. Rather, "Indian," like "identity," must be understood in its sociability, emerging in the social relations that engage human beings in time. History is inseparable from social processes of understanding; and this holds true not only for those Andeans who, in seventeenth-century Peru, were mobilized by a consciousness of their Indianness, but also for our own attempts to conceptualize the past and present through terms like "Indian."

Swings from noble savage to murderous savage, from shattered victim to heroic resister, from the socialist empire of the Incas to Cuzco's totalitarian tyranny have drained the life and lessons from "Indian."[91] So have similar trends, romancing "Indians" or "others" as human ideals before the European invasions or as pure challengers of European ways for ever after.[92] And so has our proclivity to demonize Spanish inquisitors and bureaucrats as greedy, fanatic megalomaniacs. Our theoretical biases, echoed in well-known penchants for oppositional thinking, have skirted the compromising social relations that make us contradictory selves, part of contradictory worlds. Traditions of critical thinking still direct us to recognize the compromises—the real limits, the unintended consequences, the missed chances, the unrecognized complicities, and the plain unknowables—that come with being part of this, our modern, colony-driven world.

I can imagine Hacas Poma wondering why it has taken us so long to confront our pollutions.

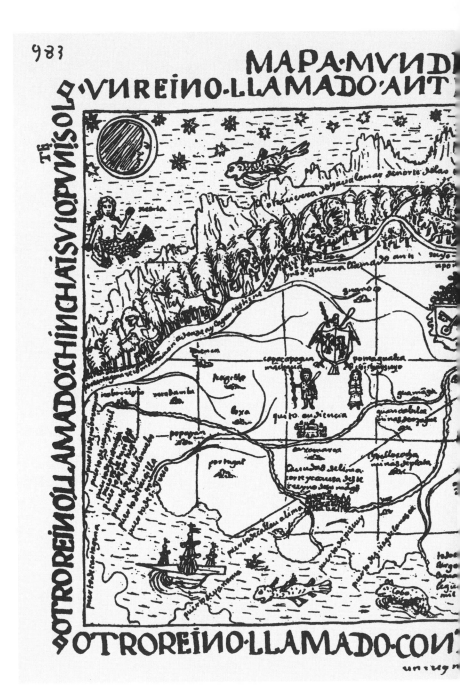

Mappamundi of the Kingdom of the Indies. From Felipe Guaman Poma de Ayala, *El primer nueva corónica y buen gobierno* (1613?).

EINO·DELAS·INS
ACIA·EL·DERECHO·DELARDENORTE MAR

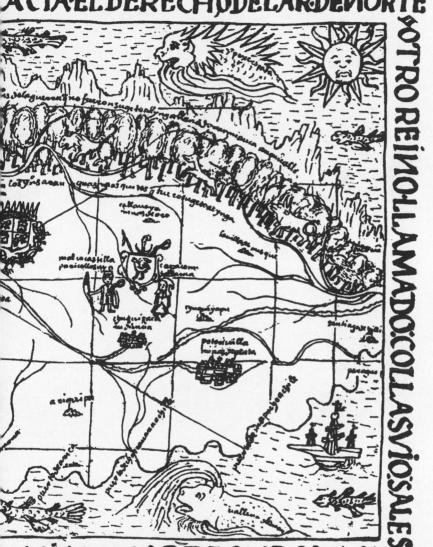

OTRO·REINO·LLAMADO·COLLASVIOSALESO

HACIALAMAR·DE·SVR·LLAI·Mx

AFTERWORD

[R]ace is, politically speaking, not the beginning of humanity but its end, not the origin of peoples but their decay, not the natural birth of man but his unnatural death. —HANNAH ARENDT, *The Origins of Totalitarianism*

For every image of the past that is not recognized by the present as one of its concerns threatens to disappear. —WALTER BENJAMIN, "Theses on the Philosophy of History"[1]

The West's Subterranean Stream

HANNAH ARENDT BELIEVED that the nineteenth-century colonial world had set the precedent for the savagery of the twentieth century—that it was the source of the West's "subterranean stream" of terror and violence that was to erupt in fascism. Colonialism's governing principles—race thinking and bureaucratic rule—triggered the West's most barbaric acts and presaged, she argued, the extraordinary belief that one nation was destined to command the world as a master race. Arendt's model was the nineteenth-century imperialism of England and France, but the globe had experienced Europe's barbarous civilizing missions nearly three centuries before, when Spain was at the Continent's vanguard of state-making and colonialism. Life in the seventeenth century was very different from life in the nineteenth, of course; but it was Spain's colonial efforts, not northern Europe's, that initiated the "civilizing" mix of bureaucracy and race thinking that Arendt found so damning.

Our sense of modernity changes once we trace its elementary forms back from the nineteenth century to the seventeenth.[2] We can then grasp how essential colonialism, race thinking, and bureaucracy have been to the making of the modern world; and we can ask ourselves why we have been so blind.

But blindness seems to be an unavoidable feature of civilization: we make sense of—we capture—many experiences of modern life by fetishizing them. Expanding "fetishism" from a critique of capitalism into a critique of politics demands a reappraisal of the bedrock of our common political sense—that "race" and "state" are objects, things, givens of human experience. Fetishism obscures our appreciation that Indian, New Christian, black, Spaniard, slave, merchant, tribute-payer, bureaucrat, woman, and man are not "states of being" but are social relations, inescapably part of one another and inescapably immersed in the swings of power. Turning these relations into fetishes stops us from seeing their history—our history—or even inquiring about it.

By virtue of our past, race thinking and state-making were of a piece. The modern state took "government in the name of truth" as its charge;[3] and one of the most profound social truths for state officials to judge was the nature of human personhood. Inquisitors' day-to-day activities, like that of other viceregal officeholders, included specification of that truth when they placed human beings into one of the official categories of the empire's social community. Inquisitors, as imperial officials, working through and in state structures, secured bureaucratic, racialized ways of defining the world, judging both the world and being-in-the-world.

Arendt asks how any group of human beings could acquire the confidence—and arrogance—to make these kinds of decisions over the lives of others. Seventeenth-century inquisitors, it seems, were bolstered by their unshakable faith in the justice of their cause; and, that faith, in turn, was braced twice over—by a religion giving them God's grace to expand the world and by the day-to-day practices of bureaucracy itself. With God's word in one hand and rational procedures in the other, inquisitors convinced themselves (and others) that they were working for the larger good and in society's (i.e., the world's) interest. The racial schemes that put Spaniard—and, in their case, "pure" Spaniard—at the top of the social order could only reinforce that confidence and arrogance.

Inquisitors, however, didn't have the only word on race. Their understandings, although shared by many, were not shared by everyone in Peru —sometimes neither by fellow bureaucrats nor by the people they were cataloguing. We find that Indians and missionaries disagreed over the meaning of Indian; Indians and Spaniards disagreed over the meaning of Spaniard; inquisitors and New Christians disagreed over the meaning of Spaniard; inquisitors and royal bureaucrats disagreed over the meaning Spaniard. Moreover, debates and identities changed over time so that Andeans could become Indians; Castilians and Viscayans could become Spaniards; the Inca could become stereotypically Indian; New Christians could—and could not—become Spaniards; and some Peruvians—Spaniards, mestizos, mulatos, blacks, and Indians—could begin to envision a creole common ground. These tensions—and not a juggernaut State—animated the cultural dialectic of colonialism: the cultural dialectic that institutionalized, and set directions for, modern race thinking.

But, of course, this was a lopsided dialectic, as imperial muscle and magnetism buoyed Spanish desires over all others. Sure, inquisitors did not always have their way: their own bureaucratic homage to regulations and standards kept some of their activities in check; and royal authorities made it clear that they, and not the tribunal, were Peru's preeminent bureaucracy. Nonetheless, by the seventeenth century (if not earlier) the colonial framework was in place. And it was clear that inquisitors and other bureaucrats, even when—or especially when—they were in conflict, never questioned the signature triad (Spanish, Indian, black) of the new modern order. It took two centuries, and the Wars of Independence, for part of that design to be successfully challenged. Some would argue that its essential form has yet to be replaced.

There was no Spanish nation as such in the seventeenth century. What we call Spain consisted of local kingdoms or principalities under the rule of the Hapsburgs. But there was a sense of "Spanishness," and that sense emerged as early modern colonialism took form. In 1532 Peru's first conquistadors called themselves "Christians," armed to fight the infidels; it was only decades later, when Iberian immigrants were forging the colonial Peruvian state, that "Spaniards" or "Spanish" became a term of reference. Political scientists of the early seventeenth century, writing when the modern state was coming into being, theorized about the Spanish people and about the Spanish character. Their forays into Spanishness, however, took place when representatives of Castile were colonizing the globe—civilizing Indians, enslaving Africans, and distinguishing themselves from the lower orders by calling one another "Spanish." The historical meeting of state-making, colony-making, and merchant capitalism meant that the two senses of "Spanishness" penetrated each other. Further, that penetration was braced by race thinking. Conquistadors brought the curse of the New Christians—the concept of stained blood (*sangre manchada*)—to the Americas, and when colonizers similarly condemned the blood of Indians, blacks, mestizos and mulatos, they provided "Spanishness" with another common ground.[4] Spanish blood was pure blood. Not only was the Spanish caste racialized, so was its contemporary partner—the potential Spanish nation. There are benefits to exploring civilization's elementary forms, and one such benefit is a more transparent—and stunning—view of this process.

We have lost sight of these silent, chameleonlike exchanges because we have denied colonialism its rightful place at the core of modern life. From its birth, the modern world was global in scope and hierarchical in structure. Yet we have ignored our foundation in colonialism and, as a result, we ignore that the twin hierarchies of global politics and racialized humanity are inherent to modern (civilized) life. As Hacas Poma, Manuel Bautista Pérez, and Hannah Arendt knew too well, these hierarchies are its marrow.

The historical circumstances joining colonialism and European state-making linked different social relations and different ideologies of personhood and, in the process, spawned new kinds of social beings: modern social beings. The social relations of power that structured life before the modern age were circumscribed, specific, and personal. But modern hierarchies, coming out of that melange of state and colonialism, were built on the exploitation of one class of people by another: they were built on abstractions, which were at once vast and intimate. Modern hierarchies were born in global geopolitics and thus created mammoth social boxes, capable of absorbing peoples everywhere, the world over. Those mammoth social boxes, however, were inhabited by stripped-down individuals, with colored skin, and by discarded, opaque social relations.

Modern political thought made "races" appear to be autonomous and independent; definable classes of humanity that existed before their momentous and foundational historic encounters. The portrayal of racial categories of state—whether black, Spaniard, or Indian, New Christian/Old Christian, or Castilian/Portuguese/English/French—as distinct entities, fixed by "blood stain," obscured the social relations at the very center of modern life, along with their violent birth. "Race think" categories, then, along with "state think" categories, were magical: they made the social relations of colonialism and state formation disappear; they made the social relations of colonialism and state formation appear to be external to the creation and identity of social being. As a result, "race" and "state" have come to be perceived as real, material entities; while, in social practice, they are very real but nonetheless illusory avenues through which we understand and experience modern existence.

These machinations of state and race were accomplished in dialectic with that other modern, abstract invention—the "individual." It is a commonplace that modern identity is rooted in the concept of the individual; or, as Marx saw it, the abstract individual could not exist apart from the abstract state; or as Foucault saw it, conjoined processes of totalizing and individuating marked the experience of modern life. Foucault pinpointed the confession as a paradigm of individuating practice; Gilroy, the act of enslavement; Marx, the collapse of feudal society. In all cases the erosion of traditional social bonds, or the forced uprooting of individuals from their traditional moorings, set in play the illusion that an individual—the embodiment of inherent, personal qualities—was the center of contemporary being. When inquisitors demanded that each prisoner articulate his or her vital statistics for bureaucratic consumption, then, they were framing a very modern bond between personhood, individuated political experience, and the state.

But modern life, associated so wholeheartedly with the emergence of the "individual" and the "state," was inseparable—in its origin and its history—from race thinking. The demand that state subjects identify their "casta y generación" was party to that achievement. By branding someone as New Christian or quadroon, using percentages to create caste subsets, or demanding to know which ancestors were Castilian or Portuguese, tribunal members—like all colonial state-makers—were constructing modern individuals, and they were doing so via modern race thinking. Race thinking embodied that modern, contradictory recipe of totalizing and individuating. Race thinking imparted concreteness and biology to the experience of being an "individual" and, at the same time, put the "individual" in a broader, abstract place. And once the social bedrock of "race" disappeared, once "caste" was jettisoned, race could become both obscenely personal—reduced to a calculus of stains and biology—and obscenely generalizing, with traits and capabilities extended to an entire set of humanity.

Race thinking was both a homogenizing force (a broad, universal category of human being) and a specifying one (a demand for personal calculation). Maybe the dialectic of state and individual—a dialectic of abstraction and individuation—was a threesome (at the least); and their interaction imparted an impression of tangibility, a sensation of autonomous, embodied existence, to what were (are) the principal abstractions of modern life. Perhaps by the very act of being separated into these global, abstract, racialized categories of humanity—not in spite of that act—the modern world is a world of individuals.

Ideologies of race and state—under the cover of reason—brewed a melange of irrationalities, along with an invidious measure of abilities and stains. Colonial fictions attached to national fictions, forging ideas of self and personhood on both sides of the Atlantic, were anything but "true." It was an ugly dance, that of state and race: fashioning a cultural milieu that encouraged subjects to see themselves as individuals, but through racialized state designs; making race and state an intrinsic part of their being, but then cutting off their political, exploitative, human moorings. These were the processes joining "race magic" and "state magic"; these were the processes making the modern world and our modern selves; these were the processes that have absorbed, promoted, and obscured civilization's— our—terrible subterranean stream.

Modern Inquisitions

This book has spent many pages alleging that the Spanish Inquisition was a modern institution and that Spain was an emerging modern nation; yet, few Anglos would consider either one to have been part of the modern experience. In our eyes Spain and particularly the Inquisition would represent just the opposite: examples of the horrors, of the barbaric irrationalities, of the cruelty and ruthlessness people were forced to endure before our way of life claimed victory over the planet. But if this book has been at all convincing, it should make us question ourselves—beginning with the discrepancy between the past and our understanding of it. What might our distorted common sense imply about us—we who claim the mantle of modernity as our own? What does it say about the way we conceive of ourselves, define ourselves and, ultimately, legitimize ourselves as a nation? *Modern Inquisitions* cannot do justice to these concerns; but, at the least, we can inquire—in a critical spirit—into the history of our confusions.

American imaginations were not the first to have made Spain and the Spanish Inquisition into foils against which modern successes could be judged. Both nation and institution have served as counterpoints to civic virtues for centuries—and they did so in the service of our Anglo forebears.

From its beginnings, England was obsessed with Spain. England had to confront Spain before it, too, could become a player in the West's new political order, and their battles were fought on religious as well as secular grounds. Protestantism became a badge of English nationalism once the Church of England broke from Rome; and during the last decades of the sixteenth century, England saw itself as the bearer of the true faith, a chosen people, with Catholic Spain as its nemesis. The Inquisition—defender of Catholicism and false arbiter of heresy—became in England's propaganda wars (the "Black Legend"), the emblem of Spain's moral and political degeneracy.[5]

Like most forms of government, monarchy had a language of legitimacy, and much of its rhetoric turned on the concept of tyranny. Seventeenth-century state-making put issues of law in the limelight, and European monarchs, as absolutist as they might appear, were not only constrained by legal mandates but understood them to stand for the best of modern government. In the hands of British propagandists, the Inquisition represented Spain's most glaring affront to the standards of civilization. With displays of vitriol that became all too familiar, the British pilloried the Inquisition for its abuse of law and contempt for justice.[6] John Foxe, called the Inquisition "this dreadful engine of tyranny" and, in international comparison, praised England as a country "not cursed with such an arbitrary court."[7] The tribunal was not only a model of government gone wrong, but a throwback to the past: proof that Spain disdained the political principles of a modern nation.[8] In these tracts, Spain's backwardness was made all the more evident by the progressive light of England's modern, "legitimate" approach to power.[9]

English critics commonly argued that Spain's miserable treatment of Indians was proof that she did not deserve to enter the ranks of modern civilization.[10] One of England's first travel writers, Richard Hakluyt, opened his compatriots' eyes to the curiosities and cruelties of the globe. And many of those cruelties were Spanish. Spaniards, he claimed at the turn of the sixteenth century, might talk about bringing salvation to the untutored, but "in truth [they sought] not [infidels] but their goods and riches." Ironically, Hakluyt grounded his argument in the bishop of Chiapas, Bartolomé de Las Casas's scathing critique of his countrymen's behavior toward Indians, the *Brevíssima relación de la destruyción de las Indias*. Once translated into English, Las Casas's jeremiad—with its extensive exposes of Spanish brutality in the Americas—became abundant grist for the British propaganda mills. Citing Las Casas, Hakluyt denounced Spanish ruthlessness as "most outrageous and [even] greater than Turkish cruelties." Spaniards, Hakluyt claimed, had done little more in the colonies than "tear [the Indians] in pieces, kill them, martyr them, afflict them, torment them, and destroy them by strange sorts of cruelties, never either seen or read or heard of the like."[11]

Denunciations of Spanish brutality in the Americas went hand in glove with British anxiety over Spain's global pretensions. It was with Spain in mind—and her decision to incorporate native peoples as colonial subjects—that Hakluyt critiqued the imperial mission of ancient Romans, "who imposed not only their ensigns and victories but also their laws, customs and religion in those provinces they had conquered with force of arms. . . . [R]uin and overthrow . . . are the effects and rewards of all such as being pricked forward with their Roman and tyrannical ambition will go about thus to subdue strange people."[12] England, however, had global designs of her own. British apologists were in a bit of a bind: they wanted to stake a claim to the world's riches, yet, at the same time, distance themselves from Spain. They did so by deprecating colonialism, or direct state control over conquered populations. Their weapon of choice was trade and their not so innocent rhetoric was to guarantee the creation of a world of sovereign nations united by the free market.

Hakluyt suggested the arguments. The "effects" produced by "tyrannical ambition" were "contrary to the profit which those shall receive which only are affectioned to the common benefit . . . to the general policy of all men, and endeavor to unite them one with the other as well by traffic and civil conversations."[13] In other words, although the creation of a universal monarchy would lead to "ruin," the creation of a universal market would not. Trade relations, the search for common profits, would be "an end so much more commendable as it is far from all tyrannical and cruel government."[14] As we might have expected, our author nevertheless went on to write that if the "savages will not yield unto the endeavors so much tending to their profit," the conquest by "military virtues and force of arms" would be justified.[15]

This is just one representation of a more complex English vision of its role in late sixteenth- and seventeenth-century colonialism, but it is a telling one. The goal would be to build a global network of commerce between sovereign nation-states, with whom England could favorably conduct business.[16] But if the natives would not oblige voluntarily, then England would have no choice but to learn something from Spain about political coercion.

Thus began an Anglo sleight of hand, born in the Black Legend, that would elevate the free market as an instrument of equality—of mutual benefit—while muffling its unholy attachment to the state and the unholy effect of its practices.[17] The United States is this ideology's most notable heir.

With the defeat of the Spanish armada, England struck an early and decisive blow to empire; more than three centuries later, the United States effectively destroyed what remained—or, better said, took it over. For, with its victory in the Spanish-American War, the United States embarked on its own imperial agenda. Like England, the United States concocted a vocabulary to both legitimize its international designs and to sharply distinguish itself—and American-style colonialism—from its Spanish predecessors. In an updated version of the modern/premodern divide, the United States spoke about itself as a modernizing force, a nation bringing virtue and freedom to people stymied by a feudal oppressor. The United States was not really a colonizer, it brought civilization.[18]

We Americans have our own origin myths, our own collective representations that filter how we understand history and our rightful place in it. We tend to see ourselves as exceptional: we vaunt our democratic foundations; we speak of our uniqueness as a republic, born free of the social and political constraints that hobbled Europe. We praise ourselves as a nation of individuals, living in a world of equality, justice, and capitalism. We celebrate our entrepreneurial spirit. We express our right—as a people of such exception—to spread the American way of life to the entire community of nations.[19]

We downplay state structures—or anything smacking of social forces—whenever we envision and account for our own experience in the world. The institutions and institutionalizing that Philip Corrigan and Derek Sayer deem so crucial to modern life—in the realm of law or education or national security—are only weakly present in our definitions of what constitutes modernity. For we are a nation of enterprising individuals, separately and equally endowed to make our fortunes and failures. We deny that state institutions have had much to do with our successes in the world or that social forces can profoundly effect the life chances of our citizens.

The American version of the West's liberating potential has done a remarkable job of hiding our structures of privilege and our global shenanigans—along with their subtle, and sometimes not so subtle, support from state institutions. In apparent homage to an earlier Anglo discourse, our imaginations have made the power of state institutions disappear behind a screen of free-market rhetoric. These mysteries of state have allowed most of us to deny that we are or ever have been a colonial (or neocolonial) power. After all, the free market is innocent, impartial, and certainly not colonial.

Like England, we have made Spain and its iconic Inquisition into our antiselves. While our fantasies of horror are fed by many sources (and our fears take many shapes), the Inquisition would be on any list of institutions we associate with a cruel and unreasonable past. Our Inquisition nightmares tell of profound injustices: men and women rotting away in cells, screaming on the rack, and ultimately burned at the stake because of premodern irrationalities. They tell of baffling intolerance, of the capriciousness of personal whims, of the inexplicable use of torture. All reveal a kind of societal perversity—extreme arrogance on the part of state officials, debauched feelings of entitlement, and an almost unquestioned sense of power over the life and death of others. All reveal the evils of the absolutist state—a monster that was never able to establish itself on American soil. That monster, our antiself, stands in stark contrast to our virtues, to our exceptionalism.

Yet, the emotions and horrors linked to the Inquisition—its terrors and its tortures—are not foreign to us. Neither is its bureaucratic face nor its projection as an institution of modern rationality. Of course, we are not seventeenth-century Spain; we have the good fortune to live in a nation that protects civil rights and liberties, that allows freedom of speech, that defends political and religious diversity. But we are also responsible for shameful times, when our forthright ideals and reasoned standards have been ignored or disgraced or simply justified away. Some of our national myths, like that celebrating our exceptional character or our role as civilization's beacon, divert our attention from that shameful underside, that shameful subterranean stream. We have to yet to confront our illusions.

Myths of American exceptionalism, buttressed by the free market, might dismiss the power of social forces to shape American lives and possibilities, might ignore the ability of America's political class to sidestep democratic procedures and undermine principles of accountability. They might disregard how appeals to national security can silence opposition at home and legitimize the use of force abroad. They might fail to notice how appeals to reasons of state can make punishment appear just and violence appear reasonable. They might overlook the attempts of some to exclusively define what it means to live an American—as opposed to an un-American (heretical)—way of life.

What, then, is our relation to Spanish contributions to the making of the modern world? Was the Inquisition—our icon of premodern irrationality and cruelty—the opposite of Anglo-dominated modernity? Or an unheralded ancestor?

This is a cautionary tale.

Appendix
Notes on Bias and Sources

Modern Inquisitions has a bias: we focus on the connections between the seventeenth century and "modern" life, not on the distinctions between them. Because of that bias—and our focus on modern institutions like bureaucracies, colonialism, and race—we risk encouraging the perception that little of substance changed between the seventeenth century and the nineteenth. That, of course, was not the case.[1]

Seminal differences distinguish the early modern world from later centuries. The creation of nation-states built on individual sovereignty and the secularization of life—along with enormous shifts in the conceptions and practices of power that ensued—are among the most crucial. In fact, the great differences between our world and the seventeenth century gives that time a feeling of strangeness. You have encountered this "strangeness" in Inquisition testimony—in assumptions about social hierarchies and human nature, in the weakness of subjects vis-à-vis state institutions, in the literalist interpretation of the Bible, in the intricacies of state rituals, in rhetorical arrogance, and in musings about devils and Jews (among others).

A focus on difference also points to a seminal lesson about bureaucracies. Bureaucracies do not exist outside of power relations; they are always part of, and do the bidding of, larger political systems.

A significant body of Renaissance scholars have sought to emphasize the uniqueness of the period. Some of the peculiarities of Renaissance life involve the way political authority was effected and conceptualized: we are shocked by the seemingly unchecked powers of governing institutions and startled by the political culture of personal monarchies, with their ritual celebrations of kingly divinity.[2] Contra the thrust of *Modern Inquisitions*, these historians would be reluctant to use "state" to characterize either early modern politics or the emerging bureaucracies of the seventeenth century. They would consider it premature, arguing that even though Spain's governing institutions, like the Inquisition, could limit monarchal power, they did not have sufficient autonomy to gain "statedom."[3]

Those who contend that personal monarchies dominated virtually all political contexts look at power from the center—which, of course, is necessary for any serious comprehension of seventeenth-century politics. But the view at the center can be quite different from the view in the colonies. Political authority had different shadings. The king might have been an important figure in colonial imaginations and in colonial policy, but his reach was slow and short. Inquisitors were the king's men, but they could ignore him in ways unheard of in Europe. Moreover, although inquisitors were the king's men, they also talked about themselves as officeholders in a bureaucracy that served the public weal, with its own rules and its own authority. Inquisitors were the king's men, but they were still forging an institution that would transcend individual bureaucrats as well as kings.

The different views of the same past that appear to characterize seventeenth-century historiography should perhaps remind us that inquisitors, like kings—and like their various subjects—inhabited several worlds. They sought favors and they believed in merit; they were entrepreneurs and acted like aristocrats; they were Spaniards and they were derided as creoles; they were worldly wise and they were ignorant of the world around them. Early moderns were party to remarkable transformations and to unsparing incongruities; they were party to the incompatible social relations, values, and institutions that characterized state-making's (and colonialism's) beginnings.[4] Instead of seeing a dichotomy between state and monarch, between royal power and expanding bureaucracies, we interpreters might do better by capturing their dialectic, by capturing that long and untidy process wrenching the "body politic" from the body of the king.

A somewhat analogous debate over the nature of Spanish colonialism has involved literary critics, anthropologists, and historians. J. Jorge Klor de Alva, in a provocative article, contended that "colonial discourse" (as used in reference to eighteenth- and nineteenth-century events) should not be applied to the Spanish enterprise. Klor de Alva claimed that Indian communities in colonial New Spain were so little transformed by Spanish institutions that to use the term colonialism, as we understand it, would be misleading.[5] Rolena Adorno, standing on Klor de Alva's shoulders and contributing to a debate stimulated by an important review article and commentary by Patricia Seed,[6] argued that Spain was "irrelevant to the colonial discourse paradigm."[7] Adorno contended that the kinds of questions regarding authoritative meaning that were introduced by "postcolonial" theorists, like Homi Bhabha and Edward Said, would be out of play in the Spanish case because Spanish writers had not absorbed the same kinds of political assumptions as their British counterparts. I appreciate and respect Adorno's and Klor de Alva's concern about misplaced and mistaken similarities and support their enterprise to challenge heretofore undisputed assumptions. Nonetheless, I don't think that their arguments are meaningful critiques of the biases presented here. First, Klor de Alva's reconstruction of Mexican Indian peasant life seems to be far from Peruvian colonial reality, where many native communities were profoundly transformed by such Spanish colonial institutions as the "reducciones" or the forced labor drafts in the mines, or by priestly vigilance, or by the tremendous population decline introduced with European disease. Adorno depended on Klor de Alva's projection of Spanish colonialism to argue that its colonial rhetoric—shaped by the conventions of the times—would not resemble the race- and power-induced tensions of its English colonial equivalent. My readings of seventeenth-century Peruvian documents, including the administrative accounts, missionary manuals, and legal compendia used in this book, suggest, on the contrary, something very close to the nineteenth-century rhetoric of European exceptionalism that is critiqued by the British postcolonial theorists.

Inquisition documents, like their cousins from the campaigns to extirpate idolatry, share a rocky stature in history, and I imagine after reading this book you can see why. We turn to these sources for information about early state-making, but we also turn to them because, for an age in which few diaries or personal correspondence remain, they take us within reach of the minds and hearts of colonial Andeans. But do they? Can they? Aren't they so compromised, so refractory, that in the end they tell us little about the lives or beliefs or habits of those being tried?

Very respected scholars of the Inquisition and of the "extirpation of idolatry" campaigns have made that argument. Benzion Netanyahu in his masterwork about the Spanish Inquisition and Henríque Urbano in his assessment of the idolatry campaigns contend that these trial transcripts chiefly reflect the understandings, interests, and motives of priests and magistrates.[8] They have pointed to the problems besetting any juridical system based on confessions, denunciations, and torture. You have read about coerced testimony: how, under the threat of torture or because of a desire to dampen punishment, the accused became obliging witnesses, expanding their confessions to include more and more people and more and more (expected) heretical acts. Testimonies are also suspicious because they are so ritualized and stereotyped. You are familiar with the standard litany of Judaizing charges: wearing one's best clothes on Saturday, cleaning the house on Saturday and changing the sheets, refusing to eat pork, celebrating the festivals of Queen Esther, the Day of Atonement, or the Hebrew New Year. In the idolatry trials, we find these recurring accusations: worshiping the Sun, worshiping the Moon, making prayers to the Earth, giving offerings to the mountain gods. Inquisition and extirpation trials alike might appear to tell us more about what the judges wanted to hear, or what the accused believed the judges wanted to hear, than anything else.

But expert historians, like Yosef Yerushalmi and Carlo Ginzburg, have shown how Inquisition documents can be used to flesh out the lives and understandings of tribunal suspects.[9] With careful reading, testimony leaps out because it goes against the grain, clashes with expectations—just seems surprising. Ginzburg makes the case that these strange, bizarre, and unexpected statements constitute precisely the leads that historians should follow. All transcripts are dialogues, he reminds us, and even if the testimony is lopsided, even if it so mutes the defendants' desires and beliefs that they seem to disappear, something of the accused remains in the text. This is a lesson in power, to be sure, and about how those in power shape what appear to be "objective" records; but it is also a lesson in the limited ability of those in power to utterly crush the will of others.

Henríque Urbano, in the strongest and most extreme case against the extirpation records, argues that they have little to say about Andean religion and everything to say about the misconceptions, stereotypes, interests, and motives of the extirpators.[10] But extirpation trials also have their moments of incongruity and surprise: natives worshiping guacas that had been burned by doctrineros decades before; elaborate descriptions of local divinities—and their adventures—that go well beyond Church stereotypes. And we have corroborating evidence of Andean religious practices in burial sites, offerings, and other material remains.[11]

The vexing question of native religion in the colonies is a good example of vexing knowledge. Our richest source of information about native religion in the seventeenth century comes from the idolatry campaigns. However, those campaigns were not systematically waged over time, nor were they uniformly waged across Peru's dispersed native population. Lima's bishops seem to have been the most aggressive, or at least they have left us the most records. Except for early-print ecclesiastic manuals and some descriptions by chroniclers, we do not have abundant evidence about native religion outside the Lima diocese. Does that mean "idolatries" didn't exist?

Let's look at the cases of colonial Ayacucho, Cuzco, and Arequipa. Given the documents, it would be hard to claim that natives living there were anything but faithful Catholics. Yet the Andeans living in these areas today maintain practices that would have scandalized doctrineros three centuries ago. Does this suggest that idolatries were more deeply rooted in the countryside than the record allows? Were some bishops unwilling or unable to mount campaigns against the native peoples they were responsible for?[12] I would imagine so. And were these "heresies" as vitriolic, as resolutely anti-Spanish, as those found in Hacas Poma's Cajatambo? Impossible to know.

Avila's sermons are helpful, tantalizing, but they also point to muddles. His sermons, published at the time Hacas Poma was brought before ecclesiastic judges, reflect a pointed awareness of native dissatisfaction with life under colonial rule as well as of the religious idiom expressing dissent. In one sermon, Avila had an imaginary Indian say the following things: "[The Christian god] won't do for us Indians"; "We are not like *españoles*"; "We '*indios*' . . . are not of God's flock nor is the Spaniards' god our own."[13] Avila spent time as an idolatry hunter in Huarochirí, a village in the area where extirpation campaigns flourished; and he was also familiar with other Andean regions, like Cuzco. Was Avila generalizing from his Lima experience, or had he found similar beliefs elsewhere?

Indians were not a uniform community: some lived in cities, others in the sierra; some were noblemen; others, peasants. Different religious opportunities and experiences might then be reflected in their commitment to Christianity. Wouldn't we expect to find more pro-Christian sentiment in urban settings, where the opportunities to participate in Catholic institutions were more abundant? Or among the nobility, who, privileged by the colonial regime, would have much to lose if their heresies were uncovered? Yes, and these are significant lines of differentiation. But they, too, are suggestive at best; not conclusive. Hacas Poma, for example, was a member of the local nobility and had been highly respected by Spanish authorities—until his idolatries were uncovered; similarly, Juan Santos Atahuallpa, trained in a Jesuit school for the Indian elite, fluent in Latin and Spanish, led the longest Indian revolt witnessed in the viceroyalty.[14]

Indian beliefs changed over time, and not necessarily in one direction: Catholics could abandon the faith (also suggested by Avila); Indianists could return to it. In this, they appear to be like those other heretics under inquisitorial surveillance.

Inquisition and extirpation records are at the core of this book; and so, therefore, are the institutions that produced them. Occupying center stage, they assume an exaggerated importance, and as the reviewers of my manuscript reminded me, I must be clear about their limits. In spite of the Lima records, it is unlikely that native religion was everywhere about to explode into a militant, anti-Spanish nativism. Similarly, in spite of the Inquisition records, the tribunal did not have an immediate hold on all viceregal lives. I do not want to exaggerate the consequence of either institution.

The Inquisition, according to its self-presentation and to our stereotype, was an imposing, nearly monolithic power, able to reach into souls and uncover every heretical thought. But how much was it really a factor in people's lives? Think of it: Lima's few magistrates were responsible for nearly all of South America—an impossible task, as they constantly reminded their superiors. Given the relatively few men and women actually punished over the course of the seventeenth century, was the tribunal much of a force at all? Was it all sound and fury?

How to gauge its impact? If we calculate in terms of the number of people arrested, then the tribunal had, obviously, very little. But what about vaguer properties? Like its influence, or even simply its perceived presence, or weight, as an institution of state?

The Inquisition's appeal—and mystique—were tied to the Church, and Peruvians, it appears, were churchgoers. Although I have no statistics, diaries and travelers' accounts depict religious activity as a fulcrum of daily life.[15] Churches and chapels were a prominent part of the colonial landscape, flourishing in cities and existing in villages that today would be considered isolated pueblos. For example, the city of Huamanga, Department of Ayacucho, had over thirty colonial chapels, and although Sarhua, a village where I did fieldwork, boasted a colonial church along with other colonial buildings, there was almost no contemporary government presence in 1979. As to the success of Church teaching, I can't assess Peruvian morality, but I can attest that almost everyone brought before the Inquisition was familiar with basic doctrine and the catechism.

It would have been difficult to ignore the tribunal's presence in Lima, especially when autos-da-fé were celebrated. And outside Lima? The Inquisition was made known by other means: by arrests in regions far from Lima (like Potosí, Trujillo, Cuzco, Tucumán, or Sucre); by Church occasions, i.e. in sermons and in the annual edicts of faith read throughout the viceroyalty; and, no doubt, by an ever vibrant popular imagination stoked in verbal renderings, tales, and rumors.[16]

I don't want to exaggerate the Inquisition's powers: it was not an all-seeing, all-knowing institution; its tentacles did not extend into the farthest corners of the empire. And although this book is devoted to men and women accused of heresies, I do not want to leave the impression that Peru was amok with witches and hidden Judaizers, all being chased by inquisitors or their familiars. Nonetheless, the tribunal was not an inconsequential institution. Its notoriety extended well beyond its current ventures, well beyond its immediate reach. The Inquisition had a viceregal and an imperial (even international) presence.[17]

So, where does that leave us? The problems raised by tribunal and extirpation records are overwhelming—to the extent that some renowned scholars consider their use, except in very restricted efforts, to be futile. At times, today's intellectual cynicism seems to enhance this despair. But knowledge, as we know, is always uncertain. Still, documents and fieldwork, checking and counterbalancing, mark out a potential, if debatable, path. We owe it to those who are central to our lives—including those people whose lives are crucial for our scholarship—not just to recognize the limitations of knowledge but to explore its possibilities.

NOTES

Prologue

1 Arendt, *The Origins of Totalitarianism*, ix.

2 Scarred by standoffs over royal prerogatives on the Peninsula, Castile would never allow colonists the liberties secured by Catalonia or the Basque country. Viceregal "vecinos" would meet in municipal councils like their European counterparts, but they never enjoyed the same right to limit royal demands. The viceroy always had the final word. For overviews of Spanish conquest and colonization see Elliott, "The Spanish Conquest" and "Spain and America before 1700"; Gibson, "Indian Societies under Spanish Rule"; and Spalding, *De indio a campesino*.

3 Colonization, of a piece with Spanish state-making, took various specific forms over time and across the empire's vast reach.

4 See Gibson, "Indian Societies under Spanish Rule"; Elliott, "Spain and America before 1700"; and Spalding, *De indio a campesino*, 31–126. Spain also recognized the "noble" standing of native headmen, who, as intermediary agents for the Crown, were exempted from tribute and labor obligations. Spalding, *De indio a campesino*, 31–60. For a classic study of colonial categories of race see Mörner, *Race Mixture in the History of Latin America*.

5 See Corrigan and Sayer, *The Great Arch*.

6 Of course, students of Spanish history have long known of the Inquisition's bureaucratic sophistication. See Elliott, *Imperial Spain, 1469–1716* (1964), and Kamen, *The Spanish Inquisition*.

7 Kamen, *The Spanish Inquisition*, 193. The Inquisition's emphasis on regulations and standards was part of a significant trend in early modern jurisprudence and administration. See Francisco Tomás y Valiente, *La tortura en España*; Lewin, *El Santo Oficio en América*, 113–34, for a comparison of the law and the practice of torture; and Herzog, *La administración como un fenómeno social*. Corrigan and Sayer make a similar point about English jurisprudence in *The Great Arch*, esp. 31–72, as do Wolfram Fischer and Peter Lundgreen about England and other European states, "The Recruitment and Training of Administrative and Technical Personnel," in Tilly, ed., *The Formation of Nation-States in Western Europe*, 456–61. For a more detailed exploration of the ways in which the Inquisition's judicial apparatus—and its reliance on denunciations in particular—favored the prosecution, see my chapter "Inquisition as Bureaucracy"; for more about the use of torture, see my chapter "Mysteries of State."

8 Again, and not to be underemphasized, the Spanish Inquisition, unlike other European tribunals, was under the control of the Crown, not the pope. So, even though the In-

quisition had a religious purpose, and therefore was tied indirectly to the Church, the Spanish Crown oversaw the tribunal's functioning.

9   Medina, *Historia del Tribunal del Santo Oficio de la Inquisición en México*, 27, 41–51. The three New World offices had much in common. All were players in the jostling for power within their respective viceroyalties and between their local offices and Madrid, and denunciations against accused heretics found their way from one office to another. The sin of Judaizing provoked the most vicious response in the three tribunals, and accused Judaizers were the most likely to be burned at the stake (see my chapter "New Christians and New World Fears," esp. note 3, for more detail on accused Judaizers). All three offices tried accused witches, although it appears that magistrates in Lima and Cartagena sought to prosecute them more aggressively than the Mexico office (for more detailed comparisons, see my chapter "The Inca's Witches," esp. note 1). The most comprehensive, recent studies of the Mexican Inquisition have been conducted by Alberro, *Inquisición y sociedad en México, 1571–1700*. For Cartagena see Splendiani, Sánchez Bohorquez, and Luque de Salazar, *Cincuenta años de inquisición en el Tribunal de Cartagena de Indias 1610–1660*. Much of the variability in the actual prosecution of heretics rests on the particular history of each tribunal office, which is why a local perspective is so important.

10   Cited in Castañeda Delgado and Hernández Aparicio, *La Inquisición de Lima*, 1:101, 102.

11   Ibid., 1:101. For example, asserting preeminence over royal authorities, the tribunal claimed the right to judge its own employees in most criminal and civil cases. During times of crisis, Inquisition personnel's first responsibility was to the tribunal and not to royal authority. Eventually, secular government did some clipping of the Inquisition's wings. Some of the most serious sniping between the two bureaucracies was in the arena of protocol and etiquette — the public, visible dimension of social rank. While many of these squabbles appear petty to us (size of chair, kind of seat, cushions or no cushions, place in a procession), they were not so to the participants, who were well aware that ritual place was another name for status and power. Pérez Villanueva and Escandell Bonet, eds., *Historia de la inquisición en España y América*, 2:12–13; Castañeda Delgado and Hernández Aparicio, *La Inquisición de Lima*, 1:105–7, 126.

12   The Inquisition's jurisdiction did not extend to the colony's native populations, whose moral behavior and customs were monitored by the bishops. See Medina, *Historia del Tribunal del Santo Oficio de la Inquisición de Lima*, 2:27–28.

13   No conviction but no release; i.e., kept "on hold."

14   Thus, we must understand the Inquisition as a dynamic of interests and possibilities. This perspective focuses on the context of decisions made by midlevel officials, on the Lima magistrates' internal conflicts, as well as on conflicts between them and the accused, and between them and their Madrid higher-ups. In this regard, *Modern Inquisitions* hopes to extend the path begun by important new scholarship in the area of early modern legal structures and in ethnographies of the state. More detail is provided in my chapter "Inquisition as Bureaucracy," esp. in note 2.

15   See Duviols's classic and magisterial work *La lutte contre les religions autochtones dans le Pérou colonial*, as well as his *Cultura andina y represión*. My chapter "Becoming Indian" is based on the records generated by the "extirpation of idolatry" campaigns.

16   The AAL records in the Campaigns to Extirpate Idolatry section, like Inquisition records, are very problematic. See "Appendix: Notes on Bias and Sources."

17   Weber also wrote about the dehumanizing aspects of bureaucratic order that accompanied the "disenchantment" of the world. Seventeenth-century Peru, however, was still an enchanted world.

18   Some historians would not use the term "state" to characterize the polities of early modern Europe. They would consider the state to be a phenomenon of the eighteenth and nineteenth centuries and, therefore, prematurely applied to the emerging bureau-

cratic institutions of the seventeenth century (more about this later). One such scholar, the important historian of early modern Spain Antonio Feros, would center political history on issues of kingship, on Europe's "personal monarchies" in which the king, as the axis of all power, "reigned supreme" (*Kingship and Favoritism in the Spain of Philip III*). Feros, I believe, would conceptualize Spain's central governing institutions as imposing limits on the monarchy, but would be reluctant to grant them the political autonomy associated with state structures.

19   Foucault cited in Burchell, Gordon, and Miller, eds., *The Foucault Effect*, 87–104.

20   Bourdieu, *Practical Reason*, 35–74.

21   Abrams, "Notes on the Difficulty of Studying the State."

22   Ibid., 82.

23   Ibid., 77.

24   Corrigan and Sayer, *The Great Arch*, 1–13, 166–208.

25   Ibid., 15–41.

26   Ibid., 59.

27   Ibid., 42–71.

28   Ibid., 70–71.

29   See the epigraph opening this chapter.

30   See Weinstein, *The Amazon Rubber Boom, 1850–1920*, however, for a discussion showing that the Putumayo region was an exception in boss–laborer relations. The Putumayo region was notably brutal.

31   Taussig, "Culture of Terror—Space of Death."

32   Taussig, "Maleficium."

33   Ibid.

34   Ibid.

35   Also see Herzfeld, *The Social Construction of Indifference*, for a Durkheimian analysis of bureaucratic rationality as ideology.

36   Taussig, "Culture of Terror—Space of Death."

37   Coronil, "Beyond Occidentalism." Also see the foreword to Joseph, LeGrand, and Salvatore, eds., *Close Encounters of Empire*, ix–xv. Other examples of this important critical literature include Mignolo, *Local Histories/Global Designs*, among his many works; Amin, *Eurocentrism*; Dussel, "Beyond Eurocentrism"; Lander, "Eurocentrismo y colonialismo en el pensamiento social latinoamericano"; and, of course, the iconic Ribeiro, *The Americas and Civilization*, and Gilroy's *The Black Atlantic*. For earlier studies of the economic underpinning of modernity's inequalities see Williams and Frank, *Capitalism and Underdevelopment in Latin America*, and Wallerstein, *The Modern World-System*. For an essay that stresses the importance of the colonial experience for the metropole, see Cooper and Stoler, "Between Metropole and Colony."

38   See Holt, *The Problem of Race in the Twenty-first Century*, and the pathbreaking Trouillot, *Silencing the Past*.

39   Here, of course, I am indebted to so many scholars who have provided a critical and historical view of race. See ibid.; Hall, "Gramsci's Relevance for the Study of Race and Ethnicity"; Stuart Hall, *Critical Dialogues in Cultural Studies* (London: Routledge, 1996); Donald and Hall, eds., *Politics and Ideology*; Gilroy, *Against Race*; Trouillot, *Silencing the Past*; Ribeiro, *The Americas and Civilization*; Baker, *From Savage to Negro*; Balabar and Wallerstein, *Race, Nation, Class*; and Gilroy, *The Black Atlantic*. For a careful analysis of the relationship between colonialism and race see Memmi, *Racism*, and Fanon's classic *Black Skin, White Masks*. For a recent review of critical race theory in Latin America, see Warren and Twine, "Critical Race Studies in Latin America." Also see Stoler, *Carnal Knowledge and Imperial Power* for the pioneering examination of the relationship between imperialism, race, gender, and sexuality. As Bianca Premo has pointed out, some of the early formulations of the "race question" in Latin America remain provocative, particularly the work of Charles Wagley, who stressed race's "so-

cial" nature and its "entanglements" with "social and cultural criteria." See Wagley, "On the Concept of Social Race in the Americas," in *Actas del XXXIII Congreso Internacional de Americanistas* (San José, 1959), 403–7, cited by Premo in her unpublished manuscript.

40 Beetham, *Bureaucracy*; Kamenka, *Bureaucracy*.

41 Marx, "On the Jewish Question"; Marx, *The Grundrisse*, 16–22, 77.

42 These tensions, of course, were present within any of the unmixed race categories. Ann Stoler has most insightfully shown that colonialism's dominant race had to be constructed; see Stoler, *Carnal Knowledge and Imperial Power*.

43 Anónimo portugués, *Descripción del virreinato del Perú*, 73.

44 Cobo, *History of the Inca Empire* (1979), 68.

45 Anónimo portugués, *Descripción del virreinato del Perú*, 39, 70.

46 Ibid., 32–40, 54, 55, 68, 70.

47 Ibid., 32–40; also Mills and Taylor, eds., *Colonial Spanish America*, 169–70 with a short selection from Anónimo portugués trans. into English at 170–75. Special thanks to Bianca Premo, currently working on an important book about "minority" in colonial Peru, who shared with me some insights into Lima from her unpublished manuscript.

48 Anónimo portugués, *Descripción del virreinato del Perú*, 69–70.

49 The category of mestizo/mulato was most likely underrepresented, with many whom we would designate as "mixed race" joining Spanish or Indian populations.

50 I am taking these 1614 census numbers from Mills and Taylor, eds., *Colonial Spanish America*, 165–66. They remind us that these numbers should be seen as approximations, as should the estimate by Buenaventura de Salinas y Córdoba.

51 Ibid., 165. The silver ore of Potosí, along with the Indian labor that produced it, are icons of what Marx would have called capitalism's relentless drive for "primitive accumulation."

52 An exciting and growing literature exists concerning colonial Peruvian religiosity. Santa Rosa de Lima, the first canonized saint from Latin America, showed the world (and especially Andeans) that the colonies, not just Europe, could nurture saints. *Limeñas* who lobbied on her behalf emphasized to the Vatican that it would be good for *criollos*, women and men of Spanish descent but born in Peru, to recognize that a saint could emerge from their midst. See Glave, *De Rosa y espinas*, and Hampe Martínez, "Santa Rosa de Lima como prototipo divino y humano." The three-session symposium "Santidad y perversión," where Hampe Martínez presented his paper at the fifty-first Congreso Internacional de Americanistas (2003) was noteworthy. Also see Kathleen Ann Myers, "'Redeemer of America': Rosa de Lima (1586–1617), the Dynamics of Identity and Canonization," in Greer and Bilinkoff, eds., *Colonial Saints*, 251–76, and Flores Araoz et al., eds., *Santa Rosa de Lima y su tiempo*.

There is also a new and significant literature on indigenous Catholicism. The Virgin of Copacabana, a statue carved by an Indian and initially rejected by Spanish authorities, attracted adherents throughout South America (including Rio de Janeiro). Although first gaining renown at Lake Titicaca, where her first chapel was built, the Virgin of Copacabana captivated believers in Lima, where a chapel to her was built during the first decades of the seventeenth century. Ramos, *Historia de Copacabana y de la milagrosa imagen de su Virgen*. For recent research see Sordo, "Nuestra Señora de Copacabana y su legado en el Potosí colonial," another paper presented at the "Santidad y perversión" symposium (2003). Some of the most fascinating new scholarship focuses on the appeal of Catholicism to indigenous elites. See, for example, the articles in Decoster, ed., *Incas e indios cristianos*, as well as Dean, *Inka Bodies and the Body of Christ*. For an important collection focusing on the engagement of native religion and Christianity see Cervantes and Griffiths, eds., *Spiritual Encounters*, particularly the article by Osorio, "El Callejón de la Soledad." Also see Mills, "Diego de Ocaña's Hagiography of New and Renewed Devotion in Colonial Peru." For further discussions of indigenous religiosity see my chapter "Becoming Indian"; that chapter, however, focuses on a movement in Andean religious belief that excoriated Christian things.

Another of Peru's saints who lived during the colonial period was San Martín de Porres, the illegitimate son of a Spanish nobleman and a freed slave. San Martín became the first black American saint. Although miracles were attributed to him after his death, San Martín was not beatified until 1873 and was not canonized until 1962 (Patron Saints Index, Catholic Community Forum, www.catholic-forum.com/saints/indexsnt.htm).

53 One of the most vexing problems was that presented by the *beatas*, women who claimed a special relationship to God. Several such women, cherished by a broad sector of vice-regal society—from laundresses to artisans, from clergymen to royal officials—were damned by the Inquisition for doing the devil's work. Inéz de Jesús was one, and you will be encountering others, like María Pizarro and Angela Carranza. For another example, from colonial Buenos Aires, see Fraschina, "De bruja a 'elegida de Dios'"—yet another paper presented in 2003 at the "Santidad y perversión" symposium. For further examination of women in religious life, see Iwasaki, "Mujeres al borde de la perfección"; van Deusen, *Between the Sacred and the Worldly*; and Burns, *Colonial Habits*.

54 These bold contradictions are what make seventeenth-century religious life so fascinating to us. See above for examples of the growing literature exploring the dynamism of colonial Andean religious life. For a broader look at the formation of saints in colonial America see Greer and Bilinkoff, eds., *Colonial Saints*.

55 I chose these trials not only because of their interest, but because their records are complete and, therefore, more integral and coherent than others. Although most other dossiers are not as full or rich, they do reveal similar processes at play.

56 Hannah Arendt's paradigm for bureaucratic rule was nineteenth-century colonialism, and the bureaucratic arrogance she criticizes comes from the very nature of colonial administration. British colonial officials were ultimately accountable to political authorities in London. Of course there were enormous political differences between seventeenth-century Spain and nineteenth-century England—not the least being democratic governance at home. Viewed from the colonies, though, the tribunal bureaucracy of the seventeenth century and the imperial administration of the nineteenth century had certain similarities, including principles of representation and accountability.

57 This expression is an allusion to Coronil's *The Magical State*, and Taussig's *The Magic of the State*.

58 Centuries later, during the first half of the twentieth century, a new regional political movement would surface in Peru. Its ideology stressed Peru's distinctiveness because of its Indian past, and it became both a way for local regional elites to separate themselves from the Lima establishment and a way for Peru to differentiate itself from Western powers.

59 It is very difficult to assess the breadth or depth of these indigenous notions of Indian self-identity. Certainly they did not shape the vision of all Andeans. I argue that the dynamic here was one dimension in the process of building colonial hegemony. During the last twenty years students of the processes of nation-building have been exploring the dynamics of class relations, state formation, and cultural practices. Nourished by the work of Antonio Gramsci, they have complicated the meaning of "culture" and insisted on the ways in which power permeates the living experiences of people in state-ruled societies. For the most part, their studies have explored the roads to nation-building and capitalist development, but I believe Gramscian insights are germane to the early colonial state as it helped make our modern world. The literature on these processes has grown enormously, so I will cite here only those works that most influenced my project. Along with Corrigan and Sayer, *The Great Arch*, see the following: Thompson, "Eighteenth-Century English Society"; Williams, *Marxism and Literature*, 75–144; and Genovese, *Roll Jordan Roll*. Jean and John Comaroff have used Gramsci, along with Corrigan and Sayer, in their important discussions of the cultural dimensions of the En-

glish colonial state in South Africa; see Comaroff and Comaroff, *Ethnography and the Historical Imagination*. I have relied on Gramsci in my exploration of the crisis of social categories at the heart of the colonization process; see Silverblatt, "Political Memories and Colonizing Symbols" and "Becoming Indian in the Central Andes of Seventeenth-Century Peru."

Three Accused Heretics

1 Benjamin, "Theses on the Philosophy of History," 256.
2 These three cases were chosen because of their great interest and because the completeness of the dossiers makes their transcripts more integral and coherent than others. Other transcripts, while not as rich, manifest similar processes at play. All translations are mine unless otherwise noted. I have standardized and occasionally modernized spelling to help avoid confusion.
3 The Inquisition was established in Castile and tribunals were set up in different Spanish cities as early as 1478. However, in 1483, a papal bull initiated the process that united the Inquisitions of the Spanish Crown under a single jurisdiction. See Kamen, *Inquisition and Society*, 18–43, and Gitlitz, *Secrecy and Deceit*, xiv–xvi, 18–25.
4 For a more detailed discussion of this period see Caro Baroja, *Los judíos en la España moderna y contemporánea*, 125–64; Kamen, *The Spanish Inquisition*, 1–65; and Gitlitz, *Secrecy and Deceit*, 3–34.
5 In practice, New Christians held offices and entered universities in spite of the prohibitions. See my chapter "Inquisition as Bureaucracy" as well as the histories of many of the arrested, described in later chapters.
6 Kamen, *The Spanish Inquisition*, 202–4.
7 Gitlitz, *Secrecy and Deceit*, 75. Estimates range from 50,000 to 120,000, with the lower end seeming most likely. See Kamen, *The Spanish Inquisition*, 267, for the numbers of Jews living in Portugal.
8 Scholars have stressed the significance for New Christian communities of this early history of Portuguese Jews, converted as a block to Christianity. See Kamen, *The Spanish Inquisition*, 287–90; Yerushalmi, *From Spanish Court to Italian Ghetto*, 1–51; Caro Baroja, *Los judíos en la España moderna y contemporánea*, 207–26; and Lockhart and Schwartz, *Early Latin America*, 225–26.
9 The commercial interests of New Christians and Jews, along with their international ties, have been well noted. Among the many analyses see Jonathan I. Israel's several pathbreaking accounts, among them *Empires and Entrepôts* and *European Jewry in the Age of Mercantilism, 1550–1750*. Of the 62 men and women who were penanced for Judaizing in the 1639 auto-da-fé, 44 had occupations associated with commerce or trade. For interesting cases against merchants brought before the Lima Inquisition, see Francisco Núñez de Olivera, AHN, Inq., lib. 1029, fols. 45v–49v; Antonio Fernández, AHN, Inq., lib. 1029, fols. 57v–59v; Balthasar de Lucena, AHN, Inq., lib. 1029, fols. 61–65; Duarte Núñez de Zea, AHN, Inq., lib. 1029, fols. 65v–67v; Bernabé López Serrano, AHN, Inq., lib. 1030, fols. 280–80v; Alvaro Méndez, AHN, Inq., lib. 1030, fols. 367–69; Raphael Pérez de Freitas, AHN, Inq., lib. 1030, fols. 418–19v; Luis de Valencia, AHN, Inq., leg. 1647, no. 12; Andrés Núñez Xuárez, AHN, Inq., lib. 1029, fols. 53v–55v; Duarte Méndez, AHN, Inq., lib. 1028, fols. 339–44; Manuel Anríquez, AHN, Inq., lib. 1028, fols. 364–69; Diego López de Fonseca, AHN, Inq., lib. 1031, fols. 89–95; Juan de Acevedo, AHN, Inq., lib. 1031, fols. 77–87; Manuel Albarez, AHN, Inq., lib. 1031, fol. 83; Rodrigo Báez Peryra, AHN, Inq., lib. 1031, fol. 84; Juan Rodríguez de Silva, AHN, Inq., lib. 1031, fol. 99; Antonio de la Vega, AHN, Inq., lib. 1031, fol. 104; Bartolomé de Silva, AHN, Inq., lib. 1031, fol. 136v; Martías Delgado, AHN, Inq., lib. 1031, fols. 138v–39; Gonzalo de Valcázar, AHN, Inq., lib. 1031, fol. 141; Sebatián Duarte, AHN, Inq., lib. 1031, fols. 186–95v;

Manuel Henríquez, AHN, Inq., leg. 1647, no. 11; Manuel Bautista Pérez, AHN, Inq., leg. 1647, no. 13.

10 Gitlitz, *Secrecy and Deceit*, 51–53; Kamen, *The Spanish Inquisition*, 287–90. Portuguese not of Jewish descent were often outraged that they were assumed to be Jewish. See Boxer, *The Portuguese Seaborne Empire, 1415–1825*.

11 Elliott, *Imperial Spain* (1990), 249–84, 337–49; Lockhart and Schwartz, *Early Latin America*, 221–27, 251; Gitlitz, *Secrecy and Deceit*, 43–46.

12 Altolaguirre, ed., *Colección de las memorias o relaciones que escribieron los virreyes del Perú...*, 194–297; Suardo, *Diario de Lima de Juan Antonio Suardo (1629–1639)*, 1:259–61.

13 Although it is difficult to identify allegiances with great accuracy, evidence suggests that Brazil's New Christian population held divided loyalties: while some, principally crypto-Jews, might have sided with Holland, many, perhaps even the majority, fought to keep Brazil under Iberian control. See the excellent study by Novinsky, *Cristãos novos na Bahia*. In a 1997 conference, "Jews and the Expansion of Europe: 1450–1800," hosted by the John Carter Brown Library (Brown University, Providence, R.I.), Novinsky reiterated her belief that a significant proportion of New Christians remained loyal to Spain. In a similar vein, a commonplace of the time (one that is still heard today) held that Portuguese Jews had controlling interests in the Dutch West Indies Company. After a careful examination of company records, Jonathan Israel concluded that although some Jews had investments in the Dutch West Indies Company, they never dominated it (*Empires and Entrepôts*, 356n2). Also see Kamen, *The Spanish Inquisition*, 42–43, 64–65, 290, 293–94, 297–98; and Gitlitz, *Secrecy and Deceit*, 61–62.

14 See AHN, Inq., Cartas, rollo 9, fol. 51, letter from inquisitors Juan de Mañozca, Andrés Gaytán, and Antonio de Castro y del Castillo to Muy P. Señor, May 18, 1636; also Lockhart and Schwartz, *Early Latin America*, 250. Part of the preceding discussion comes from Silverblatt, "New Christians and New World Fears in Seventeenth-Century Peru."

15 Israel, *Empires and Entrepôts*, 160, 247–56, 360, 362.

16 Ibid., 315; AHN, Inq. rollo 9, fols. 166–81. Even officers of the Inquisition jumped onto the bandwagon. Felipe IV's confessor, the inquisitor general, noted positively that "the 'Portuguese' who are here would be capable of drawing off from Holland many of those who have most capital there, if some concession were made to them concerning a pardon for past offences, should they undertake to live in the future without offence to the Catholic faith" (cited in Israel, *Empires and Entrepôts*, 362).

17 Fernando de Montesinos, "Descripción del auto de fe de la 'complicidad grande'" ("Auto de la fe celebrado en Lima a 23 de enero de 1639"), in Lewin, *El Santo Oficio en América*, app. 1:155–189; citation at 159.

18 AHN, Inq., leg. 1647, no. 10, fols. 35–35v.

19 AHN, Inq., leg. 1647, no. 10, fols. 1–1v.

20 AHN, Inq., leg. 1647, no. 10, fol. 1.

21 AHN, Inq., leg. 1647, no. 10, fol. 2v.

22 AHN, Inq., leg. 1647, no. 10, fols. 3v–4v. As you will see, it was common to claim that the "feast of Esther," or Purim, took place in September—the period of high holidays; but Purim usually falls in March.

23 AHN, Inq., leg. 1647, no. 10, fols. 2–4v.

24 AHN, Inq., leg. 1647, no. 10, fols. 7–7v.

25 AHN, Inq., leg. 1647, no. 10, fol. 8.

26 AHN, Inq., leg. 1647, no. 10, fols. 9v–10.

27 AHN, Inq., leg. 1647, no. 10, fols. 9v–10. This testimonial pattern—confessing when subject to torture, recanting, being tortured again, recanting again—held for most of the witnesses against Doña Mencia. Rodrigo Báez, the husband of Doña Mencia's niece, kept to this pattern, except he did not name Doña Mencia in his second round of confessions. And, as good bureaucrats, magistrates underscored this fact for the record. There were exceptions. One of the witnesses who at first denied Judaizing but then, after con-

fessing, never retracted his testimony was Antonio Gómez de Acosta. See AHN, Inq., leg. 1647, no. 10, fol. 15. Bachiller Francisco Maldonado de Silva, who changed his name to Elí el Nazareno in the Inquisition cells, was the one witness who never denied practicing some form of Judaism (Montesinos in Lewin, *El Santo Oficio en América*, app. 1:182).

28 Medina, *Historia del Tribunal del Santo Oficio de la Inquisición de Lima*, 2:56.

29 Ibid.

30 AHN, Inq., leg. 1647, no. 10, fols. 18–18v.

31 AHN, Inq., leg. 1647, no. 10, fol. 19.

32 AHN, Inq., leg. 1647, no. 10, fols. 22, 27v.

33 For Doña Mayor, see AHN, Inq., leg. 1647, no. 10, fols. 20v–27v. She was also convicted of trying to send messages to her daughter. Her most successful scheme was to write with lemon juice, a kind of invisible ink, that became legible when heated by a flame. Medina, *Historia del Tribunal del Santo Oficio de la Inquisición de Lima*, 2:132. For Doña Isabel see AHN, Inq., leg. 1647, no. 10, fols. 28–32. Both were reconciled in the 1639 auto-da-fé and, as an additional punishment for letter writing, were put on donkeys and publicly whipped through Lima's main streets. Medina, *Historia del Tribunal del Santo Oficio de la Inquisición de Lima*, 2:132. For Doña Mencia, see AHN, Inq., leg. 1647, no. 10, fols. 35–35v.

34 AHN, Inq., leg. 1647, no. 10, fol. 35.

35 AHN, Inq., leg. 1647, no. 10, fol. 39v.

36 AHN, Inq., leg. 1647, no. 10, fol. 41.

37 AHN, Inq., leg. 1647, no. 10, fol. 37v.

38 AHN, Inq., leg. 1647, no. 10, fols. 38v–39.

39 AHN, Inq., leg. 1647, no. 10, fols. 39–40v.

40 AHN, Inq., leg. 1647, no. 10, fol. 40v.

41 AHN, Inq., leg. 1647, no. 10, fols. 48v–49. One witness declared that Doña Mencia hated intermarriage between Old and New Christians, and that men who needed to be encouraged to marry fellow Jews "would, in particular, go to talk with [her]."

42 AHN, Inq., leg. 1647, no. 10, fol. 41–54v.

43 AHN, Inq., leg. 1647, no. 10, fol. 41.

44 AHN, Inq., leg. 1647, no. 10, fols. 57, 57v.

45 AHN, Inq., leg. 1647, no. 10, fol. 58v.

46 Lewin, *El Santo Oficio en América*, 122.

47 Ibid.; AHN, Inq., leg. 1647, no. 10, fol. 59.

48 AHN, Inq., leg. 1647, no. 10, fol. 59.

49 AHN, Inq., leg. 1647, no. 10, fol. 59.

50 AHN, Inq., leg. 1647, no. 10, fol. 59.

51 AHN, Inq., leg. 1647, no. 10, fol. 59v.

52 AHN, Inq., leg. 1647, no. 10, fol. 59v.

53 AHN, Inq., leg. 1647, no. 10, fols. 59v–60.

54 AHN, Inq., leg. 1647, no. 10, fols. 60v–61.

55 AHN, Inq., leg. 1647, no. 10, fol. 65v.

56 AHN, Inq., leg. 1647, no. 10, fols. 68–68v.

57 AHN, Inq., leg. 1647, no. 10, fol. 70v.

58 García de Proodian, *Los judíos en América*, 545.

59 AHN, Inq., leg. 1647, no. 11, fol. 56v.

60 AHN, Inq., leg. 1647, no. 11, fol. 57.

61 AHN, Inq., leg. 1647, no. 11, fol. 58.

62 AHN, Inq., leg. 1647, no. 11, fols. 57v–58.

63 AHN, Inq., leg. 1647, no. 11, fol. 59. Interestingly, Henríquez's Spanish showed a Portuguese inflection, as noted by Pedro Báez in this deposition; and when Henríquez indicated the days when rites were observed, he did so in Portuguese, not in Castilian.

64 AHN, Inq., leg. 1647, no. 11, fol. 60.

65 AHN, Inq., leg. 1647, no. 11, fol. 60.

66 Some examples: Don Simón Osorio, befriending Henríquez on the voyage from Seville to Cartagena, promised to help establish him in the viceroyalty, if he would return to Judaism ("[Don Simón] said in order for you to be rich and save your soul you should follow the Law of Moses"); the brothers Jorge and Antonio de Espinosa assured Henríquez they would always buy corn from him and that "they were happy as long as he said he was Jewish" (as he was led to the stake, Antonio de Espinosa requested a final confession in which he denounced Henríquez for perjury). AHN, Inq., leg. 1647, no. 11, fols. 60–67v. Note the stereotype: Jews are rich, and Jews unfairly help one another.

67 AHN, Inq., leg. 1647, no. 11, fol. 79.

68 AHN, Inq., leg. 1647, no. 11, fols. 81v–82.

69 AHN, Inq., leg. 1647, no. 11, fol. 90v.

70 AHN, Inq., leg. 1647, no. 11, fols. 90v, 13–14v. In a round of remarkable and illicit correspondence—which spanned nearly half a continent—Henríquez found out that Acuna had been right.

71 AHN, Inq., leg. 1647, no. 11, fol. 95. According to Henríquez, Acuna had very successfully induced fellow prisoners to memorize detailed plots of Judaizing and then to confess them to the tribunal. See AHN, Inq., leg. 1647, no. 11, fols. 90–91.

72 AHN, Inq., leg. 1647, no. 11, fol. 91v.

73 AHN, Inq., leg. 1647, no. 11, fol. 99.

74 AHN, Inq., leg. 1647, no. 11, fol. 92v.

75 AHN, Inq., leg. 1647, no. 11, fol. 91v.

76 AHN, Inq., leg. 1647, no. 11, fols. 106–26.

77 AHN, Inq., leg. 1647, no. 11, fol. 106.

78 AHN, Inq., leg. 1647, no. 11, fols. 121, 124v, 129v.

79 AHN, Inq., leg. 1647, no. 11, fol. 129v.

80 AHN, Inq., leg. 1647, no. 11, fol. 130v.

81 AHN, Inq., leg. 1647, no. 11, fol. 132.

82 AHN, Inq., leg. 1647, no. 11, fol. 132.

83 AHN, Inq., leg. 1647, no. 11, fol. 132.

84 AHN, Inq., leg. 1647, no. 11, fol. 136v.

85 AHN, Inq., leg. 1647, no. 11, fol. 141.

86 AHN, Inq., leg. 1647, no. 11, fol. 141v.

87 AHN, Inq., leg. 1647, no. 11, fols. 152–52v.

88 AHN, Inq., leg. 1647, no. 11, fol. 154.

89 AHN, Inq., leg. 1647, no. 11, fols. 154–54v.

90 AHN, Inq., leg. 1647, no. 11, fol. 56v; AHN, Inq., leg. 1647, no. 11, fol. 155. At this stage, Henríquez added to the confusion by introducing several different versions of the events leading to his arrest in Coimbra. AHN, Inq., leg. 1647, no. 11, fols. 157v–60, 162v, 169.

91 AHN, Inq., leg. 1647, no. 11, fol. 162v.

92 AHN, Inq., leg. 1647, no. 11, fol. 169.

93 "Relaxación" meant death. The condemned were "relaxed," or remanded, to the secular branch of government for execution.

94 Before writing this testimony, Henríquez listed outstanding debts to his brother-in-law, his uncle, two colleagues, and his aunt who were living in Spain. AHN, Inq., leg. 1647, no. 11, fol. 172.

95 AHN, Inq., leg. 1647, no. 11, fols. 173v–75.

96 AHN, Inq., lib. 1031, fol. 359.

97 AHN, Inq., leg. 1647, no. 11, fol. 175v.

98 Medina, *Historia del Tribunal del Santo Oficio de la Inquisición de Lima*, 2:176–77.

99 García de Proodian, *Los judíos en América*, 543.

100 AHN, Inq., leg. 1647, no. 13, fol. 13.

101 AHN, Inq., leg. 1647, no. 13, fols. 241–42.

102 AHN, Inq., leg. 1647, no. 13, fol. 54.

103 AHN, Inq., leg. 1647, no. 13, fol. 54; AHN, Inq., leg. 1647, no. 10, fol. 6; AHN, Inq., leg. 1647, no. 11, fol. 91.

104 AHN, Inq., leg. 1647, no. 13, fol. 78v. Pérez was also renowned for his extensive library, no doubt one of the finest in Peru. Inquisitors thought it contained books on Judaism, but inventories showed that in addition to histories, accounting manuals, and theological treatises, the only religious material was lives of the saints. AHN, Inq., leg. 1647, no. 13, fols. 78v–79v, 104–5.

105 AHN, Inq., leg. 1647, no. 13, fol. 248v.

106 AHN, Inq., leg. 1647, no. 13, fols. 246–47v.

107 AHN, Inq., leg. 1647, no. 13, fol. 249.

108 AHN, Inq., leg. 1647, no. 13, fol. 251v.

109 AHN, Inq., leg. 1647, no. 13, fol. 260.

110 AHN, Inq., leg. 1647, no. 13, fol. 263; also see fols. 264v, 265, 265v.

111 AHN, Inq., leg. 1647, no. 13, fols. 264v, 265, 267v.

112 AHN, Inq., leg. 1647, no. 13, fol. 263v.

113 AHN, Inq., leg. 1647, no. 13, fol. 266.

114 AHN, Inq., leg. 1647, no. 13, fol. 266.

115 AHN, Inq., leg. 1647, no. 13, fols. 271, 271v, 273, 278, 300v, 307. Follow-up testimony regarding specifics of the treatise dedicated to Pérez is found at fol. 309v.

116 AHN, Inq., leg. 1647, no. 13, fol. 281.

117 AHN, Inq., leg. 1647, no. 13, fols. 272–72v.

118 AHN, Inq., leg. 1647, no. 13, fol. 278v.

119 AHN, Inq., leg. 1647, no. 13, fols. 278v–79.

120 AHN, Inq., leg. 1647, no. 13, fol. 279v.

121 AHN, Inq., leg. 1647, no. 13, fols. 312v–14v. Communications between prisoners and between prisoners and the outside depended on both the connivance of tribunal employees and the help of slaves. In this case, a "house slave," named Antonio, had carried the message from Pérez's home and delivered it to his cell. Pérez also explained how he managed to get messages out with the help of his servants and the tribunal's workers: when Jusepe, one of the Inquisition's attendants (referred to as the "young attendant") deposited Antonio in Pérez's cell and then left them alone together for more than four hours, Pérez used the time to compose a letter for Antonio to take back to Diego Rodríguez de Lisboa. The cost of writing material was 120 pesos. See fols. 314–15, 317.

122 AHN, Inq., leg. 1647, no. 13, fol. 318v.

123 AHN, Inq., leg. 1647, no. 13, fols. 318v–19.

124 AHN, Inq., leg. 1647, no. 13, fols. 339v–40.

125 AHN, Inq., leg. 1647, no. 13, fol. 345v.

126 AHN, Inq., leg. 1647, no. 13, fol. 338v.

127 AHN, Inq., leg. 1647, no. 13, fol. 342v.

128 AHN, Inq., leg. 1647, no. 13, fols. 342v–43.

129 AHN, Inq., leg. 1647, no. 13, fol. 352v. Apparently other men and women had spoken on Pérez's behalf, but the tribunal's evaluators declared their testimonies inadmissible because they were members of his household (Sebastián Duarte; Doña Guiomar, his wife; Simón Báez, brother-in-law; García Báez, brother-in-law; Domingo González, mayordomo). It is noteworthy that if the testimonies supported the prosecutor's charges, household membership did not matter. AHN, Inq., leg. 1647, no. 13, fol. 1v.

130 AHN, Inq., leg. 1647, no. 13, fols. 363–364v, 365v–67v.

131 AHN, Inq., leg. 1647, no. 13, fol. 385v.

132 AHN, Inq., leg. 1647, no. 13, fols. 388–90.

133 AHN, Inq., leg. 1647, no. 13, fol. 406v.
134 AHN, Inq., leg. 1647, no. 13, fol. 406v.
135 AHN, Inq., leg. 1647, no. 13, fol. 410.
136 Medina, *Historia del Tribunal del Santo Oficio de la Inquisición de Lima*, 2:150.
137 Báez or Vaz (Portuguese) are the same.
138 *Taita* means "father" in Quechua.
139 AHN, Inq., leg. 1647, no. 13, loose sheet, not paginated.

Inquisition as Bureaucracy

1 Kamen, *The Spanish Inquisition*, 144.
2 The Inquisition, then, was similar to other emerging bureaucracies of the day. Although some theorists, like Foucault, have presented state power as if it were a directive from on high, inevitably carried out, *Modern Inquisitions* in general and this chapter in particular point to the contingent nature of outcomes. Here we can see not only the importance of middle-level functionaries in determining the actual outcomes of bureaucratic or legal mandates, but also the surprising limits imposed on inquisitors' desires by the institution's rules and procedures. Our approach follows an encouraging trend in early modern legal scholarship, as well as in contemporary anthropological studies of the state, that focuses on the actual processes of decision making and, consequently, on the role of lesser judicial officials and local contexts. Much of the historical scholarship looks at England. See the many works of C. W. Brooks, including *Pettyfoggers and Vipers of the Commonwealth*; Herrup, *The Common Peace*; and Hindle, *The Experience of Authority in Early Modern England*. For South America see, Herzog, *La administración como un fenómeno social*. For the "social history" of one Peruvian inquisitor see Gabriela Ramos, "La fortuna del inquisidor." For ethnographies of the state that focus on local decision-making processes see Herzfeld, *The Social Production of Indifference*, and Gupta and Ferguson, eds., *Culture, Power, Place*.
   Of course, the Crown precipitated the downfall of the royal bureaucracy in the middle seventeenth century when, strapped for cash, it began to sell offices. See Andrien, "The Sale of Fiscal Offices and the Decline of Royal Authority in the Viceroyalty of Peru."
3 There is an extensive literature on the Spanish Inquisition and a growing one on the Lima office. Some of the works I have consulted are these: Kamen, *The Spanish Inquisition*; Castañeda Delgado and Hernández Aparicio, *La Inquisición de Lima*; Pérez Villanueva and Escandell Bonet, eds., *Historia de la inquisición en España y América*; Millar Carvacho, *Inquisición y sociedad en el virreinato peruano*; Hampe Martínez, "Recent Works on the Inquisition and Peruvian Colonial Society, 1570–1820," and *Santo Oficio e historia colonial*; Mannarelli, *Hechiceras, beatas y expósitas*; van Deusen, *Between the Sacred and the Worldly*; the essays in *Inquisición y sociedad en América Latina*; Palma, *Anales de la Inquisición de Lima*; Medina, *Historia del Tribunal del Santo Oficio de la Inquisición de Lima*; Pérez Villaneuva, ed., *La Inquisición española*; Sánchez, *Mentalidad popular frente a ideología oficial*; Lewin, *El Santo Oficio en América*; and Caro Baroja, *Inquisición, brujería y criptojudaísmo*.
4 Castañeda Delgado and Hernández Aparicio, *La Inquisición de Lima*, 1:12, 16, 50, 69, 114.
5 Nonsalaried employees included the commissioners (the inquisitors' eyes and ears in the countryside) and consultants.
6 See Castañeda Delgado and Hernández Aparicio, *La Inquisición de Lima*, 1:1–68. Like the empire's other important bureaucrats, most came from Spain's "lesser nobility." Of the nine inquisitors working from 1570 to 1635, all were born in Spain and all came from the *baja nobleza* except for one whose father was a merchant and whose grandfather was a "worker"; his mother and maternal grandparents, however, were "hidalgos and

very renowned." Lima's magistrates, well experienced, all held offices in other tribunals, royal government or university before coming to Peru. Ibid., 1:3–5.

7 The relationship between inquisitor and prosecuting attorney, or *fiscal*, could be contentious. The fiscal had an ambiguous position in the tribunal's hierarchy—one of great responsibility, requiring background and training much like the inquisitor's, but not carrying equal prestige. A classic case was that of the attorney general, Juan Alcedo de la Rocha, who complained that he was given inferior seating when autos were held inside the church. In an attempt to avert problems, the Lima tribunal relieved Alcedo of his obligation to attend the autos. But the Supreme Council, or Suprema, was not satisfied with Lima's ad hoc decision and, insisting that precedent be followed and rules be kept, ordered Alcedo to attend the ceremonies and remain in his customary place with the tribunal's other officers. By intervening the way it did, the Suprema took advantage of a chance to clarify the fiscal's place in the bureaucracy's chain of command and further assert control over its hinterland operations—something it deemed necessary in the Lima case. Ibid., 1:17–18.

8 Ibid., 1:6–9. Five were given the opportunity to be bishops or archbishops in the Americas. Juan de Mañozca, one of Lima's more infamous inquisitors and the mastermind behind the Great Jewish Conspiracy of 1635–39, was asked to be chancellor of the Suprema in Madrid. Following that appointment he was named president of the Chancery of Granada, and three years later he was celebrated as the archbishop of Mexico, one of the most important archdioceses of the Americas.

9 Kamen, *The Spanish Inquisition*, 193.

10 Ibid.

11 As Henry Kamen pointed out, rules and safeguards were not always carried out. He has also presented a strong case that the Inquisition's cells were as humane as any of the secular jails of any European nation of the time. This is not to diminish the horrors of being detained by the tribunal, only to point out that as an institution, the Inquisition showed at least some concern for the physical well-being of its prisoners. Ibid., 182–87.

12 Much of this overall description is based on Kamen (ibid., 193–213). Manuel Bautista Pérez, one of Lima's wealthiest subjects, attempted to use the cache of local "experts" to his advantage, and the list of witnesses assembled to testify in his favor is a roll call of renowned men, well credentialed to judge character and faith. One of his star witnesses, Father Juan de Córdoba, was considered so distinguished an authority in Christian ethics that the inquisitors had appointed him as one of their consultants. The weight of the consultants' opinions, however, did not go in his favor. When the tribunal deliberated Manuel Bautista's fate for the last time, inquisitors joined with experts, "learned and educated men" all, to sentence him to the stake. AHN, Inq., leg. 1647, no. 13, fols. 388–410.

13 Castañeda and Hernández, *La Inquisición de Lima*, 1:1–68. The tribunal's economic transactions were carefully recorded; an accountant, with staff, was charged with supervising all commercial activity, including inventories of the prisoner's personal goods and confiscated property.

14 Instrucciones de 1569, AHN, Inq., lib. 352, fols. 4–10, cited ibid., 1:17.

15 Ibid., 1:22–29, 51.

16 Trial transcripts included witnesses for the defense. See Manuel Bautista Pérez's list for the lengthiest; he claimed two or three hundred persons might have had a grudge to bear, and he gave the inquisitors an extensive list (AHN, Inq., leg. 1647, no. 13, fols. 24v, 260, 332–34). Doña Mencia de Luna claimed that torture produced her enemies (AHN, Inq., leg. 1647, no. 10, fols. 41, 49–54). Transcripts also included weak prosecution witnesses—like Witness no. 21, who constantly reminded the tribunal that whatever he said about the suspected Jew Manuel Bautista Pérez was no more than hearsay and rumor (AHN, Inq., leg. 1647, no. 13, fol. 338v).

17 When Jorge de Silva, a principal witness against Doña Mencia de Luna, left her off a sec-

ond deposition full of accused Judaizers, it was duly noted: "does not name Doña Mencia" (AHN, Inq., leg. 1647, no. 10, fol. 10). We find the same annotation when Rodrigo Báez left her off his extensive list of hidden Judaizers (fol. 15).

18 AHN, Inq., leg. 1647, no. 3, is the transcript of Vicente's trial; this part of Alonso's testimony is to be found in fols. 1–1v.

19 AHN, Inq., leg. 1647, no. 3, fols. 2–11.

20 AHN, Inq., leg. 1647, no. 3, fol. 11v.

21 His mother and sister had been burned at the stake for remaining "negative" (i.e., denying they were closet Jews), while another sister, his aunt, uncle, and their two sons were penanced. Another uncle died in prison, while a third escaped and was last seen in Rome. And then Vicente's wife, her mother, her uncle, four of her mother's half siblings, along with two great aunts had been apprehended by the tribunal: the aunts were executed, the grandmother died in jail but was burned in effigy, and the rest were punished and reconciled. AHN, Inq., leg. 1647, no. 10, fols. 11v, 44.

22 AHN, Inq., leg. 1647, no. 10, fols. 46v–48; cite at 47v–48.

23 AHN, Inq., leg. 1647, no. 10, fol. 63v.

24 AHN, Inq., leg. 1647, no. 10, fol. 64.

25 AHN, Inq., leg. 1647, no. 10, fol. 42.

26 AHN, Inq., lib. 1029, fols. 507–13; Medina, *Historia del Tribunal del Santo Oficio de la Inquisición de Lima*, vol. 2. Inquisitors also followed the paper trail of accused witches. Given the gravity of the crime (particularly in the viceroyalty) and the prevailing sense that innate weaknesses propelled women to commit witchcraft heresy, inquisitors were anxious to track down women who had been previously detained. See the cases of Ana Almanza, Ana de Contreras, Luisa Ramos, Luisa Vargas, and Francisco de la Pena, whose previous witchcraft offenses, the details of which were archived in Lima or Potosí, loomed large in the investigations leading to their subsequent arrest (AHN, Inq., lib. 1030, fol. 371, and lib. 1031, fols. 4, 6, 331v–32). When Doña Luisa de Castro Lizárraga appeared before the tribunal a second time, the tribunal also noted a previous arrest on bigamy charges—further evidence of her flawed character (AHN, Inq., lib. 1031, fol. 201).

27 For example: Juan Rodríguez Mesa was arrested in Cartagena (Viceroyalty of Nueva Granada) during the height of the "complicidad grande" (spring 1636). In the course of taking the stand, he denounced several men, already in Lima's jails, including Antonio de Acuna, Antonio Gómez de Acosta, Manuel Henríquez, Manuel Bautista Pérez, and Jorge de Silva. As a (purported) eyewitness account and—even more significant—an account registered independently of the Lima depositions, Rodríguez's accusations were accorded sizable weight and ended up playing a considerable role in the Peruvian trials. AHN, Inq., leg. 1647, no. 11, fol. 46v.

28 As Henríquez feared, once their numbers escalated, the accused stood to gain by condemning one another—not by declaring the truth.

29 Medina, *Historia del Tribunal del Santo Oficio de la Inquisición de Lima*, 2:48–50.

30 AHN, Inq., lib. 1031, fols. 31, 32–32v.

31 Decades earlier, in the case of Duarte Núñez de Cea, the Suprema had restrained the local court from carrying out its death sentence until it had carefully reviewed the matter—a process taking years, from 1594 to 1600. AHN, Inq., lib. 1029, fols. 65–67v.

32 Medina, *Historia del Tribunal del Santo Oficio de la Inquisición de Lima*, 2:145.

33 For the most part, investigations of witchcraft at midcentury followed protocol, but there were exceptions. For example, Antonia de Urbina, a repeat offender, was arraigned by fiat but against regulation: not a single outside consultant participated in the deliberations, nor had the prosecutor presented formal charges against her. Madrid demanded a reckoning. Lima proffered a rationale we have heard before: "they feared she would go into hiding" to avoid arrest, since "many of her accomplices had already been detained by the tribunal" (AHN, Inq., lib. 1031, fol. 392). In 1675 the Suprema uncov-

ered gross irregularities in sentencing: some accused witches suffered punishment—reclusion or exile—even though their cases had been suspended. A vigilant headquarters demanded an accounting, and scrawled on Sabina Junto's transcript: "Explain what the motives were to suspend the case, since the prisoner was already forewarned and there was testimony against her," adding, "and why was she condemned to go into exile if the case was suspended?" AHN, Inq., lib. 1032, fol. 182.

34 Castañeda and Hernández, *La Inquisición de Lima*, 1:70–71.

35 Ibid., 1:80; AHN, Inq., lib. 352, fol. 46, letter from the Suprema, October 7, 1570.

36 At one point Madrid blamed the Peruvians for the mess, claiming that they were delaying the nomination process by not "fill[ing] out the forms" properly. Ibid., 1:85–86.

37 Ibid., 1:81; AHN, Inq., lib. 352, fol. 216, letter of October 10, 1595.

38 Ibid., 1:82; AHN, Inq., lib. 1037, fols. 30–32, letter of April 26, 1602.

39 Ibid., 1:82; AHN, Inq., lib. 1039, fols. 16, 20. Mañozca's scathing letter is an example of his deep concern about the ability of those who did not have proper genealogies to take up positions of importance in the colonies.

40 According to statute, candidates' wives were also subject to background checks, as were fiancées; candidates were denied positions if their wives did not pass the test, and bachelors were forbidden to marry until their fiancée's "purity of blood" was certified. In practice, as Castañeda Delgado and Hernández Aparicio point out, these statutes were often ignored or subverted. In 1613 the Suprema in Madrid gave conditional approval to the marriages of two Lima officials, pending their wives' final review. Several years later, Lima inquisitors invoked this precedent to authorize the marriage of a regional nuncio. Ibid., 1:82–86.

41 The entire transcript of the proceedings involving María Pizarro can be found in AHN, Inq., leg. 1647, no. 5; also see Medina, *Historia del Tribunal del Santo Oficio de la Inquisición de Lima*, 1:57–110.

42 María Pizarro was not married, nor had she reached formal adult standing. For two reasons, then, a legal guardian would have been required to represent her.

43 Ibid., 1:86.

44 Ibid., 2:34.

45 Ibid.

46 Ibid., 2:35, letter from Gaytán, May 1, 1624. Luisa Melgarejo was one of several "sainted women" whose perplexing cases spurred the local tribunal to ask for advice. Others, like Ana María Pérez, garnered an equally loyal and diverse following: "Some thought she was drunk, others crazy, and others a good thing" (AHN, Inq., lib. 1030, fol. 231v).

47 See Lewin, *El Santo Oficio en América*, 135–54, and Liebman, *The Inquisitors and the Jews in the New World* (1975).

48 Seven were penanced as "sospechosos" (suspect), forty-four as severe and vehement Judaizers, and twelve were "relajados," or condemned to death—including one who was burned in effigy.

49 AHN, Inq., lib. 1031, fols. 1, 14–26. Although not the case in the complicidad grande, indicted heretics could be released by "conquering torture"—insisting on their Christian beliefs in spite of the pain. In 1624 Manuel Bautista Pérez and Henrique Núñez were given suspended sentences because they would not budge. AHN, Inq., leg. 1647, no. 13, fol. 98.

50 Scurrying to justify his fecklessness, Gaytán stressed that there had been grounds for a guilty verdict, in any case, and that headquarters would understand once they had a chance to scrutinize the abundant, indictable evidence. AHN, Inq., letter from Andrés Gaytán to the Consejo, June 8, 1641 (rollo 10, fols. 63–64). Gaytán was pressured by the inquisitor general, Mañozca, who, no political novice, was not beneath behind-the-scenes manipulation. Because of Gaytán's intransigence, Mañozca asked the Suprema for permission to skirt some principal directives: viz., that local tribunals remit capital cases to Madrid and that a unanimous vote be required for execution. In his words:

"there is one among us who is so impiously pious that he will dissent in many, if not all, [of the cases]." Mañozca continued: this "impiously pious" man was just one among ten "serious and learned persons," and the consequences of respecting his dissent would be dire, for "there will be an irredeemable delay such that this entire enterprise will be stymied, greatly endangering the Church, and public welfare (*causa pública*), and undermining the authority of the Holy Office and at great cost to our finances." AHN, Inq., letter from Juan de Mañozca and Antonio de Castro y del Castillo to the Consejo, August 3, 1637 (rollo 9, fols. 63–63v).

51 The tribunal was also appalled at the extraordinary success of his sons in colonial society. One son was a canonical priest; another, named Antonio, became Latin America's first bibliographer; another, Diego, was a jurist and scholar (more about him will follow).

52 AHN, Inq., letter from Mañozca, Gaytán, and Castro, to the Consejo, May 15, 1640 (rollo 9, fols. 257–63). With the same sort of equivocation found in other cases (e.g. Manuel Henríquez and Manuel Bautista Pérez), the witness said that Diego López de Lisboa was "known to be a very devout man."

53 AHN, Inq., letter from Domingo de Aroche to the Consejo, July 12, 1647 (rollo 10, fols. 450–55).

54 AHN, Inq., letter from Domingo de Aroche to the Consejo, July 12, 1647 (rollo 10, fol. 450v).

55 AHN, Inq., letter from Domingo de Aroche to the Consejo, July 12, 1647 (rollo 10, fols. 453–53v, 454). One last example: that same year, 1638, inquisitors received another denunciation, with testimony as arbitrary as Guzmán's. Doña María Flores claimed that on the Easter past, she saw Don Diego López, who happened as usual to be carrying the archbishop's train at the service, "become so furious at Our Savior" that he seemed "possessed by the devil" (fol. 454v).

56 AHN, Inq., letter from Domingo de Aroche to the Consejo, July 12, 1647 (rollo 10, fol. 454v).

57 Letter from Gaytán, Castro, and Bentancurt to the Consejo, July 9, 1647 (rollo 10, fol. 449). We should not forget that religious events constituted much of public culture in the seventeenth century, and the figure of Don Diego holding the archbishop's train would not have gone unnoticed.

58 Letter from Gaytán, Castro, and Bentancurt to the Consejo, July 9, 1647 (rollo 10, fol. 449).

59 Kamen, *The Spanish Inquisition*, 187–91. Nor should we forget that civilized nations, including the United States, have continued to condone torture and other forms of intimidation.

60 Much of the following discussion derives from Kamen (ibid., 188–91); the quotation from the *Instructions* to inquisitors is from p. 188. Kamen also argues that Spanish policy regarding torture compares favorably with that followed elsewhere throughout Europe.

61 Madrid suggested that local officials warn detainees about torture at the time of indictment. They claimed forewarning would better prepare detainees for the eventuality, thereby "upsetting them less." Some scholars, including Boleslao Lewin, have suggested that the mere mention of torture constituted threat and intimidation (Lewin, *El Santo Oficio en América*, 30). Certainly Doña Luisa de Vargas and Francisca de Bustos, accused of witchcraft and warned about the possibility of torture, were sufficiently "upset" to elaborate their confessions considerably. See Doña Luisa de Vargas, AHN, Inq., lib. 1031, fol. 387; Francisca de Bustos, AHN, Inq., lib. 1032, fol. 116v.

62 Here are some regulations found in *Inquisitorial Jurisprudence; or, The Inquisitors' Manual*:

[T]orture is justified when a prisoner changes his mind about the circumstances [under which heresy was committed], denying the principal act. Second, if someone is a known heretic, and it is public knowledge, and there is testimony against him, even if it is only one witness who declares he heard or saw him say or do something against the faith, because in this case, the witness plus the prisoner's bad reputation are two indications that form nearly complete proof (*semi-plena probanza*) and this is enough to raise the question of torture. Third, even when there is no witness, but there are many very strong indications of a heretical character. . . . Fourth, even if the prisoner is not a known heretic, if there is one witness who has heard or seen him say or do something against the faith, adding to this factor one or more very strong indications (*uno o muchos indicios vehementes*), that is enough to warrant torture. Generally speaking, given the following factors—one eyewitness, a poor reputation in questions of faith, one very strong indication (*un indicio vehemente*)—one alone is not sufficient; two are necessary and sufficient to call for torture.

Nicolás Eymerich, *Jurisprudencia inquisitorial o Manual de inquisidores* (Buenos Aires, 1864), 98–99, cited by Lewin, *El Santo Oficio en América*, 119.

63 AHN, Inq., lib. 1031, fols. 42–45. Magistrates not only believed "voluntary" testimony to be more reliable, they promised leniency to those who confessed willingly. Examples include a slew of women who admitted to witchcraft practices in Potosí: Doña Francisca Maldonado, Mariana Clavijo, Doña María de Aguilar, and Constanza Ordóñez (AHN, Inq., lib. 1028, fols. 502, 506v, 507–8, 511–11v, 515v–16; AHN, Inq., lib. 1030, fols. 369v–73). I put "voluntary" in quotes because these testimonies were usually coerced—if not by torture, by the fact that the detained knew that others had already accused them of witchcraft. Certainly inmates recognized the value given by the tribunal to torture-free confessions. Jorge de Silva's voluntary disclosure of guilt, so incriminating in Doña Mencia's case, was equally damaging to Manuel Bautista Pérez. There is little question that it, and others (like Manuel Henríquez's torture-free accusation) contributed to Pérez's decision to submit his own guilty plea. AHN, Inq., leg. 1647, no. 10, fols. 68–68v; AHN, Inq., leg. 1647, no. 3, fol. 51v. Also see Gaspar López Suárez, AHN, Inq., lib. 1031, fol. 342.

64 AHN, Inq., leg. 1647, no. 11, fols. 51v–52.

65 See AHN, Inq., leg. 1647, no. 10, passim; Catalina Baena, AHN, Inq., lib. 1030, fols. 361v–62; Doña Luisa Castro de Lizárraga, AHN, Inq., lib. 1030, fol. 205; Doña Luisa de Vargas, AHN, Inq., lib. 1031, fol. 423.

66 Kamen, *The Spanish Inquisition*, 189, whose source for the estimate in Spain is Michèle Escamilla-Colin, *Crimes et châtiments dans l'Espagne inquisitoriale* (Paris, 1992), 1:599.

67 The Holy Office in Lima was ransacked during the Spanish American Wars of Independence, and its terrible "secrets"—no longer protected by the institution's bureaucracy—were exposed for the first time to public view: "In the middle of the torture chamber was a table eight feet long. At one end you could see a collar made out of iron, opening in the middle, in which was placed the neck of the victim, and strong straps to tie his arms and legs, arranged in such a way that when a man was stretched out on the table, and a wheel turned, he was violently pulled in opposite directions, and his joints dislocated. There was also a pillory placed against the wall, with one large hole and two smaller ones. The victim, with his neck and wrists in the pillory . . . couldn't see the face of the layman who whipped him. There were whips (*disciplina*) of leather and iron, of different types and stained by blood, and horsehair shirts that the prisoners had to wear after they were whipped. There were rings put on [victims'] fingers . . . and a person would be suspended by them two or three feet from the ground." Palma, *Anales de la Inquisición de Lima*, cited in Lewin, *El Santo Oficio en América*, 121.

68 Lewin, *El Santo Oficio en América*, 118.

69 Ibid., 119. Lewin noted that the intent of the relevant papal bull was circumvented by inquisitors, who would temporarily "interrupt" torture sessions in order to "continue them" at a later time. See AHN, Inq., leg. 1647, no. 11, fols. 135v–36. In another case, Antonio de Acuna remained in agony for eight hours, until he could stand it no longer (AHN, Inq., leg. 1647, no. 11, fols. 90v–91).

70 AHN, Inq., leg. 1647, no. 10, fol. 58v.

71 AHN, Inq., leg. 1647, no. 10, fol. 41.

72 AHN, Inq., leg. 1647, no. 10, fol. 59.

73 See Medina, *Historia del Tribunal del Santo Oficio de la Inquisición de Lima*, 2:50–51.

74 Ibid., 2:51.

75 The conspiracy to confess guilt was remarkable with respect to the extent that inmates were able to communicate with one another, to recruit fellow prisoners, to concoct testimony, to distribute the scripts, and to rehearse the participants (you will read more in the upcoming trial accounts and in following chapters). AHN, Inq., lib. 1031, fol. 86; ibid., 2:183.

76 AHN, Inq., leg. 1647, no. 11, fols. 27–32v; García de Proodian, *Los judíos en América*, 525. For an example in a witchcraft case, see Doña María de Córdoba: 1) arrested for witchcraft, claimed innocent of "implicit pact with devil," but guilty of consulting "hechiceras" for predictions about love; 2) admitted more serious acts; 3) revoked the serious charges; 4) revoked rest of the charges, except for coca chewing; 5) whipped and put in seclusion; 6) confessed and testified against others; 7) ratified charges. AHN, Inq., lib. 1031, fols. 374v–77v, 405–6, 417–18, 420v, 444v–49, 458–64.

77 Lewin, *El Santo Oficio en América*, 173, 176. Of the men and women condemned for being "observers of the Law of Moses" and accomplices in the "complicidad grande," seventeen were charged with revoking testimony. Bartolomé de León, Rodrigo Fernández, Enrique Núñez, Jorge de Silva, Tomás de Lima, Manuel de Espinosa—each saw his penance grow. For example: Bartolomé de León, sentenced to perpetually wear a sanbenito, to life imprisonment, and to exile from the Indies, received 200 lashes and ten years in the galleys for revocations and perjury; Rodrigo Fernández, also sentenced to life imprisonment, perpetual sanbenito, and exile, received 200 lashes and five years in the galleys for "variations, revocations, and false testimony." Rodrigo Fernández is listed as Gerónimo Fernández in the Fernando de Montesinos early print account of the 1639 auto-da-fé (for the text see Lewin, *El Santo Oficio en América*, app. 1). Since there are no trial records for "Gerónimo Fernández," and since "Rodrigo," for whom there are extensive records, does not appear in Montesinos, I believe there was a printing error. Note that the prisoner after "Gerónimo Fernández" was another "Gerónimo."

78 Lewin, *El Santo Oficio en América*, 183.

79 Letter from Juan de Mañozca et al. to the Suprema, May 18, 1636, in Medina, *Historia del Tribunal del Santo Oficio de la Inquisición de Lima*, 2:48–76; citations at 59, 71.

80 Ibid., 2:149.

81 Ibid.; AHN, Inq., lib. 1031, fols. 80v, 87.

82 AHN, Inq., leg. 1647, no. 11, fol. 25.

83 AHN, Inq., leg. 1647, no. 11, fols. 99, 91v.

84 AHN, Inq., leg. 1647, no. 13, fols. 315v, 339v–40.

Mysteries of State

1 Kafka, *The Trial*, 40.

2 For a fuller introduction to state reasons and state mysteries see the Prologue. My analysis owes much to Abrams and the rich legacy he engendered with "Notes on the Difficulty of Studying the State." Corrigan and Sayer followed up on Abrams's wisdom with their monumental study of English state-making, *The Great Arch*. Foucault (see Burchell, Gordon, and Miller, eds., *The Foucault Effect*), Bourdieu (*The State Nobility*), and Elias (*The Civilizing Process*) have also investigated theoretical aspects of state-building and state magic, focusing on early modern Europe. Also see Coronil, *The Magical State*, and Taussig, *The Magic of the State*, who have looked at state chicanery in South America. Comaroff and Comaroff (*Ethnography and the Historical Imagination*) have pioneered the use of Abrams in colonial contexts.

3 See Taussig, "Maleficium."

4 We can demystify "state mystery," but never completely. For we are burdened with similar, nearsighted language and imagine through similar, nearsighted concepts, as have all men and women of the modern world from the seventeenth century on.

5 In *Discipline and Punish* Foucault provides a panoramic view of the history of state punishment, making special note of the transformation from "spectacular" displays of force, in which criminals were publicly and violently punished, to the more modern regulative and reform-oriented style of today's disciplinary systems. Foucault's dualistic schema is too stark to understand seventeenth-century Peru (or Peru today, for that matter). While the Inquisition is infamous for its public autos-da-fé, it is not as well known for its attempts to "reform" prisoners. But the aim of the Inquisition was to "reconcile" heretics to the one true faith, not to burn them at the stake. Since the goal was to return heretics to the fold, prisoners were not just dumped in prison, but were visited by priests who instructed them in their error and encouraged them to "behave" in approved ways. The Inquisition was not a "panopticon"; in their "reformist" mode, though, inquisitors were engaging in a more "modern" form of discipline than Foucault would have us expect. Also see note 21, below.

6 Montesinos, "Auto de la fe celebrado en Lima a 23 de enero de 1639," app. 1 in Lewin, *El Santo Oficio en América*, 161–64. I've translated *vara* as one yard. The viceroy and inquisitors shared the same landing, although the inquisitors had preferred seating. This was the moment when inquisitors had precedence over secular authority.

7 Ibid., 164–66.

8 AHN, Inq., leg. 1647, no. 11, fol. 58.

9 AHN, Inq., leg. 1647, no. 13, fols. 249v, 279v; also no. 11, fol. 58.

10 Arendt, *Eichmann in Jerusalem*.

11 Bourdieu, *The State Nobility*.

12 One notable exception is Bourdieu (ibid.).

13 To paraphrase E. P. Thompson, bureaucrats and state subjects (like England's working classes) were present at their own creation.

14 Elliott, "The Spanish Conquest," esp. 12–14. For an indication of the breadth of exclusionary thinking see Kaplan, "Political Concepts in the World of the Portuguese Jews of Amsterdam during the Seventeenth Century," esp. 51–53.

15 Inquisitors met the challenge of bypassing procedure, like bureaucrats throughout history, by respecting the rules even as they ignored them. When inquisitors arrested Judaizers without following the rules and then were obliged to account for their actions, they did so with a backhanded appeal to bureaucratic measures: suspect cases like Manuel Henríquez's or Manuel Bautista Pérez's, the magistrates argued, eventually accrued more than sufficient eyewitness testimony to have warranted indictments. Disregarding procedure could be justified, in other words, but only in a bureaucratic way.

16 AHN, Inq., leg. 1647, no. 11, fol. 91.

17 AHN, Inq., leg. 1647, no. 11, fols. 91–91v. Montesinos made it public record that magistrates wasted hours with accomplices in the confession conspiracy (see Lewin, *El Santo Oficio en América*, 183).

18 There is a long tradition, associated with the Frankfurt school, of critiquing these "Enlightenment" traditions: Theodor Adorno, *Negative Dialectics*; Horkheimer and Adorno, *Dialectic of Enlightenment*; Marcuse, *Studies in Critical Philosophy*.

19 The past two centuries have witnessed a change in how public officials treat records of violence. The kind of detailed accounting provided by the Inquisition annals has mostly disappeared, often replaced by what amounts to accepted intimidation in the name of "truth," but one that no longer records its actions for public view. Our judicial system is not commensurate with the Inquisition, by any means, but the comparative point is that, today, we would have a very difficult time finding written accounts of the physical abuse suffered by civilization's citizens.

20 Scott, *Seeing Like a State.*

21 In *Discipline and Punish*, Foucault analyzed transformations in the systems of punishment effected in modern times. He describes a change from the spectacle of public punishment, in which the criminal's body parts were posted as warnings to potential transgressors, to the more "civilized" punishments that remove criminals from public life and keep them, and the citizenry at large, under surveillance. Modern systems of discipline require the establishment of government bureaucracies to keep tabs on state subjects—to keep statistics. Foucault, however, is never very clear about when these major "epistemic" shifts occur. He does talk about the development of disciplinary bureaucracies in the seventeenth century (see my Prologue); and the present description of Inquisition recordkeeping, along with that from an earlier chapter, "Inquisition as Bureaucracy," would appear to support his case. But how to make sense, then, of the tribunal's monumental autos-da-fé, which Foucault would certainly characterize as premodern. What Foucault doesn't do very well is account for the processes of change; as a consequence, he is unable to account for seeming anachronisms. There have been important times in modern history when the two punishment systems play off each other—often to spectacular effect. Two recent examples in the United States would be the execution of the Rosenbergs in the 1950s and the execution of Timothy McVeigh only a few years ago. See note 5, above, for more inconsistencies.

22 The use of state-sanctioned physical force to control the behavior of citizens and subjects has undergone some telling transformations over the centuries. Perhaps one of the most stunning changes is its growing invisibility. In today's civilized world, the use of physical means to exact information, or "truth," is illegal and morally reprehensible, running counter to the reasoned, enlightened way in which information is to be garnered. However, as we occasionally find out—usually when extreme excesses result in scandal—torture and abuse are not foreign to the ways our public officials, police, and prison guards carry out their mission in the name of order and reason.

23 Nearly every man released with a "suspended" sentence somehow managed to hold fast to Catholicism through all the pain of torment: Luis Vela de los Reyes, Henrique Núñez, Manuel Bautista Pérez, and Pérez's cousin Diego Rodríguez de Lisboa are all examples. See Medina, *Historia del Tribunal del Santo Oficio de la Inquisición de Lima*, 2:179; AHN, Inq., lib. 1030, fols. 174–79, and leg. 1647, no. 13, fols. 249, 279v.

24 Some accused witches—Sabina Junto, Petrona Arias, and Josefina Llanos—had their cases "suspended" for lack of convincing grounds (AHN, Inq., lib. 1032, fols. 182–82v, 186v–87, 188v–89). Another, Doña Luisa de Vargas, quit the tribunal's jail cells in 1649 because, as she and her lawyer pointed out, she had been tried and convicted for witchcraft by the royal authorities several years before, and on the same charges now being used as the basis for the new case: "she had [already] done penance for the crime and the law does not allow two punishments for the same crime" (AHN, Inq., lib. 1031, fol. 382). Luisa de Vargas was arrested again in 1655, but this time she was punished (AHN, Inq., lib. 1031, fol. 423).

25 In Lewin, *El Santo Oficio en América*, 186. Montesinos went out of his way to assure the reader that inquisitors reached decisions based on the merit of each case, not because "they had been petitioned by the parties involved." For good measure, he staked the magistrates' skills and reputations on divine judgment: "that any jurist who would have done differently, would have mortally sinned."

26 Ibid.

27 I have found one case, that of Manuel López, in which the prisoner refused to swear an oath to the truth and to the institution. He was called crazy. AHN, Inq., lib. 1029, fol. 69v.

28 AHN, Inq., leg. 1647, no. 10, fol. 41.

29 AHN, Inq., leg. 1647, no. 10, fols. 59, 59v.

30 Henríquez claimed he had been prosecuted unjustly in Coimbra, for "he was never

charged [with a crime], nor was he assigned a legal guardian" (his right as a minor), nor were all the mandatory procedures followed—the required ratifications, the warnings of indictment. AHN, Inq., leg. 1647, no. 11, fol. 157v.

31 AHN, Inq., leg. 1647, no. 11, fol. 56v.

32 AHN, Inq., leg. 1647, no. 11, fol. 6.

33 AHN, Inq., leg. 1647, no. 11, fol. 272.

34 AHN, Inq., leg. 1647, no. 13, fol. 279v.

35 AHN, Inq., leg. 1647, no. 13, fol. 281.

36 AHN, Inq., leg. 1647, no. 13, fols. 278v–79.

37 Pérez had his aunt "find" his baptismal records in one of Seville's churches.

38 Anónimo portugués, *Descripción del virreinato del Perú*, 13.

39 AHN, Inq., lib. 1028, fol. 384v; AHN, Inq., lib. 1029, fols. 55v–56v, 68, 115.

40 AHN, Inq., lib. 1030, fols. 359v–62, 369v–73, 374v.

41 AHN, Inq., lib. 1028, fols. 502–16.

42 The Inquisition could be used as a threat, even in the realm of domestic relations. Doña Bernada Cerbantes's husband, furious to find her with another man, threatened to haul her off to the Inquisition. AHN, Inq., lib. 1032, fol. 221.

43 AHN, Inq., leg. 1647, no. 11, fol. 6; AHN, Inq., leg. 1647, no. 11, fol. 165.

44 AHN, Inq., lib. 1028, fol. 384v.

45 AHN, Inq., lib. 1028, fol. 384v; leg. 1647, no. 13, fol. 28; lib. 1031, fols. 162v–63. Also: AHN, Inq., Lima, leg. 4805, fol. 3, cited in Quiroz, "La expropiación inquisitorial de cristianos nuevos portugueses en Los Reyes, Cartagena y México (1635–1649)," n. 29. Among the many voices are Antonio Leal, Manuel Núñez, A. Méndez, Diego López, Sebastián Duarte, Antonio Cordero, and Francisco Botello.

46 Pérez Villanueva and Escandell Bonet, eds., *Historia de la Inquisición en España y América*, 2:12–13; Castañeda Delgado and Hernández Aparicio, *La Inquisición de Lima*, 1:6–9.

47 Mannarelli, *Hechiceras, beatas y expósitas*.

48 AHN, Inq., lib. 1030, fols. 214–17v; citations at fols. 214–14v, 217v.

49 Kamen, *The Spanish Inquisition*, 255–82.

50 We know this because in a letter written by Licenciado Castro y del Castilla to the Suprema in 1641, the magistrate justified his role in the 1639 auto by appealing to the tribunal's substantial popular backing. He described the tremendous interest shown by young men when the highly coordinated arrests were under way. AHN, Inq., lib. 1031, fol. 265v.

51 Town criers announced the autos in churches around Lima and residents were expected to attend. Medina, *Historia del Tribunal del Santo Oficio de la Inquisición de Lima*, 1:124–25.

52 Vázquez de Espinosa, *Compendium and Description of the West Indies*, 447–50. The spectacular autos-da-fé and their popularity are suggestive of the elaborate public celebrations that validated personal monarchies and that were characteristic expressions of early modern authority (see "Appendix: Notes on Bias and Sources"). Also see Mugaburu and Mugaburu, *Chronicle of Colonial Lima*, 92, 166. Vázquez de Espinosa sang the Lima Inquisition's praises, claiming that "no matter what commissioner represents [the tribunal] he is highly regarded in every city and village." Vázquez also judged that "although all over Christendom the Holy Tribunal is esteemed and reverenced . . . the Kingdom of Peru leads them all" (*Compendium and Description of the West Indies*, 447).

53 Medina, *Historia del Tribunal del Santo Oficio de la Inquisición de Lima*, 2:260–61.

54 See Rolena Adorno's fundamental study, *Guaman Poma de Ayala*.

55 Guaman Poma de Ayala, *El primer nueva corónica y buen gobierno*, 1:276.

56 Ibid., 1:279. To show the comparison's limits Guaman Poma added that "no one was sentenced to the galleys because they did not exist."

57 Ibid., 2:549.

58 Ibid., 2:585.
59 Ibid., 2:538.
60 Ibid.
61 Ibid., 2:445.
62 AHN, Inq., lib. 1028, fol. 339.
63 Medina, *Historia del Tribunal del Santo Oficio de la Inquisición de Lima*, 2:57–58.
64 Inquisitors, for their part were furious whenever they discovered that the law had been violated. Joan Vicente was asked over and over and over, "Didn't you, having been penanced, think that leaving your country and coming to these parts without a permit from the Inquisition was an offense." AHN, Inq., leg. 1647, no. 3, fol. 47.
65 AHN, Inq., lib. 1030, fol. 173.
66 AHN, Inq., lib. 1030, fol. 225v.
67 AHN, Inq., lib. 1032, fol. 228v.
68 Silva's overt struggle to remain a practicing Jew while in custody and his dramatic death at the stake made him Peru's most famed martyr to the Jewish faith; at times, however, his identity was confused with other New World martyrs. See Kohut, "The Trial of Francisco Maldonado de Silva."
69 In Lewin, *El Santo Oficio en América*, 182.
70 Ibid.
71 Benjamin, "Theses on the Philosophy of History."

Globalization and Guinea Pigs

1 Avila, *Tratado de los evangelios*, 1:297, 479.
2 Avendaño, *Sermones de los misterios de nuestra santa fe católica*, 1:99v, emphasis mine.
3 Ibid., 1:71v–72. An example: "the reason why Providence commanded that there be poor men in the world was so that the republics and cities would be well ordered."
4 Ibid.
5 Ibid. Protest was also futile. Indians, "like the pot, cannot question the potter who made it."
6 Avila, *Tratado de los evangelios*, 1:105.
7 Ibid., 2:97–98.
8 Ibid., 1:475. One fanega = approximately 1.58 bushels.
9 Ibid., 1:466.
10 Each Andean polity was associated with a founding pair (or pairs), and origin stories usually had them emerging from sacred sites in the local landscape—caves, springs, underground tunnels. See my chapter "Becoming Indian" for the political directions such beliefs could take.
11 See Urton, *Inca Myths*; also, my chapter "Becoming Indian."
12 Avila, *Tratado de los evangelios*, 1:295, 477, 478; for Avendaño, *Sermones de los misterios de nuestra santa fe católica*, 1:81v. Also see "Becoming Indian." Both Avila and Avendaño explained that the Indians' great suffering was part of God's design: an initial punishment leading to eventual salvation.
13 Avila, *Tratado de los evangelios*, 1:297; Avendaño's fire-and-brimstone sermons accused Indians of "heretical blasphemy" for denying God's omnipotence. To think that God was not powerful enough to create Indians was, in Avendaño's words, "a grave sin against the one true God." Avendaño, *Sermones de los misterios de nuestra santa fe católica*, 1:45v.
14 This is two centuries before nineteenth-century race thinking posited a different solution to the color conundrum.
15 Avila, *Tratado de los evangelios*, 1:297.
16 Ibid.

17 Ibid., 1:479.

18 Avila critiqued the idea that other physical characteristics, like shape, or size, or body hair, were of any real significance. With humor (I think), Avila sermonized about a trait that native Peruvians, from the time of conquest until the present day, point to in order to differentiate themselves from "españoles": "and all that talk about having a lot or not much of a beard (*barbas*), don't pay [that] any mind; and many of you, if you weren't combing [your beards and mustaches] at every opportunity, would have full ones, too." Ibid., 1:479.

19 "Moro" is the term always used in the text, and that is why I am using it. In general, they were referring to Muslims.

20 Ibid., 1:511.

21 Ibid., 1:512. One Isabel, further identified only as "negra," expressed a version of this unholy trinity when she swore she was neither witch nor Moor nor Jew. AHN, Inq., lib. 1030, fol. 213v.

22 Avendaño, *Sermones de los misterios de nuestra santa fe católica*, 2:16v–17.

23 Conflating "moros" and "turcos" as they did, Avila and Avendaño were expressing an assumption that the Moors, Muslims from North Africa, were necessarily allied with the Ottomans, the largest Muslim political entity of the age. Yet the North African caliphs who dominated Iberia were, over the course of history, sometimes at odds with the Ottomans and sometimes their allies.

24 Pena Montenegro, *Itinerario para párrocos de indios* (1658), 326.

25 See Avila, *Tratado de los evangelios*, 1:66–67, 77, 88, 160–62, 236–37, 283, 330, 390, 451, 2:62, 96–99; Avendaño, *Sermones de los misterios de nuestra santa fe católica*, 1:48v. Although Indians were said to have been punished primarily because of idol worship, other charges were that Atahuallpa had murdered his brother, Huáscar, and that Indians refused to listen to Saint Thomas when he traversed the continent centuries before. See Avila, *Tratado de los evangelios*, 2:96–99, 236.

26 Avila, *Tratado de los evangelios*, 2:96–99. Avila reminded his Spanish countrymen that they would be subject to the same fate if they ignored God's mandate: "our homes and wealth and even our lives will be taken away like the Romans did to the Jews, and the Spanish did to the Incas."

27 Arriaga, *The Extirpation of Idolatry in Peru*, 9.

28 Ibid. For Moors had been expelled from Spain twice: in 1492 when they, like Jews, had to accept baptism or leave the Peninsula, and in 1609 when, in response to a rebellion, the Crown banished all moriscos from the realm, regardless of faith. See Kamen, *The Spanish Inquisition*, 214–29.

29 Arriaga, *The Extirpation of Idolatry in Peru*, 6.

30 Avila, *Tratado de los evangelios*, 1:233.

31 Avendaño, *Sermones de los misterios de nuestra santa fe católica*, 1:17v.

32 We know that Lima's Archbishop Villagómez found the situation deeply troubling and that he wrote a directive to all clergy working with natives: "You well know that . . . the devil deceives men and especially those who are less capable and with diminished talents to understand." Avila concluded that missionaries would have to "accommodate the [natives'] diminished capacity" by writing extremely simple homilies. Villagómez, cited by Avila, *Tratado de los evangelios*, 1:prologue. This distinction also affected Indians' legal rights and was the basis for the special protections afforded them by the colonial state. "An Indian's understanding is less than a Spaniard's," Pena Montenegro argued, and for this reason the Crown decreed that "the attorney general of the Royal Court be their . . . protector." Pena Montenegro, *Itinerario para párrocos de indios* (1658), 142–44.

33 Pena Montenegro, *Itinerario para párrocos de indios* (1658), 306.

34 Ibid., 165, 523.

35 Ibid., 427, 95.

36 Ibid., 141. References to this perspective (ibid., 9, 142–44) are legion in Pena Montenegro's work.

37 Ibid., 533–34.
38 See Spalding, *De indio a campesino*, 61–88.
39 Avendaño, *Sermones de los misterios de nuestra santa fe católica*, 2:6v, 33v–34. Also see my chapter "Becoming Indian."
40 Pena Montenegro, *Itinerario para párrocos de indios* (1658), 523.
41 Ibid., 152–53; also 146, 167.
42 Avila, *Tratado de los evangelios*, 1:15.
43 Pena Montenegro, *Itinerario para párrocos de indios* (1658), 339.
44 Ibid., 278–79.
45 Ibid., 76–77 (note that the morisco's ignoble customs included eating on the floor, sitting on cushions, not using a table).
46 Ibid., 141.
47 Ibid.
48 Ibid.
49 Ibid., 178–79.
50 Ibid., 226.
51 Avila, *Tratado de los evangelios*, 1:278–79.
52 Pena Montenegro, *Itinerario para párrocos de indios* (1658), 370.
53 Avila, *Tratado de los evangelios*, 1:289.
54 Ibid.
55 Chimu ("Chimo" in Avila's account) was a large coastal state defeated by the Incas. Their capital was close to the Spanish city of Trujillo.
56 Ibid.
57 Popayán is an exception to the list of otherwise Inca locales.
58 Ibid.
59 Ibid., 1:289–90.
60 Quechua = "Huacca muchhaccuna"; in Spanish, "Hereges."
61 Avendaño, *Sermones de los misterios de nuestra santa fe católica*, 1:100v.
62 Ibid., 2:47.
63 Avila, *Tratado de los evangelios*, 1:290, 156; Avendaño, *Sermones de los misterios de nuestra santa fe católica*, 1:45v.
64 Avila, *Tratado de los evangelios*, 1:95.
65 While the evangelists distinguish among "naciones blancas" (e.g. France, Spain, Italy), or speak of the "indios" of China and Japan and the different nations of "indios" in the Andes, Africa tends to be seen as a block. See, for example, Avendaño, *Sermones de los misterios de nuestra santa fe católica*, 1:8v. For whatever reason and in spite of many opportunities, Avila and Avendaño do not give Moors a place in their color scheme. Thus, contrary to expectations, it would appear that Moors were not considered to be "negro." There seems to be some contemporary confusion about the relationship between "moro" and "moreno" (brown), and it is important to stress that these words have different etymological roots.
66 Avila, *Tratado de los evangelios*, 2:38.
67 Avendaño, *Sermones de los misterios de nuestra santa fe católica*, 1:99v, emphasis mine.
68 Avila, *Tratado de los evangelios*, 1:80, 2:471, also see 1:159, 204, 290, 296–99, 479; Avendaño, *Sermones de los misterios de nuestra santa fe católica*, 1:95, 99v.
69 Avila, *Tratado de los evangelios*, 1:80. Of all the color divisions, the one least used was "brown," to stand for indios. I have never heard the term applied in contemporary Peru.
70 Avendaño, in one of his earlier sermons, spoke of humanity in various terms. First he presented the straightforward triad of colonial cultural order: God created all mankind, "indios, negros, y españoles." Then he elaborated on differences, including physical aspects like skin color: "everyone—Indians, blacks, and whites" was descended from God's first human creation. See Avendaño, *Sermones de los misterios de nuestra santa fe católica*, 1:45v.

1   Guaman Poma de Ayala, *El primer nueva corónica y buen gobierno*, 2:504, 3:878.
2   AHN, Inq., leg. 1647, no. 11, fol. 91v.
3   See Balabar and Wallerstein, *Race, Nation, Class*. This collection of essays is an important contribution to understanding the complexities of the ideologies of race and nation. Balabar makes the argument that in our contemporary world, culture or ethnicity is becoming the modern version of race ("Is There a Neo-racism," 17–28).
4   This chapter has benefited from earlier studies of race and caste in colonial Latin America, particularly from the important debate that took place in the pages of the *Colonial Latin American Review*. See Kuznesof, "Ethnic and Gender Influences on 'Spanish' Creole Society in Colonial Spanish America" (1995); Schwartz, "Colonial Identities and the 'Sociedad de Castas'"; and Kuznesof, "Ethnic and Gender Influences on 'Spanish' Creole Society in Colonial Spanish America" (1996). Mary Weismantel has also edited a very important collection of articles looking at questions of race and ethnicity in the contemporary Andes; see the *Bulletin of Latin American Research* 17, no. 2 (1998). The following articles were particularly helpful to me: Weismantel and Eisenman, "Race in the Andes"; Cadena, "Silent Racism and Intellectual Superiority in Peru"; Mendoza, "Defining Folklore" and "'Dirty Indians,' Radical *Indígenas*, and the Political Economy of Social Difference in Modern Ecuador," 185–206; and Orlove, "Down to Earth." Also see two recently published monographs: Cadena, *Indigenous Mestizos*, and Poole, *Vision, Race, and Modernity*.
5   See Hall, "Gramsci's Relevance for the Study of Race and Ethnicity," for a particularly thoughtful argument using Gramsci's notion of hegemony in the study of race. Herzfeld, *The Social Construction of Indifference*, emphasized the importance of local contexts in the study of bureaucracy. Also see Gupta, "Blurred Boundaries."
6   When Manuel Henríquez and Manuel Bautista Pérez were asked to name "casta y generación," they declared themselves to be New Christian (AHN, Inq., leg. 1647, no. 11, fol. 56v; AHN, Inq., leg. 1647, no. 13, fols. 246–47v, 248v, 249). But accused "converted" New Christians, like Duarte Méndez, Vasco de Xerez, and Joan Vicente, claimed to be New Christians "of Jewish descent" (AHN, Inq., lib. 1028, fols. 300, 339; also leg. 1647, no. 3, fol. 47). Others, skipping over New Christian, claimed to be of the "casta y generación de judíos" or, in the words of the repentent Joan López, of the "evil (*mala adventurada*) generación de judíos" (AHN, Inq., lib. 1028, fol. 347v).
7   Solórzano Pereira, *Política indiana*, bk. 2, chap. 29, 437–38. Henry Kamen, while importantly stressing the controversies surrounding purity-of-blood statutes, noted that by the mid-seventeenth century the concepts of honor in matters of religion and race were equated in published treatises; see *The Spanish Inquisition*, 235–54.
8   Solórzano Pereira, *Política indiana*, bk. 2, chap. 29, 436.
9   Ibid., 437. There were disagreements about racial calculations; this was Solorzano's understanding after examining a set of conflicting decrees.
10 Ibid., 436–38.
11 Solórzano argued that Indians, even "if descended from fathers or grandfathers who were pagan, should be admitted to the priesthood." Ibid., 436.
12 Pena Montenegro, *Itinerario para párrochos de indios, en que se tratan las materias . . .* (1658), 368–69.
13 The debates surrounding illegitimacy turned on two reservations: first, that "the incontinence of the fathers would be inherited by the children"; second, that "dishonor" and "infamy" would forever enshroud them. These burdens made anyone from an illegitimate background suspect, or "irregular"; but, Pena Montenegro strongly contended, the Church provided an opening — a bishop's dispensation could override all shortcomings. He was also very explicit that the drawbacks of illegitimate birth cut across colonial boundaries ("whether the person be español or mestizo") and, likewise, the means to override them. Ibid., 366–68.

14   Ibid., 368–69.

15   Some blacks, he added, "have even inspired great devotion." Ibid., 370–71.

16   Ibid., 370.

17   Ibid., 371–72.

18   See Burns, *Colonial Habits*. For more studies of Andean religiosity, see notes 52 and 53 to the Prologue, above.

19   The López de Lisboa family comes to mind.

20   Pena Montenegro says yes, basing his argument on two papal decrees from the previous century. Pena Montenegro, *Itinerario para párrocos de indios, en que se tratan las materias . . .* (1658), 394–404.

21   "Mestizo" here is narrowly defined as the offspring of two pure "castes." "Mestizo" could also refer to a general state of racial mix.

22   For similar disputes over the dispensations needed to contract marriage within the third degree, see Pena Montenegro, *Itinerario para párrocos de indios, en que se tratan las materias . . .* (1658), 488.

23   Here we are looking at one version of the official blood language, not actual social practice. Pena Montenegro's precise delineations seem unusual for seventeenth-century Peru, where mestizo, mulato, sambo or, at times, quadroon were as detailed as blood language would get. The confusions over what "mestizo" refers to reflects the common use of the broader, more inclusive terminology. Pena Montenegro was most likely forced into this precision by the particular questions he was raising; but, in any case, he was expressing a vision of race that was then taking root in viceregal culture. Over time, this vision was to become more apparent, and by the eighteenth century, it was made evident in paintings and legal codes. One of its manifestations was in the "casta paintings," those works depicting, with a scientific sensibility, the viceroyalty's numerous racial types. For an excellent discussion of colonial classifications and the more complex racial categories of the eighteenth century, see Cahill, "Colour by Numbers." Casta paintings were also found in eighteenth-century Mexico; see Carrera, *Imagining Identity in New Spain*.

24   Pena Montenegro, *Itinerario para párrocos de indios, en que se tratan las materias . . .* (1658), 403–4.

25   Ibid.

26   Ibid., 370.

27   AHN, Inq., lib. 1031, fols. 497, 382; lib. 1032, fol. 220v. Also see the case of Diego Cristóbal, the son of a Spanish man (Old Christian) and a mestiza woman; therefore, he was called a quarter mestizo (AHN, Inq., lib. 1030, fol. 390).

28   AHN, Inq., lib. 1029, fol. 499; lib. 1031, fols. 495v, 497, 527.

29   AHN, Inq., lib. 1031, fol. 332v; lib. 1032, fol. 380. Also see Cahill, "Colour by Numbers," which underscores the social construction of these categories, their instability, and the ways that class, ethnicity, and race intertwined. "Samba" could also be spelled "zamba."

30   AHN, Inq., lib. 1032, fol. 228v; lib. 1030, fols. 360v, 213v, 383v; lib. 1031, fol. 494.

31   AHN, Inq., leg. 1647, no. 11, fol. 46v.

32   AHN, Inq., lib. 1031, fol. 339.

33   AHN, Inq., lib. 1029, fol. 49.

34   AHN, Inq., lib. 1031, fol. 121.

35   AHN, Inq., lib. 1031, fol. 136v.

36   One exception: Manuel Anríquez, called New Christian by every witness, tentatively claimed he might be "half Old Christian" because "some of his relatives said they were Old Christian," AHN, Inq., lib. 1028, fol. 365. The Lisbon Inquisition, however, did impose "percentages"; in a 1658 auto, they registered Paula de [or da] Crasto, "half a New Christian," and Thereza María de Jesús, "more than half a New Christian." See Kohut, "Martyrs of the Inquisition in South America," 172.

37   See my chapter, "The Inca's Witches," for more on this.

38   See Spalding, *De indio a campesino*, 181. There was special concern about Indians pass-

ing, since that would reduce the numbers of men available to fulfill labor and tribute obligations.

39 See AHN, lib. 1029, fols. 8–8v, 250v; AHN, Inq., lib. 1032, fols. 113v, 421; AHN, Inq., lib. 1031, fols. 497, 382.

40 AHN, Inq., lib. 1028, fols. 274v, 299v; AHN, Inq., leg. 1647, no. 12, passim; AHN, leg. 1647, no. 12, fols. 38, 61v, 84. Also note that Bachiller de Valencia, most likely Luis de Valencia's brother, was educated in the most elite universities of the times—Salamanca and Coimbra (AHN, Inq., lib. 1029, fols. 59–59v; Medina, *Historia del Tribunal del Santo Oficio de la Inquisición de Lima*, 2:114–15; AHN, Inq., lib. 1030, fol. 154).

41 AHN, Inq., lib. 1028, fols. 422–22v.

42 AHN, Inq., lib. 1031, fol. 224. There were confusions regarding racial calculations. A royal cédula of 1539 pronounced that the Christian grandchildren of Judaizers would have permission to travel to the New World (Lewin, *El Santo Oficio en América*, 84–85). That is not necessarily the same thing as a determination of "Old" Christian standing.

43 Guaman Poma de Ayala, *El primer nueva corónica y buen gobierno*, 2:617.

44 Ibid., 2:533.

45 Ibid., 3:863; also see 871.

46 Ibid., 3:882.

47 AHN, Inq., lib. 1030, fol. 367; AHN, Inq., lib. 1031, fols. 160, 186.

48 Guaman Poma de Ayala, *El primer nueva corónica y buen gobierno*, 3:887.

49 Ibid., 2:421, 3:908.

50 Ibid., 2:498. I have written about Guaman Poma's insistence that the only way for the indigenous population to return to its pre-Columbian levels would be for the "races" to remain strictly separate. For this reason he reserved special venom for "mestizos" (predominantly Spanish father and Indian mother, and illegitimate) and for Indian women whose sexual excesses, he argued, also contributed to the destruction of the Indian population. See Silverblatt, "Family Values in Seventeenth-Century Peru."

51 Guaman Poma de Ayala, *El primer nueva corónica y buen gobierno*, 3:857–58.

52 Ibid., 1:207, 2:380 (where I translated *cacique principal* as "Indian nobility"; also see 2:711). The anonymous Portuguese chronicler echoed Guaman Poma's sentiments about low-ranking Spaniards who manifested presumptions of grandeur once in the New World. See Anónimo portugués, *Descripción del virreinato del Perú*, 68.

53 Guaman Poma de Ayala, *El primer nueva corónica y buen gobierno*, 2:511, 3:1025.

54 Ibid., 2:692.

55 See Silverblatt, "Family Values in Seventeenth-Century Peru."

56 Guaman Poma de Ayala, *El primer nueva corónica y buen gobierno*, 1:189, 2:498, 504, 509.

57 Ibid., 2:470.

58 Ibid., 2:620, 659, 725, 3:878.

59 Ibid., 3:858.

60 Therefore, in line with Guaman Poma's political protest, the viceroyalty's governors were illegitimate.

61 Because of the confusions of race and status inherent in colonial categories, Guaman Poma sometimes merged racial stains and class stains in ways that complicated the global racial picture. He would thus put Spanish peasants in the same basket as the castes "of color": "Spanish peasant, Jew, Moor mestizo, mulato" (ibid., 3:1064; also 3:1025). Or he would place Indian elites in the same basket as Spaniards (2:726).

62 Ibid., 2:342, 1:96.

63 Ibid., 3:878.

64 Ibid.

65 Ibid. As far as I know, this is a first for English "stains."

66 Ibid., 2:504. Guaman Poma also thought people should dress according to caste for easy recognition (see 2:511).

67 Letter of May 18, 1636, in Medina, *Historia del Tribunal del Santo Oficio de la Inquisición*

de Lima, 2:48–76; Montesinos, "Auto de la fe celebrado en Lima a 23 de enero de 1639," app. 1 in Lewin, ed., *El Santo Oficio en América*.

68   Vázquez de Espinosa, *Compendium and Description of the West Indies*, 447; Suardo, *Diario de Lima de Juan Antonio Suardo (1629–1639)*, 2:113, 114, 119, 120, 125.

69   I am indebted to the great Spanish historian José Antonio Maravall, who analyzed sermons as the popular culture of the times. See his book *Culture of the Baroque*.

70   AHN, Inq., lib. 1030, fol. 67.

71   Epithets like "children of Portuguese" or even "grandchildren of Portuguese" were quite ordinary. Other examples include Manuel Anríquez, AHN, Inq., lib. 1028, 367; Bernabé López Serrano, AHN, Inq., lib. 1030, fol. 280; Martín López de Taide, AHN, Inq., 1030, fol. 344; Tomás de Lima, AHN, Inq., leg. 1647, no. 11, fol. 23v; Alvaro Rodrigo de Acebedo, AHN, Inq., lib. 1032, fol. 195v; Alvaro Núñez, AHN, Inq., lib. 1029, fol. 282; and Antonio de Espinosa, AHN, Inq., lib. 1031, fol. 104.

72   AHN, Inq., lib. 1029, fol. 39v; AHN, Inq., lib. 1031, fol. 160; AHN, Inq., lib. 1031, fol. 224; AHN, Inq., lib. 1029, fol. 89.

73   AHN, Inq., lib. 1030, fol. 188.

74   AHN, Inq., lib. 1030, fol. 294.

75   AHN, Inq., leg. 1647, no. 3, fol. 60.

76   AHN, Inq., leg. 1647, no. 13, fols. 70–71.

77   AHN, Inq., leg. 1647, no. 13, fols. 54, 78v–79v.

78   AHN, Inq., leg. 1647, no. 11, fol. 82v.

79   AHN, Inq., lib. 1030, fol. 263v.

80   AHN, Inq., lib. 1030, fol. 266.

81   AHN, Inq., lib. 1030, fol. 269.

82   AHN, Inq., lib. 1031, fol. 160.

83   AHN, Inq., lib. 1031, fol. 186; AHN, Inq., leg. 1647, fols. 246–47v, 248v, 249.

84   AHN, Inq., lib. 1030, fol. 367.

85   For a discussion of the different backgrounds of Portuguese settlers in Mexico, see Israel, *Empires and Entrepôts*, 320–22, 328–42. The Old Christian Portuguese who tended to be small farmers and artisans—not merchants—resented being called Jews. Loyalty to Portugal could override, however, internal divisions of occupation and background, especially when one was speaking of oppression by the Castilian monarchy.

86   AHN, Inq., leg. 1647, no. 13, fol. 51.

87   AHN, Inq., leg. 1647, no. 13, fols. 49v, 31v.

88   AHN, Inq., leg. 1647, no. 13, fol. 51.

89   Bartolomé de León—one of the first to be apprehended in the "complicidad grande," the first to be tortured, the first to recant—offered a comment on the retraction deluge that owed much to the racial premises of tribunal justice, but turned around. Explaining to the tribunal why he wanted to revoke the accusations he had made against so many, León blurted out that "the Honorable Tribunal had said they only wanted the truth, which [he had] understood to mean that he had testified against an Old Christian" (AHN, Inq., leg. 1647, no. 13, fol. 86). Magistrates presumed that the innocence of Old Christians was self-evident because their stain-free blood and stain-free character were inherited, just as they presumed that the guilt of New Christians was self-evident.

90   Henríquez and company tried to reinforce their argument by articulating what was quite well known: New Christians had risen to the highest (and noblest) positions in the Spanish court, as knights in Castile's elite military orders and as "asentistas," the most respected and influential advisers to king and council. Wouldn't these achievements, plus the visible acceptance of New Christians by court society, prove that Portuguese could be authentic Spaniards as well? See AHN, Inq., rollo 9, fols. 166–81; AHN, Inq., lib. 1029, fols. 59–59v. The conspiracy also accused Old Christian Portuguese of Judaizing. One man exonerated by the tribunal was a Portuguese merchant; another, the Portuguese Antonio de los Santos, was one of the Inquisition's "familiars"; so was Am-

brosio de Morales, another native of Portugal who had been falsely accused. I imagine that by choosing to make false charges against Portuguese, the confession conspirators were aiming to show, once again, the bankruptcy of the tribunal's assumptions. Portuguese, contrary to stereotype, were not necessarily New Christians or Judaizers; and all merchants were not Jews. See Medina, *Historia del Tribunal del Santo Oficio de la Inquisición de Lima*, 2:186–87.

91 AHN, Inq., lib. 1031, fol. 89. For more examples, see Andrés Rodríguez, AHN, Inq., lib. 1029, fol. 32v; Isabel Catana, AHN, Inq., lib. 1028, fol. 262.

92 Henrique Tavares, AHN, Inq., lib. 1031, fol. 339.

93 AHN, Inq., leg. 1647, no. 10, fols. 18, 22, 27v.

94 This charge played into assumptions that New Christians/Jews would not marry outsiders. Yosef Kaplan, in fact, has argued that Amsterdam's Sephardic community was highly endogamous, even excluding Ashkenazic Jews from their cemetery. In any case, endogamy was considered to be something that defined Jewish behavior. Thus, verbal support for marriage prohibitions was one of the identifying characteristics of a Judaizer. See Kaplan, "Political Concepts in the World of the Portuguese Jews of Amsterdam during the Seventeenth Century."

95 AHN, Inq., leg. 1647, no. 10, fol. 35.

96 We know (but it is not clear that the Lima inquisitors knew) that three decades before, Doña Mencia and her immediate family, classed as "Portuguese and New Christian," had been condemned by the Lisbon tribunal. Hidden in a 1603 deposition is testimony that Doña Mencia had been imprisoned. Isabel de Sosa, Joan Vicente's wife, explained that she had been apprehended along with "the parents and siblings of Gonzalo de Luna." (Isabel and her husband had long-standing ties with the wealthy Luna, who was a sponsor of Joan Vicente's business dealings in the viceroyalty.) Isabel de Sosa "had been put in the same cell as Doña Mencia de Luna, Gonzalo de Luna's younger sister." Somehow the inquisitors trying the Luna clan three decades later missed this testimony, and never brought it to bear as evidence against Doña Mencia. The inquisitors disputed Doña Mencia de Luna's age (about twenty years difference). Perhaps Doña Mencia was trying to keep them off her brother's trail. AHN, Inq., leg. 1647, no. 3, fols. 14–14v, and no. 10, fols. 35–35v.

97 AHN, Inq., leg. 1647, no. 10, fol. 41.

98 This concept was conveyed by the Peninsula's early "policy wonks," the seventeenth-century political thinkers who, as Foucault suggested, were the first to articulate the "state" as a concept of governance. Some of them were beginning to address their elaborate plans for economic improvement (or sometimes their elegant assessments of national character) to "Spain" rather than to Castile. See Cellorigo, *Memorial de la política necesaria y útil restauración a la República de España y estados de ella, y del desempeño universal de estos reynos*, and López Madera, *Excelencias de la monarchía y reyno de España*. Outspoken critics of the empire spoke about the evils of "Spain" as well: when Manasseh Ben Israel petitioned Cromwell to allow his New Christian kinsmen to resettle in Britain, he situated the Jews' terrible dilemma in relation to the politics of "England, France, and Spain." See Ben Israel, *The Hope of Israel*. Also see the discussions of culture and political authority toward the end of my Prologue.

99 For references to "cristianos" and "mezquitas" see Pizarro, "Carta de Hernando Pizarro" [1533], 123, 124, 125, 127; and Mena, "La conquista del Perú" [1534], 136, 138, 139, 141, 142, 145, 151, 153, 156. Arce's "Advertencia" [1545] uses "cristiano" and "español" (409, 410, 416, 419).

100 Avila, *Tratado de los evangelios*, 1:60. Another example of regionalism can be seen in descriptions of culinary preferences in which "Castile and Spain" were set apart from "Catalonia, Majorca and France." Pena Montenegro, *Itinerario para párrocos de indios* (1658), 460.

101 Avila, *Tratado de los evangelios*, 1:390.

102 Ibid., 41. As today, another area where "Castile" emerges is in the description of language. Avendaño, in a sermon about the world's multitudinous languages, noted that the Spaniards arrived in Peru speaking Castilian; nevertheless, Avila explained that *testigo* "en lengua española" meant "witness"; and Pena Montenegro described "El Inca" Garcilaso de la Vega, author of a multivolume chronicle about the Incas and the conquest, as writing in a Spanish style. Avendaño, *Sermones de los misterios de nuestra santa fe católica*, 1:113; Avila, *Tratado de los evangelios*, 1:72; Pena Montenegro, *Itinerario para párrocos de indios* (1658), "Aprobación."

103 Avila, *Tratado de los evangelios*, 2:75.

104 Avendaño, *Sermones de los misterios de nuestra santa fe católica*, 1:102v; compare with 2:47. Of the two, "España" was more likely.

105 Avila, *Tratado de los evangelios*, 1:152.

106 Avendaño, *Sermones de los misterios de nuestra santa fe católica*, 1:77v–78.

107 Avila, *Tratado de los evangelios*, 1:236.

108 Ibid., 97–98; also see 152.

109 In sermons laying out the colonial scheme of things, Avila and Avendaño would equate "español" to "gente blanca" (including Portuguese) whenever Spanish or white was counterposed to people "of color" (indios and negros). When the "Portuguese" faithful died (including those reconciled and punished by the tribunal), they were buried in the Lima cemetery designated for Spaniards. One example is Luis de Valencia, registered as "español" at his death, who was taken to the cemetery by one of Manuel Bautista Pérez's brothers-in-law. AHN, Inq., leg. 1647, no. 12, fol. 129.

110 Be wary of the "Hebrew nation," the Suprema admonished its Lima affiliates, for they were in the habit of accusing "non-Portuguese" of engaging in Judaizing habits. AHN, Inq., lib. 1031, fol. 31.

111 Although there were extensive purity-of-blood·statutes limiting the functions of New Christians, the chief impact on colonial hierarchy had to do with the various rights and privileges reserved for españoles. Actual social practices, of course, were another story.

112 One exception was Doña María de Aguilar, described as a "mestiza," who was married to the "procurador," or fiscal officer, of Potosí, a high position in government. AHN, Inq., lib. 1028, fols. 511–15.

113 Solórzano Pereira, *Política indiana*, bk. 1, chap. 11, 113.

114 See my chapter "Globalization and Guinea Pigs." Avila and Pena Montenegro accounted for the limitations of Indians and blacks by calling on the same terminology applied to New Christians: they were said to have stained blood, *sangre manchada*.

New Christians and New World Fears

1 Arendt, *The Origins of Totalitarianism*, xvi.

2 This chapter is a significantly revised version of my article "New Christians and New World Fears in Seventeenth-Century Peru," *Comparative Studies in Society and History* 42, no. 3 (2000): 524–46.

3 Three New World branches of the Spanish Inquisition tried men and women who were accused of secretly practicing Judaism. And, in every case, reconciled Judaizers faced the most severe sentences and convicted Judaizers were almost inevitably executed. A refusal to desist from Judaizing was the principal cause of a sentence of execution. According to Liebman in *The Inquisitors and the Jews in the New World* (1975), which is a compendium of *procesos* (trials) with bibliography, the Mexican Inquisition was the most active. Forty-nine convicted Judaizers were burned at the stake, 50 died in their cells, 4 became insane, and 192 were sent to the galleys (p. 33). In Peru, 39 were burned at the stake, 139 were reconciled, 2 were declared insane, and 14 were either suspended or absolved (these numbers are all approximate because of inconsistent information).

The hunt for Jews came in waves, and the apogee in the Americas was reached between 1635 and 1649. During this period, inquisitors in Mexico and Peru talked about "great conspiracies" of hidden Jews. The Great Jewish Conspiracy in Lima (1635–39) was followed by Mexico's roundup and 1649 auto-de-fé. The "great conspiracies" are an example of how the tribunal's dependence on confessions and denunciations could have a wavelike effect on prosecutions (as we saw with the Manuel Henríquez trial in my chapter "Three Accused Heretics"). No doubt, these prosecutions were also spurred by the hostilities between Castile and Portugal (see "Three Accused Heretics" for background on these conflicts, along with Liebman, *The Inquisitors and the Jews in the New World*, 31–32).

Inquisitors in the Americas not only maintained ties with Iberia, but they established important communications links among themselves. Testimony in Cartagena could condemn a prisoner in Lima (see Manuel Henríquez's trial), and testimony in Lima could condemn a prisoner in Mexico (Medina, *Historia del Tribunal del Santo Oficio de la Inquisición en México*, 175). Once in the tribunal's ken, Judaizers fleeing Mexico for Lima became suspect (see the case of Felipa López, AHN, Inq., lib. 1029, fols. 39–43v).

4   See Kohut, "The Trial of Francisco Maldonado de Silva." Jonathan Israel estimates that 25 percent of the "Spanish" population in Buenos Aires and almost 10 percent in Cartagena were "Portuguese." See Israel, *Empires and Entrepôts*, 277.

5   AHN, Inq., Cartas, rollo 9, fol. 7, letter from Don León de Alcayaga Lartaun to Muy Poderoso S., May 15, 1636.

6   Adler, ed. and trans., "A Contemporary Memorial Relating to Damages to Spanish Interests in America Done by Jews of Holland" [1634].

7   After a careful examination of company records, Israel concluded that while some Jews might have invested in the company, they never dominated it (*Empires and Entrepôts*, 356n2).

8   Adler, "A Contemporary Memorial Relating to Damages to Spanish Interests in America Done by Jews of Holland," 48.

9   Ibid., 49.

10 Kohut, "The Trial of Francisco Maldonado de Silva," 166–67.

11 AHN, Inq., lib. 1028, fol. 365. For additional examples, including cases against merchants and well known to the inquisitors, see AHN, Inq., lib. 1028, fols. 339–44; lib. 1028, fols. 373v–75v; lib. 1028, fols. 422–23; lib. 1029, fols. 53v–55v. In the twelve cases of Judaizing punished by the Inquisition in the auto-da-fé of 1595, not one presents the stereotype linking Jews with riches.

12 AHN, Inq., lib. 1029, fols. 41–41v. Only three cases from the 1590s included claims that Jewishness could "make you rich"; and in all three, the overwhelming evidence for heresy rested on Judaizing practices and not on economics. AHN, Inq., lib. 1028, fols. 222–27v, for the case of Francisco Díaz, and lib. 1028, fols. 404–13v for the case of Pedro de Contreras. AHN, Inq., lib. 1029, fols. 57–59 for case of Antonio Fernández. Similarly, while Joan Vicente, described as getting merchandize and credit from other "Portuguese," the quantities were extremely modest, in line with his financial possibilities. AHN, Inq., leg. 1647, no. 3, fols. 19v, 45v.

13 AHN, Inq., lib. 1030, fol. 68v.

14 AHN, Inq., Cartas, rollo 7, fols. 111–17; citation at 113v.

15 AHN, Inq., leg. 1647, no. 11, fol. 61v.

16 AHN, Inq., leg. 1647, no. 11, fols. 61–61v, 62, 62v, 64–64v.

17 AHN, Inq., leg. 1647, no. 13, fol. 53. This same theme peppers testimonies throughout Manuel Bautista Pérez's case. Also see AHN, Inq., leg. 1647, no. 13, fols. 105v–6, 153–65.

18 AHN, Inq., leg. 1647, no. 13, fols. 105v–6v.

19 AHN, Inq., lib. 1031, fol. 95.

20 AHN, Inq., leg. 1647, no. 11, fol. 66v.

21 AHN, Inq., lib. 1031, fol. 95v.

22 AHN, Inq., leg. 1647, no. 12, fol. 71v.

23 AHN, Inq., leg. 1647, no. 13, fol. 263. It is not surprising, then, to find that in 1656 Luis de Ribero was denounced for "being a Jew, with impure blood (*sangre infecta*), who came here on the run, concealing and favoring other Jews." Moreover, we should note that this stereotype was contradicted in other testimony: Luis Valencia refused to be associated with certain people precisely because they had been penanced by the Inquisition; see AHN, Inq., leg. 1647, no. 12, fol. 65. In addition, Manuel Bautista Pérez was disturbed by the growing number of immigrants to Peru, because he felt "he was being persecuted by the many poor Portuguese who asked him for handouts and support"; see AHN, Inq., leg. 1647, no. 13, fol. 31v.

24 AHN, Inq., leg. 1647, no. 13, fol. 52v.

25 AHN, Inq., leg. 1647, no. 13, fol. 54v.

26 Kohut, "The Trial of Francisco Maldonado de Silva," 166–67.

27 AHN, Inq., Cartas, rollo 9, fol. 7, letter from Lartaun to Muy Poderoso S., May 15, 1636.

28 AHN, Inq., Cartas, rollo 9, fol. 51, letter from inquisitors Juan de Mañozca, Andrés Gaytán, and Antonio de Castro y del Castillo to Muy P. Señor, May 18, 1636.

29 Letter of May 18, 1636 (see n. 28 above).

30 Letter of May 18, 1636 (see n. 28 above).

31 Letter of May 18, 1636 (see n. 28 above).

32 Letter of May 18, 1636 (see n. 28 above). See Quiroz, "La expropiación inquisitorial de cristianos nuevos portugueses en Los Reyes, Cartagena y México (1635–1649)." In his fascinating article, Quiroz uses expropriation records to flesh out these complicated trading networks. Here is one example: Manuel Bautista Pérez sold slaves in Lima that he bought from Blas de Paz Pinto, Manuel de Fonseca, and Antonio Núñez Gramajo. With Amaro Dionis Coronel and Antonio Gómez Acosta, he was part of the pearl trade from Cartagena, headed by Manuel Fonseca Enríquez. Pérez sold merchandise from China and Mexico that was on consignment for Simón Váez, who was headquartered in Seville. These merchants provided merchandise and credit to middlemen and to the peddlers who traversed the sierra (pp. 413, 416).

33 See AHN, Inq., Cartas, rollo 9, fols. 150–54, letter from Gaspar Mato y Ribero, December 1636, which is a summary of the case against Simón Báez de Fontes, born in Portugal, resident of Amsterdam, who was captured when his boat capsized off the coast of Spain. Also see Israel, *Empires and Entrepôts*, 363–64, 374, 429.

34 It is true that Portuguese trade networks were worldwide and extensive. Manuel Bautista Pérez's business ventures were considerable, and frequently kinship channeled the structure of his endeavors. Taken together, Pérez, his brothers, and his cousins were engaged in commercial activities touching Portugal, Spain, South Asia, Africa, and the Americas. Within the viceroyalty, Pérez had extensive links—via traders, agents, and shopkeepers under his employ—to towns along the coast and in Peru's highland interior: Pativilca, Huaura, Chancay, Tiahuanaco, Potosí, Huamanga, Ica, Pisco, Arica, Arequipa, and Cuzco. In addition, two of Pérez's relatives were important bankers. See Israel, *Empires and Entrepôts*, 278; AHN, Inq., leg. 1647, no. 13, fols. 246–47v; Reparaz, *Os Portugueses*, 82–84; and AHN, Inq., leg. 1647, no. 11, fols. 56v, 38, 173v–75. Also, for a more detailed reconstruction of Portuguese trading networks, see Quiroz, "La expropiación inquisitorial de cristianos nuevos portugueses en Los Reyes, Cartagena y México (1635–1649)."

35 AHN, Inq., leg. 1647, no. 11, fols. 62, 67v.

36 AHN, Inq., leg. 1647, no. 13, fols. 116v–19, 342v–43.

37 AHN, Inq., Cartas, rollo 7, fol. 35v, letter from Juan de Yzaguirre to the Consejo, March 12, 1625.

38 Letter of May 18, 1636 (see n. 28 above). Alfonso Quiroz suggests where some of the inquisitorial venom might have come from. He intimates that members of the Con-

sulado, the board overseeing the Crown monopoly of trade, saw themselves as being in competition with Portuguese merchants and might have lobbied the Inquisition accordingly. Although some Spaniards were part of the Portuguese network, the great majority involved in credit operations were in debt to the Portuguese. See Quiroz, "La expropiación inquisitorial de cristianos nuevos portugueses en Los Reyes, Cartagena y México (1635–1649)," 246–48.

39 AHN, Inq., lib. 1031, fols. 264–64v; brief (dated May 14, 1642) of letter from Castro y del Castillo to the Suprema, June 8, 1641.

40 Kamen, *The Spanish Inquisition*, 42–43, 64–65, 290, 297–98.

41 Lewin, *El Santo Oficio en América*, 40. The decree went on to accuse New Christians of opening South American ports to Spain's enemies, for purposes of business and sedition.

42 Solórzano Pereira, *Política indiana*, 252:262.

43 AHN, Inq., Cartas, rollo 9, fol. 59, letter from Mañozca, Gaytán, and Castro y del Castillo, May 18, 1636.

44 Cobo, *History of the Inca Empire* (1979), 21–22, 31–32; Anónimo portugués, *Descripción del virreinato del Perú*, 40; Altolaguirre, ed., *Colección de las memorias o relaciones que escribieron los virreyes del Perú . . .*, 9. Note the similarities in stereotypes about women's susceptibility to diabolic influences: see Silverblatt, *Moon, Sun, and Witches*; Altolaguirre, ed., *Colección de las memorias o relaciones que escribieron los virreyes del Perú . . .*, 13, 179, 194–297; and Suardo, *Diario de Lima de Juan Antonio Suardo (1629–1639)*, 1:259–61. One viceroy wrote: "[T]here are over twenty-two thousand *negros* living in Lima and its surroundings, and if they were ever to see the Spanish losing in [battles with the enemy] there is little to assure us of them, because . . . generally they love liberty . . . and for similar reasons one has to be suspicious of *indios*, for everywhere, in these occasions, danger grows" (Altolaguirre, ed., *Colección de las memorias o relaciones que escribieron los virreyes del Perú . . .*, 43). For other examples see Suardo, *Diario de Lima de Juan Antonio Suardo (1629–1639)*, 1:146, 206, 225, 246, 296, 297, 299, 301; 2:5, 20, 24, 109 as well as Altolaguirre, ed., *Colección de las memorias o relaciones que escribieron los virreyes del Perú . . .*, 13–14 for the 1620s, 111–12 for the 1630s, 297–98 for the 1640s; Palma, *Anales de la Inquisición de Lima*, 69; AHN, Inq., Cartas, rollo 7, fols. 34, 36, letter from Yzaguirre to the Consejo, March 12, 1625; and Medina, *Historia del Tribunal del Santo Oficio de la Inquisición de Lima*, 1:231, 289. Also see Steve Stern, "Introduction," in Stern, ed., *Resistance, Rebellion, and Consciousness in the Andean Peasant World, 18th to 20th Centuries*, for an overview of peasant revolts.

45 AHN, Inq., leg. 47, no. 13, fol. 266.

46 "[E]ven though [the tribunal] just employed '*negros bozales*,' recently captured and transported to Peru . . . the Portuguese could understand them." Montesinos, "Auto de la fe celebrado en Lima a 23 de enero de 1639," in Lewin, *El Santo Oficio en América*, 160–61; note also the memo about "Moses Coen," sabotage, and special language requirements (p. 140).

47 AHN, Inq., leg. 1647, no. 13, fols. 314–14v.

48 Vázquez de Espinosa, *Compendium and Description of the West Indies*, 18–21, 24. This was a highly contentious issue. See Cobo, *History of the Inca Empire* (1979), 48, for a discussion of the debates.

49 Buenaventura de Salinas y Córdoba, *Memorial de las historias del Nuevo Mundo Pirú*, 11. We have few sources referring to how Jews (or at least New Christians) and Indians perceived their relationship to one another, but what we do have suggests that neither group was quick to claim the other as kin. See Guaman Poma de Ayala, *El primer nueva corónica y buen gobierno*, 1:14, 49, 3:852. Manasseh Ben Israel recounts the story of a Portuguese merchant who, although believing he had encountered one of the Lost Tribes, insisted that they had a different origin from that of Andean natives. See Ben Israel, *The Hope of Israel*, 105–6, and Kaplan, "Political Concepts in the World of the Portu-

guese Jews of Amsterdam during the Seventeenth Century." Also see the case of Luis de Valencia, who refused to admit that "Hebrews" and natives had the same origin (AHN, Inq., leg. 1647, no. 12, fol. 32).

50 Vázquez de Espinosa, *Compendium and Description of the West Indies*, 24.

51 AHN, Inq., Cartas, rollo 7, fols. 34, 36, letter from Yzaguirre to the Consejo, March 12, 1625.

52 Medina, *Historia del Tribunal del Santo Oficio de la Inquisición de Lima*, 1:231, 289.

53 Altolaguirre, ed., *Colección de las memorias o relaciones que escribieron los virreyes del Perú . . .* , 206.

54 AHN, Inq., Cartas, rollo 7, fol. 35v, letter from Yzaguirre to the Consejo, March 12, 1625.

55 Reparaz, *Os Portugueses*, 82–84.

56 AHN, Inq., leg. 47, no. 13, fol. 53.

57 AHN, Inq., leg. 47, no. 13, fols. 53–53v.

58 AHN, Inq., leg. 47, no. 13, fol. 53v.

59 AHN, Inq., leg. 47, no. 13, fol. 266.

60 AHN, Inq., leg. 47, no. 13, fol. 266.

61 AHN, Inq., leg. 47, no. 13, fol. 278v.

62 AHN, Inq., leg. 47, no. 13, fols. 278v–79.

63 AHN, Inq., leg. 47, no. 13, fols. 278v–79. Sometimes he made a show of using tobacco— "he would pretend he wanted to have some and he would take the tobacco pouch (*tabaquero*) and shake it [etc.]"—but it would most likely be done in mockery.

64 See Murúa, *Historia general del Perú*, 436–37, for similar descriptions of the use of coca.

65 Cobo, *History of the Inca Empire* (1983), 179–81; Guaman Poma de Ayala, *El primer nueva corónica y buen gobierno*, 2:441–45.

66 Anónimo portugués, *Descripción del virreinato del Perú*, 74.

67 AHN, Inq., leg. 1647, fol. 90v; tragically this was not to be the case. For an additional critique of the baselessness of the arrests of Portuguese in Europe, see AHN, Inq., lib. 1031, fol. 193v.

68 Montesinos, "Auto de la fe celebrado en Lima a 23 de enero de 1639," in Lewin, *El Santo Oficio en América*, 183.

69 Some examples: Manuel Henríquez, AHN, Inq., leg. 1647, no. 11, fols. 5v–6; Pero Luis Enríquez, AHN, Inq., lib. 1028, fol. 205v; Isabel Báez, AHN, Inq., leg. 1647, no. 3, fol. 11; Antonio de Acuna, AHN, Inq., leg. 47, no. 13, fol. 27v; Pasqual Núñez, AHN, Inq., lib. 1028, fols. 381v–82. Also see AHN, Inq., Cartas, rollo 7, from ? to the Consejo, January 11, 1628, for concern expressed by inquisitors regarding genealogies. Jacinto del Pino, a Portuguese merchant, supposedly told Manuel Henríquez that he pretended to be an Old Christian in remote places like Caylloma (a mining town in the Arequipa highlands); if inquisitors asked for his casta y generación, he added defiantly, he would tell them the same thing. AHN, Inq., leg. 1647, no. 11, fol. 67.

70 AHN, Inq., lib. 1029, fol. 25; AHN, Inq., lib. 1028, fol. 369; AHN, Inq., leg. 1647, no. 10, fols. 10–10v, 17v–18, 21v–22.

71 AHN, Inq., lib. 1028, fol. 422. Also note Francisco de Silva, who said he was Old Christian but the grandson of Portuguese (AHN, Inq., lib. 1031, fol. 224).

72 AHN, Inq., leg. 1647, no. 11, fols. 133–33v, 148v–49v, 67. Don Simón tried to hide his Portuguese roots by saying he was a Gallego (i.e. from Galicia, a region in Spain bordering on Portugal and where Portuguese is spoken).

73 AHN, Inq., leg. 1647, no. 12, fols. 60–61v.

74 AHN, Inq., leg. 1647, no. 12, fols. 37, 37v.

75 AHN, Inq., lib. 1029, fol. 48v; also see fols. 45v–49v.

76 AHN, Inq., lib. 1028, fols. 59–61.

77 AHN, Inq., leg. 1647, no. 12, fols. 2, 113–15v, 118.

78 AHN, Inq., rollo 9, fols. 166–80.

79 Luis de Valencia was ordered to pay a large fine and was exiled, in perpetuity, from

the Indies. However, he never left. He was buried as an "español" in Lima, in December 1641, accompanied by Father Buysas, a Jesuit, and one of Manuel Bautista Pérez's brothers-in-law. AHN, Inq., leg. 1647, no. 13, fol. 129.

80 Reparaz, *Os Portugueses*, 36–38; AHN, Inq., leg. 47, no. 13, fols. 2–37v et pass.

81 AHN, Inq., leg. 1647, no. 13, 271–73, 278x, fols. 104–5.

82 AHN, Inq., leg. 1647, no. 13, fol. 309v.

83 AHN, Inq., leg. 1647, no. 13, fols. 308–9v.

84 Reparaz, *Os Portugueses*, 105–9. Lively gatherings with intellectual substance could all too easily fit stereotypes of covert Sabbaths and unsavory rites. There were too many Portuguese in one Limeñan venue to be suspicion-free, especially when it belonged to someone called "the oracle of the Hebrew nation," "the captain," "the rabbi," and "the most knowledgeable Jew in Lima." Jorge Rodríguez Tavares thought inquisitors must have doubted his faith because he used to visit Manuel Bautista Pérez; and Rodrígues Tavares played on that hunch when he testified against Portuguese men, whom he seemed to suspect primarily because they talked to one another. So did Bartolomé de León, who suggested that the books belonging to Pérez were manuals for Judaizing; as did Luis de Vega, who had misgivings about the serious discussions of history overheard in Pérez's office. AHN, Inq., leg. 1647, no. 13, fols. 49v–51, 78v–79v, 108v, 111–11v; AHN, Inq., Cartas, rollo 9, fol. 53, letter from Mañozca et al. to Muy P. Señor, May 18, 1636.

85 Much of the wealth that allowed merchants to become aristocrats was ill-gotten. Portuguese were supposedly banned from trading in the Indies (although they were often royally reprieved), and contraband trade—where, again, Portuguese were salient—seemed to be thriving. As we can see from our records, the trade laws appear to have been violated with abandon.

86 AHN, Inq., lib. 1031, fol. 414; AHN, Inq., Cartas, rollo 7, fols. 111–17, and rollo 8, fols. 250–51. Barahona, a well-positioned administrator of the "obrajes" of the Countess of Lemos, was fined 200 pesos and, to his great detriment, exiled from the Viceroyalty of Peru.

87 From the early years of Spanish colonialism, Spaniards in the New World were accused of exploiting its native peoples and resources out of greed. The most significant denunciations came from fellow Spaniards, from priests like Bartolomé de Las Casas or from government officials, even from the king. Concerns about avarice often went hand in hand with concerns about the devastation of Peru's indigenous population. See Solórzano Pereira, *Política indiana*, 252:166–67; Altolaguirre, ed., *Colección de las memorias o relaciones que escribieron los virreyes del Perú . . .*, 234–35; Guaman Poma de Ayala, *El primer nueva corónica y bien gobierno*, 1:49; Buenaventura de Salinas y Córdoba, *Memorial de las historias del nuevo Mundo Perú*, 182; Córdoba y Salinas, *Corónica franciscana de las provincias del Perú*, xliii–xliv.

88 Solórzano Pereira, *Política indiana*, 252:150.

89 Fr. Jerónimo Mendieta, in Bayle, "Historia peregrina de un Inga andaluz," 27 (78): 51.

90 Anónimo portugués, *Descripción del virreinato del Perú*, 74.

91 From *Colección de documentos inéditos para la historia de España*, 118:236, cited in Bayle, "Historia peregrina de un Inga andaluz," 52.

92 AHN, Inq., Cartas, rollo 9, fol. 7, letter from Don León de Alcayaga Lartaun to Muy Poderoso S.

93 AHN, Cartas, rollo 9, fol. 59, letter from Mañozca, Gaytán, and Castro y del Castillo to Muy P. Señor, May 18, 1636.

The Inca's Witches

1 This chapter is a revised version of my contribution "The Inca's Witches: Gender and the Cultural Work of Colonization in Seventeenth-Century Peru," in *Possible Pasts: Be-*

coming Colonial in Early America, ed. Robert St. George, 109–30 (Ithaca: Cornell University Press, 2000).

The Lima witchcraft trials are somewhat different from the trials in Mexico or Cartagena. Witchcraft did not seem to be a major concern in Mexico, where women were principally charged with carrying out "superstitious acts," or throwing lots and conjuring (see Medina, *Historia del Tribunal del Santo Oficio de la Inquisición en México*, 150, 163, 166, 173, 209, 348; and Alberro, *Inquisición y sociedad en México, 1571–1700*, 183–85, 321). The indigenous plant that drew the magistrates' concern and ire was peyote, used by natives and, according to José Toribio Medina, by "not [just] a few Spaniards." Eventually, the tribunal condemned its use. See Medina, *Historia del Tribunal del Santo Oficio de la Inquisición en México*, 186. Alberro describes Mexican witchcraft as an amalgam of Spanish, African, and Indian influences, with the Spanish being predominant (*Inquisición y sociedad en México, 1571–1700*, 303). Nonetheless, Indian "magic" seemed to be the most sought after, Alberro notes, since accused witches were more likely to have hunted for Indian herbs and knowledge than any other (ibid., 301, 305, 318, 320; also see his app. 3, where we see that at least half of the accused used Indian herbs, 338–41). But while Mexico's accused witches used Indian herbs and powders, they did not conjure pre-Columbian deities or political rulers. In trials from both Mexico and Peru, we find reference to women of African ancestry who had special, clairvoyant skills. These women were called "zahori." For Mexico, see Alberro (339); and for Peru, see my discussion of the case of María Martínez in the present chapter.

Unlike the tribunal in Mexico but like the tribunal in Peru, however, the Cartagena tribunal was very preoccupied with witchcraft. But, in contrast to the Peruvian case, witchcraft allegations and confessions in Cartagena turned on explicit, sexual pacts with the devil. The Sabbaths, resembling Europe's, were said to be enormous celebrations, covens, in which witches overtly repudiated Christianity as a prelude to devil worship. Some of the "diablos" participating in the covens possibly had African names. For examples, see the witch trials brought to judgment in 1627 and 1628. See Splendiani, Sánchez Bohgorquez, and Luque de Salazar, *Cincuenta años de inquisición en el Tribunal de Cartagena de Indias 1610–1660*, 2:263–70.

Moreover, Peru's, Cartagena's, and Mexico's accused witches came from a variety of backgrounds: some were Spanish—usually from poorer sectors but not always, others were blacks (slaves and free), or mulatos or mestizos; some were married, others were widows or single. Ruth Bejar, in a study of eighteenth-century witchcraft, has pointed out the symbolic power of witchcraft for women—particularly *castas*—who were otherwise powerless and marginalized in colonial society (Bejar, "Sexual Witchcraft, Colonialism, and Women's Powers").

How to account for Peru's distinctiveness and its threat? Perhaps the Peruvian witches' turn to the Inca and to all things native might reflect—and be part of—creole Peru's general identification with its indigenous past, an identification that continues into the present.

For a compendium of articles about women's encounters with the tribunal see Giles, *Women in the Inquisition*.

2 Medina, *Historia del Tribunal del Santo Oficio de la Inquisición de Lima*, 2:17–18.

3 Ibid., 2:35–41; citation at 38.

4 Henningsen, *The Witches' Advocate*; Levack, *The Witch-hunt in Early Modern Europe*, 201–6. Studies of colonial women accused of practicing witchcraft in the New World constitute a small but growing field. See Mannarelli, "Inquisición y mujeres," for an important first examination of women tried for witchcraft in colonial Peru, as well as her equally important overview of women in the Inquisition, *Hechiceras, beatas y expósitas*. Also see van Deusen's significant work *Between the Sacred and the Worldly*, and Karlsen's *The Devil in the Shape of a Woman*, a pioneering analysis of the gendered aspects of New England witch-hunts vis-à-vis women of European descent. For important feminist analysis of witchcraft practices among Spaniards and mestizos in eighteenth-century

Mexico, see Bejar, "Sex and Sin, Witchcraft and the Devil in Late Colonial Mexico" and "Sexual Witchcraft, Colonialism, and Women's Powers." For an analysis of indigenous women accused of practicing witchcraft in colonial Peru see Silverblatt, *Moon, Sun, and Witches*.

5 Corrigan and Sayer, *The Great Arch*.

6 Indeed, this dynamic was the basis of colonial hegemony.

7 Medina, *Historia del Tribunal del Santo Oficio de la Inquisición de Lima*, 2:37–38.

8 Although the early records do not record occupation, later ones do. Thus we find that some earned their survival sewing, hawking wood, peddling fruits, vending sex, or selling their unorthodox skills.

9 For the period 1592–98, see AHN, Inq., lib. 1028, fols. 233–234, 234v–35, 262–64v, 282v, 319v–21, 330v–31, 515–16, 517–19, 522–23v.

10 Moorish women were commonly held to be experts in occult matters, and Isabel de Espinosa, who left Seville to escape her husband, confessed that she learned how to tell the future from "moriscas" (women of Moorish descent). AHN, Inq., lib. 1028, fols. 233–34.

11 AHN, Inq., lib. 1028, fols. 502–5. One prayer also includes men who had been either hanged or decapitated; their bones were considered very potent as well. Juan Antonio Suardo, in 1632, mentions a mulato and an español arrested for possessing bones from hanged men that were to be used in witchcraft (*Diario de Lima de Juan Antonio Suardo (1629–1639)*, 1:231).

12 Was she disturbed, or was she trying to gain the tribunal's mercy? Cases like this show the great difficulty in ferreting out motivation from the testimonies alone.

13 AHN, Inq., lib. 1028, fol. 519v.

14 AHN, Inq., lib. 1028, fol. 520.

15 AHN, Inq., lib. 1028, fol. 506v.

16 AHN, Inq., lib. 1028, fols. 512, 514; also see AHN, Inq., lib. 1028, fols. 507–11.

17 AHN, Inq., lib. 1028, fol. 326. Feeling undone by the testimony against her, Francisca Gómez ended up turning herself in.

18 Although men were only infrequently charged with witchcraft (they tended to be accused of blasphemy or of speaking heretical propositions), by 1622 two men had been condemned for using sorcery to uncover another magical attraction of Indian life: *guacas* or *huacas*, the native burials rumored to conceal vast quantities of treasure. Both men enjoyed substantial reputations as clairvoyants who could find lost property—from pilfered silver trays or stolen merchandize to escaped slaves and the colony's "lost" property of underground Indian riches. AHN, Inq., lib. 1030, fol. 225. Señor Navarrete's fame extended to Lima's Indian artisans; he had been brought in front of the Inquisition because a native tailor charged him with taking a silver picture frame in payment for services (to find who had stolen some bolts of cloth), services that were never rendered. AHN, Inq., lib. 1030, fols. 225–25v.

19 AHN, Inq., lib. 1029, fols. 499–99v.

20 AHN, Inq., lib. 1029, fol. 501.

21 AHN, Inq., lib. 1029, fols. 502–2v.

22 AHN, Inq., lib. 1029, fols. 500v–501.

23 AHN, Inq., lib. 1029, fols. 504, 504v. Violence against women was a constant problem that witches were asked to rectify.

24 AHN, Inq., lib. 1029, fol. 502v.

25 AHN, Inq., lib. 1029, fol. 504v.

26 Martin, *Daughters of the Conquistadores*, 280–309; citation at 280. My discussion of the tapadas is indebted to Martin's work; he pairs the tapadas with another ubiquitous symbol, the beatas.

27 Tapadas turned veils into a means of engaging the public life that colonial women were traditionally denied; this use is in strong contrast to veiling in the contemporary Muslim world, where it is a means of enforcing women's exclusion. (Muslim women, how-

ever, have also used veils to good advantage; Algerian women fighting against French occupation is a case in point.) We see, then, the dangers of abstract generalizations and the great importance of historical context.

28 See Barco Centenera, *La Argentina*, 192–92v.

29 Martin, *Daughters of the Conquistadores*, 302.

30 Altolaguirre, ed., *Colección de las memorias o relaciones que escribieron los virreyes del Perú.*
     . . .

31 Suardo, *Diario de Lima de Juan Antonio Suardo (1629–1639)*, 1:10, 2:46, 158. Sermons preached by Joseph Aguilar at the end of the seventeenth century again singled out tapadas for their veiled threat to moral and civic order in Lima. See Vargas Ugarte, *La elocuencia sagrada en el Perú en los siglos XVII y XVIII*, 48.

32 See Pinelo, *Velos antiguos i modernos en los rostros de las mugeres sus conveniencias, i daños.*
     . . .

33 AHN, Inq., lib. 1029, fol. 503v.

34 AHN, Inq., lib. 1029, fols. 499, 507.

35 AHN, Inq., lib. 1029, fols. 506–6v.

36 AHN, Inq., lib. 1030, fol. 194v.

37 AHN, Inq., lib. 1030, fol. 201v.

38 AHN, Inq., lib. 1030, fols. 194v, 201v.

39 AHN, Inq., lib. 1030, fol. 360.

40 AHN, Inq., lib. 1030, fol. 360v. Note that blacks and, at times, mulatas are often listed only by their first names in the record—an indication of their racial standing.

41 AHN, Inq., lib. 1030, fol. 360.

42 AHN, Inq., lib. 1030, fol. 360.

43 AHN, Inq., lib. 1030, fol. 361.

44 AHN, Inq., lib. 1030, fol. 361.

45 AHN, Inq., lib. 1030, fol. 360.

46 Although Catalina de Baena was penanced for engaging in witchcraft, the court did not believe that the bones she brought had contributed to Isabel de Mendia's illness. AHN, Inq., lib. 1030, fols. 361–61v.

47 See Fanon, *The Wretched of the Earth*, and Taussig, *Shamanism, Colonialism and the Wild Man*; also see Bejar, "Sexual Witchcraft, Colonialism, and Women's Powers." A confusion of race and name got Catalina in trouble, when the wife of the Royal Lieutenant (*alférez*)—also named Francisca and also said to "have some *mulata* in her"—thought Catalina de Baena had been accusing her in the bone-excavation scandal. "Some *mulata* in her" must have been an important marker in the Andean mining region, one that not only bedeviled Catalina (who was threatened as a result), but bedeviled the wife of a very important local official. AHN, Inq., lib. 1030, fols. 360–61v.

48 AHN, Inq., lib. 1030, fols. 360, 361v. We should note that the appeal to women's simple-mindedness was part of a standard rhetoric of mercy petitions. Another common appeal was to necessity; many of the witches were single women for whom "witchcraft" was a form of financial support. Catalina de Baena, the owner of slaves, put herself into the impoverished category. It is impossible, from the information at hand, to know Catalina's wealth, but we cannot forget that "Spanishness," in the viceroyalty, was defined in some measure by the possession of slaves.

49 AHN, Inq., lib. 1030, fol. 361v.

50 AHN, Inq., lib. 1030, fol. 381.

51 AHN, Inq., lib. 1030, fols. 380v–82.

52 AHN, Inq., lib. 1030, fol. 381.

53 AHN, Inq., lib. 1030, fol. 382.

54 AHN, Inq., lib. 1030, fol. 381.

55 One slave even met her labor obligations by selling her witchcraft talents and turning over the earnings to her master. See Catalina Ormache, AHN, Inq., lib. 1030, fol. 382v.

56 AHN, Inq., lib. 1030, fol. 380v.

57 AHN, Inq., lib. 1030, fol. 381.

58 AHN, Inq., lib. 1030, fol. 381.

59 AHN, Inq., lib. 1030, fol. 380v.

60 AHN, Inq., lib. 1031, fol. 121.

61 AHN, Inq., lib. 1030, fol. 382v.

62 Medina, *Historia del Tribunal del Santo Oficio de la Inquisición de Lima*, 2:35.

63 Although men were rarely tried as witches, some certainly believed in their own special powers. The records have given us only a few examples of men accused of witchcraft; however, we have many examples of men who availed themselves of witchcraft magic. These cases also show the gendered basis for making charges. Women who consulted witches are often accused as co-conspirators or accomplices, while men are not (e.g., AHN, Inq., lib. 1030, fol. 354–end; also lib. 1031, fols. 1–147v).

64 AHN, Inq., lib. 1031, fols. 376, 446v.

65 The trial records for accused witches during this time period are not to be found in the record group I am working with. Although witches were penanced, without the trial records I do not know of their beliefs etc. until trial records appear again in 1646.

66 AHN, Inq., lib. 1031, fol. 332v.

67 AHN, Inq., lib. 1031, fols. 374v–77v, 405–6v, 420v, 444v–49.

68 AHN, Inq., lib. 1031, fols. 374v–75.

69 AHN, Inq., lib. 1032, fols. 417–18, 458–64.

70 AHN, Inq., lib. 1031, fol. 375.

71 AHN, Inq., lib. 1031, fols. 376, 446v. Other devilish figures—Barrabás, Satanás, the lame devil—appeared in the earliest chants.

72 AHN, Inq., lib. 1031, fol. 375.

73 AHN, Inq., lib. 1031, fol. 445v.

74 Over time, the number of witches said to remove Christian objects when practicing their craft increased. Antonia de Ibarra, a "mulata," was said to have claimed, "[H]ow could you read [the images in the porcelain bowl] in front of Christ, when you were calling the '*sopai*' [*supay*]." AHN, Inq., lib. 1031, fol. 455v. *Supay* is the Quechua term given by evangelists to mean "devil," but its meanings did not necessarily coincide with official European definitions. See Silverblatt, *Moon, Sun, and Witches*, 177–78.

75 AHN, Inq., lib. 1031, fols. 349v, 382.

76 AHN, Inq., lib. 1031, fol. 449v.

77 AHN, Inq., lib. 1031, fols. 349v, 382.

78 AHN, Inq., lib. 1031, fol. 382v.

79 AHN, Inq., lib. 1031, fol. 386.

80 AHN, Inq., lib. 1031, fol. 383.

81 AHN, Inq., lib. 1031, fols. 382–87.

82 AHN, Inq., lib. 1031, fols. 382v–83.

83 AHN, Inq., lib. 1031, fols. 349v–50, 385.

84 AHN, Inq., lib. 1031, fols. 384–84v; I don't know what the literacy rates were for women, but I was surprised at the number of witches who seemed to know how to read and write.

85 AHN, Inq., lib. 1031, fol. 363v. This conjure was underlined in the text. "Inga" was a common spelling for Inca.

86 AHN, Inq., lib. 1031, fol. 383. Accused witches, with similar stories—meeting in groups, praying to the Inca, and using coca—are found through the rest of the seventeenth century. Some of the more interesting cases include Antonia Abraca, AHN, Inq., lib. 1031, fol. 378; Doña Anna Balleja, AHN, Inq., lib. 1031, fol. 388; Antonia de Urbina, AHN, Inq., lib. 1031, fol. 392; Doña Petronilla de Guebara, AHN, Inq., lib. 1031, fol. 498; Doña Ana de Sarate, AHN, Inq., lib. 1031, fol. 497; Doña Josepha de Lievana, AHN, Inq., lib. 1031, fol. 498v; Doña Magdalena Camacha, AHN, Inq., lib. 1031, fol. 499v; Doña Cata-

lina Pizarro, AHN, Inq., lib. 1031, fol. 501; Francisca Arias Rodríguez, AHN, Inq., lib. 1032, fol. 178v; Francisca de Urriola, AHN, Inq., lib. 1032, fol. 188; Lorenza de Balderrama, AHN, Inq., lib. 1032, fol. 424; María Jurado, AHN, Inq., lib. 1032, fol. 181; Sabina Junto, AHN, Inq., lib. 1032, fol. 182; and Doña María Magdelena de Aliaga, AHN, Inq., lib. 1032, fol. 198.

87 AHN, Inq., lib. 1031, fols. 497, 498v.

88 AHN, Inq., lib. 1031, fol. 383.

89 Huayna Capac, often designated the eleventh Inca king, died before the Spanish conquest. Two of his other sons were fighting for the title when the Spanish arrived. Melchor was Huayna Capac's great-grandson; his grandfather was Paullu Thupa Inca, a Spanish ally. From 1602, Don Melchor spent part of his life at the Royal Court in Madrid, petitioning for recompense on the grounds of both his royal blood and his grandfather's help in "pacifying" the Andes. On Don Melchor, see Garcilaso de la Vega, *Royal Commentaries of the Incas and General History of Peru*, 620, 625.

90 AHN, Inq., lib. 1032, fol. 534. Common medicinal claims for coca were that it was a good dentifrice and helped stomach disorders (see AHN, Inq., lib. 1031, fol. 460). Some women who claimed to have developed an addiction, like Doña María de Córdoba, said they began chewing for health reasons. Also see Francisca de Bustos, tried in 1669. She claimed that when she was very ill, some Indian women, *curanderas*, helped her by having her chew coca. Once she saw how much it did help her, she continued until now she chewed it "por vicio." See AHN, Inq., lib. 1032, fols. 114–14v. Coca (as opposed to cocaine) is not considered to be physiologically addictive. See Allen, *The Hold Life Has*, 221–23.

91 AHN, Inq., lib. 1031, fol. 500.

92 María de Castro Barreto y Navarrete also portrayed colonial bureaucrats, merchants, and artisans as commanding figures, only she called them "devils": the devils of the notary publics, merchants, silversmiths, fishmongers, royal governors, blacksmiths, and shopkeepers. AHN, Inq., lib. 1031, fols. 380v–81.

93 AHN, Inq., lib. 1032, fol. 380. There were priests and secular officials who used coca and consulted witches. See, for example, Francisca de Bustos, AHN, Inq., lib. 1032, fols. 113v–16v.

94 AHN, Inq., lib. 1032, fol. 375.

95 AHN, Inq., lib. 1032, fols. 418, 421.

96 See discussion of the Taqui Onqoy in my chapter "Becoming Indian."

97 AHN, Inq., lib. 1032, fol. 421.

98 AHN, Inq., lib. 1032, fols. 388v, 389v.

99 AHN, Inq., lib. 1032, fol. 391.

100 AHN, Inq., lib. 1031, fol. 399v.

101 See Sarmiento de Gamboa, *Historia general llamada indica*, and Córdoba y Salinas, *Crónica franciscana de las provincias del Perú*.

102 Contemporary analysis, sensitive to the social matrix of Inca government, has suggested that much of the Incas' reported absolute power actually rested in the local Andean "ethnic" polity, the *ayllu*. See Murra, *La organización económica del estado inca*.

103 Avendaño, *Sermones de los misterios de nuestra santa fe católica*, 1:114–15.

104 Ibid., 1:24v.

105 Ibid., 1:33v–34.

106 Avila, *Tratado de los evangelios*, 1:43, 63, 126, 270. Also see Cobo, *History of the Inca Empire*, 239.

107 Anónimo portugués, *Descripción del virreinato del Perú*, 91.

108 Guaman Poma de Ayala, *El primer nueva corónica y buen gobierno*, 2:524, 525.

109 Ibid., 2:558, 3:857.

110 Bayle, "Historia peregrina de un inga andaluz."

111 On Calchaquí-Spanish conflict, see Altolaguirre, ed., *Colección de las memorias o rela-*

ciones que escribieron los virreyes del Perú . . . , III, and Suardo, *Diario de Lima de Juan Antonio Suardo (1629–1639)*, 231, 289.

112 The Andalusian Inca was captured and executed by royal authority in 1667. Bohorquez's treason must have added fuel to colonial fears, coming as it did on the heels of an aborted uprising by Indians from the empire's civilized center (Bayle, "Historia peregrina de un inga andaluz"; Mugaburu and Mugaburu, *Chronicle of Colonial Lima*, 108, 109).

113 AHN, Inq., lib. 1031, fol. 529v.

114 Peru's seventeenth century has often been called a century of political stability. But it took decades for the Crown to assert its dominion, challenged as much by an Inca resistance as by colonists who refused to submit to royal sovereignty. Colonial efforts to consolidate Spain's institutional presence, inspired by the successes and failures of Spanish state-making on the Iberian Peninsula, ushered in what many historians have called the "mature colonial state." The measure of "maturity" of the Peruvian colony lay in the relative political calm marking the following century and a half of Spanish hegemony. See Spalding *Huarochirí*, 168–238.

115 See Andrien, *Crisis and Decline*.

116 See León Pinelo, *Mando que se imprimiesse*. . . .

117 See Guaman Poma, *El primer nueva corónica y buen gobierno*, 1:276–79.

118 See Arriaga, *The Extirpation of Idolatry in Peru*.

119 See Altolaguirre, ed., *Colección de las memorias o relaciones que escribieron los virreyes del Perú* . . . , 26–27, 229–30; Arriaga, *The Extirpation of Idolatry in Peru*; Acosta, "Escritos menores," 249–386.

120 Arriaga, *The Extirpation of Idolatry in Peru*, 145, 152.

121 Ibid., 96.

122 Ibid., 63; Hernández Príncipe, "Mitología andina."

123 AAL, leg. 4, exp. XIV.

124 Altolaguirre, ed., *Colección de las memorias o relaciones que escribieron los virreyes del Perú* . . . , 71–72.

125 Ibid., 194, 297, 298.

126 See Silverblatt, *Moon, Sun, and Witches*, 159–96.

127 Murúa, *Historia del origen y genealogía real de los reyes incas del Perú*, 301; Acosta, "Historia natural y moral de las indias," 172.

128 AAL, leg. 1, exp. XII.

129 Silverblatt, *Moon, Sun, and Witches*, 169–81.

130 AHN, Inq., lib. 1030, fol. 426; Medina, *Historia del tribunal del Santo Oficio de la Inquisición de Lima*, 2:145–46.

131 AHN, Inq., lib. 1031, fol. 389v.

Becoming Indian

1   AAL, leg. 2, exp. XIV, 12v.

2   This chapter is a revised version of my essay "Becoming Indian in the Central Andes of Seventeenth-Century Peru," in *After Colonialism: Imperialism and the Postcolonial Aftermath*, ed. Gyan Prakash, 279–98 (Princeton: Princeton University Press, 1995). The documents from the AAL's Campaigns to Extirpate Idolatry section, like the Inquisition records, are full of hazards for the historian. See "Appendix: Notes on Bias and Sources," for a fuller discussion of the problems and difficulties they raise.

Hacas Poma spoke fighting words, and we can ask why he felt secure enough to voice them. These were dangerous sentiments to express openly, especially at a time of idolatry campaigns. But I imagine that Hacas Poma was expressing deeply held convictions about what were, after all, life-and-death concerns, and that he felt he could no longer suppress them, regardless of the consequences. I also imagine that Hacas Poma counted on his ayllu's support and on its discretion. We should not forget that much of this illicit worship was taking place in very remote areas, high in the *puna* tablelands, where Spanish priests were unlikely to go. It seems that Indian parishioners were well aware of the need to dissemble when they went to confession or to church.

3 Duviols, *Cultura andina y represión*, 277. One of the difficulties presented by the trial records is that they are recorded only in Spanish. And this quotation, from one of Hernando Hacas Poma's "dogmatizing" efforts, is a case in point. We do not know the actual words he used when preaching in Quechua. While he might have used the Spanish term "indios" to designate the category of native Andeans, *runa* (a generic Quechua term for "people") is another possibility. One priest, the very astute chronicler Bernabé Cobo, who noted the colonial origin of "Indian," claimed that natives called one another "runa" and not "indio," which they took to be a derogatory term. Spaniards were not considered "runa." Cobo, *History of the Inca Empire* (1983), 8.

Duviols, *La lutte contre les religions autochtones dans le Pérou colonial*, and Huertas, "La religión de una sociedad rural andina," are pioneering analyses of the extirpation campaigns and of various aspects of native religion that the "Idolatrías" section of the AAL reveals. Subsequent important studies include Millones's examination of a sixteenth-century nativist movement, "Un movimiento nativista del siglo XVI"; Spalding, *Huarochirí*, 239–69; and Stern, "The Struggle for Solidarity." More recent studies of the confrontations between priests and native religionists include Mills's excellent *Idolatry and Its Enemies* and Griffiths, *The Cross and the Serpent*. I have used the rich documentary resources of the AAL "Idolatrías" section to shed light on the gendered construction of Andean cultural resistance, "Andean" witchcraft, and the participation of women in native religious structures (see Silverblatt, *Moon, Sun, and Witches*) as well as in my discussion of the making of native colonial religious ideologies (see Silverblatt, "Political Memories and Colonizing Symbols"). I first worked in the AAL when conducting my dissertation research, and I was able to do follow-up work in the summers of 1988, 1989, and 1991.

Duviols's edited collection of trial manuscripts from the Cajatambo region (*Cultura andina y represión*, cited above) is of major importance. Ana Sánchez has edited a series of "idolatría" documents from Chancay: *Amancebados, hechiceros y rebeldes*. See MacCormack, *Religion in the Andes*, for an important study of the intellectual traditions shaping Spanish versions of Andean religion.

4 See "Appendix: Notes on Bias and Sources."

5 One local curaca asked inquisitors if he could have the honor of carrying a statue in the processional leading to the Lima auto-da-fé. We know that Guaman Poma de Ayala accompanied priests in their extirpation missions; Inca descendants sponsored elaborate celebrations of Corpus Christi; the curaca who sculpted the Virgin of Copacabana spurred the creation of new Andean saints; indigenous women joined convents, participated in cofradías, and as "beatas" followed the route to "blessedness." See Medina, *Historia del tribunal del santo oficio de Lima*, 2:105; Guaman de Ayala, *El primer nueva corónica y buen gobierno*, 2:661–63; Dean, *Inka Bodies and the Body of Christ*; Griffiths and Cervantes, eds., *Spiritual Encounters*; and especially Osorio, "El Callejón de la Soledad." Also see Decoster, ed., *Incas e indios cristianos* and Sordo, "Nuestra Señora de Copacabana y su legado en el Potosí colonial."

6 See Silverblatt, "Political Memories and Colonizing Symbols."

7 For a discussion of the difficulties of using the AAL's Extirpación de Idolatrías records and what can be drawn from them, see "Appendix: Notes on Bias and Sources."

8 By the eighteenth century, however, Enlightenment notions were influencing Church doctrine, and the extirpation campaigns and the Inquisition were both in decline. See Bartolomé Escandell Bonet, "Reformismo borbónico y declive inquisitorial en América," in Pérez Villanueva and Escanell Bonet, eds., *Historia de la Inquisición en España y*

América, 1:1211–22; and, for extirpation campaigns in Huarochirí, see Spalding, *Huaro-chirí*, 267–69. Which is not to say that persecutions of native beliefs completely stopped. See Mills, *Idolatry and Its Enemies*; also Nicholas Griffiths, "Andean *curanderos* and Their Repressors: The Persecution of Native Healing in Late Seventeenth- and Early Eighteenth-Century Peru," in Cervantes and Griffiths, eds., *Spiritual Encounters*, 185–97, which describes the case against the healer Juan Vásquez, who was accused of "the superstitious use of herbal remedies" (185). In the twentieth century, versions of liberation theology encouraged the view that native myths incorporated understandings of God; for the Cuzco region see the journal *Allpanchis: Revista del Instituto Pastoral Andina* (1969–1972).

9   See Silverblatt, "Imperial Dilemmas, the Politics of Kinship, and Inca Reconstructions of History," especially for discussions of the contradictions Inca rule generated.

10   For the fullest discussion of the figure of the curaca see Spalding, *De indio a campesino*, 31–90.

11   See Silverblatt, "Imperial Dilemmas, the Politics of Kinship, and Inca Reconstructions of History."

12   For Inca economics see Murra, *La organización económica del estado inca*; Silverblatt, "Imperial Dilemmas, the Politics of Kinship, and Inca Reconstructions of History."

13   Gibson, "Indian Societies under Spanish Rule"; Spalding, *De indio a campesino*.

14   For a study of Indian migration in response to labor drafts, see Ann Wightman, *Indigenous Migration and Social Change*; for gender, see Silverblatt, *Moon, Sun, and Witches*, 159–96.

15   Silverblatt, "Imperial Dilemmas, the Politics of Kinship, and Inca Reconstructions of History."

16   Gibson, "Indian Societies under Spanish Rule."

17   It was also a fusion that made possible a sense of "blackness." I have been able to uncover only very little about colonial Peru's negros. They are the least studied of colonialism's racial trio, and much more research needs to be done. Today there is a thriving African-Peruvian movement with roots going back many decades; it is championed by renowned singers like Susana Baca. "Indianness" was dependent on the breakdown of ayllu boundaries; in this regard, it is similar to other broad identity movements (e.g., the diasporic movements of Zionism or Pan-Africanism) that develop in response to conditions of forced exile.

18   My principal documentary source for the Taqui Onqoy is Millones, ed., *La información de Cristóbal de Albornoz*. In *El retorno de las huacas*, Millones has revised and republished the archival material along with important accompanying essays. Cristóbal de Albornoz, the priest who was responsible for investigating the Taqui Onqoy, briefly describes the movement in his "Instrucción para descubrir todas las guacas del Pirú y sus camayos y haciendas," reprinted in the *Journal de la Société des Américanistes* 56 (1967): 17–39.

   Also see Stern, *Peru's Indian Peoples and the Challenge of Spanish Conquest*, 51–70, for an insightful discussion of the Taqui Onqoy. Other studies include Millones, "Un movimiento nativista del Siglo XVI," and Wachtel, "Rebeliones y milenarismo."

19   Colonials transformed the meaning of guaca from "sacred place and deity" to "burial site" (see my chapter "The Inca's Witches"). I am keeping with the colonial spelling here; in contemporary writing about the Andes, "guaca" is usually spelled "huaca."

20   Millones, ed., *La información de Cristóbal de Albornoz*, 25–149.

21   Worsley, *The Trumpet Shall Sound*.

22   Stern, *Peru's Indian Peoples and the Challenge of Spanish Conquest*, 51–62.

23   Millones, ed., *La información de Cristóbal de Albornoz*, 25–149. Local visionaries of the coming apocalypse saw the great mountains of the Andes doing battle: although the renowned guacas-mountains of Ayacucho and Apurimac dominated the scene, the great Chimborazo from Ecuador (also worshiped by Doña Ynés de la Penallilo) was among the ranks.

24 It is difficult to determine how influential the movement actually was or how far it spread beyond the department of Ayacucho. It is also difficult to determine if it was tied to the armed resistance movement of Manco Inca or if its militancy extended to a cache of arms uncovered to the north, in Jauja.

25 Rowe, "The Incas under Spanish Colonial Institutions"; Spalding, *Huarochirí*, 136–67.

26 Spalding, *Huarochirí*, 179–80, 214–16. However, ayllus of Sarhuas and Chuschis in the Río Pampas region of Ayacucho still live in what had been colonial reducciones.

27 Guaman Poma de Ayala, *El primer nueva corónica y buen gobierno*, 2:415.

28 Spalding, *Huarochirí*, 252–53.

29 See Solórzano Pereira, *Política indiana*, in *Biblioteca de Autores Españoles*, 252:371–83.

30 Pagden, "Identity Formation in Spanish America," 66.

31 AAL, leg. 6, exp. XI, fols. 9–9v, 47.

32 Indianism must have been compelling in these difficult times, but it was also fragile. Competing ideologies and allegiances—to ayllus or curacas, or even priests—might rip into its strength. Unfortunately, with our sources' limitations, there is so much about the movement that we will never know.

33 AAL, leg. 1, exp. X and leg. 6, exp. XI; Duviols, *La lutte contre les religions autochtones dans le Pérou colonial*, 385.

34 My arguments have been influenced by an extensive literature on "hegemony," including Williams, *Marxism and Literature*, 1–144; Genovese, *Roll Jordan Roll*; and Guha and Spivak, eds., *Selected Subaltern Studies*.

35 Any study of Andean utopian thought, with its ties to a belief in the Inca's return, is indebted to Flores Galindo's pathbreaking work *Buscando un Inca*. The commemoration of past relations with the Inca empire, described in the present chapter, while part of a configuration drawing on Inca experience, does not (yet) represent a full-blown belief in the Inca's coming. However, it could serve as part of the ideological landscape from which the figure of an Inca king might eventually be drawn.

36 See Rappaport, *The Politics of Memory*, for a wonderful study of the uses of the past in the political present.

37 AAL, leg. 4, exp. s.n., and leg. 6, exp. XI.

38 Hernández Príncipe, "Mitología andina," 52–63; Silverblatt, *Moon, Sun, and Witches*, 94–100; Zuidema, "Kinship and Ancestor Cult in Three Peruvian Communities." *Capaccocha*, or unblemished infants, were also sacrificed.

39 AAL, leg. 6, exp. XI, fol. 117; Duviols, *Cultura andina y represión*, 169.

40 Duviols, *Cultura andina y represión*, 350.

41 Flores Galindo, *Buscando un Inca*.

42 Silverblatt, *Moon, Sun, and Witches*, 109–96.

43 In Duviols, *La destrucción de las religiones andinas*, 42–43.

44 AAL, leg. 6, exp. XI, fols. 33v, 37, 39.

45 AAL, leg. 4, exp. XVIII, fols. 7–7v; also see AAL, leg. 6, exp. XI, and leg. 6, exp. X.

46 AAL, leg. 6, exp. XI, fol. 13. It is interesting that, in the original, two Spanish terms were used to refer to a nativist minister: *sacerdote*, or "priest," and *hechicero*, or "witch."

47 Duviols, *Cultura andina y represión*, 198, 455.

48 AAL, leg. 6, exp. XI, fol. IV.

49 AAL, leg. 6, exp. XI, fol. 10.

50 Duviols, *Cultura andina y represión*, 235.

51 See Silverblatt, *Moon, Sun, and Witches*; also ibid., 267–68.

52 AAL, leg. 4, exp. XVIII, fols. 5v, 6.

53 Duviols, *Cultura andina y represión*, 268.

54 AAL, leg. 6, exp. XI, fol. 54v.

55 Several Indian attempts to organize rebellions failed because priests found out about them in the confessional. Spalding, *Huarochirí*, 273.

56 Some nativist worship was so exuberant that it became reckless in its public display.

Licenciado Ygnasio Oserín was awakened one evening by the loud noise of drums winding throughout the streets of the pueblo he was inspecting. Realizing these were the accompaniments of Indian rites, he got out of bed and grabbed all the Indians he could and punished them (Duviols, *Cultura andina y represión*, 222). The idolatry trials describe heroic attempts to maintain the proper order of native religion. In the face of startling demographic declines and the forced reconstruction of Andean social units, some founding guacas were left either without ministers or without sufficient adherents. So as not to allow the collective memory to die, one curaca, along with a renowned preacher—both of whom had followings beyond their local communities—would hold worship for the guacas; meanwhile, the two remaining tributaries of a neighboring ayllu, neither of whom was a proper "minister," turned to the same preacher to conduct the necessary sacrifices and offerings for their *malquis* (ibid., 169). Another committed nativist, the only man left in his ayllu "who was not an *hechicero* by either inheritance or election," took it upon himself to take care of his group's five or six guacas and two malquis (ibid., 451).

57   Duviols, *Cultura andina y represión*, 152; citation at 156. Also see AAL, leg. 6, exp. XI, fols. 6–6v, 10. This reads almost like a page from the New Christian conspiracy trials.

58   Spalding, *Huarochirí*, 179–80, 214–16, notes that after a century of reducciones only a small percentage of Huarochirí's Indians actually lived in them.

59   AAL, leg. 2, exp. XXVII, fols. 1, 8. One of Toledo's most important reforms was to force Indians into the nucleated settlements called "reducciones."

60   Duviols, *Cultura andina y represión*, 453.

61   AAL, leg. 2, exp. XIV, fol. 12v.

62   AAL, leg. 2, exp. XIV, fol. 12v.

63   See Hill, *The World Turned Upside Down*.

64   Silverblatt, *Moon, Sun, and Witches*, 169–96.

65   Ibid.

66   AAL, leg. 4, exp. XIV, fol. 3v.

67   See AAL, leg. 4, exp. XVIIIa.

68   During the ritual alluded to here, people who were not of Inca origin had to leave the imperial capital for several days, after which they were invited back and given special foods by the aclla. Silverblatt, *Moon, Sun, and Witches*, 105–6.

69   The following discussion of Guaman Poma's thinking comes from Silverblatt, "Family Values in Seventeenth-Century Peru."

70   Guaman Poma de Ayala, *El primer nueva corónica y buen gobierno*, 1:162, 205, 207, 2:474, 413–14, 421, 566, 800, 801, 816, 3:896, 1019–20.

71   Ibid., 1:48–49; also see 1:54, 56, 89, 275, 2:720, 3:871.

72   Ibid., 1:199.

73   Ibid., 2:800.

74   Ibid., 3:1019–20.

75   Ibid., 1:190–92.

76   Seed, *To Love, Honor and Obey in Colonial Mexico*, 17–94.

77   Guaman Poma de Ayala, *El primer nueva corónica y buen gobierno*, 1:189, 2:498, 504, 509.

78   Ibid., 2:534, 542–47, 610, 618–19.

79   Ibid., 2:816.

80   Ibid., 1:122.

81   Ibid.

82   AAL, leg. 4, exp. XVIII.

83   Duviols, *Cultura andina y represión*, 52.

84   See Silverblatt, "Political Memories and Colonizing Symbols," 174–94, which analyzes the merged mountain gods and Santiago in more detail. Also see Urbano, "Dios Yaya, Dios Churi, Dios Espíritu."

85   Esquivel y Navia, *Anales de Cuzco*, 222.

86 Note that in contemporary Peru, mountain gods are still portrayed with blond hair and blond beards. This depiction has even found its way into tourist art made by indigenous migrants living in Lima. In their "tablas" or painted stories, the mountain gods are painted sitting around a table with other gringo-looking types, fingering the piles of money in front of them.

87 AAL, leg. 4, exp. XXI; AAL, leg. 6, exp. VIII; AAL, leg. 6, exp. XI; AAL, leg. 4, exp. XVIII; AAL, leg. 2, exp. XVIII; AAL, leg. 3, exp. X; AAL, leg. 1, exp. XII.

88 AAL, leg. 2, exp. XVIII; AAL, leg. 4, exp. XVIII; AAL, leg. 3, exp. X; AAL, leg. 1, exp. XII.

89 For descriptions of violence and acts of rebellion in the Huarochirí region, see Spalding, *Huarochirí*, 203, 247, 248, 270–93.

90 See Clifford, *The Predicament of Culture*; Warren, *The Symbolism of Subordination*, and *Indigenous Movements and Their Critics*; and Taussig, *Shamanism, Colonialism and the Wild Man*, and *The Nervous System*.

91 See Vargas Llosa, "Questions of Conquest." In this lead article in *Harper's*, Vargas Llosa describes Peru's Indians as an indistinguishable mass, whose religious fanaticism—blind devotion to an all-powerful "totalitarian" ruler, the Inca—led to their easy defeat at the hands of Spanish conquistadors. In Vargas Llosa's words, the Inca Empire "disintegrated like ice in water" (49–50).

92 I include myself. See Silverblatt, *Moon, Sun, and Witches*, 3–39, 67–80.

Afterword

1 Arendt, *The Origins of Totalitarianism*, 157; Benjamin, "Theses on the Philosophy of History," 255.

2 "Elementary forms," of course, alludes to Durkheim's classic work, *The Elementary Forms of the Religious Life*; John and Jean Comaroff apply the notion beyond Durkheim's original intent in their work on British colonialism in Africa, *Ethnography and the Historical Imagination*. I found their suggestion very helpful.

3 Again, I refer to Michel Foucault's understanding of governmentality and the emergence of the state.

4 Nothing as graphic as stained blood was required to incorporate race-thinking into other designs for colonialism or nationalism.

5 See Gibson, *The Black Legend*. The late Edward Said, certainly one of the most provocative, brilliant, and sensitive of postcolonial theorists, was also hobbled by Black Legend reasoning. In a commentary comparing England and France with Spain, Said had this to say about Spanish colonialism: "[T]he major distinguishing characteristic of Western empires (Roman, Spanish and Portuguese) was that the earlier empires were bent on loot, as Conrad puts it, on the transport of treasure from the colonies to Europe, with very little attention to development, organization, or system within the colonies themselves" (*Culture and Imperialism*, 89).

6 These accusations cut a little thin, given England's track record.

7 Cited in Kamen, *The Spanish Inquisition*, 305–6.

8 Ibid., 306.

9 See Helgerson, "Camões, Hakluyt, and the Voyages of Two Nations," 51, and Lepore, *The Name of War*, 7–13.

10 The English treatment of Indians was hardly a model; see Lepore, *The Name of War*. To my knowledge, England never produced a defender of Indians like Las Casas, who stood as a beacon for a substantial school of Spanish critics of the treatment of native peoples.

11 See Hakluyt, *The Original Writings and Correspondence of the Two Richard Hakluyts*. The quotation is in Helgerson, "Camões, Hakluyt, and the Voyages of Two Nations," 51, and all my Hakluyt citations are from Helgerson's study. This section is based on Hel-

gerson's excellent account and I have followed his insightful argument. The image of Spanish butchery has been sustained for centuries. Over two hundred years after the first tirades, a British historian was to write: "[The Inquisition] taught the savages of India and America to shudder at the name of Christianity. . . . It was a bench of monks without appeal, having its familiars in every house, diving into the secrets of every fireside, judging and executing its horrible decrees without responsibility" (quoted in Kamen, *The Spanish Inquisition*, 306–7).

12 In Helgerson, "Camões, Hakluyt, and the Voyages of Two Nations," 54.

13 Ibid.

14 Ibid.

15 Ibid.

16 Ibid., 55–56. British colonialism took many forms, and Hakluyt's conceptualization of the first wave of British colonialism was just one. In any case, Hakluyt's contrast between mercantilist England and colonial Spain—a point brought out by Helgerson—is fascinating. Although issues of direct versus indirect rule play a role in Hakluyt's critique of Spain, they were part of a more general critique rooted in English "enlightened tutelage" versus Spanish "brutal oppression."

17 The consequences of the Black Legend were felt long after the years when England and Spain first locked horns. Contemporary anglophone social theory, for example, has consistently denied Spain a role in the creation of the modern world. Even if Spain did successfully conquer native peoples in the Americas, so the argument goes, it was not capable of governing them in any way approximating political legitimacy. Spain dominated its colonies by brute force alone, rather than by any form of recognizable government. No less a scholar and activist than Edward Said saw Spanish rule in this way; see n.5 above. For more on the Black Legend, see Gibson, *The Black Legend*.

18 For a powerful critique of American exceptionalism, see Said, *Culture and Imperialism*, 54–57.

19 I am sure I need not belabor the brutality that has often accompanied these efforts to spread our way of life—whether in the Americas, Asia, or the Middle East—nor our failures at establishing this same way of life at home, attested to by our unyielding legacies of race thinking and poverty.

Appendix

1 In spite of the familiarities, the early modern world was indeed strange, and analyses with an eye toward its distinctiveness would be a welcome complement to this study.

2 Peter Burke has influenced a generation of cultural historians, who have focused on the historical differences of the sixteenth and seventeenth centuries. See, for example, Bertelli, *The King's Body*.

3 One such scholar, an important historian of sixteenth- and early seventeenth-century Spain, is Antonio Feros. See his *Kingship and Favoritism in the Spain of Philip III*. The aforementioned insights into seventeenth-century politics are kin to scholarship in cultural history that focuses on the play between the king's "two bodies"—his physical body and his reincarnation as the body politic. See Kantorowicz's seminal work *The King's Two Bodies*.

4 Whether to understand kingship as being so dominant as to override the potential of governing institutions, or to see it as social and political relations in the making is a complex question of interpretation.

5 See J. Jorge Klor de Alva, "Colonialism and Postcolonialism as (Latin) American Mirages," *Colonial Latin American Research Review* 1, nos. 1–2 (1992): 3–23.

6 Patricia Seed, "More Colonial and Postcolonial Discourses," *Latin American Research Review* 27, no. 3 (1993): 146–52, and "Colonial and Postcolonial Discourses," *Latin American Research Review* 26, no. 3 (1991): 181–200.

7   Rolena Adorno, "Reconsidering Colonial Discourse for Sixteenth- and Seventeenth-Century Spanish America," *Latin American Research Review* 28, no. 3, (1993): 135–45; citation at 144.

8   See the critique by Yosef Hayim Yerushalmi of B. Netanyahu's *The Marranos of Spain from the Late XIVth to the Early XVIth Century According to Contemporary Hebrew Sources* (New York, 1966), in Yerushalmi, *From Spanish Court to Italian Ghetto*, 22n31; and Henrique Urbano, "Poder y violencia en los Andes: Apuntes para un debate," in Urbano, ed., *Poder y violencia en los Andes* (Cuzco: Centro de Estudios Regionales "Bartolomé de Las Casas," 1991), 21–22.

9   Yerushalmi, *From Spanish Court to Italian Ghetto*, 21–31; Carlo Ginzburg, *Clues, Myths, and the Historical Method* (Baltimore: Johns Hopkins Press, 1989), 96–125 and 156–64.

10 Urbano, "Poder y violencia en los Andes," 21–22.

11 See Hernández Príncipe, "Mitología andina." If we assume that these testimonies reflect little of Andean religion, we run the risk of giving Spaniards the enormous powers that they, in their most arrogant moments, presumed to have. See the essays in Axel, *From the Margins*, for discussions of the difficulties of writing anthropological histories, and especially his excellent introduction, 1–46.

12 María Marsili argues that there were plenty of idolatries in Arequipa's Collca Valley, but the Jesuit missionaries in charge of the region were reluctant to mount campaigns for reasons of local politics. See Marsili, "El diablo en la familia."

13 Avila, *Tratado de los evangelios*, 1:295, 477, 478. Also see my chapter "Becoming Indian." Both Avila and Avendaño explained that Indians' great suffering was part of God's design: an initial punishment leading to eventual salvation. See Avendaño, *Sermones de los misterios de nuestra santa fe católica*, 1:81v.

14 Spalding, *Huarochirí*, 270–72.

15 Published diaries and traveler accounts portray the significance of religious activity in the lives of Peru's subjects. See Vázquez de Espinosa, *Compendium and Description of the West Indies*, 447–50. Also see Mugaburu and Mugaburu, *Chronicle of Colonial Lima*, 92, 166. For a more detailed discussion see my chapter "Mysteries of State." Even during the moments when anti-Catholic ideology was celebrated, natives attended church—in large part, of course, because they had no option. See my chapter "Becoming Indian."

16 For an exploration of the popularity of the Inquisition and of the autos-da-fé in the viceroyalty, see my discussion in "Mysteries of State."

17 See my chapter "Mysteries of State."

BIBLIOGRAPHY

AAL. Archivo Arzobispal de Lima.
AHN. Archivo Histórica de la Nación, Madrid.

Abrams, Philip. 1988. "Notes on the Difficulty of Studying the State." [1977]. *Journal of Historical Sociology* 1(1):58–89.

Acosta, José de. 1954a. "Historia natural y moral de las indias" [1590]. In *Obras, Biblioteca de autores españoles*, vol. 73, 3–250. Madrid: Ediciones Atlas.

———. 1954b. "Escritos menores" [1571–1578]. In *Obras, Biblioteca de autores españoles*, vol. 73, 249–386. Madrid: Ediciones Atlas.

Adler, Cyrus, ed. and trans. 1909. "A Contemporary Memorial Relating to Damages to Spanish Interests in America Done by Jews of Holland." [1634] *American Jewish Historical Society* 17:45–51.

Adorno, Rolena. 1986. *Guaman Poma de Ayala: Writing and Resistance in Colonial Peru*. Austin: University of Texas Press.

Adorno, Theodor W. 1983. *Negative Dialectics*. Trans. by E. B. Ashton, New York: Continuum.

Alberro, Solange. 1988. *Inquisición y sociedad en México, 1571–1700*. Mexico City: Fondo de Cultura Económica.

———. 1991. "Prólogo." In José Toribio Medina, *Historia del Tribunal del Santo Oficio de la Inquisición en México* [1905]. Mexico City: Consejo Nacional de la Cultura y Artes.

Albornoz, Cristóbal de. 1967. "Instrucción para descubrir todas las guacas del Pirú y sus camayos y haciendas" [c. 1580s]. *Journal de la Société des Americanistes* 56:17–39.

Allen, Catherine. 1988. *The Hold Life Has*. Washington: Smithsonian Institution.

Allpanchis: Revista del Instituto Pastoral Andina. 1969–1972. Vols. 1–3. Cuzco: El Instituto de Pastoral Andina.

Altolaguirre, Angel de, ed. 1930 *Colección de las memorias o relaciones que escribieron los virreyes del Perú acerca del estado en que dejaban las cosas generales del reino*. Madrid: Imp. Mujeres Españolas.

Amin, Samir. 1989. *Eurocentrism*. Trans. by Russell Moore. New York: Monthly Review Press.

Andrien, Kenneth J. 1982. "The Sale of Fiscal Offices and the Decline of Royal Authority in the Viceroyalty of Peru." *Hispanic American Historical Review*. 62(1):49–71.

———. 1985. *Crisis and Decline: The Viceroyalty of Peru in the Seventeenth Century*. Albuquerque: University of New Mexico Press.

Anónimo Portugues. 1958. *Descripción del virreinato del Perú* [1610]. Ed. by Boleslao Lewin. Rosario: Imprenta de la Universidad Nacional del Litoral Santa Fe.

Arce, Juan Ruiz de. 1968. "Advertencia" [1545]. In *Biblioteca peruana*, ser. 1, vol. 1, 407–37. Lima: Editores Técnicos Asociados.

Arendt, Hannah. 1964. *Eichmann in Jerusalem: A Report on the Banality of Evil*. New York: Viking Press.

——. 1973. *The Origins of Totalitarianism*. New York: Harcourt Brace and Jovanovich.

Arriaga, Pablo José de. 1968. *The Extirpation of Idolatry in Peru* [1621]. Trans. by L. Clark Keeting. Lexington: University of Kentucky Press.

Avendaño, Fernando de. 1648. *Sermones de los misterios de nuestra santa fe católica, en la lengua castellana y la general del Inca*. 2 vols. Lima: Jorge López de Herrera.

Avila, Francisco de. 1648. *Tratado de los evangelios, que nuestra madre la iglesia . . .* 2 bks. Lima: Comenjado.

Axel, Brian. 2002. *From the Margins: Historical Anthropology and Its Futures*. Durham: Duke University Press.

Baker, Lee D. 1998. *From Savage to Negro: Anthropology and the Construction of Race, 1896–1954*. Berkeley: University of California Press.

Balabar, Etienne, and Immanuel Wallerstein. 1991. *Race, Nation, Class: Ambiguous Identities*. London: Verso.

Barco Centenera, Martín del. 1912. *La Argentina* [1602]. Buenos Aires: A. Estrada.

Bayle, Constantino. 1927. "Historia peregrina de un inga andaluz" [1658]. In *Razón y Fe*. Madrid. 27 (78):49–58, 239–50, 412–22; (79):146–56, 207–18; (80):314–2; (81):337–50.

Beetham, David. 1996. *Bureaucracy*. Minneapolis: University of Minnesota Press.

Bejar, Ruth. 1987. "Sex and Sin, Witchcraft and the Devil in Late Colonial Mexico." *American Ethnologist* 14(1):35–55.

——. 1989. "Sexual Witchcraft, Colonialism, and Women's Powers: Views from the Mexican Inquisition." In *Sexuality and Marriage in Colonial Latin America*, ed. by Asunción Lavrin, 178–206. Lincoln: University of Nebraska Press.

Ben Israel, Manasseh. 1987. *The Hope of Israel* [1652]. Ed. by Henry Mechoulan and Gerard Nahon; intro. and notes Moses Wall; trans. from French by Richenda George. Oxford: Oxford University Press.

Benjamin, Walter. 1986. "Theses on the Philosophy of History." In *Illuminations*, ed. by Hannah Arendt, 253–64. New York: Schocken.

Bertelli, Sergio. 2001. *The King's Body: The Sacred Rituals of Power in Medieval and Early Modern Europe*. Trans by R. Burr Litchfield. University Park: Pennsylvania State University Press.

Bourdieu, Pierre. 1998. *Practical Reason*. Stanford: Stanford University Press.

Boxer, C. R. 1969. *The Portuguese Seaborne Empire, 1415–1825*. London: Hutchinson.

Brooks, C. W. 1986. *Pettyfoggers and Vipers of the Commonwealth: The "Lower Branch" of the Legal Profession in Early Modern England*. Cambridge: Cambridge University Press.

Burchell, Graham, Colin Gordon, and Peter Miller, eds. 1991. *The Foucault Effect: Studies in Governmentality*. Chicago: University of Chicago Press.

Burns, Kathryn. 1999. *Colonial Habits: Convents and the Spiritual Economy of Cuzco, Peru*. Durham: Duke University Press.

Cadena, Marisol de la. 1998. "Silent Racism and Intellectual Superiority in Peru." *Bulletin of Latin American Research* 17(2):143–64.

——. 2000. *Indigenous Mestizos: The Politics of Race and Culture in Cuzco, 1919–1991*. Durham: Duke University Press.

Cahill, David. 1994. "Colour by Numbers: Racial and Ethnic Categories in the Viceroyalty of Peru, 1552–1824." *Journal of Latin American Studies* 26:338–46.

Caro Baroja, Julio. 1961. *Los judíos en la España moderna y contemporánea*, vol. 1. Madrid: Ediciones Arión.

——. 1972. *Inquisición, brujería y criptojudaísmo*. Barcelona: Ediciones Ariel.

Carrera, Magali Marie. 2003. *Imagining Identity in New Spain: Race, Lineage and the Colonial Body in Portraiture and Casta Paintings*. Austin: University of Texas Press.

Castañeda Delgado, Paulino, and Pilar Hernández Aparicio. 1989. *La Inquisición de Lima*. 3 vols. Madrid: Demos.

Cellorigo, Martín González de. 1991. *Memorial de la política necesaria y útil restauración a la República de España y estados de ella, y del desempeño universal de estos reinos*. [1600]. Madrid: Instituto de Cooperación Iberoamericana.

Clifford, James. 1988. *The Predicament of Culture*. Cambridge: Harvard University Press.

Cobo, Father Bernabé. 1979. *History of the Inca Empire*. Ed. and trans. by Roland Hamilton. Austin: University of Texas Press.

Colloredo-Mansfeld, Rudi. 1998. "'Dirty Indians,' Radical Indígenas, and the Political Economy of Social Difference in Modern Ecuador." *Bulletin of Latin American Research* 17(2): 185–206.

Comaroff, Jean, and John Comaroff. 1992. *Ethnography and the Historical Imagination*. Boulder: Westview Press.

Cooper, Frederick and Ann L. Stoler. 1997. "Between Metropole and Colony: Rethinking a Research Agenda." In *Tensions of Empire: Colonial Cultures in a Bourgeoise World*. Ed. by Frederick Cooper and Ann L. Stoler, 1–58. Berkeley: University of California Press.

Córdoba y Salinas, Diego de. 1957. *Crónica franciscana de las provincias del Perú*. [1651]. Washington: Academy of American Franciscan History.

Coronil, Fernando. 1996. "Beyond Occidentalism: Towards Non-imperial Geohistorical Categories." *Cultural Anthropology* 11(1):51–87.

——. 1997. *The Magical State: Nature, Money, and Modernity in Venezuela*. Chicago: University of Chicago Press.

Corrigan, Philip, and Derek Sayer. 1985. *The Great Arch: English State Formation as Cultural Revolution*. Oxford: Basil Blackwell.

Dean, Carolyn. 1999. *Inka Bodies and the Body of Christ: Corpus Christi in Colonial Cuzco, Peru*. Durham: Duke University Press.

Decoster, Jean-Jacques, ed. 2002. *Incas e Indios Cristianos: Elites indígenas e identidades cristianas en los Andes coloniales*. Cuzco: Centro de Estudios Regionales Andinos Bartolomé de Las Casas.

Donald, James, and Stuart Hall, eds. 1986. *Politics and Ideology: A Reader*. Philadelphia: Open University Press.

Durkheim, Emile. 1995. *The Elementary Forms of the Religious Life*. Trans. and intro. by Karen E. Fields. New York: Free Press.

Dussel, Enrique. 1998. "Beyond Eurocentrism: The World System and the Limits of Modernity." In *The Cultures of Globalization*. Ed. by Fredric Jameson and Masao Miyoshi, 3–31. Durham: Duke University Press.

Duviols, Pierre. 1971. *La Lutte contre les religions autochtones dans le Perou colonial: L'extirpation de l'idolâtrie entre 1532 et 1660*. Paris: Institut Français d'Etudes Andines.

——. 1977. *La destrucción de las religiones andinas (durante la conquista y la colonia)*. Trans. by Albor Maruenda. Mexico City: Universidad Nacional Autónoma de México.

——. 1986. *Cultura andina y represión: Procesos y visitas de idolatrías y hechicerías Cajatambo, siglo XVII*. Cuzco: Centro de Estudios Rurales Andinos "Bartolomé de las Casas."

Elias, Norbert. 1982. *The Civilizing Process*. New York: Pantheon.

Elliott, J. H. 1964. *Imperial Spain, 1469–1716*. New York: St. Martin's Press.

——. 1987. "Spain and America before 1700." In *Colonial Spanish America*, ed. by Leslie Bethell, 59–111. Cambridge: Cambridge University Press.

——. 1990a. *Imperial Spain*. London: Penguin.

——. 1990b. "The Spanish Conquest." In *Colonial Spanish America*, ed. by Leslie Bethell, 12–14. Cambridge: Cambridge University Press.

Escamilla-Colin, Michèle. 1992. *Crimes et châtiments dans l'Espagne inquisitoriale*, vol. 1. Paris: Berg Internacional.

Fanon, Frantz. 1968. *The Wretched of the Earth*. New York: Grove.

——. 1991. *Black Skin, White Masks*. New York: Grove.

Feros, Antonio. 2000. *Kingship and Favoritism in the Spain of Philip III: 1598–1621*. Cambridge: Cambridge University Press.

Flores Araoz, José, et al., eds. 1999. *Santa Rosa de Lima y su tiempo*. Lima: Banco de Crédito del Perú.

Flores Galindo, Antonio. 1986. *Buscando un Inca: Identidad y utopía en los Andes*. Havana: Casa de las Américas.

Foucault, Michel. 1995. *Discipline and Punish*. New York: Vintage Books.

Fraschina, Alicia. 2003. "De bruja a 'elegida de Dios': La experiencia de una beata jesuítica en el Buenos Aires colonial." Paper presented to the fifty-first Congreso Internacional de Americanistas, Santiago, Chile.

García de Proodian, Lucía. 1966. *Los judíos en América: Sus actividades en los virreinatos de Nueva Castilla y Nueva Granada, S. XVII*. Madrid: Instituto Arias Montano.

Genovese, Eugene D. 1974. *Roll Jordan Roll*. New York: Pantheon.

Gibson, Charles. 1971. *The Black Legend, Anti-Spanish Attitudes in the Old World and the New*. New York: Random House.

———. 1987. "Indian Societies under Spanish Rule." In *Colonial Spanish America*, ed. Leslie Bethell, 361–99. Cambridge: Cambridge University Press.

Giles, Mary. 1999. *Women in the Inquisition: Spain and the New World*. Baltimore: Johns Hopkins Press.

Gilroy, Paul. 1993. *The Black Atlantic: Modernity and Double Consciousness*. Cambridge, Mass.: Harvard University Press.

———. 2002. *Against Race: Imagining Political Culture beyond the Color Line*. Cambridge, Mass.: Harvard University Press.

Gitlitz, David M. 1996. *Secrecy and Deceit: The Religion of the Crypto Jews*. Philadelphia: Jewish Publication Society.

Glave, Luis Miguel. 1998. *De Rosa y espinas: Economía, sociedad y mentalidades andinas, siglo XVII*. Lima: Instituto de Estudios Peruanos.

Greer, Allen, and Jodi Bilinkoff, eds. 2003. *Colonial Saints: Discovering the Holy in the Americas, 1500–1800*. New York: Routledge.

Griffiths, Nicholas. 1997. *The Cross and the Serpent: Religious Repression and Resurgence in Colonial Peru*. Norman: University of Oklahoma Press.

Griffiths, Nicholas and Fernando Cervantes, eds. 1999. *Spiritual Encounters: Interactions between Christianity and Native Religion in Colonial America*. Lincoln: University of Nebraska Press.

Guaman Poma de Ayala, Felipe. 1980. *El Primer nueva corónica y buen gobierno* [1615]. Ed. by John Murra and Rolena Adorno. Trans. and textual analysis of Quechua by J. Urioste. 3 vols. Mexico City: Siglo Veintiuno.

Guha, Ranajit, and Gayatri Spivak, eds. 1988. *Selected Subaltern Studies*. New Delhi: Oxford University Press.

Gupta, Akhil. 1995. "Blurred Boundaries: The Discourse of Corruption, the Culture of Politics, and the Imagined State." *American Ethnologist* 22(2):375–402.

Gupta, Akhil and James Ferguson, eds. 1997. *Culture, Power, Place: Explorations in Critical Anthropology*. Durham: Duke University Press.

Hakluyt, Richard. 1935. *The Original Writings and Correspondence of the Two Richard Hakluyts*. London: Hakluyt Society.

Hall, Stuart. 1983. "Gramsci's Relevance for the Study of Race and Ethnicity." *Journal of Communication Inquiry* 10(2):5–27.

Hampe Martínez, Teodoro. 1996. "Recent Works on the Inquisition and Peruvian Colonial Society, 1570–1820." *Latin American Research Review* 31(2):43–63.

———. 1998. *Santo Oficio e historia colonial: Aproximaciones al Tribunal de la Inquisición de Lima (1570–1820)*. Lima: Ediciones del Congreso del Perú.

———. 2003. "Santa Rosa de Lima como prototipo divino y humano: Una perspectiva diacrónica." Paper presented to the fifty-first Congreso Internacional de Americanistas, Santiago, Chile.

Helgerson, Richard. 1992. "Camões, Hakluyt, and the Voyages of Two Nations." In *Colonial-*

ism and Culture, ed. by Nicholas B. Dirks, 27–64. Ann Arbor: University of Michigan Press.

Henningsen, Gustav. 1980. *The Witches' Advocate: Basque Witchcraft and the Spanish Inquisition, 1609–1614*. Reno: University of Nevada Press.

Hernández Príncipe, Rodrigo. 1923. "Mitología andina." [1621]. *Inca*. 1:24–68.

Herrup, Cynthia B. 1987. *The Common Peace: Participation and the Criminal Law in Seventeenth-Century England*. Cambridge: Cambridge University Press.

Herzfeld, Michael. 1992. *The Social Production of Indifference: Exploring the Symbolic Roots of Western Bureaucracy*. Chicago: University of Chicago Press.

Herzog, Tamar. 1995. *La administración como un fenómeno social: La justicia penal de la ciudad de Quito (1650–1750)*. Madrid: Centro de Estudios Constitucionales.

Hill, Christopher. 1972. *The World Turned Upside Down*. London: Temple Smith.

Hindle, S. 1996. *The Experience of Authority in Early Modern England*. New York: St. Martin's Press.

Holt, Thomas C. 1996. *Critical Dialogues in Cultural Studies*. London: Routledge.

——. 2000. *The Problem of Race in the Twenty-first Century*. Cambridge, Mass.: Harvard University Press.

Horkheimer, Max, and Theodor W. Adorno. 1972. *Dialectic of Enlightenment*. Trans. by John Cumming. New York: Herder and Herder.

Huertas, Lorenzo. 1969. "La religión de una sociedad rural andina: Cajatambo en el siglo XVII." Tesis para bachiller, Facultad de Letras, Universidad Nacional Mayor de San Marcos, Lima.

Inquisición y sociedad en América Latina. 1989. *Cuadernos para la Historia de la Evangelización en América Latina*. Vol. 4. Cuzco: Centro de Estudios Rurales Andinos "Bartolomé de las Casas."

Israel, Jonathan I. 1989. *European Jewry in the Age of Mercantilism, 1550–1750*. Oxford: Clarendon.

——. 1990. *Empires and Entrepôts: The Dutch, the Spanish Monarch and the Jews, 1585–1713*. London: Hambledon Press.

Iwasaki, Fernando. 1993. "Mujeres al borde de la perfección." *Hispanic American Historical Review*. 73(4):581–613.

Joseph, Gilbert M, Catherine C. LeGrand, and Ricardo D. Salvatore, eds. 1998. *Close Encounters of Empire*. Durham: Duke University Press.

Kamen, Henry. 1985. *Inquisition and Society in Spain*. Bloomington: Indiana University Press.

——. 1998. *The Spanish Inquisition: A Historical Revision*. New Haven: Yale University Press.

Kamenka, Eugene. 1979. *Bureaucracy: The Career of a Concept*. New York: St. Martin's Press.

Kantorowicz, Ernst H. 1997. *The King's Two Bodies* [1957]. Princeton: Princeton University Press.

Kaplan, Yosef. 1989. "Political Concepts in the World of the Portuguese Jews of Amsterdam during the Seventeenth Century: The Problem of Exclusion and the Boundaries of Self-Identity." In *Menasseh Ben Israel and His World*, ed. by Y. Kaplan, H. Mechoulan, and R. Popkin, 45–62. Leiden: E. J. Brill.

Karlsen, Carol. 1987. *The Devil in the Shape of a Woman*. New York: Norton.

Kohut, George Alexander. 1896. "Martyrs of the Inquisition in South America." *American Jewish Historical Society* 4:101–87.

——. 1903. "The Trial of Francisco Maldonado de Silva." *American Jewish Historical Society* 11:163–79.

Kuznesof, Elizabeth Anne. 1995. "Ethnic and Gender Influences on 'Spanish' Creole Society in Colonial Spanish America." *Colonial Latin American Review*. 4(1):153–76.

——. 1996. "Ethnic and Gender Influences on 'Spanish' Creole Society in Colonial Spanish America" (Response). *Colonial Latin American Review*. 5(1):129–35.

Lander, Edgardo. 1999. "Eurocentrismo y colonialismo en el pensamiento social latinoamericano." In *Pensar (en) los Intersticios: Teoría y practica de la crítica poscolonial*, ed. by Santiago Castro-Gómez, Oscar Guardiola-Rivera, and Carmen Millán de Benavides, 45–54. Bogotá: Instituto Pensar.

León Pinelo, Diego de. 1661. *Mando que se imprimiesse . . . cerca de la enseñanza y buen tratamiento de los indios.* Lima: s. n.

Lepore, Jill. 1998. *The Name of War: King Philip's War and the Origins of American Identity.* New York: Knopf.

Levack, Brian. 1987. *The Witch-hunt in Early Modern Europe.* London: Longman.

Lewin, Boleslao. 1950. *El Santo Oficio en América; y el más grande proceso inquisitorial en el Perú.* Buenos Aires: Sociedad Hebraica Argentina.

Liebman, Seymour B. 1975. *The Inquisitors and the Jews in the New World: Summaries of Procesos, 1500–1810, and Bibliographical Guide.* Coral Gables: University of Miami Press.

Lockhart, James, and Stuart B. Schwartz. 1983. *Early Latin America: A History of Colonial Spanish America and Brazil.* Cambridge: Cambridge University Press.

López Madera, Gregorio. 1597. *Excelencias de la monarchía y reyno de España.* Valladolid: Diego Fernández á de Cordova.

MacCormack, Sabine. 1991. *Religion in the Andes: Vision and Imagination in Early Colonial Peru.* Princeton: Princeton University Press.

Mannarelli, Maria Emma. 1985. "Inquisición y mujeres: Las hechiceras en el Perú durante el siglo XVII." *Revista Andina.* 3:141–56.

———. 1998. *Hechiceras, beatas y expósitas: Mujeres y poder inquisitorial en Lima.* Lima: Ediciones del Congreso del Perú.

Maravall, José Antonio. 1986. *Culture of the Baroque: Analysis of a Historical Structure.* Trans. by Terry Cochran. Minneapolis: University of Minnesota Press.

Marcuse, Herbert. 1973. *Studies in Critical Philosophy.* Boston: Beacon Press.

Marsili, María. 2003. "El diablo en la familia: Herejía, idolatría y hechicería en Arequipa colonial." Paper presented to the fifty-first Congreso Internacional de Americanistas, Santiago, Chile.

Martin, Luis. 1989. *Daughters of the Conquistadores: Women of the Viceroyalty of Peru.* Dallas: Southern Methodist University Press.

Marx, Karl. 1971. *The Grundrisse.* Ed. and trans. by David McLellan. New York: Harper and Row.

———. 1983. "On the Jewish Question." In *The Portable Karl Marx,* ed. by Eugene Kamenka, 112–14. New York: Penguin.

Medina, José Toribo. 1956. *Historia del Tribunal del Santo Oficio de la Inquisición de Lima (1569–1820)* [1887]. 2 vols. Santiago, Chile: Imprenta Gutenberg.

———. 1991. *Historia del Tribunal del Santo Oficio de la Inquisición en México* [1905]. Prologue by Solange Alberro. Mexico City: Consejo Nacional de la Cultura y Artes.

Memmi, Albert. 2000. *Racism.* Trans. by Steve Martinot. Minneapolis: University of Minnesota Press.

Mena, Cristóbal de. 1968. "La conquista del Perú" [1534]. In *Biblioteca peruana,* ser. 1, vol. 1, 135–69. Lima: Editores Técnicos Asociados.

Mendoza, Zoila. 1998. "Defining Folklore: Mestizo and Indigenous Identities on the Move." *Bulletin of Latin American Research.* 17(2):165–84.

Mignolo, Walter. 1999. *Local Histories/Global Designs: Essays in Colonial Legacies, Subaltern Studies and Border Thinking.* Princeton: Princeton University Press.

Millar Carvacho, René. 1998. *Inquisición y sociedad en el virreinato peruano: Estudios sobre el tribunal de la Inquisición de Lima.* Lima: Instituto Riva-Agüero, Pontificia Universidad Católica del Perú.

Millones, Luis. 1973. "Un movimiento nativista del siglo XVI: El Taki Onqoy." In *Ideología mesiánica del mundo andino,* ed. by Juan Ossio, 83–94. Lima: Ignacio Prado Pastor.

———, ed. 1971. *La información de Cristóbal del Albornoz: Documentos para la historia del Taki Onqoy.* Cuernavaca: CIDOC.

———. 1990. *El retorno de las huacas. Estudios y documentos sobre el Taki Onqoy, siglo XVI.* Lima: Instituto de Estudios Peruanos and Sociedad Peruana de Psicoanálisis.

Mills, Kenneth. 1997. *Idolatry and Its Enemies: Colonial Andean Religion and Extirpation, 1640–1750*. Princeton: Princeton University Press.

———. 2003. "Diego de Ocaña's Hagiography of New and Renewed Devotion in Colonial Peru." In *Colonial Saints: Discovering the Holy in the Americas, 1500–1800*, ed. by Allan Greer and Jodi Bilinkoff, 51–76. New York: Routledge.

——— and William B. Taylor, eds. 1998. *Colonial Spanish America: A Documentary History*. Wilmington, Del.: Scholarly Resources.

Montesinos, Fernando de. 1950. "Auto de la fe celebrado en Lima a 23 de enero de 1639." In *El Santo Oficio en América; y el más grande proceso inquisitorial en el Perú*, ed. by Boleslao Lewin, app. 1. Buenos Aires: Sociedad Hebraica Argentina.

Mörner, Magnus. 1967. *Race Mixture in the History of Latin America*. Boston: Little, Brown.

Mugaburu, Josephe, and Francisco Mugaburu. 1975. *Chronicle of Colonial Lima: The Diary of Josephe and Francisco Mugaburu, 1640–1694*. Trans. and ed. by Robert Ryal Miller. Norman: University of Oklahoma Press.

Murra, John V. 1978. *La organización económica del estado inca*. Mexico City: Siglo Veintiuno.

Murúa, Martín de. 1946. *Historia del origen y genealogía real de los reyes incas del Perú*. [1590]. Madrid: Consejo Superior de Investigaciones Científicas, Instituto Santo Toribio de Mogrovejo.

———. 1987. *Historia general del Perú*. Madrid: Historia 16.

Novinsky, Anita. 1972. *Cristãos novos na Bahia*. São Paolo: Editora Perspectiva.

Orlove, Benjamin S. 1998. "Down to Earth: Race and Substance in the Andes." *Bulletin of Latin American Research* 17(2):207–22.

Osorio, Alejandra. 1999. "El Callejón de la Soledad: Vectors of Cultural Hybridity in Seventeenth-Century Lima." In *Spiritual Encounters. Interactions between Christianity and Native Religions in Colonial America*, ed. by Fernando Cervantes and Nicholas Griffiths, 198–229. Lincoln: University of Nebraska Press.

Pagden, Anthony. 1987. "Identity Formation in Spanish America." In *Colonial Identity in the Atlantic World, 1500–1800*, ed. by Nicholas P. Canny and Anthony Pagden, 51–93. Princeton: Princeton University Press.

Palma, Ricardo. 1910. *Apéndice a mis últimas Tradiciones peruanas*. Barcelona: Tipografía Maucci.

———. 1937. *Anales de la Inquisición de Lima*. Buenos Aires: Imprenta "La Vanguardia."

———. 1997. *Anales de la Inquisición de Lima* [1833–1919]. Madrid: Ediciones del Congreso de la República.

Pena Montenegro, Alonso de la. 1658. *Itinerario para párrocos de indios*. Madrid: Joseph Fernández de Buendía.

———. 1678. *Itinerario para párrocos de indios, en que se tratan las materias . . .* Lyon: Joan A. Hugetan.

Pérez Villanueva, Joaquín, ed. 1980. *La Inquisición español: Nueva visión, nuevos horizontes*. Madrid: Siglo Veintiuno de España.

Pérez Villanueva, Joaquín, and Bartolomé Escandell Bonet, eds. 1984–. *Historia de la inquisición en España y América*. 3 vols. Madrid: Biblioteca de Autores Cristianos: Centro de Estudios Inquisitoriales.

Pinelo, Antonio León. 1641. *Velos antiguos i modernos en los rostros de las mugeres sus conveniencias, i daños . . .* Madrid: Juan Sánchez.

Pizarro, Hernando. 1968. "Carta de Hernando Pizarro" [1533]. In *Biblioteca Peruana*, ser. 1, vol. 1, 119–30. Lima: Editores Técnicos Asociados.

Poole, Deborah. 1997. *Vision, Race, and Modernity: A Visual Economy of the Andean Image World*. Princeton: Princeton University Press.

Quiroz, Alfonso W. 1986. "La expropiación inquisitorial de cristianos nuevos portugueses en Los Reyes, Cartagena y México (1635–1649)." *Histórica* 10:237–303.

Ramos, Alonso. 1867. *Historia de Copacabana y de la milagrosa imagen de su Virgen*. Lima: J. E. del Campo.

Ramos, Gabriela. 1989. "La fortuna del inquisidor." In *Cuadernos de la Historia de la Evangelización en América Latina*. 4:89–122.

Rappaport, Joanne. 1990. *The Politics of Memory: Native Historical Interpretation in the Colombian Andes*. Cambridge: Cambridge University Press.

Reparaz Ruiz, Gonzalo de. 1976. *Os Portugueses no Vice-Reinado do Peru: (séculos XVI e XVII)*. Lisbon: Instituto de Alta Cultura.

Ribeiro, Darcy. 1971. *The Americas and Civilization*. Trans. by L. Barrett and M. Barrett. New York: Dutton.

Rowe, John H. 1957. "The Incas under Spanish Colonial Institutions." *Hispanic American Historical Review*. 37:155–99.

Sánchez, Ana. n.d. *Mentalidad popular frente a ideología oficial: El Santo Oficio en Lima y los casos de hechicería (siglo XVII)*. Cuzco: Centro Bartolomé de las Casas.

———. 1991. *Amancebados, Hechiceros y Rebeldes (Chancay, Siglo XVIII)*. Cuzco: Centro Bartolomé de Las Casas.

Said, Edward. 1993. *Culture and Imperialism*. New York: Knopf.

Salinas y Córdoba, Fray Buenaventura de. 1957. *Memorial de las Historias del Nuevo Mundo Piru* [1653]. Lima: Universidad Nacional Mayor de San Marcos.

Sarmiento de Gamboa, Pedro. 1960. *Historia general llamada indica* [1572]. In *Biblioteca de autores españoles*, vol. 135, 195–280. Madrid: Atlas.

Schwartz, Stuart B. 1995. "Colonial Identities and the 'Sociedad de Castas.'" *Colonial Latin American Review* 4(1):185–201.

Scott, James C. 1998. *Seeing Like a State: How Certain Schemes to Improve the Human Condition Have Failed*. New Haven: Yale University Press.

Seed, Patricia. 1988. *To Love, Honor and Obey in Colonial Mexico: Conflicts Over Marriage Choice, 1574–1821*. Stanford: Stanford University Press.

Silverblatt, Irene. 1987. *Moon, Sun, and Witches: Gender Ideologies and Class in Inca and Colonial Peru*. Princeton: Princeton University Press.

———. 1988a. "Imperial Dilemmas, the Politics of Kinship, and Inca Reconstructions of History." In *Comparative Studies in Society and History* 30(1):83–102.

———. 1988b. "Political Memories and Colonizing Symbols: Santiago and the Mountain Gods of Colonial Peru." In *Rethinking History and Myth: Indigenous South American Perspectives on the Past*. ed. Jonathan D. Hill, 174–94. Urbana: University of Illinois Press.

———. 1995. "Becoming Indian in the Central Andes of Seventeenth Century Peru." In *After Colonialism: Imperial Histories and Postcolonial Displacements*, ed. by Gyan Prakash, 279–98. Princeton: Princeton University Press.

———. 1998. "Family Values in Seventeenth Century Peru." In *Native Traditions in the Postconquest World*, ed. by Elizabeth Boone and Tom Cummins, 63–89. Washington: Dumbarton Oaks Research Library and Collection.

———. 2000a. "The Inca's Witches: Gender and the Cultural Work of Colonization in Seventeenth-Century Peru." In *Possible Pasts: Becoming Colonial in Early America*, ed. by Robert Blair St. George, 109–30. Ithaca: Cornell University Press.

———. 2000b. "New Christians and New World Fears in Seventeenth-Century Peru." *Comparative Studies in Society and History* 42(3):524–46.

Solorzano Pereira, Juan de. 1972. *Política Indiana* [1647]. In *Biblioteca de autores españoles*, vols. 252–56: Madrid: Ediciones Atlas.

Sordo, Emma María. 2003. "Nuestra Señora de Copacabana y su legado en el Potosí colonial." Paper presented at the fifty-first Congreso Internacional de Americanistas, Santiago, Chile.

Spalding, Karen. 1974. *De indio a campesino*. Lima: Instituto de Estudios Peruanos.

———. 1984. *Huarochirí: An Andean Society under Inca and Spanish Rule*. Stanford: Stanford University Press.

Splendiani, Anna María, José Enrique Sánchez Bohgórquez, and Emma Cecilia Luque de Salazar. 1997. *Cincuenta años de inquisición en el Tribunal de Cartagena de Indias 1610–1660*. 4 vols. Bogotá: Centro Editorial Javeriano.

Stern, Steve. 1982. *Peru's Indian Peoples and the Challenge of Spanish Conquest*. Madison: University of Wisconsin Press.

——. 1983. "The Struggle for Solidarity: Class, Culture, and Community in Highland Indian America." *Radical History Review*. 27:21–45.

——. 1987. "Introduction." In *Resistance, Rebellion, and Consciousness in the Andean Peasant World, 18th to 20th Centuries*, ed. by Steve Stern. Madison: University of Wisconsin Press.

Stoler, Ann. 2002. *Carnal Knowledge and Imperial Power: Race and the Intimate in Colonial Rule*. Berkeley: University of California Press.

Suardo, Juan Antonio. 1936. *Diario de Lima de Juan Antonio Suardo (1629-1639)*. 2 vols. Lima: Universidad Catóica del Perú.

Taussig, Michael. 1987. *Shamanism, Colonialism and the Wild Man*. Chicago: University of Chicago Press.

——. 1992a. "Culture of Terror—Space of Death: Roger Casement's Putumayo Report and the Explanation of Torture." In *Colonialism and Culture*, ed. by Nicholas Dirks, 135–74. Ann Arbor: University of Michigan Press.

——. 1992b. "Maleficium: State Fetishism." In *The Nervous System*, ed. by Michael Taussig, 111–40. New York: Routledge.

——. 1992c. *The Nervous System*. New York: Routledge.

——. 1997. *The Magic of the State*. New York: Routledge.

Thompson, E.P. 1978. "Eighteenth-Century English Society: Class Structure without Class?" *Social History* 3(1):133–65.

Tilly, Charles, ed. 1975. *The Formation of Nation-States in Western Europe*. Princeton: Princeton University Press.

Tomás y Valiente, Francisco. 1973. *La Tortura en España: Estudios históricos*. Espluges de Llobregat, Catalonia: Editorial Ariel.

Trouillot, Michel-Rolph. 1995. *Silencing the Past: Power and the Production of History*. Boston: Beacon.

Urbano, Henrique. 1980. "Dios Yaya, Dios Churi, Dios Espíritu." *Journal of Latin American Lore* 6:111–28.

Urton, Gary. 1999. *Inca Myths*. Austin: University of Texas Press.

van Deusen, Nancy. 2001. *Between the Sacred and the Worldly: The Institutional and Cultural Practice of Recogimiento in Colonial Lima*. Stanford: Stanford University Press.

Vargas Llosa, Mario. 1990. "Questions of Conquest: What Columbus Wrought and What He Did Not." *Harper's*. (December 1987):45–53.

Vargas Ugarte, Rubén. 1942. *La elocuencia sagrada en el Perú en los siglos XVII y XVIII*. Lima: Academia Peruana.

Vázquez de Espinosa, Antonio. 1942. *Compendium and Description of the West Indies*. [1630]. Tran. by Charles Upson Clark. Washington: Smithsonian Institution.

Wachtel, Nathan. 1973. "Rebeliones y milenarismo." In *Ideología mesiánica del mundo andino*. ed. by Juan Ossio, 103–42. Lima: Ignacio Prado de Pastor.

Wallerstein, Immanuel. 1974. *The Modern World-System*. New York: Academic Press.

Warren, Jonathan W., and France Winddance Twine. 2002. "Critical Race Studies in Latin America: Recent Advances and Recent Weaknesses." In *A Companion to Racial and Ethnic Studies*, ed. by John Solomos and David T. Goldberg, 538–60.

Warren, Kay B. 1978. *The Symbolism of Subordination: Indian Identity in a Guatemalan Town*. Austin: University of Texas Press.

——. 1998. *Indigenous Movements and Their Critics: Pan-Maya Activism in Guatemala*. Princeton: Princeton University Press.

Weinstein, Barbara. 1983. *The Amazon Rubber Boom, 1850-1920*. Stanford: Stanford University Press.

Weismantel, Mary, and Stephen F. Eisenman. 1998. "Race in the Andes: Global Movements and Popular Ontologies." *Bulletin of Latin American Research* 17(2):121–42.

Wightman, Ann. 1990. *Indigenous Migration and Social Change: The Forasteros of Cuzco*. Durham: Duke University Press.

Williams, Eric, and André Gunder Frank. 1967. *Capitalism and Underdevelopment in Latin America: Historical Studies of Chile and Brazil.* New York: Monthly Review Press.

Williams, Raymond. 1977. *Marxism and Literature.* Oxford: Oxford University Press.

Worsley, Peter. 1968. *The Trumpet Shall Sound.* 2nd ed. New York: Schocken.

Yerushalmi, Yosef Hayim. 1971. *From Spanish Court to Italian Ghetto: Isaac Cardoso, A Study in Marranism and Jewish Apologetics.* New York: Columbia University Press.

Zuidema, R. T. 1977. "Kinship and Ancestor Cult in Three Peruvian Communities. Hernández Príncipe's Account of 1622." *Bulletin de l'Institut Français d'Etudes Andines* 2:16–23.

INDEX

Bureaucracy, 4–5, 82–83, 86, 93–95, 110, 120, 122, 124, 134, 175, 184, 196–97, 204, 210, 214, 217–19, 221, 225, 227–28, 322; Inquisition and, 4–5, 10–11, 23, 34, 50, 57–75, 84–85, 88, 136; modernity and, 9; torture and, 83–84. *See also* State
Bustos, Dona Francisca de, 70, 127, 249 n.61

Cabali, Miguel, 94
Cabrera, Lic. Don, 36–37
Calchaquí Indians, 177, 181
Capitalism, 21, 33, 114–15, 218, 225. *See also* Mercantalism
Carranza, Angela de, 90
Cartagena, 6, 41–42, 50, 74, 113, 143, 147, 150, 152–53, 163, 167–68, 263–64 n.3, 265 n.32, 268–69 n.1
Casas, Bartolomé de las, 158, 223, 268 n.87
Casta y generación (caste and lineage). *See* Race Thinking: *casta y generación*
Castaneda, Ana de, 126, 167–70
Caste. *See* Race Thinking: caste and
Castile, 19–20, 33–34, 41, 106, 114, 129, 131, 136–39, 143, 159, 169, 218–21, 263–64 n.3
Castillo, Doña Ana del, 179
Castro Barreto, María, 126, 178
Castro y del Castillo, don Antonio de, 36, 40, 132, 148
Catholic Church, 6–7, 15, 21–22, 25–27, 35, 37–41, 47–49, 51–52, 59–61, 66, 71–72, 94–96, 106, 122–23, 128, 149–50, 155, 158, 160, 163, 165–67, 169, 170–71, 173, 174, 176–77, 180–82, 184–85, 197, 219, 222, 230–33; converts and conversion to 4–5, 57, 107–8, 110–11, 179–80, 182–85, 189–90, 192–93, 197, 201–2, 204, 210; internal conflicts in 66–68, 88–91, 178–79; nationalism and 7, 31–32
Catholicism. *See* Catholic Church
Centenera, Martin del Barco, 168
Chile, 111, 113–14
China, 15, 20, 111, 147, 265 n.32
Clifford, James, 214
Cobo, Father Bernabé, 21
Coca, 26, 164–65, 174–79, 182, 184, 200–201
Cochabamba, 167
Coen, Mosen. *See* Peixotto, Diego
Cola nut, 49–50, 87, 152–53
Colmenares, Gabriela 127
Colonialism. *See* Spanish: colonialism and
Color, and race. *See* Blacks; Brown; Whites; Race Thinking: color and

Complicidad grande. See Great Jewish Conspiracy
Contreras, Ana María de, 61, 174, 247 n.26
Conversos. See New Christians
Cordero, Antonio, 35, 61–63, 72, 89, 133, 254 n.45
Cordoba, Doña María de, 73, 174–76, 178, 251 n.76
Cordoba, Juan de, 59, 246 n.12
Coronil, Fernando, 16, 96
Corrigan, Derek, 12–14, 80–81, 225
Cuello, Jorge 154
Curacas, 109, 129, 190–91, 193, 195–99, 201, 203, 206–7, 209–10. *See also* Indian elite
Cutido, Sebastián, 146
Cuzco, 4, 21, 40, 42, 91, 107, 113, 124, 139, 148, 154, 166, 174–75, 179–80, 191–92, 197–99, 204–5, 210, 212, 230–32, 265 n.34

Dandrade, Rodrigo, 176
Despinosa, Francisca, 167, 170
Despinosa, Manuel Alvarez, 133
Doctrineros. See Missionaries
Dominicans, 66, 170
Duarte, Sebastián, 50–52, 89, 133, 254 n.45
Durkheim, Emile 15, 81
Dutch. *See* Holland
Dutch West Indies Company, 144

Elí el Nazareno. *See* Silva, Francisco Maldonado de
England, 75, 96, 106, 114; Amazon and, 14; colonialism of, 20, 223–24; imperialism and, 3, 217; Spain and, 221–26, 228–29; state making and, 12–14
Enríquez, Alvarez, 127
Enríquez, Dona Guiomar, 51, 68, 160, 244 n.129
Enríquez, Simón Vaz. *See* Baez, Simón Henríquez
Espinosa, Antonio de, 42, 243 n.66
Espinosa, Jorge de, 42, 73, 146, 243 n.66
Evora (Portugal), 59–61
Expulsos, 123
Extirpation of Idolatry Campaigns, 4, 57, 107–8, 174, 180, 183, 190–91, 196–202, 205, 207–8, 210–11, 229–32

Fanon, Franz, 172
Fascism, 3–4, 174, 217
Felipe II, king, 5, 33–34
Felipe III, king, 91
Felipe IV, king, 33–34, 156

Irene Silverblatt is a professor in the Department of Cultural Anthropology at Duke University. She is the author of *Moon, Sun, and Witches: Gender Ideologies and Class in Inca and Colonial Peru* (1987).

Library of Congress Cataloging-in-Publication Data
Silverblatt, Irene Marsha.
Modern Inquisitions : Peru and the colonial origins of the civilized world / Irene Silverblatt.
p. cm. — (Latin America otherwise)
"A John Hope Franklin Center book."
Includes bibliographical references and index.
ISBN 0-8223-3406-2 (hardcover : alk. paper)
ISBN 0-8223-3417-8 (pbk. : alk. paper)
1. Inquisition—Peru. 2. Peru—Church history—17th century.
3. Catholic Church—Peru—History—17th century. I. Title.
II. Series.
BX1740.P5S55 2004   272'.2'0985—dc22   2004011219